CONTEMPORARY POETRY IN AMERICA

CONTEMPORARY POETRY IN AMERICA

Essays and Interviews

Edited by Robert Boyers

SCHOCKEN BOOKS · NEW YORK

Contents

Preface

THIS VOLUME GREW out of a special issue of *Salmagundi* magazine, also entitled *Contemporary Poetry in America*, which originally appeared in the spring of 1973. The earlier collection, including a number of original poems that had to be dropped from this book, was decidedly less ambitious in scope and intention. The present volume should serve the needs of teachers and students, inside and outside the classroom, who are interested in the current poetry scene and wish to develop a critical apparatus for dealing with the work of a variety of poets.

In my earlier preface I conceded that a collection of this kind cannot be definitive, in the sense that "the verse of our time is wonderfully various, and the range of real achievement very great." The judgment accurately estimates the limitations of this book as well as of the *Salmagundi* issue, though we have fleshed out the volume substantially. Even with the addition of essays on Lowell, Roethke, Jarrell, Plath, Olson, Merwin, and Dugan, there is a great deal we have not covered. It is difficult to imagine a course in contemporary poetry that would need to consider more than one or two poets not treated here, but an editor would be hard put to identify which those "other poets" might be. This is only to say that everyone who reads poetry in our time will approve the efforts of a Lowell or a Nemerov or an Ammons, but that only a proportion of readers will admire the efforts of contemporaries not included here.

How, then, do I explain the inclusion of materials on poets who are not universally admired—poets like Wagoner and Belitt, even Galway

Kinnell? Such poets are my choices. They seem to me every bit as distinguished as better-known writers whose verses are more regularly anthologized, and I am confident that literary professionals will in time come to study and teach their writings with a seriousness they have occasionally misdirected. This volume ought to encourage, at the very least, such modest adjustments in our orthodox perspectives.

Readers will note that there is no consistent "line" in the reflections published here. My aim has been a reasonably generous representation of the dominant urgings in our verse, and especial representation of achievements that to some of us matter most. No idols are toppled, but I have been anxious to elbow a little room for poetry considered old-fashioned or intellectually severe or literally splendid in ways not acceptable to contemporaries bent always on making it natural. If I've worked toward anything in particular, by way of a vision of the essential in contemporary verse, it would take the form of a declaration that neither intelligence nor splendor need be any longer suspect among us, as though they could compromise our serious poetry.

The items included are various indeed. Some of the essays argue from the perspective of the American cultural heritage, attempting to look at our poetry in terms of the fulfilling of large prophecies and promises. Such are the essays on Ashbery and Ammons. Others, like those on Belitt and Nemerov and Roethke, linger lovingly over a body of work, noting its strengths and illuminating its dynamics. Still others work largely to locate symptomatic weaknesses, or to distinguish between the inspired and the false note in works that have been uncritically or carelessly embraced—such are the essays on Rich, Wright, and Dickey. And there are others. The interviews are extraordinary documents as well, whether for particular insights they develop or for the sense they convey of the way our best poets relate to their own work and to their contemporaries.

I am grateful to a variety of people with whose help and encouragement I have come to know my own feelings about the verse of our time. Among these I must single out for particular thanks Ben Belitt and Jerome Mazzaro, to whom, however, none of the faults and omissions in this volume may be attributed.

ROBERT BOYERS

Saratoga Springs, N.Y.
June, 1974

T. Roethke   [signature] '72

THEODORE ROETHKE

Robert Lowell

John Berryman   Pollard '72

JOHN BERRYMAN

ADRIENNE RICH

HOWARD NEMEROV

John Ashbery

Poetry & Meaning

BY HOWARD NEMEROV

WHAT I HAVE TO SAY TO YOU is very simple; so simple that I find it hard to say. It is that poetry is getting something right in language, that this idea of rightness in language is in the first place a feeling, which does not in the least prevent it from existing; if it is subjective, which I doubt, it is not "merely subjective" (as students say, and o dear, how often they say it); that this feeling of rightness has largely been lost, if not eagerly assaulted with destructive intent, by people who if they ever wake up are going to find it extremely hard to recapture or even to remember what that feeling was.

One possible, and to me likely, consequence of these simplicities will have to be contemplated; it is that poetry in English is coming to an end. I have hesitated fearfully for a long time before that statement, realizing that coming from a middle-aged poet it will helplessly be heard as one more variant of the common cry of middle-aged poets, I had talent once, where did it go? And yet it seems as though the evidence is massive that not poetry alone but a great deal to do with language in relation to mind is fast approaching an end where it will be transformed into something unrecognizably other. To some of this evidence I shall return later on; meanwhile I can at least show that the thought of such an end or such a transformation is not one I hold all by myself.

To show that the question has been seriously entertained I may cite the instance of H. G. Wells and his last work, a little pamphlet called *Mind at the End of Its Tether*. It was written just after the Second World War and in the last year of the author's life, and in it this great progressive, humanitarian, scientifically-minded and positivist intelligence — who had predicted in one work after another so much that has come literally true — turned right round to the opposite and declared that intelligence and world, which had for the length of history run on parallel courses, were now separating, like two ships whose paths diverge in the night, or like two celestial bodies that approach one another only to fall away into illimitable dark. Admitted that Wells was old, tired, mortally ill, we have still to inquire whether he was saying something true, or at least probable enough to be given the steadiest consideration, or whether he was merely expressing one more symptom of his malady.

A. M. Turing once said that the question "Can machines think?" was too meaningless to deserve discussion, and suggested that the proper short answer was "Can people?" But he added this: "Nevertheless, I believe that at the end of the century the use of words and general opinion will have altered so much that one will be able to speak of machines thinking without expecting to be contradicted." You will observe that to this scientist the point is not that superior machines will be invented, though they almost undoubtedly will be; it is that we will have changed our ways of using words, so that thinking will no longer mean what it did. Indeed, this change may in large measure already have taken place. Hannah Arendt says of this, "If we compare the modern world with that of the past, the loss of human experience . . . is extraordinarily striking. It is not only and not even primarily contemplation which has become an entirely meaningless experience. Thought itself, when it became 'reckoning with consequences,' became a function of the brain, with the result that electronic instruments are found to fulfill these functions much better than we ever could" (*The Human Condition*).

And Owen Barfield, possibly the clearest and most searching thinker of the present time, says — though he calls it a provocative heterodoxy — "I have been coming to feel for some time that imagination, *as an end in itself*, is a vein that has been, or very soon will be, worked out. I am in doubt whether much more that is really significant can be done with it" (see *Interpretation: The Poetry of Meaning*).

There is at least a funnier way of viewing the matter. Otto Rank says somewhere that it took long ages for soul, or spirit, or what we call mind, to work its way up into the head. In some cultures this vital principle inhabited the soles of the feet — the Buddha's footprint is holy — and in others the genitals, the stomach, bowels, heart, liver, and solar plexus were its abode. But among us for a couple of centuries or more thought is commonly believed to be something done in the head, and its sacred function is protected from contamination by the lower parts of the body by collar and tie; compare the expression "white-collar worker" for someone whose business is mental.

Considering this progression we might reasonably ask by way of extrapolation where this principle of life has left to go. And the student of such matters might look long and hard at the sudden efflorescence of hair styles, including beards and wigs, among the young in late years. It suggests sadly enough people's coming to the dismayed realization that the only thing about yourself you have the power to change, until you go bald, is hair; and it irresistibly reminds me of that species of scientific thought, becoming every day more common, which observes that hair grows out of the head and goes on to infer that the head is full of hair. We are already assured by science that the head does not contain thoughts or words, but only neurons — to which I suppose the teacherly response would be, "Which of you neurons said that?"

Turning from this topic for the present, I remark that the spectacle, now some centuries long, of western man patiently endeavoring to reason himself out of thought and read himself out of the universe, would be as fit a subject for a comic poet as for a tragic one, were its consequences not so brutal and so lamentable.

I return now to my first assertion: poetry is a way of getting something right in language, poetry is language doing itself right. This idea came first, as ideas have a way of doing, as a thoughtless phrase. I am a most inefficient teacher of verse-writing — but imagine what a monster an efficient one would be! — and term after term, no matter what resolutions of patience and good-will I began with, three weeks later I found myself saying to the students about their productions such things as: But it's not right, it just simply isn't right . . . and even more cruelly on occasion: if there's nothing right what's the use of trying to say what's wrong with it? And sometimes I would rhap-sodize to my poor class about how poetry was simply language doing itself right, language as it ought to be, language as it was in the few hours between Adam's naming the creation and his fall. The whole art of poetry, I would say, consists in getting back that paradisal condition of the understanding, the condition that says simply "yes" and "I see" and "it is so." Naturally enough, it doesn't happen often. But it does happen.

My students, though accustomed to classes in which their instruc-tors explained themselves, explained literature, and in fact left nothing unexplained that could possibly be explained, and now confronting a teacher who apparently couldn't or wouldn't explain one blessed thing, and especially not the one blessed thing they were there to have explained to them, were understandably puzzled. All the same, they behaved very kindly about it. At most, the ones inclined to philosophize would point out to me that my criterion of rightness could never be defined and in any event was merely subjective.

Meaning I could never *prove* anything was right.

I do have a reply to that objection, though unfortunately it is a rather unwieldy one because it has to include some consideration of our intellectual habits with respect to subjects and objects, or, as Coleridge used to say when drinking, sumjects and omjects.

It was Coleridge, I am told, who introduced the words subjective and objective into our language. Ruskin, who was very funny on the theme, hated the words and said they were foisted on us by a combination of German dullness and English affectation. However that may be, I call it to your attention as significant that whole populations which had formerly been able to express their thoughts without resort to the words subjective and objective — whole populations, by the way, including Chaucer and Shakespeare and Milton — now, less than two centuries after their entrance into the language, can scarcely get through a classroom hour without leaning heavily on them. Students in particular appear to experience from their use some kind of magical resolution of any difficulty of thought.

I am not trying to take away these terms, which seem to stand to our intellectual astronauts as space-craft and space respectively. But I would point out first that though Coleridge introduced the words into philosophizing in English he was far indeed from denigrating thought, feeling, or belief by calling them "merely" subjective. In fact I came by chance on a place where he does just the opposite and refers to the natural world as "all that is merely objective" (in Barfield's essay in *Interpretation*).

The great dictionary is pretty funny, as well as illuminating, on *subjective* as a philosophe word, now obsolete, "Pertaining to the real or essential being of that which supports qualities, attributes, or relations; substantial; real"; for it adds, after what might be a thoughtful pause, "objective in the modern sense." Funny, as the sight of great learning trapped in its words may often be, and illuminating about the great change in the mind of the world from a time when true subjectivity could strictly be attributed only to God, to a time when saying that something or someone is being subjective means a considerable variety of things, all pejorative, e.g., you think it's so but it's not; maybe, but it's not important; you're being emotional when you ought to be reasonable.

It is by some such process as is represented in the changed meaning of such a word as subjective that the mind has reached its present most familiar predicament, ludicrous and pathetic by turns, whereby a learned discipline begins its course of studies by excluding as far as possible all feeling, including especially the feeling of interest, curiosity, pleasure, delight that prompted the study itself, and winds up several years and thousands of pages later plaintively asking itself about human values and wondering where they are to be found. The entire development is of the greatest historical interest, but in the result, it is rather like the man found by a policeman searching under a streetlight for his lost watch. Did you lose it here? asks the policeman, one would have thought unnecessarily. No, I lost it over there, but I'm looking here because the light's better.

This distinction of the whole world into subjective and objective probably began with Galileo's, and then Locke's, division of the qualities into primary and secondary. The dictionary gives the former as bulk, figure, number, situation, and motion or rest, "which are in the object as in our perception of it," while the secondary qualities, tastes, sounds, colors, &c., "are modes of our perception induced by some character in the object which does not coincide with the perception itself." One notices immediately that the primary qualities have the air already of being what are called "hard facts," while the secondary ones are already a touch sentimental and unmanly. And the scientific way of developing this distinction had the effect of progressively reducing even the primary qualities to quantity, or number, alone, so that only what is enumerable is effectively regarded as real. With this fateful distinction, which indeed did not rest as a distinction but became a division, much else separated that had formerly been one and the object of a single attention; poetry, for example, in the eyes of most of the world, became "only poetry." I shan't pause to drop a tear for "only poetry," but would suggest that poetry, and literature generally, may be the last remaining place where that about subjective and objective does not apply; and that an appropriate emblem for this characteristic of literature is the situation you have in *Hamlet,* where the Ghost is neither subjective, for the soldiers can see it just as well as Hamlet, nor objective, for when it next appears Hamlet alone can see it, while his mother can see "Nothing at all; yet all that is I see." I've a sense that we all incline by training and study to be like Gertrude about our ghosts. Wallace Stevens poignantly varies Gertrude's line, speaking of "a mind of winter" and of

> the listener, who listens in the snow,
> And, nothing himself, beholds
> Nothing that is not there and the nothing that is.
> —"The Snow Man," *Collected Poems*

Now there is one great trouble with the intellectual, learned, school of approach to the art of poetry; it is a trouble that secretly afflicts, I am convinced, a great part of our thoughts about a good many things, and it is this: we are much too concerned to turn our experience into a result, something tangible, and in the course of doing this we forget what the experience felt like in the first place, and, still more important, how through all our studies we remain related to time in two ways, biographical and historical. This is a simple enough thought, and that may be why it is almost always forgotten, though sometimes I've the feeling of its being deliberately excluded. But it bears importantly on this business of poetry as getting things right in language. For the lover of poetry would never have become a lover of poetry, much less a student of poetry, had he not at first had this feeling of rightness and certainty about some piece of language. That came before all question of study, of English courses, of why it was so; enough that it simply was so. James Dickey writes in an essay that he remembers what first attracted him to poetry; it was the rightness of the expression "to sweat it out," in relation to the soldier's experience of war.

That brings me to another point about the experience of the rightness of language, and to another thing that is dreadfully wrong about the idea of poetry as a subject to be studied in schools.

It is most important to any inquiry into this idea of rightness in poetry that we be as candid as possible about our actual relation, of feeling and thought, to the phenomena; and with respect to this problem I begin by observing that neither teaching nor criticism is very often quite candid about this relation. For there is always present a temptation, which we almost always yield to, to make our experience of poetry both more intellectual and more pretentious than it is or ought to be. There is a somewhat comic, somewhat vulgar and mercantile, aspect to our serious and no doubt well-meaning endeavors to convince others and even possibly ourselves that the experience we are getting from poetry is certifiably profound, lofty, sublime, organic, harmonious . . . even pleasurable. You may supply other adjectives, from whatever schools of criticism, as you care to.

Without denying that our experience of poetry is sometimes one or more of those things, I think it proper to acknowledge that it is not always like that, and may not often be like that. A primary pleasure in poetry is surely something low enough to be beneath the notice of teacher or critic — the pleasure of saying something over for its own sweet sake, and because it sounds just right. For myself, certainly, and for you if you will remember how it truly was, the thing said over will not necessarily be A Great Thought, though great thoughts are not necessarily excluded either; it may be as near as not to meaningless, especially if one says it without much attention to its context. For instance, a riddling song has the refrain: Sing ninety-nine and ninety. I can remember being charmed enough with that to say it over and over to myself for days, without ever having a single thought about its meaning except for a certain bemused wonder about how different it was from singing a hundred and eighty-nine.

Or else it may be something proverbially helpful, that you say to yourself when things are going wrong: "Time and the hour runs through the roughest day." Perhaps this would not have meant so much to me without the little grammatical oddity of "runs" instead of "run." And here are a couple of lines from *The Comedy* that delight me as much now as they did when I first came across them so many years ago:

> Cosi di ponte in ponte, altro parlando
> Che la mia commedia cantar non cura.

No deep insight here, nor lofty wisdom; he is talking in effect about what he is not going to talk about; though it is wonderfully appealing to be told that Dante and Virgil said things to one another in Hell that we are never going to know, that is not the whole charm of the lines —

> So from bridge to bridge, talking of other things
> That my comedy cares not to sing.

It loses much of its delightsomeness in English; loses that lovely, offhanded strolling lilt that makes the Italian of the second line especially so wonderful to say. There's a clue in that, maybe, in that *ambulando* rhythm that imitates the two poets walking along; for Paul Valéry gave perhaps the shortest definition of poetry recorded: it is what it says.

One more example. I sang to my children a nursery rhyme I must have missed in childhood:

> Fiddle dee dee, fiddle dee dee,
> The fly has married the bumble bee.
>
> Said the fly said he, will you marry me
> And live with me sweet bumble bee?
> Said the bumble bee, I'll laugh and sing
> And you'll never know I carry a sting.
>
> Fiddle dee dee, fiddle dee dee,
> The fly has married the bumble bee.

I don't know in the least what there is about this that made me so happy I went about the house chanting it for days on end, in all sorts of situations . . . until I observed that when I did my wife was beginning to look sideways at me, as though this little verse was turning into A Dark Thought About Marriage.

Which suggests a further step. It is part of the power of a poem to generate meanings from what may originally be meaningless. Perhaps what I am thinking of as rightness in language is this abstract power, or power gained from being very abstract (as Stevens said a supreme fiction had to be) — the power to handle a great many situations at once, the power of poetry to be somewhat more like a mind than a thought. These apparently trivial examples of things that one repeats to oneself rather as though they were talismans, are they not after all the stuff and substance itself of poetry, and more visibly so for not being so cluttered with meanings that we can't see the things themselves? After all, delight itself may mean nothing. Love may mean nothing. The world appears to have every prospect of never meaning anything again. But love and delight and, so far, the world remain.

In an earlier essay I made a detailed comparison between the mechanisms visible in certain sorts of poetry and the mechanisms of jokes. I found the comparison illuminating even if it would not hold equally for all kinds of poetry (I never claimed it would). But in connection with the question of rightness in language as over against the claim that such rightness is "merely subjective" it is appropriate to draw on that earlier essay for a moment, in order to say as follows.

1. When you understand a joke, you laugh. In fact, your laughter quite simply is your understanding, which doesn't express itself in a separate verbal form.

2. When you fail to understand a joke, in a company where everyone else seems to understand it and laughs, you either say "I don't get it," or you give one of those fake and feeble laughs which you know everyone else will see through at once. What do you not do?

3. I submit that what you never do in this situation is say that the joke is subjective or merely subjective.

4. If someone explains or interprets the joke to you, your difficulty will perhaps be cleared up, but too late; you won't laugh as hard as you would have, had you understood immediately, that is, without the mediation of more words.

5. Therefore a joke is a way of getting something right in language.

6. A poem too is a way of getting something right in language, save that the proper response will be not laughter but silence, or the acknowledgment that it is so, it is as it is; that the miracle has happened once again: "something understood," as Herbert says finally and ever so quietly about prayer.

7. It is in this sense that poems ought to be approached as sacred objects. One expects not so much to learn them as to learn from them. They give a certain definition to experience, and it may be that it is to experience we should refer them, rather than to exegesis. By contrast, definitions given in dictionaries break up experiences into units in order to make them — the units, unhappily, not the experiences — easier to understand; but dictionary definitions will at last be found to be circular, hence not definitive, while a poem is "the burning bow that once could shoot an arrow out of the up and down" (Yeats).

You will no doubt have been thinking for some time that this is all very well, but when are we to have an example? other than, of course, those agreeable trivialities he quoted a few minutes back. But I have deliberately withheld examples because I want the idea of rightness to be as open, contentless, empty if you like, as may be. For I am not at all certain it is so important for each of us to have the same ideas about the same things, even if it is that particular species of what Lovejoy called "metaphysical pathos" that more than anything else informs and sustains the university and the culture. What is important to each of us is to have the idea of rightness, to grasp it feelingly. If we do not have it, perhaps poetry is not for us; music goes on though many are tone deaf and few have absolute pitch; absolute pitch has never been accused of being subjective on that account. If you are in the presence of a greater vision than your own — Shakespeare's for instance — and do not see what he is talking about, you don't say he sees nothing, for that would be like telling a microscope that it exaggerated.

In keeping with a somewhat oriental style of going at a subject, a style that abstains from saying what the subject is directly, but hopes to produce an immediate vision of it by indirect means and dark hints — this negative approach is usually translated as "no-knowledge," and commentators warn us not to confuse it with "no knowledge" — I shall present, instead of examples of rightness in poetry, a couple of examples in which, as far as I am able to see, nothing went right at all.

The first is by a student, who has generously allowed me to make use of his effort. In fact it was this student who kindly put me straight by telling me that my idea of rightness was purely subjective.

OPUS 125

The hall of deafness still had heaped
a confusion of memories,
a pile awaiting craftsman's wit;
but he wished he could hear his sobs
when pain forced and hacked into tears,
or, the huge laugh like a giant's
that knew that after all it was
hard work setting sounds in order . . .

I forbear to quote the remainder. I don't want to make fun of it either. It's sad. You can see it's about Beethoven writing the Ninth Symphony, and you can feel that it is very sincere, but it's awful. I said to the student, who by the way is a very intelligent one, "Here you are, you've read and probably understood half the literature of the past four hundred years — but you've never heard anything." Maybe the motto of the English Department could be this line varied from Eliot:

We missed the experience, but we had the meaning.

My second example of getting it wrong is professional work, so far as poets may be said to be professionals. Anyhow, it appeared in *Poetry* magazine, a title in which, I have often thought, the word "poetry" has exactly the force that the word "beauty" does in the title "beauty shoppe." Beyond that, not wishing to be invidious, I shall not identify the author; the following is how he begins a piece of some sixty lines:

A small voice is fretting my house in the night
A small heart is there . . . Listen,
I who have dwelt at the root of a scream forever,
I who have read my heart like a man with no hands
reading a book whose pages turn in the wind,
I say listen, listen, hear me
in our dreamless dark, my dear.

If I read that in a sufficiently sonorous and reverential tone, some of you will doubtless have thought it beautiful, but you are wrong. (It is best, I think, for me to say such a thing plainly and without qualification.) That is one of the unmentioned and possibly unmentionable dangers to poetry recitations, that any old garbage will go down all right if it's read with conviction.

About that passage I shall comment briefly. For if silence is the appropriate response to rightness, it may be that the real use of talk is about wrongness.

To read the book of the heart is an ancient, conventional expression, hence not good enough for our poet, who wishes to be simultaneously intense, complex, rhapsodic, and desperately not to mention modern. Still, he is unable to resist this honorable old figure, the heart as a book to be read. So he fancies it up a bit. The speaker is reading the book of the heart? well, chop off his hands at the wrists to show that this is no easy matter; now to clinch the point home, spring up a wind and start the pages of the book flapping; compared to the speaker's problems here, it would be a cinch for him to dwell at the root of a scream forever. This poetry is intense, indeed, with the grim intensity of someone trying to masturbate too soon after having masturbated.

Maybe from examples such as these we can see the beauty even of wrongness, that from it we infer that a right way of doing things does exist, even that many right ways of doing things must exist, even as from the idea of getting lost we infer the existence of roads and destinations.

I began by saying that I thought this idea of rightness had largely been lost, or destroyed, and that on that account we might have to contemplate the end of poetry as we have known it. And I promised to return to that thought and the evidence for it, knowing that everyone likes a bit of an apocalypse to finish on.

It is a sound maxim for a prophet to hold before him, that when he is about to peer into the future and say that something awful is going to happen, he might well turn around and ask himself if it hasn't happened already. Blake said of this, that prophecy meant simply, If you go on doing thus, the result will be thus. And I add that my favorite prophet is Jonah both for being short-winded and for being wrong about the destruction of Nineveh, that great city wherein, says the Lord in one of his infrequent jokes, are more than sixscore thousand persons that cannot discern between their right hand and their left hand; and also much cattle. Which a poet once brought up to date as follows:

> The Lord might have spared us the harsh joke;
> Many that live in Nineveh these days
> Cannot discern their ass from a hot rock.
> Maybe the word 'cattle' refers to these.

I hope that I, like Jonah, am wrong; though if I should be I too might be displeased exceedingly.

There is a sense, utterly true but not very helpful, in which everything is always ending and always beginning. The fabric of the generations simply is woven that way, seamlessly, and only the work of the historical intellect divides it up. Imagine someone living through the fall of the Roman Empire in a provincial town, in Marseille, say, or London; he would live his life day by day, as we all do, and never know that he had lived through the fall of the Roman Empire. He would notice, perhaps, certain signs of neglect; the garrison might go slovenly and unshaven, the roads might not be so well kept up, proclamations would be fewer than they used to be . . . and when people began to notice the absence of something called the Roman Empire they nostalgically replaced it with a Holy Roman Empire and pretended it was the same thing, sort of. So it may be with my subject. I will present my evidences as best I can.

For one thing, the posture of the literary mind seems these days to be dry, angry, smart, jeering, cynical; as though once people had discovered the sneaky joys of irreverence they were quite unable to stop. This is one typical process of Shakespeare's tragedies, where the intelligent and crafty young destroy the stupid old and, with them, the sacred something that these complacent dodos by some accident had in their charge, and the intelligent and crafty young at last, as Ulysses says, eat up themselves.

This symptom in itself is perhaps not much. Literary quarrels have usually been acrimonious, indeed are less personally spiteful now than in the Age of Pope; and the world has always been as full of people plugging their friends as of people unplugging their enemies. Yet the public discussion, the criticism, that attends on poetry, has appeared to me as coming close to the point at which a smart shallowness and verbal facility will jettison meaning altogether; and the same thing has been happening in poetry itself. I shall not now give examples, but I ask you to consider whether it is not as I have said. Not only the terms of abuse, but more importantly the terms of praise, appear in a language whose vagueness of sense is closely related to the extravagance of its claims.

This kind of shrillness may be the sign of considerable unacknowledged anguish of spirit. As though everyone felt some big thing was breaking up, and made bigger and louder noises to pretend that all is as it was. For it ought now to be possible to turn and look back over the modern period, as it foolishly goes on being called, and see how some one thing — I should date it perhaps from the middle of the last century, from Baudelaire and Swinburne, say — was gathering momentum in a direction and was assembling armies of adherents, but that not so long ago this momentum, giant as it was, divided itself among the members of the armies, diminished, and may now be flickering out in brief contingencies.

I don't know just what name would be right for this momentum. It had to do with a slow collapse in the idea of meaning which progressed simultaneously with an imposing acceleration of the rate at which knowledge was accumulated. Everyone who thinks much about poetry will have observed how in the early years of this century it abruptly became much harder to understand. Not all of it by any means, but I need mention only Eliot, Pound, Hart Crane, as instances. By heroical efforts of criticism and exegesis Eliot's poems, which seem to have impressed many of their first readers as being written in Linear B, were made part of the common language, so that even ball games now may end not with a bang but a whimper. The same has not happened to the *Cantos* of Ezra Pound, and I incline to doubt it will happen.

What I am calling the slow collapse in the idea of meaning, which made poetry so very hard to understand and consequently conferred on English Departments a large part of both their real and their spurious importance, evidently did not happen in poetry alone. It happened even more conspicuously and at about the same time in physics, in painting, in music; the whole world suddenly became frightfully hard to understand. And there is a corollary to this that I find most interesting: the mind responded magnificently to the challenge of all this difficulty in ever so many ways . . . and from asking concerning the meaning of this poem or that, went on to ask concerning meaning itself and in general. Again, I need mention only a few names: Kenneth Burke, William Empson, I. A. Richards, all seem to have begun by inquiring about the meaning of poems and then to have felt themselves irresistibly drawn to the question beyond:

what is meaning, and how does it happen to arise? And the new science of linguistics here enters the picture. Men are now beginning to understand, doubtless as yet in a fumbling and vague sort of way compared to what may be coming, what sort of entity a language is and what relations, of possibility and of limitation, it has to thought. Realizing that language is an abstract and utterly arbitrary but totally articulated system of relations, men now begin to see that they may invent other languages for other purposes—indeed, they do so already.

Anthropology too, with its close relations, folklore and comparative religion and mythology, gets into the act, and for the first time men begin to have a clear and coherent understanding of how literature arose, and what it is, and even a little what it does.

Now these are very real and reckonable advances. I am not anti-science, though I do think that our ways of thinking about what science does and is doing are inadequate and even stupid, and I am not against the accumulation and coordination of knowledge. But I think it is clear that to understand a given matter will have its effect on doing. Students of what is called nowadays The Creative Process do not observably turn into artists. And when the depths of things are exposed to the dry light of reasoned explanation, they may well dry up. For it is paradoxical, and therefore, in a round world true, that a great deal of knowledge may come to resemble a great insanity. That may be why I am forced to contend that a vast increase in knowledge was simultaneous with a slow collapse in the idea of meaning.

It is commonplace to observe that we today are the beneficiaries and victims of more language than any people has ever been subjected to in the history of the world. Even going for a walk or drive in the country, we see that the landscape more and more carries written messages — signs. Two strange and related consequences come from this circumstance.

For one, the public language of press and the other media imposes upon us a public dream, a fantasy written in a language that is neither right nor wrong but, say, serviceable. Not so much that it tells us what to think, though it tries to do that as well, but it makes of no avail our freedom of thought by telling us what we must have these thoughts about, and by progressively and insensibly filling us with a low, dull language for thinking them.

The second consequence seems to be that the languages of art and of learning grow ever more recondite, as if they were the distorted mirror-images of the public language, which they relate to, perhaps, more or less as a dream relates to a newspaper.

Yet here too the opposites coincide, for the public dream that is the daily dream of all appears as no less insane, and no less under the threat of an ultimate meaninglessness, than the private dream that is the nightly dream of each alone. And if the languages of the arts and sciences grow progressively harder to understand, the matching phenomenon on the other side is that in the public language it is getting progressively harder to say anything that refers to reality.

I think I can now give a name to the period that is over. I shall assert that it lasted from the middle of the last century to the middle of this one, and I shall call it The Age of Art, or The Aesthetic Age. Its dominant characteristic was the claim that salvation was by art alone. What that salvation would be, or would be like, was specified in ever so many different ways by different artists, but it scarcely ever failed to be asserted that the way and the truth and the life was by art.

Matthew Arnold has often been rebuked for suggesting that art would be the religion of the future, but if you take his statement not as a slogan to wave but as a statement of what was going to happen, it would seem that he was historically accurate, or prophetic.

And if you ask why I hazard a guess that the great period of art may now be over, I can but suggest that, while holding that idea firmly in mind, you look around you. And I would remind you that even if I am somewhat right about what is happening, it may not be altogether a disaster. The world is a very deep place, no matter how much of it we explain, and explain away, and the end of a particular form of experience does not mean the end of experience. Forms are there to be transformed, and of all this something kind and good may come one day. Or so I hope.

Some Thoughts on American Poetry Today

BY M. L. ROSENTHAL

The United States is a large country, and there are hundreds and hundreds of poets in every section. There are little baby poets, and teen-age poets, and college poets, and soldier poets, and elderly widow poets, and "professional" poets most of whom need another profession to pay for typewriter ribbons and postage stamps. (For purposes of thumb-rule, a professional poet may be defined as a poet whose name appears on pages 1-88 of *A Directory of American Poets*, published in January 1973 by Poets and Writers, Inc.) Each of these groups produces some interesting poems *daily*; this is not only because the level of mediocrity has risen considerably of late, but also because genuine sensitization to poetry has taken place within groups hitherto immune and because the one positive result of the schools' failure to open the young to the literature of the past is that they have grown less awestruck at the Muse's rigorous expectations.

This is a country in which everyone is encouraged to be a beginner in the arts (and in all matters of the intellect) but in which there is virtually no interest in the nature of actual developed accomplishment. It seems absurd to attempt assessing the present state of American poetry when so pathetically few names of poets are known to the general reader. The best work often remains totally unreviewed in the weekly and monthly publications of general circulation that discuss books regularly. Promising young poets and even accomplished older ones are hard put to get their books published. It would be easy to say that the bland indifference of publishers exactly matches the bland indifference of the aforesaid weeklies and monthlies, and that they have little interest in literary values. But the blame is economic and social rather than personal. Without a climate or a center of mature discussion, literary reputation becomes an affair of public relations — and this even when everyone concerned is essentially honorable. Momentarily prestigious persons and cliques promote their own candidates for fame. But what is the value of praise or prizes from people too complacent or too simply uninterested in the unfamiliar to know who is writing what?

I write this from the viewpoint of those who do not think that literature, and poetry least of all, has become obsolete, and who agree with Wallace Stevens that a book of poems is "a damned serious thing." Had the American Academy of Arts and Science taken poetry seriously, they would have honored the late Ezra Pound with their Emerson-Thoreau prize because his work, with all that can be said against him and it, embodied everything in life that counted for him and was mobilized toward the creation of a self-transcendent art. Pound took the risk demanded in Emerson's challenge: "We do not with sufficient plainness or sufficient profoundness address ourselves to life, nor dare we chaunt our own times and social circumstance." These aims are simple, perhaps too simple to meet all the requirements of genuine art, and yet they look toward ends nobler and more thrilling than most criticism seems aware of today. Safe tributes to talented mediocrity are the order of the day, even under the Nobel Prize. In Pound's poetry we see the "sufficient profoundness" of passionate and tragic artistic confrontation of life. He locates the enduring conflict within himself and within our civilization. Sometimes he does so painfully, sometimes exquisitely, sometimes wrongheadedly or disgustingly — but he succeeds because, through his images and language, his energetic genius seeks out the elusive realities of human consciousness. The repudiation of Pound by the Academy (once their committee had recommended doing him honor), a quarter-century after the political acts for which he had paid dearly by a dozen years in a mental asylum, was the act of people who would not give two cents for poetry in its own right. They would be unable to name a single one of the many younger poets, anything *but* fascist, whose master has been Pound. They do not know that if you plunge into his work, which even at this late date stands with the most advanced and brilliant of the age, you are in the midst of the most disturbing and enlightening intellectual and spiritual play with the essential matter of modern consciousness. I make these points so insistently to try to counteract the basic triviality of vision that seems to be coming into the foreground with the current attempt to discredit and demean the high artistic aims and genuine historical relevance of great poetry.

Pound was, however he distorted the position, in the tradition of the Enlightenment and of Thoreau's and Emerson's individualism. He insisted on his understanding of the realities rather than yielding to prevailing opinion. His courage — *and* foolhardiness, since it pitched him into the abyss — in going beyond the bounds of cultural consensus was surely Concord independence pushed to the extreme. For the same reason Imamu Amiri Baraka should be heeded despite his black racism; though his poetry and plays cannot be said to compare with Pound at his best, they nevertheless at their most interesting follow intractably through into an artistic vision that rights the balance in its own way. I think that Baraka draws a false distinction when he says that "Blacks in the street learn the truth about the society's real values from television — 'The Beverly Hillbillies' and Jack Paar — rather than through exposure to the profundities of Western culture which produce confusion in the minds of Negroes." Though the distinction is meaningless the concern with the realities that guide the imagination is not.

Before returning to Baraka and, more concretely, to his poetry, I want to note that poetry in English has been experiencing an exhaustion of the vein of pure sensibility. When he speaks of "Western Culture" in the way I have just cited, Baraka — I see I have returned to him already, though not for long — is at least partly speaking of that poetry of emotional self-exploration that found one culmination a few years back in the Confessional poetry of Lowell and others. He is calling for attention to literal social realities that will break the circuit of introspective entrancement. In so doing, he closely resembles a number of other figures who have reinforced their formal experimentation by a heavy use of myths, symbols, and ritual motifs from cultures that antedate or resist the modern state and the specific conformations of modern civilization.

I could cite the late Charles Olson as an obvious instance, with his interest in Mayan and Indochinese clues to alternative cultural sets. But it would be useful to suggest that this sort of contemporary development is hardly exclusively American. The Black Mountain poets have emphasized an inner, organic motivation centered in consciousness realizing itself about some process of the mind or of external relationship and reality. But we find something similar in certain current British tendencies — for instance, in the later Ted Hughes (and implicit, actually, in his tightly structured earlier work). His *Wodwo* was so loosely held together that, when he published it in

1967, he felt compelled to note that the whole thing — the separate poems, the prose, the dramatic section — is to be read as a single unit. A couple of years later he was well into *Crow,* and described it to me in a letter:

> I've been writing a long saga about a bird or a quasi-bird. It's been going on too long — now trying to finish it. It's about a Crow — it began as a device to justify the plainest and ugliest language possible within limits, but it's become a bit of an epic.
>
> It's the other pole to the style of "Cadenza."

No doubt the assertion that *Crow* "began as a device to justify the plainest and ugliest language possible within limits" was deliberately unpretentious and self-protective. Hughes's desire for language free of any gentility is akin in motive to Baraka's stress on the brutal side of white America's consciousness, and he took intellectual clues from a book on shamanism and from certain interests of Vaska Popa's. But anyone can see how much his earlier poetry, whatever it's *about,* is intimately in search of a language so hard and fierce it will taste of blood. His animal poems in *Lupercal* are concentrations of that search, projections of a sophisticated and even decadent neo-primitivism. When he broke out of their thematic grip, he still kept the same aim of making the intensity of his language, in itself, his symbolic means. "Cadenza," the poem in *Wodwo* to which his letter alluded, is perhaps Hughes's most purely lyrical poem despite its violent buffoonery at the very end. It consists of a series of images, proliferating in singing couplets after the one-line opening stanzas, evoked by a violin solo. The images are of death-terror, lost love, and mourning. They make for a dazzling surrealist elegy, and the rhythmic idiom inevitably recalls, because it echoes and summons up their very tone and pitch, the voice and tone of Sylvia Plath's poetry, especially the title-poem of *Ariel.* Her miraculous buoyancy and, simultaneously, her suicidal death-consciousness reverberate in many of the lines and couplets of "Cadenza":

> The full, bared throat of a woman walking water,
> The loaded estuary of the dead . . .

In *Crow,* Hughes tries to suppress that voice which stamped itself into his own spirit even while Sylvia Plath was going through the terrible phase, at once passionate and charged with deadly hatred, defined by the poems in *Ariel.* Husband and wife, as young poets developing together with a definitely reciprocal influence on one another despite their quite individual minds and styles, had shared a desire to be ruthlessly true to their perceptions and to the demands of language. One can actually see, in certain poems of the *Crow* sequence, a continuation of that reciprocity. They present both a fused voice and an ongoing dialogue. Meanwhile, the larger vision of the sequence as a whole pushes toward a kind of negative transcendence, archaic, archetypal, anti-lyrical, and obliterative of personality. The process by which Hughes creates a context for "the plainest and ugliest language" while guiding the interplay of opposites into what he calls "a bit of an epic" makes *Crow* an improvisational structure just as surely as are the superficially more diffuse great American sequences.

I want, though, to return now to the American scene specifically. Let us not speak of movements; for the moment, at least, the very word is wearying. Nor do I wish to call attention to the better-known figures among, or influenced by, the Black Mountain poets, the Confessional poets, and so on. Instead, I should like to make a few suggestions about some other figures and about one or two neglected considerations in current American poetry. One reason that I have mentioned Hughes's work is that it is of the same order as some of the most interesting American work of the age. It represents a formal ordering of a kind that the best American poetry has been after for a long time but that British critical hostility has made it difficult for English poets to pursue. Such a triumph is always internationally significant, and the explosive violence in Hughes's poetry seems especially expressive to Americans at this moment.

Indeed, American sensibility has in the past decade suffered a renewed exposure to violence in ways we did not expect and hardly yet realize. One poetic result is a morbid, sickened assimilation of the shock into the language of feeling generally. The phenomenon, though not the emotion, is comparable to the way in which the exploration of the New World in earlier centuries enabled a poet to address his girl exuberantly as "O my America, my new-found-land." An instance of what I am talking about in contemporary America is Baraka's poem "BLACK DADA NIHILISMUS." Here the poet contrives a rhetoric of rage that acts out the role assigned the black man by his most paranoid oppressor. It is important to note, as with Hughes, that the violent, simple affect exists in a sophisticated intellectual context. The very title of the poem shows a deliberate marshaling of motifs from literary and political revolutionary tradition and from black magic. Jones assimilates the syntax, the cultural

tokens, and the vocabulary of uneducated blacks to his highly literate
context of reference:

> Why you stay, where they can
> reach? Why you sit, or stand, or walk
> in this place, a window on a dark
>
> warehouse. Where the minds packed in
> straw. New homes, these towers, for those
> lacking in money or art. A cult of death,
>
> need of the simple striking arm un'der
> the streetlamp. The cutters, from under
> their rented earth. Come up, black dada
>
> nihilismus. Rape the white girls. Rape
> their fathers. Cut the mothers' throats.
> Black dada nihilismus, choke my friends
>
> in their bedrooms with their drinks spilling
> and restless for tilting hips or dark liver
> lips sucking splinters from the master's thigh.

At the end of his poem, Baraka finds a rationale for this summons
to a symbolic holocaust destroying all whites, including his own
white friends:

> money, God, power,
> a moral code, so cruel
> it destroyed Byzantium, Tenochtitlan, Commanch
> > (*got it, Baby!*)
>
> For tambo, willie best, dubois, patrice, mantan, the
> bronze buckaroos.
>
> > For Jack Johnson, asbestos, tonto, buckwheat,
> > billie holiday.
>
> > > For tom russ, l'overture, vesey, beau jack,
>
> (may a lost god damballah, rest or save us
> against the murders we intend
> against his lost white children
> black dada nihilismus)

The author of these lines has something of a political power base
in one of our great, crisis-ridden American cities: Newark, New
Jersey. His poems and plays have explored the subjective effects of
the dominant whites' violation of black mentality, and at the same
time have acted out psychologically and in fantasy the politics of
intransigent confrontation. No American poet since Pound has come
closer to making poetry and politics reciprocal forms of action. That
is not necessarily a good thing. When the reciprocity comes out of
the very nature of the language and feeling that engage the poet, when
it amounts to a discovery as of the awakening of the senses, then we

have to do with an accomplishment whose moral and aesthetic character are inseparable values: as in *Hamlet* or *Coriolanus* or, less grandly, in Shelley's glorious chorus in *Hellas*: "The world's great age begins anew." In such work the quality of the poet's engagement with truth makes him incapable of using language dishonestly. But in part of "BLACK DADA NIHILISMUS" Baraka's political rhetoric cheapens his poem and dilutes its intended but merely contrived barbaric ferocity. His catalogue of names, for example, places Lumumba in the same category of race victims as characters in American comic strips and radio serials, nightclub performers, and prizefighters, so that he weakens and at last loses the poem's original incantatory force.

Even in this poem, however, as the last stanza quoted shows, Baraka has not betrayed himself entirely through an oversimplified rhetoric. He is the victim of his own best human qualities, a man who refuses to let himself slide out from under the burdens of less privileged black Americans. The psychological and political dangers of his position are obvious, for his own problems of poetic perspective are almost engulfed by the demands of his insistent militancy. Many of his poems are the deliberate invention of an intellectual poet setting out to internalize the violence of the poor blacks' experience and convert it into an equal and opposite reaction, and one just about as acceptable as a promise of national enlightenment. But in his best work he is guided by the subjective pressures underlying this process. His poem "An Agony. As Now." begins with a finely accurate self-identification:

> I am inside someone
> who hates me. I look
> out from his eyes. Smell
> what fouled tunes come in
> to his breath. Love his
> wretched women. . . .

I won't say that the feeling here is peculiarly American. It *is,* nevertheless, *specifically* American though we can, no doubt, find the same kind of racial, national, or class pathology, in many variations, expressed in the literature of other countries as well. The speaker cannot sort himself out from the degraded image of himself stamped into him by the ruling culture. He lives in a ghetto of the sensibility, seeing himself through eyes not his own. The condition is maddeningly confusing, for conscious, objective analysis teaches him one thing but inward realization is something else again. Now, to get this all right is an artistically precarious affair. It is easy to slip from the rigorous truthfulness of "An Agony. As Now." to the easy political tendentiousness of most of "BLACK DADA NIHILISMUS" and of the many imitations of Baraka's work by younger black poets. Understanding the *poetic* problems involved is essential to do something more sustained in its achievement than Baraka has yet done.

This brings us, for a moment, back to Pound. His *Mauberley*, with its balance between the rhetorical first movement and the introspective second movement (with various subtle shifts and modulations within each of the two main divisions of the sequence), is one valuable model still for dealing with poetic issues at once social and private. One can find many individual poems by many poets of the past two decades that betray the way poets must continue to grapple with comparable questions of balance if their work as a whole is to sustain the promise of occasional pieces. Thus, James Dickey's "The Firebombing" discovers and sustains an ambiguous moral awareness deeply true to the situation of having bombed unknown people and their homes in war — a guilt held in abeyance and, in fact, declared non-existent that yet persists. In other poems, though, Dickey slips away from the sustained sensitivity of "the Firebombing" into the cultivation of a sense of confusion for its own sake, one almost masquerading as vision. In many poems he focuses on some simple literal situation and then blurs his subject — not the same thing as poetic exploration. As Baraka and other poets lapse into sloganizing, so Dickey and others lapse into undifferentiated meandering within portentously isolated private states without perspective.

There is little question that the war in Vietnam, and the sense of government as an impersonal, impervious, complex engine of destruction, has murderously colored the sense of spiritual desolation of much recent American poetry. Within that context the poetic issue we have been discussing becomes even more insistent. Galway Kinnell's *The Book of Nightmares* meets Emerson's challenge more bravely and consistently than most recent work. At the center of this sequence we find two poems. The first, "In the Hotel of Lost Light," fixes on the poet's sense of being at one with all trapped and defeated beings; a fly caught by a spider, a down-and-out drunk found dead in a hotel room — these become nuances of himself in a world of symbolic possibilities. This is the key-poem of the sequence, locating the speaker:

> in March, of the year Seventy,
> in my sixteen-thousandth night of war and madness,
> in the Hotel of Lost Light, under the freeway
> which roams out into the dark
> of the moon, in the absolute spell
> of departure, and by the light
> from the joined hemispheres of the spider's eyes.

I need hardly point out that the word "war" here takes on a particular strength and meaning in the American context of the poem. So does the word "freeway," with its connotation of endless stretches of superhighway with their innumerable high-powered, speeding cars. The final lines of the passage just quoted charge the desolate scene with a malign, "absolute" spell —

> the absolute spell
> of departure, and by the light
> from the joined hemisphere of the spider's eyes.

This is the closest Kinnell comes to the fierce unsentimentality of *Crow,* though he compensates — if that is the word — by the human immediacies of his poem which test its involvement with ordinary life more than Hughes allows himself to do. Marriage, birth, thwarted love, the atmosphere of particular places, the voices of soldiers — all these set off the moments when the impersonality of the universe suddenly freezes the poem's temperature and a music of personal loneliness in the face of the actual takes over:

> when the Maud moon
> glimmered in those first nights,
> and the Archer lay
> sucking the icy biestings of the cosmos,
> in his crib of stars,
> I had crept down . . .
> and there learned my only song.

But these moments are enwombed in literal human realization. The second of the poems at the center of the sequence is "The Dead Shall Be Raised Incorruptible." It begins:

> A piece of flesh gives off
> smoke in the field —
>
> carrion,
> caput mortuum,
> orts,
> pelfs,
> fenks,
> sordes,
> gurry dumped from hospital trashcans.
>
> *Lieutenant!*
> *This corpse will not stop burning!*

This last cry is repeated at the end of the poem and thus becomes its ultimate refrain. In between we have a monologue by a soldier who has come to love seeing the "little black pajamas jumping / and falling" and in fact has had all his senses awakened by war's distorted passion:

> "I love the *sound*
> of them, I guess I just loved
> the *feel* of them sparkin' off my hands . . ."

The longest segment of "The Dead Shall Be Raised Incorruptible" is a testament after Villon (whom Kinnell has translated superbly), in which Christian man bequeaths his soul and various parts of his body to selected recipients. The ironic tone is set by the opening stanza:

> In the Twentieth Century of my trespass on earth,
> having exterminated one billion heathens,
> heretics, Jews, Moslems, witches, mystical seekers,
> black men, Asians, and Christian brothers,
> every one for his own good . . .
>
> I, Christian man, groan out the testament of my last will.

Amid the sardonic, raucous, and obscenely jeering notes, one stanza sustains the deeper motifs of tragic pain and anger suffused by regret that derive from the continuing shock of a series of more and more meaningless wars:

> To the last man surviving on earth
> I give my eyelids worn out by fear, to wear
> in his long nights of radiation and silence,
> so that his eyes can't close, for regret
> is like tears seeping through closed eyelids.

I cite these various passages merely to suggest, without extended analysis or any attention to its weakness, the complex and interesting character of Kinnell's sequence. I wanted to show its shifting tones and voices and intensities. As Pound, Eliot, and Williams all discovered in their experiments with open form that yet *remains* form, or at least strives toward it, the extended development of a complex and serious theme requires such a variety of affects handled musically. The whole work serves as a context, fluid, alive, afloat on the overall developing consciousness of the work's total voice, within which the individual affect finds its place. *The Book of Nightmares* stands with Robert Lowell's *Life Studies,* Charles Olson's *The Maximus Poems,* Robert Duncan's *Passages,* and Ramon Guthrie's *Maximum Security Ward* among the touchstones of high poetic endeavor of the past decade and a half. It is of some interest that, among these works, only Lowell's has been recognized for one of the yearly national awards given to poets. Perhaps a pair of lines in Guthrie's sequence, written to a quite different end, will explain why this should be so:

> Our God is innocent. He holds forth such awards
> as only the very innocent could ever prize.

I want, especially, to call attention to Guthrie's sequence — not to depreciate the others, but only to wonder, after all, that it has not received more attention. Its unpretentious and humorous colloquialism, its apparently effortless moments of rich and exquisite music, and its simple dramatic situation and continuity (the desperate illness of the poet in a real American hospital) would almost warrant its being called popular poetry, if people of moderate education were at all encouraged to read poetry in our country. Guthrie is probably the most learned of the poets I have named, but he uses his learning to help him get at feelings and meanings and make them available to his reader. The central, autobiographical situation of the sequence easily carries the poem's symbolism. The protagonist's struggle to hold on to all that means life to him is engrossing in the way that Proust (one of Guthrie's great models and sources) is engrossing. At the same time, the morale of poetry itself is at issue here; there is no question of Guthrie's faith that personal and social sanity and the poetic art are intertwined at all points along the emotional scale.

Guthrie's sequence is simple, not in its poetic qualities but in its dramatic immediacy. The protagonist's predicament is clear, and the ebb and flow of moods and motifs and significant memories reinforce our initial sense of what it is. In the opening poem we see him in the "maximum security ward," his term for the intensive care unit in which he has been trapped into becoming a "frantic bramble of / glass and plastic tubes and stainless steel." That is, he is being treated with the kind of indifferent brutality that might be accorded the most extreme case in a mental hospital or prison — hence his use of "maximum security ward." He longs to hear from an old love who has refused to write to him. He imagines making one triumphant gesture at his own funeral by sitting up "with one last galvanic jerk" and declaring his disgust with life. His bitter humor and yearning, couched partly in rich American vernacular, lightly suggest his absolute need to ponder his real identity and to find a perspective that will match the agony and crisis of his present experience.

The poems of Part I of Guthrie's sequence, on the whole, develop a harsh view of existence, hostile to affirmation. The illness itself, unspecified but probably cancer, is presented in the poem "Today Is

Friday" through powerful images of physical pain and impotence and of enclosure in a "cube" — transparent and pressing in on the sufferer — that embodies death as an active principle at once intractably abstract and closing in like a ravening beast. Another poem, "Fiercer Than Wolves," presents the terrible early death of the poet's religious mother (by suicide after a tormenting series of strokes) and of his father in a fire. Another, "Polar Bear," is a remarkable symbolic rendering of the state of death-awareness and loss of articulateness the speaker had once felt when coming out from under sodium pentathol. And indeed, throughout the sequence, there is an anchoring of abstract considerations in sharply recollected events, personalities, and subjective states. In Part II, Guthrie struggles to deal with the negativism and depression of the earlier section. The poems move through various stages of counter-affirmation, then through very dark moods, then through assertions of a humanistic, secular religiosity, and finally into an aesthetic vision of the artist's ceaseless effort through the centuries to get into the deep sources of the life-principle and project them through his art. Through this projection he can encompass the conditions of existence and free us from being mere victims. Because of the convincing autobiographical evocations that have studded the sequence, the great climactic poem "The Making of the Bear" — an allegorical narrative of man's urge toward aesthetic transcendence of depressive experience — takes on a comparable conviction.

But though anchored in the literal, *Maximum Security Ward* works on us in many other ways. For one thing, Guthrie (like Pound) is quite willing to extend his range of reference through assuming various masks in addition to his empirical self. He is Icarus. He is also Marsyas, who challenged Apollo to a flute competition and, in one version, won and was honored by a statue in the Roman forum symbolizing liberty but who, in another version, lost and was flayed alive by the god. And he is both a Christ-figure and the archetypal artist of "The Making of the Bear." By humor, self-irony, quick shiftings of tone and dramatic spotlighting, and a constantly recurring introduction of key-lines and figures from preceding poems in the sequence, Guthrie virtually always holds the flow of thought, feeling, and association in order and wards off pomposity or sentimentality. The double tradition of Marsyas, as hero and as scapegoat, helps toward this end, as does Guthrie's picture of himself in "Icarus Agonistes" and elsewhere as a hero — *if* a hero, and more likely an anti-hero — who "got myself overmatched . . . from the start." In fact, the sheer multiplicity of points of attention and jostling tones both keeps the work alive and interesting and enables the poet to correct overstatement and ponderous modulations almost at once. He proposes a class of creative and spiritually absorbed men and women called "Christoi" (not "heroes," not even uniformly admirable) who find themselves becoming what they must by their natures but who hardly realize the glory of what they are, and he adapts his conception of his own various masks to the qualities of this class. Memories, some of them traumatic, of World War I and of the Paris of that war and just after color the poems.

In short, Guthrie's sequence gives us a teeming mind in full action with all its lyric excitement and redeeming memory and desolate self-confrontation brought to bear on the whole contemporary state of consciousness — my description hasn't half begun to suggest the poem's overflowing life. For instance, there is a whole dimension of sexual consciousness, centered in female deities, that affects its final character enormously. I wish there were space here to compare it with Duncan's *Passages* as they appear in scattered groupings, throughout his book *Bending the Bow*. There are some interesting convergences of theme and symbol, but many differences too. Particularly, Duncan does not so much explore as sing or state his attitudes, feelings, and desires. The elusive, disappearing music, the prophetic stance, the assumption of knowledge of mystic realities that may or may not be earned — all these make Duncan's poetic structures less open to the play of passionate meditation than Guthrie's.

It is interesting to note that, *intellectually*, our poetry is still just about at the stage of thought that Thomas Hardy reached a long time ago: jammed up against the tragicomic irony of human circumstance. In the rival world of the artist and of myth, existential irony is transcended; in great art, it is wrestled down because confronted, defined, and subordinated to the mind's plastic use of all the realities that it has to do with. There is a sense abroad that we can actually get past Hardy if we let our apperceptions and our undefined but overwhelming emotional needs organize our intelligence into some kind of balanced relationship (comparable to that which Lawrence called for in "Song of a Man Who Has Come Through"). A passage from Paul Goodman's *Tragedy & Comedy: Four Cubist Plays*, an absorbing sequence though it does not match the works I have named in sheer poetic quality, will illustrate the problem, though not the solution. It is in the play called *Structure of Pathos, after Euripides*. At the point in this play from which I am about to quote, the protagonist and the leader of the Chorus of Women have been having a highly enlightened and cynical discussion about the disparity between human meaning and the workings of nature and the gods. The protagonist has left the stage in rage and disgust, and the Chorus then speaks an incantatory prose-poetry:

> Because things happen that I don't expect, I have an inkling
>   there is an existing world, given to me and not
>   entirely made by me.
> There seems to be other persons in it like myself.
> Alas! We are lost here, as if on "an island desert and
>   frightful." I cannot turn to my fellow for help, for he
>   knows no more about it than I.
> Yet oh! I am moved and sometimes delighted by the power and
>   infinite variety of what occurs. It magnifies my diminished
>   spirit to notice just the size of the world. That cloud
>   up there — if I calculate its true size — is large enough
>   to blanket all our city. And the sky — for the ground
>   is always larger than the figure — must be enormous,
>   maybe immeasurable. I am pleased. I identify with that.

While this is hardly poetry of the order found in the sequences of Kinnell, Guthrie, and the others, it shares their preoccupation and (except for Duncan) their earthiness. Guthrie's work, like the minor poetry of fine sensibility that we have in such large supply nowadays, is often deeply interesting. But it falls short of the transcendent qualities of heroic poetry in the modern mode because it lacks genuine poetic dynamics involving a range of styles including the purely lyrical. The sustaining of a vision of reality internalized by the imagination and then projected outward in a humanized order is the structuring motive of the great modern sequences. This is what Guthrie calls the "vast innocence of Einstein, Rembrandt, Blake" that links the memory of the past and the openness to the unknown future that is the true humanistic and aesthetic tradition. Goodman stated the issues though he could not fling his poem out of himself in such a way that its very form would be an exploration, a drunken boat charting its own direction by dead reckoning.

For the moment, discussions of schools and movements in poetry have rather burnt themselves out. Our breaths are gathering for a new look at just where we are now, and then a new plunge into the unknown. I have therefore thought it useful here to speak to Emerson's old idea of "chaunting our own times and social circumstance" and to point to some poets whose genius has caught up that idea in recent years.

"Imagine Wrestling with an Angel":
An Interview with Stanley Kunitz *

INTERVIEWER: ROBERT BOYERS

Q.: *Whenever I go and visit people who are interested in poetry, there seems to be constant reference to Stanley Kunitz as the "poets' poet." Have you heard yourself described in this way? What do you think these people mean?*

KUNITZ: When it was said of Spenser, it was meant to be a compliment. Nowadays it would depend on the inflection. I'm a bit leery of it.

Q.: *I was wondering if the fact that people speak of you in these terms suggests that they have in mind another kind of poetry which is more immediately contemporary, more popular among the young on college campuses, and whether this isn't the poetry, this other poetry, that the best poets themselves consider inferior, perhaps not poetry at all?*

KUNITZ: That may be so, but it's dangerous to think of poetry as being divided into two kinds — a high art and a low art. No poet can afford to be out of touch with the commonplace. In my youth I suppose I rather willed myself on being an hermetic poet. But for years I have tried to make my work more open and accessible, without sacrificing its complex inner tissue. Film, jazz, and rock have been very much a part of my world of experience.

Q.: *You read many poetry manuscripts. Can you give us some notions of what the younger poets, those who've not published volumes, are writing?*

KUNITZ: The most notable characteristic of the poetry written by the young — in their 20's or 30's — is its variety. There is no dominant strain that I can detect. So much depends on local in-

*Edited transcript of a public interview conducted at Skidmore College in April, 1972.

terest — regional associations, university teachers who happen at the moment to be available to them as models. A few years ago it seemed to me that the New York School had many adherents over the country, but I think there are fewer now — it seems to have exhausted its potentiality. Certainly Robert Bly and company have a number of acolytes who follow their precepts thundered from on high — but that's only one aspect of the scene. You can find almost as many different styles as you can find poets.

Q.: *In particular I was interested in one poet who was awarded the Yale Series Prize, Hugh Seidman, in many ways a remarkable poet. Now many of his poems seem to me to be haphazardly put together, and he seems to trust a good deal to what one might call the "happy accident," the chance hit, which is matched, I guess, by a great many unlucky misses. I wonder if you might speak a little bit about that kind of poetry, a poetry which includes the "happy accident."*

KUNITZ: The concept of chance is inseparable from the act of poetry. Verse that is precalculated and preordained inevitably goes dead. There has to be room for accidents in the writing of a poem. You leave yourself open to the possibility of anything happening and you hope that it will work — if it doesn't that's your hard luck.

Q.: *In the volume* The Contemporary Poet as Artist and Critic, *there is a symposium having to do with your poem "Father and Son," a very beautiful poem. There is some talk in the symposium about the line in the poem which reads "The night nailed like an orange to my brow." In the course of your response, you speak of the line as an example of that special kind of risk which poets must take, and which constitutes a kind of signature, a unique signature of the poet. Could you speak a little bit about the relationship between a good risk and a bad risk in poetry?*

KUNITZ: I don't think that you can tell beforehand whether the risk is a good one or a bad one — but if you take no risks, I doubt that much will happen. I want to venture beyond what I know to be safe and correct, to grapple with a possibility that doesn't yet appear.

Q.: *And would you say that in taking the risk with a line that doesn't seem readily to yield its private associations even to a reader who's armed with the elementary biographical information, you would justify that risk simply on the basis of what you felt strongly at the time the poem was being composed? That is, must one always take into account the presence of the reader who perhaps won't be able to pick up the association?*

KUNITZ: In the first place the poet hasn't invited the reader to become the judge of his poem — he enters the scene after the event. It is the reader's choice — he can either continue to work with the poem, or he can decide that it offers him nothing, and if he so chooses, that's his privilege. The poet ought not to complain if the reader decides that he doesn't like that particular poem, or that he can't understand it, and turns to another poem, or to somebody else's work. A poet who begins by saying, "I am myself and only myself," is in no position to demand, "You must read me and love me." My own preference is for a poetry that looks fairly simple on the surface, but that moves mysteriously inside its skin.

Q.: *I'm very interested also in raising the whole question of composition, the process of composition, and I've come upon all sorts of preferences in poets who come at their poems in a great variety of ways. Roethke, for instance, speaks in the* Letters *of carrying around a phrase in his pocket, scrawled on a piece of paper for a very long time, and then of allowing that single phrase or image to develop over perhaps several years, and then watching that phrase lead to others, and finally building an entire poem out of that one single image; or I think of Dylan Thomas establishing a whole string of end rhymes and then sort of backing into the poem, filling in the text that leads to the end rhyme. How do you compose a poem?*

KUNITZ: I'm a night bird, so that most of my poems happen in the small hours and usually after a long struggle to clean my mind out — to get rid of the day — that's the first step. The poem usually ripples out from something buried. Perhaps you turn over the leaves of your notebook and come across a phrase 5 years old, or 15 years old, that leaps out of the page — it's ready now to be played with. And then you begin pushing works and rhythms around. But to me it's mainly dredging, dredging down into the unconscious — trying to find associations, links with the whole life and with the secrets of the life, not with the obvious materials. And so the poem slowly builds. I say it over and over again — whatever I have of it — the lines with which I begin — it's a kind of incantation and maybe a form of self-hypnosis, who knows, but gradually the rhythm begins to take over, and then I know that nothing is going to stop the poem from happening.

Q.: *Do you think it's possible for a reader of poems, like yourself for instance, to perceive, in reading the poem for the first time, whether it was written with one approach rather than another, whether a poem suggests in its very contours, its surface contours, whether it was constructed out of an image which gave birth to others, or whether it was originally an "idea poem," emerging from a particular thematic concern, a political idea, for instance? Do poems yield that kind of information, do you think?*

KUNITZ: In the kind of poem I'm talking about the stitching between thoughts and feelings is invisible. I don't really care much for "idea poems" as such. They're a form of illustration.

Q.: *Who were the poetic models that you adopted and followed as a young poet? Were you, for instance, taken by T. S. Eliot, as others were who came of age in the 1920's and '30's?*

KUNITZ: I was moved by him but I resisted him — I think that's the answer there — one could not help but be moved by him because he was a poetic event. Certainly "The Wasteland" shook my world at the moment of its appearance. I can still remember the thrill of picking up my copy of *The Dial* in which it appeared. Subsequently I became a kind of adversary. His definition of poetry as an objective act, a depersonalized performance, was contrary to my own conviction that the art and the life were bound together. I sought a more passionate voice. And I scorned his politics.

Q.: *Were there other models that you felt closer to in that time, in the '20's, for instance?*

KUNITZ: Contemporaries? No. The poets who meant most to me then were Yeats (the later Yeats) and Hopkins. I studied both intensively. Hardy was another of my admirations.

Q.: *Did you study Thomas a good deal, later on, in the '40's and the beginning of the '50's?*

KUNITZ: Not particularly — though there are five or six of Thomas's poems that I admire. You're talking now of literary fashions — something I have no use for. In the '20's and '30's one had to follow Eliot in order to have an audience. In the late '30's, into the '40's, one had to be Audenesque. Then Thomas was the rage. Later the Beats had their turn. And so it goes. The easiest poet to neglect is one who resists classification.

Q.: *In thinking of tastes and fashions in poetry, I've often been fascinated by a number of things the late Sir Herbert Read used to say about poetry, feeling that a sort of betrayal was involved in a poet's going back over ground that had been amply covered by other poets. Do you think that there is such a thing as regression in the life of poetry, and perhaps more to the point, what is the nature of the function of innovation in poetry? Is it necessary that great poets be radical innovators? Can you conceive of a great poet who is an aesthetic reactionary?*

KUNITZ: Pound more or less covered that ground when he set aside a category of inventors among the poets. They are not necessarily the strongest voices of an age, but they often have great influence. Pound affected his contemporaries more than, let us say, Yeats did, who was not an inventor, but I would be willing to say flatly that Yeats is the greater poet.

Q.:   *You would say, then, that the whole idea of regression in the life of poetry is not really a viable notion, that it is possible to go back over old ground, and to do things which are essentially similar to what earlier poets perfected?*

KUNITZ: The trouble with Read's idea is that the idea of regression, like the idea of progress, has no aesthetic relevance. The way backward and the way forward are the same. A rediscovery of the past often leads to radical innovation. We know, for example, that Picasso was inspired by African sculpture, that the art of the Renaissance is linked with the resurgence of classic myth. Poetic technique follows the same route. At the moment I can think of Hopkins, who went back to Old English for his sprung rhythm; of Pound, who turned his ear on Provençal song; of Berryman, who dug up inversion and minstrel patter for his *Dream Songs.* These are all acts of renewal, not tired replays of the style of another period — which is the last thing I am prepared to defend. Pound was, of course, right, in his criticism of "The Wasteland" manuscript, when he dissuaded Eliot from trying to compete with Pope in the matter of composing heroic couplets. As he said, Pope could do it better. In general, a poet has to rework — not imitate — the past, and the success of his reworking is dependent on the degree of his contemporary awareness. If a poet has an ear for the living speech — whose rhythmic pattern is ever so slightly modified from generation to generation — he has at least the foundation of a style, the one into which he was born. I recall that Roethke and I used to challenge each other to guess the dates of the most obscure poems we could find. Over a long period we became so expert at the game that we almost never missed by more than ten years. It was simply because the voice, the stylistic voice, of any decade is unmistakable.

Q.:   *Is there such a thing as a direct relation between the poet and the particular moment of his culture, conceived as a political situation? What I'm referring to is the kind of statement we've heard from Denise Levertov of late, where the claim is made that a poet who is of his time must necessarily reflect the moment of his culture, especially when that culture is in crisis and turmoil, that to indulge a strictly personal kind of poetry at a time when one's own country is engaged in destroying thousands of people in Vietnam, for instance, is to do something that is totally irresponsible and runs counter to the whole life of poetry. Does that make any sense to you?*

KUNITZ: The war disgusts and outrages me, just as it does Denise, but I'm not inclined to tell other poets what they may or may not write. Each of us has to be trusted with his own conscience. The fanatic is the direct opposite of the poet. It's no accident that most of the poetry of confrontation is such appalling stuff. What could be more spiritually stultifying than an exclusive diet of anti-war or anti-Nixon tracts? An age in crisis needs more than ever to be made aware of the full range of human possibility.

Q.:   *In that respect, what do you see as the basic function of your own art? Is it essentially designed to give pleasure, is it educative, does it serve the function of rendering the general experience more complex?*

KUNITZ: Let me try to reply in an historical context. Modern poetry, in the long view, springs out of the Age of Enlightenment and the Industrial Revolution. When faith withered and the Church could no longer satisfy the universal need for otherness, poetry became the alternative medium of transcendence. The poet assumed, or reasserted — from an earlier tribal structure — an ambiguous but socially disturbing role with prophetic or shamanistic implications. One of his functions — as Blake clearly understood — was to serve as defender of the natural universe and of natural man against the greed and ambition of the spoilers and their faceless agents. Politically, I see the poet as the representative free man, the irreconcilable adversary of the Nation-State.

Q.:   *Is there any useful connection to be made, in a general sense, between age and creativity? Many have claimed that the creative powers wane with the advancing years, yet we all know of very wonderful poets who seemed to have their powers grow stronger with the passage of the years. For me, for instance, the major period of William Carlos Williams is his final period, though that is not the case, of course, with people like Eliot or Stevens. Is there any general relationship that's worth pointing to?*

KUNITZ: The determining factor there is the relationship between the life and the work. Yeats has a phrase, "radical innocence," that I cherish. As I interpret it, it's the capacity for perpetual self-renewal, as opposed to a condition of emotional exhaustion or world-weariness; it's waking each day to the wonder of possibility; it's being like a child — which is not to say being childish. "There lives the dearest freshness deep down things" — Hopkins' line — that's an expression of radical innocence. With Blake, it's the very essence of his art and of his prophetic function. The poets of radical innocence stay alive till the day they die — and, even then, they take that last step as an adventure.

Q.: *When I think of radical innocence, I think also of Roethke's special freshness and innocence. Could you tell us a little bit about how you came to know Roethke and what he was like in your experience of him?*

KUNITZ: In the mid-'30's I was living in an old stone house in New Hope, Pennsylvania — it's the setting of a number of my poems, including the one called "River Road." Roethke drove downriver in his jalopy from Lafayette College, where he was teaching, and knocked at my door one evening late in the year. I can still remember him standing there, a big blond hulk in a raccoon coat, with my first book of poems in his hand. *Intellectual Things* had been published in 1930 and had received some attention, but I still felt almost completely isolated from the literary world. Ted was then unpublished, except for a handful of poems in magazines. The first thing he told me, after I asked him in, was that he knew several of my poems by heart; and he proceeded to prove it, after a drink or two, by reciting a couple of his favorites. Would I look at his own stuff? I would, and did. We talked through that whole night. At last I had found a friend who was as mad about poetry as I was! We were two outsiders, and we needed each other. In one respect his need was greater, since I have never been able to show unfinished work to anybody.

Q.: *He used to send you drafts of his poems, didn't he? How did he take to criticism and to suggestions for revision?*

KUNITZ: He hated criticism, most poets do. He would sulk, he was a great sulker, and if I said a poem of his didn't work he would get into a corner and ask for another drink and put his head down and breathe heavily. Oh, his silences were forbidding. He couldn't stand being rushed. A poem had to be sweated out. Eventually he would come around to doing whatever needed to be done. No one was more of a perfectionist. And he was endlessly fascinated by technique. How he despised poets who were afflicted with what he called a "tin ear"!

Q.: *Do you remember the kinds of suggestions you might charac-teristically make to Roethke about his poems, the ones he was writing in the '30's and '40's?*

KUNITZ: One of Roethke's problems in the beginning was that he was so impressionable. There was a good deal of Eliot in those early poems . . . obvious echoes. An even stronger influence was his friend Louise Bogan. The other women who influenced his work, but to a lesser degree, were Elinor Wylie and Léonie Adams. Some-times I'd find my own lines coming back to me — that was a delicate matter. Then the poems tended to be a little too fussy in their work-ing, too neatly structured and resolved. I wanted him to pry open his interior world. In those early years of our association I tried to liberate him into his own identity. When the liberation occurred, I was overwhelmed.

Q.: *Has your estimation of Roethke and his work changed much over the years?*

KUNITZ: In my review of *The Lost Son* for *Poetry* magazine in 1948, I announced that here was a good book, the voice of a superb imagination, and I haven't wavered from that conviction to this day.

Q.: *You feel as strongly about the posthumous volume,* The Far Field?

KUNITZ: It could be argued that Roethke had already gone as far in his journey as he had strength to go. Certainly not all the poems in *The Far Field* are first-rate, but enough of them are to augment any other poet's reputation. Why do critics want to fasten on the inferior poems, the failures, of a poet? It must be in order to establish the superiority of the critical act. My only interest is in the poems that will stand.

Q.: *How about your relationship to Lowell, to Lowell's poetry? When did it begin, and what can you say about him, from your knowledge of his manuscripts and working habits?*

KUNITZ: I didn't meet Lowell till the late '50's, when he was working on *Life Studies*. A few times the three of us — Roethke, Lowell, and myself — were together — but I don't recall them as

particularly happy occasions. It's difficult to talk about someone who
is close, but I can't refrain from observing that one of Cal's most
extraordinary aspects is that he doesn't so much write his poems as
rewrite them. Criticism is more important to him than to any artist
I've ever known. His imagination feeds on it, as it does on history.
His earlier associations — with Tate, Jarrell, and Elizabeth Bishop —
each a poet with a fine critical intelligence — had a major impact on
his development. At this stage he is uniquely himself, but his manuscripts and even his proof sheets still read like palimpsests. And he is
never done with a poem, not even after you would suppose it to be
finally stamped into books and anthologies. Likely as not, the next
time around, it will appear in a different version, revamped word by
word and line by line. His work, as well as his life, is always in
progress.

Q.: *Do you especially care for the work of poets whose names are
frequently linked with Lowell as part of the confessional school?
Do you feel any kinship with poets like Snodgrass, or Sylvia Plath?
Is this where the energy of our best poetry has been?*

KUNITZ: I must tell you that, like most poets, I hate labels. I'm
not quite sure what confessional poetry is, though certain critics have
seen fit to discuss me as a late convert to that school. I guess I
resent that. I've always admired a fierce subjectivity; but compulsive
exhibitionism — and there's plenty of that around — gobs of sticky
hysteria — are an embarrassment. Perhaps I sound more censorious
than I intend. One of my premises is that you can say anything as
long as it is true . . . but not everything that's true is worth saying.
Another is that you need not be a victim of your shame . . . but
neither should you boast about it. In this context maybe Roethke
showed me a way of coping with affliction. Nearly all his adult life
he was a manic-depressive, subject to intermittent crack-ups of devastating violence. In the beginning he was terribly ashamed of these
episodes and tried to conceal them, even from his closest friends.
When he was sent away to a mental hospital, he pretended that he
had gone off on vacation. The onset of his best work coincided with
his discovery that he need not feel guilty about his illness; that it
was a condition he could explore and use; that it was, in fact, convertible into daemonic energy, the driving power of imagination. At
the same time he began to read Jung, who clarified for him the act
of psychic regression, that is, of reliving one's embryonic passage
through fish-shape, frog-shape, bird-shape until one is born human.

That knowledge, that deep metamorphic awareness, became the source of Roethke's strength in his major poems. What they speak of is archetypal experience — which has nothing to do with being a "confessional" poet.

Q.: *You've spoken of your own work in terms of the note of tragic exaltation. Can you describe what this constitutes, how you see this tonality functioning in your poems? Does it bear relation to what we get in classical tragedy, for instance?*

KUNITZ: Not much — but maybe in so far as Recognition is an element of Greek tragedy. It's easier to locate the feeling than to define it. I could offer some lines as a touchstone: "I stand on the terrible threshold, and I see / The end and the beginning in each other's arms." Or Mandelstam, at a greater distance, saying: "Only the flash of recognition brings delight." Or Pascal invoking "the eternal silence of the infinite spaces." Not everybody detects the exaltation, for it's a far more secret thing than terror or despair. Imagine wrestling with an angel, the darkest one of the tribe. You know you're doomed to lose. But that weight on your shoulder!

Q.: *Do you read much besides creative or imaginative literature? Do you keep up with developments in psychoanalysis, in aesthetics, in the sciences, and so on?*

KUNITZ: I try to, except for aesthetics, which seems to me an arid subject. Astrophysics has always fascinated me. And anything to do with the natural universe. Right now I'm deep in whales.

Q.: *But you do feel that the most exciting things at the moment are still poetry, that the work of young and coming poets is still more exciting and alive than work done in other areas?*

KUNITZ: No doubt I'm prejudiced, but I honestly believe that the poetic imagination is capable of embracing the actualities of our time more fully than any other discipline, including the scientific. That's one explanation of my involvement with the graduate writing program at Columbia, with the Yale Series of Younger Poets, and with the Fine Arts Work Center in Provincetown, Massachusetts, where young writers and artists can find a loosely structured community, created for their benefit. Has anyone noticed how the poetic and scientific imaginations are beginning to draw together for mutual sustenance? Perhaps it's an instinctive alliance determined by our crisis of survival. You mentioned Seidman earlier, my first poetry choice at Yale. He was trained as a physicist, and is an expert on the computer. My second choice, Peter Klappert, was a student of zoology, who planned to be a veterinarian. Michael Casey, who came back from Vietnam with his collection of *Obscenities,* was another physics major, who expected to become an engineer, till the Yale award threw him off his course. Robert Hass's book isn't out yet, but its title, *Field Guide,* suggests that it isn't incompatible with the others. Love and botany are his twin preoccupations. Different kinds of intellect may be turning to poetry out of desperation, but it's a good sign, nevertheless.

Q.: *You mentioned last night that you've been working on a long poem. Is there any special reason why you haven't written one before now, and could you speak a little bit about the general failure of our poets to write successful long poems, in most cases even to undertake them?*

KUNITZ: The problem of the long poem, like that of the novel, is related to our loss of faith in the validity of the narrative continuum. Joyce invented a technique for coping with a new time sense, but that required a superhuman effort, which no longer seems consistent with an anti-heroic age. The collapse of Pound's *Cantos* remains a central symptomatic event. Technically he understood the problem, as his contribution to the making of "The Wasteland" proves, but his own project was too indeterminate, and he had overreached himself in the matter of scale. As a collection of fragments, of fairly limited scope, "The Wasteland" seems better adapted for enduring the weathers of an age. I suppose the last major effort to build a solid block of marble was Hart Crane's — and "The Bridge" has its magnificence, but it is the magnificence of failure. "Mistress Bradstreet" and "Howl" are passionate apostrophes, but their architecture is too frail for the weight of their rhetoric. Berryman's *Dream Songs* and Lowell's *Notebook* — to be called *History* in its next incarnation — don't aspire to the unity of the long poem. Essentially they're poetic sequences, like the sonnet cycles of the Elizabethans. I am half-persuaded that the modern mind is too distracted for the span of attention demanded by the long poem, and that no single theme, given the disorder of our epoch, is capable of mobilizing that attention. But I am only half-persuaded.

Q.: *I also wanted to ask you about the whole question of obscurity in the poem, something that Randall Jarrell suggests in a number of places to the effect that in an age which is so apt to appropriate poets, to convert them into acrobats of a sort, it may in fact be the business of the poet to be obscure, to challenge this audience, to make readers uncomfortable, to make them work for whatever pleasures they can get from the poem. Do you feel any sympathy with that?*

KUNITZ: During the heyday of the New Criticism, there were poets who trafficked in obfuscation, providing grist for the critics who trafficked in the explication of obfuscation. A beautiful symbiotic relationship! Poets today tend to be clearer — sometimes all too clear. I strive for a transparency of surface, but I should be disappointed if my work yielded all its substance and tonality at first reading. "Never try to explain," I say somewhere. A poem is charged with a secret life. Some of its information ought to circulate continuously within its perimeters as energy. And that, as I see it, is the function of form: to contain the energy of a poem, to prevent it from leaking out.

Q.: *You spoke last night at dinner of the frustrations of so many contemporary artists, and this led you to reflect on the idea of the poet as monster. Would you care to expatiate?*

KUNITZ: It's a notion that enters into several of my poems — for instance, "The Approach to Thebes," and later "The Artist," which grew out of my friendship with Mark Rothko. So many of my attachments are to the world of painters and sculptors. I recall a conversation with Mark one evening, in which I referred to Picasso — not without admiration — as a monster. And then I added Joyce's name, for good measure. Mark was troubled by my epithet. I tried to explain to him why, in the modern arts, the words "genius" and "monster" may be interchangeable. His face darkened. "You don't mean me, do you?" he asked. Less than a year later he was dead, by his own hand. What is it in our culture that drives so many artists and writers to suicide — or, failing that, mutilates them spiritually? At the root of the problem is the cruel discrepancy between the values of art and the values of society, which makes strangers and adversaries out of those who are most gifted and vulnerable. The artist who turns in on himself, feeds off his own psyche, aggrandizes his bruised ego is on his way to monsterdom. Ambition is the fire in his gut. No sacrifice is judged too great for his art. At a certain point he becomes a nexus of abstract sensations and powers, beyond the realm of the personal. That's when the transformation into monster occurs. I don't mean to imply that everybody is worthy of that designation — it requires a special kind of greatness . . . Sylvia Plath's, for example. If we search among the poets of an older generation for the masters who were whole, who excelled in their humanity, who fulfilled themselves in the life as well as in the work, whom can we name? Not most of "the best among us" — in Pound's words. Certainly not Pound himself, not Eliot, not Yeats, nor Frost, nor Stevens . . . the list could be extended indefinitely. I am told that Pasternak was a notable exception, and I know, closer to home, that William Carlos Williams was another. Then I have to pause. They make a shining pair. The young around us give me hope that eventually they'll have plenty of company. But the condition may well be the creation of a new society.

Robert Lowell: The Middle Years *

BY GABRIEL PEARSON

LOWELL'S MIDDLE POEMS LOOK informal, easy, natural: poetic forms really do appear to cleave to, and become one with, their statement. The breath's utterances and the poem's artifices grow together in the occasion of the poem's coming into being. It is all as natural as breathing, a spontaneous order, each poem unfolding without strain under its own impulse into its proper shape. But one registers this not simply as an occurrence but an intention. The poems are not innocent: the informality is part of an acknowledged design. The contrast ought to be between closed form and open or projective form, to use Charles Olson's terminology. Projective poetry, or at least its supporting mystique, assumes an open, never occupied space in front of the poem into which it grows and which it defines in the process. The law of its growth is in no wise given by the existence of literature as an institution. The poem is not a product but a process. It seeks the utmost cultural innocence by insisting upon itself as utterance, by riding off into the wilderness upon the unique breathing of the poet.

Here one must risk being contentious. The fiction of projective verse is the counterpart of an ideology whose central concern is to detach American from its European inheritance, a sticky web in which the destiny of the whole continent seems trammeled. One would wish to add that this attempt is itself part of the destiny, one which has helped construct it. The dream of innocence permits technological man to unknow, positively to unwill and so carry on—in deliberate innocence —performing his deed, freed from traditional sanctities and controls. To return poetry to some base in the physiology of the breath is the equivalent of other forms of sanctioning myth—the myth of the frontier, the myth of economic self-help, the myth of the westward move-

* This selection from a longer essay appeared before the publication of Lowell's *Notebook* and the volumes that have followed since 1968; reprinted by permission of *The Review* (London).

ment of civilization—that underwrote the exploitation and devastation of the continent. It is a form of primitivism, resisting the institutional pressure of literature as a product of history and the repository of human significance. It substitutes a vision of individual initiatives for the containing and sustaining vision of a society. Its insistence upon the atomic valency of the syllable attempts to bypass, by detouring back behind, literary institutions and precedents, returning language to some state of virginity before it became dense with societal and institutional import. Literature, let alone syntax and verse forms, is so much lumber brought in like the rats with the *Mayflower*, to be put down as quickly as possible. Clearly this view is absurd: Europe's ghosts groan in the very marrow of the language. But it retains utility as a mystique that has allowed the wildernesses, internal and external, to be dared, penetrated and devastated.

History is canvassed as wholesale myth, to be laid flat and folded back into the landscapes of a perpetual present, as it is in the *Cantos*, *Paterson*, *The Maximus Poems*. The past can always be encountered without guilt, since the present determines the past, never issues from it. And the present can be made perpetually anew, in each poem, in each act. Hence the curious innocent cheerfulness, the ontological optimism, the essential refusal of evil that we find in all these poets, in, most incredibly, the Pound of the *Pisan Cantos*. Figuratively, however horrific the landscape, the poet is always by the side of the road in the infectious hospital. He is never encountered on his way back from it. This is cheering stuff for Europeans, but such poetic versions of the propaganda of good news they breathe all their lives ought to be depressing for Americans.

The myth of Adamic innocence is a deliberate obverse of Puritan eschatology, but, as an obverse must, issues from the same stamp. How it connects with objectivism is too tangled a piece of intellectual history to unravel here. Some parallel gets established between the poem as uncensored utterance and the poet as unauthored object. In Olson's articulation of Whitmanian aesthetic, the complex of poet-poem-recipient is to exist innocently, unprivileged among the objects of the universe. The notion is obviously consolatory. Each object, unique and self-fathered by the law of its own development, cannot be held responsible to anything else. As a project the poem, admittedly lumbered with the common tongue which is as far as possible molded to local or immediate speech, takes off at right angles from the joint project of human history. It projects outward into an undetermined field of infinite space and infinite consciousness. Analogies with journeys, voyages, most pertinently with space exploration, are relevant, as is indeed the quasi-technological jargon that a theorist like Olson employs. The poem, moving ever outward, can never really be called to account in terms of any norm. Indeed, it cannot be criticized, since literature ceases to exist.

The urgency of these issues abounds in Lowell's article on Williams in *The Hudson Review* (1961–62). About Williams himself, Lowell is tender and generous. He praises Williams for his vitality, his grip on environment, even "the shock scramble of the crass and the august." Yet a disciple of Williams must feel that, despite his human community with him, Lowell is utterly out of sympathy, to the point of not being able to engage with Williams's central project. The substitution of reminiscence for discrimination indicates a wariness, a deep withholding. Lowell finally will not endorse Williams's poetics and myths. He is lucid about the implication of that refusal being, in the end, a refusal of America—as "*the* truth and *the* subject." Beneath the hesitant, modest surface of his prose ripples a claim to a more comprehensive sophistication which places Williams and could not, conceivably, be placed by him. In this paragraph praise is subtly subverted by Lowell's sense of his own sense of Williams being more complicated than Williams's sense of himself. The evocation of "Dr. Williams . . . rushing from his practice to his typewriter" is faintly patronizing. There is, too, a syntactical cringing produced by the guilt that troubles sophistication in the presence of innocence:

> The difficulties I found in Williams twenty-five years ago are still difficulties for me. Dr. Williams enters me, but I cannot enter him. Of course, one cannot catch any good writer's voice or breathe his air. But there's something more. It's as if no good poet except Williams had really seen America or heard its language. Or rather he sees and hears what we all see and hear and what is most obvious, but no one else has found this a help or an inspiration. This may come naturally to Dr. Williams from his character, surroundings and occupation. I can see him rushing from his practice to his typewriter, happy that so much of the world has rubbed off on him, maddened by its hurry. Perhaps he has no choice. Anyway, what others have spent lifetimes in building up personal styles to gather what has been snatched up on the run by Dr. Williams? When I say that I cannot enter him, I am almost saying that I cannot enter America. This troubles me. I am not satisfied to let it be. Like others I have picked up things here and there from Williams, but this only makes me marvel the more at his unique and searing journey. It is a Dantesque journey, for he loves America excessively, as if it were *the* truth and *the* subject; his exasperation is also excessive, as if there were no other hell. His flowers rustle by the super-highways and pick up all our voices.

The notion of a "Dantesque journey" (Dante being superlatively the exiled questor for spiritual and evil order) places Williams out of reach of any terms he would use for himself. Lowell labels, tickets, tames Williams, assimilating him to an idea of literary tradition whose coercions Williams's poetics is designed to evade. Yet Lowell, ungenerously at this point, grants all too willingly that Williams's poems are not artifices, but unpremeditated, natural occurrences. Hence the speculation that his subject matter "may come naturally to Dr. Williams." While, in that curious rhetorical question that looks more like an exclamation, Lowell significantly contrasts "the building up of personal styles" (the poet as architect) with "what has been snatched up on the run by Dr. Williams," as though Williams were a bank robber or a swallow. The poems come as easily as roadside or superhighwayside flowers: they are also—if I catch the right vibration of "rustle," a trifle thin-textured—victimized and undernourished by their industrial environment. And who could determine exactly what elaborate circumspection is danced out in the twice-repeated phrase "pick up"?

Knowing that Lowell has "picked up things here and there from Williams," we may suspect that his middle poetry has been loosened and relaxed by some contamination from the Williams tradition. But the casual address of the poetry should not deceive us. Each poem is in fact braced by a rigorous logic. Even where it does not display, it reaches toward a formal rhetoric that predetermines the poem's shape and destination. Each poem is brought round unmistakably *by* the poet, whose agency the poem declares, to a predestined closure. The poem always exists somewhat after some fact, idea, or event; it is not itself a fact, an idea, or an event. It affirms some order which is its ground of being. This order may, operationally, be no more than the conviction that poems should go on being written and that a literature is still required. Lowell's poems are always bent on being and making literature. If we remember this, the strategy involved in Lowell's *Imitations* becomes clearer. Lowell re-creates for his own purposes a corpus of poems belonging to other times and other cultures. He renders them in his own idiom with a freedom and confidence that raises eyebrows. Equally, however, he commits his own idiom to the corpus; he adds, offers, sacrifices it, as it were, in order to bring into existence a usable body of literature, as distinct from an eclectic aggregation, from which to derive sanctions, directives, models. The whole operation involves the exercise of a vast tact. Merely to translate would be to become the avatar of foreign cultures. To transform utterly would be to court the solipsism of all imperialisms. Lowell, in his *Imitations*, has both to honor and render alien visions, to domesticate without destroying them. *Imitations* attempts to create a tradition by an individual effort of will, because a literature without a tradition is unthinkable, and because the tradition that filters down through the academies and organs of cultural diffusion is not a possession but so much booty and plunder. To be possessed it must, in the American way, be mastered and retrieved through an individual initiative. Lowell is nowhere more native than in his determination to make Parnassus under his own steam.

For Lowell literature is a precondition for a human world, defined against the circularities and randomness of natural process—a public space in which specifically human purposes declare themselves. Where this space is threatened or extinguished, literature takes over as the repository of its values. The poet may well find himself, even to his own surprise, mounting guard over dead civic virtue. Each poem becomes a defense of literature and behind that of the public order whose disintegrations the poet now registers, but which, in an ideal state, his art exists to celebrate and sustain. Here is the explicit ground of Lowell's career. His poems do not merely perform this function, they reflect and meditate it as well. Indeed, the defensive action for its effectiveness depends upon the poetry being a conscious assumption of this martial role. Lowell confronts in "For the Union Dead" a modern urban devastation in which the civic order is being systematically dismantled. To name is in some sense to tame it. Lowell glares at it, eyeball to eyeball, exposing all his nerves, yet constructing, in the poem's own architecture, an alternative order both to that which destroys and that which is destroyed. The poet substitutes his poem for the statue whose commemorative virtue is no longer acknowledged. The statue once preserved the dead, the past, what had been wrested from the flux of history as destiny. Lowell's poem enacts the death of the statue, its final envelopment by unmeaning. The contained chaos of the aquarium has erupted into and drowned out the public domain: "a savage servility / slides by on grease." To name the horror is to encompass it in the name of a possibility that surpasses it. For the poem is not merely, weakly diagnostic, but militantly braced against the dissolution it utters. The naming is a containment. (Frye would see it as the myth of the hero's struggle with Leviathan.) Lowell redeems the impotent memorial by reinvesting it with the immediacy of flesh and blood, while denying none of its commemorative significance:

> Shaw's father wanted no monument
> except the ditch
> where his son's body was thrown
> and lost with his 'niggers'.
>
> The ditch is nearer.

In some sense, Lowell's poem unbuilds the statue in favor of the ditch, the bestial condition of abandonment and loss which the monument traditionally redeems. Characteristically, Lowell's stanza break enacts the ditch which now deepens and widens its significance to take in the gouged soil of violated Boston, the uncommemorated wholesale destruction of the last war ("There are no statues of the last war here") and the last-ditch destructions of atomic warfare. With the utmost economy, almost with elegance, Lowell brings into one focus the commercial greed that has devastated Boston and the Puritan Church that has sponsored the same destructive energies. Its contempt for natural limits, its overweening repudiation of natural death, has, paradoxically, leagued it with the turbulence of a demonic nature. Yet the ensuing atrocity is imaged in the mindless medium of an advertisement. For Lowell to be able to contain and relate both the horror and the mass media's numbing of the horror vindicates the poet's role:

> ... a commercial photograph
> shows Hiroshima boiling
> over a Mosler Safe, the 'Rock of Ages'
> that survived the blast.

Humor plays a liberating part in the effect. It is obscene that a commercial photograph should display the destruction of Hiroshima. But when the sentence carries across the stanza break, "over" (that wildly active preposition) to a Mosler Safe, we are forced into the release of something like laughter at the solemn, self-important, unironic impudence of the commercial imagination. The paradox remains that denials or dishonorings of nature (whether exploitive or theological) give birth not to the super- but the sub-natural:

> the dark downward and vegetating kingdom
> of the fish and reptile.

Hence the ambiguity involved in saying that the safe has "*survived the blast*" (a good poet wrests his meanings from the conceptual substratum of the language itself!). It "survives" only at the expense of life. Yet Lowell does not allow himself easy victories. Obviously, the Mosler Safe is available for every sort of ironic denigration. Lowell simply states; no more. He gives the devil his due. And that ability to rest in statement is in turn an aspect of Lowell's militancy. For it depends upon an ultimate conviction of the efficacy of language, despite all debasements, all dishonorings. Lowell's power of statement points to another use of language, its existence in poems, which unite the world of nature with human intention and meaning. A poem dies; and human nature can assume nature itself as its vesture in its submission to the choice of deaths. Lowell's imagery works incessantly to define, implicitly, the right, the respectful, the decent order which should govern the transactions between man and his world. Thus, "This monument sticks like a fishbone / in the city's throat" asserts it negatively, aggressively. But of Shaw himself: "He has an angry wrenlike vigilance, / a greyhound's gentle tautness. . . ." The statuary itself embodies this fusion of nature and artifice: "William James could almost hear the bronze Negroes breathe." Yet in this very line the afflatus of that fusion is chastened by a limiting precision, "almost": artifice and nature are juxtaposed, not confused through the agents that relate them: "*bronze Negroes breathe.*" The peculiar virtue of Lowell's resistance to the endemic and literal dehumanizations of American experience, his refusal to enter America, its vast material growth, slaughter of Indians, enslavement of Negroes, its spoliation of landscape, its exportation of massive violence (all themes treated by Lowell) derives from his realization of complicity in the glamour of those processes, of which his own dealings with madness, vastness, oceanic euphoria, verbal affluence are a part:

> Once my nose crawled like a snail on the glass;
> my hand tingled
> to burst the bubbles
> drifting from the noses of the cowed, compliant fish.
>
> My hand draws back.

The change of tense from past to present is significant. Merely to state a past tense represents in so sensitive a structure as this poem the act of escaping to the past, to childhood, to innocence and evading the small, drab militant virtues of watching and warding in the present. Again, the stanza break enacts the difficulty of the gesture that resists this temptation. The act of resistance means renunciation of fluency and fluidity, a half-unwilling assumption of fixity and dryness. The last line of "Home after Three Months Away" (the poem which concludes the "Life Studies" sequence) is apposite: "Cured, I am frizzled, stale and small." To burst the bubble, as the despoilers of Boston have emptied the aquarium, promises a return to the *plenum*, to become an open, undetermined, blessedly irresponsible thing, a sheer utterance, like the projectivist poem-object, to reenter the wilderness that breaks into Edwards's sober couplets:

> the bough
> Cracks with the unpicked apples, and at dawn
> The small-mouth bass breaks water, gorged with spawn.

In "For the Union Dead" Lowell sees himself simultaneously on both
sides of the glass at once, within and without, feeling over its surfaces
and seeing himself as so feeling from the other side: "My nose crawled
like a snail on the glass." The aquarium contains, renders visible, yet
resists the demonic powers of nature which have returned in parody
through the rabid growth of technology: Lowell again "presses" toward
them, but this time with the implication that the medium (and we must
consider how far these images of containments are also descriptions of
the poem itself) is cruder, improvised out of the violence of desperation
and yet less effective:

> One morning last March,
> I pressed against the new barbed and galvanized
> fence on Boston Common. Behind their cage,
> yellow dinosaur steamshovels were grunting
> as they cropped up tons of mush and grass
> to gouge their underworld garage.

Whether "underworld" is not too artful, and hence the sign of a ner-
vousness, is a question. Is Lowell again indulging in premature coercion
of his material into myth? And if so, is this a defense against the
destructuring onslaughts of technological and bestial forces? The whole
poem is held rigid and yet vibrates between the allure of self-abandon-
ment and the restrictions and tensions of control. Colonel Shaw, Puritan that he was ("he seems to wince at pleasure, / and suffocate for
privacy"), also "waits / for the blessed break" into the sinister fullness of
creation. The "Rem Publicam" of the poem's Latin motto—object of
the poem's creative act—is built on renunciation ("sparse, sincere rebellion"). The Public Thing is a deliberate artifice, something that
stands vertical against all frontal assaults, the lure and corruption of
gravity, the erosion of elements. In the very first line, "The old South
Boston Aquarium stands / . . . now." The poem, too, is to stand, like the
statue, but more, like a piece of architecture. Indeed, architectonic
analogies seem in order. The poem appears to be constructed, sustained
by a play of tensions, resistances, contained strains. It is a complex
arrangement or investment of spaces. Masses are balanced off against
each other. The reader's attention does not enter the poem, nor does
the poem envelop or absorb it. We register the various elements of the
poem as blocks of discrepant size or weight that still are locked and held
in the grip of a fierce compositional energy that ultimately distributes
and resolves itself through them. By its last stanza the poem has
achieved the demolition of the aquarium and named its destroyer. But
it has also put itself in its place. The poem concludes at an intense pitch

of what I can only call compositional irony. All the containments and restraints of civilization have collapsed. The monsters are cruising in for the kill. Yet the poem holds, tames them, at the crux of their unleashed aggression. They become compliant to Lowell's vast verbal control: "a savage servility / slides by on grease." The destroyers remain "servile" . . . and one just flirts with the possibility that this servility may be greasy because proletarian; the micks and the wops against Colonel Shaw. But this suggestion merely flickers about the image, and it is one which Lowell would have no difficulty in confronting.

Lowell knows the dangers of the militant, the statuesque, the architectural. Other poems in *For the Union Dead* explore the potential of these virtues for tyranny and petrification. In "Florence" Lowell comes out for the monsters ("tubs of guts . . . slop") against the militant Davids and Judiths, those tyrannicides who exploit and destroy them. He demonstrates how they can become agents of the corruption they should resist:

> On the circles, green statues ride like South American
> liberators above the breeding vegetation—
>
> prongs and spearheads of some equatorial
> backland that will inherit the globe.
>
> —"July in Washington"

His own bodily architecture is implicated in the subtle poem "The Neo-Classical Urn," which, like the Washington poem, connects with all those Roman allusions, styles, republican monuments which sheathe like thinnest bronze the body politic of America. Lowell, rubbing his skull, recalls by association the turtle shells, themselves prison and armor of the living creatures which he had destroyed by keeping them in a garden urn overlooked by "the caste stone statue of a nymph, / her soaring armpits and her one bare breast, / gray from the rain and graying in the shade . . ." whose classicality is rendered in a faintly Augustan idiom. Again, "Caligula" explores an insanity that tries to turn itself into marble:

> yours the lawlessness
> of something simple that has lost its law . . .

Finally, in "Buenos Aires" Lowell finds a kind of inverted version of the military virtues, which have turned totally tyrannical and petrific, the mirror image almost of the devastation of Boston. Lowell now identifies with the natural demonic forces—"the bulky, beefy, breathing

of the herds." Into the stony solemnity of the southern capital Lowell
dances like a bovine bacchus:

> Cattle furnished my new clothes;
> my coat of limp, chestnut-colored suede . . .

In "Buenos Aires / lost in the pampas / and run by the barracks" with
its glum furniture of "neo-classical catafalques . . . a hundred marble
goddesses," Lowell becomes the therapist of so much rigor:

> I found rest
> by cupping a soft palm to each hard breast.

Throughout his work Lowell oscillates between oceanic fluxes of
euphoria and horror and a corresponding drive to the security of law,
logic, stability, structure. The flux is outer and inner; often inner and
outer are one and their identification can produce weird puns:

> Now from the train, at dawn
> Leaving Columbus in Ohio, shell
> On shell of our stark culture strikes the sun . . .

which connects, in the same poem, with water, through another "striking" image:

> On Boston Basin, shells
> *Hit* water by the Union Boat Club Wharf . . .

(My italics.) Notice the similar rhyming and syntactical salience of the
word "shells." Queerer is the crude and one hopes unconscious pun that
connects "our stark culture" with one of the ancestors, only a few lines
on:

> And General Stark's coarse bas-relief in bronze
> Set on your granite shaft
> In rough Dunbarton . . .

Lowell's extraordinary feel, touch for texture, weight, density somehow transfers itself into verbal and syntactical equivalents in the poetry
itself as well as providing much of the imagery. How much, for example,
do these lines

> frayed flags
> quilt the graveyards of the Grand Army of the Republic

owe to contrasts of texture and weight? The feel of the stuffs somehow
becomes the stuff of the lines so that "Grand Army of the Republic"
may look a well-stuffed title, but one which has worn sadly thin.
Lowell's poetry returns continually to some somatic base that is

Lowell's real presence in the poetry, much more important than any grammatical ego. Here, literally, the poetry is the shadowy but persistent corpus of the man himself, his volatilized and verbally reconstituted self-image. The poem, imaged as a shell, itself oceanic, also represents the tense, elaborate thinness of his own substance, separating the chaos without from the flux within. The process is very self-conscious in "The Neo-Classical Urn."

> Poor head!
> How its skinny shell once hummed . . .

A Lowell poem, however solid its architecture, never looks other than fragile, friable, only just mastering the pulls and pressures that threaten to disintegrate it. Freud's view of the ego as a hard-won layer of self that achieves enough stability to curb—and yet be fed and thickened by—the importunate, blind drives of the id and that copes and transacts with external reality seems apposite. If Lowell is a post-Freudian poet, this is not primarily because Freud is an inescapable ingredient of secular culture, but because Lowell's poetic practice itself enacts the Freudian drama and is the therapy of the human condition that Freud divined.

Freud was concerned, as therapist, with the making of viable individual existence. He released the fantasies, whose prodigious allure he knew only too well, not to express but to desensitize and reduce them. Lowell's poetic progress could be seen, in similar terms, as a self-therapy. But the terms are too restrictive. One could put it rather that Lowell's poetic career imitates—in an Aristotelian sense—the progress of self-therapy and thereby proposes itself as a case of an ultimately viable existence. It becomes exemplary as a measure of the depth and intensity of the forces that batter the self from within and without, and describes the forms that resistance to these can assume. Lowell as poet becomes the implicit hero of his own poetry, but, of necessity, very much a debunked and debunking hero, diffident, arrogant, self-destructive, perhaps, most of all, despite all, persistent and operative.

It is in some such terms that I would wish to understand the "Life Studies" sequence. Lowell's treatment suggests not an exhibition but a cauterization of private material and emotion. Interest is not in what is revealed but in what is reserved. These nagging, haunting, futile figures, the threadbare deposits of years of private living, are indeed exhibited, not with contempt or love, but only as they can be contained in poetic architectures—like statues in niches—their features cleansed for presentation, but neither exploited nor degraded nor glamourized. The

poker-faced numbness of Lowell's handling of these figures—the balance retained between respect for their integrity and refusal of their
domination—is more important than the figures themselves. Our fascination is for how so much emotional dynamite is offloaded and safely
defused. Lowell does not permit himself or us any absorption in the
depths of memory, emotion, or childhood. We are invited rather to
participate in Lowell's craftsmanly concentration on building evanescent emotions and moments and events into solid structures from which
they will not evaporate into wistfulness or nostalgia. Lowell hardly
permits himself the luxuries of aggression or self-pity or indulges in
Hardy-like pangs at pastness. The poetry is designed to keep the past
past and the dead dead. If there is any covert emotion it is the quiet
grimness of that determination. The success of this cauterization of the
past is summed up by the last line of a poem in *For the Union Dead*:

> Pardon them for existing.
> We have stopped watching them. They have stopped watching.

This is the end result of the process initiated in "Life Studies," that
phrase that must remind us of the term "still life" and, just as usefully,
of its French equivalent *nature morte*. The deliberate deadening of
emotion becomes a kind of spiritual exercise, and even achieves a
certain perversity in the poem about bringing the dead mother's corpse
home, "Sailing Home from Rapallo":

> In the grandiloquent lettering on Mother's coffin,
> *Lowell* had been misspelled *LOVEL*
> The Corpse
> was wrapped like *panetone* in Italian tinfoil.

The sequence shows just the thinness of love in the familiar scene. But
Lowell conspicuously abstains from fastening upon the irony of "LO-
VEL." He simply hovers, brooding glumly, over it, then relinquishes it
in the noun-length line "The corpse. . . ." Even the grotesquerie of the
last couplet is not allowed to lift into any exuberance. The poem rustles
to a dry close on the phrase "Italian tinfoil."

Lowell is really a very nonintimate poet who holds his readers at arm's
length, even though much of his reputation and appeal since *Life
Studies* depends on his appearing to offer unmediated, secular experience, almost raw. Pleasure in reading him is partly that of recognition,
of being shown the artifacts and objects—many of them disheveled,
casual, almost nameless—of our common environment. Lowell has a

superbly developed sense of milieu, of the tacky and gimcrack surfaces, as well as of the bric-a-brac of our civilization of depersonalized intimacy. How characteristic that the beads that Michael clenches at the end of "Thanksgiving's Over" should be cowhorn and from Dublin. Lowell knows, notices, and with only slightly self-congratulatory hysteria uses such things. But we should notice how far these objects are reapprehended and, as it were, redeemed for attention, by being locked and cemented into larger structures. They are never really innocent, autarchic objects like Williams's red wheelbarrow. They are there because they serve a significance or are at least apt for some design. Thus, in "During Fever" the daughter's "chicken-colored sleeping bag" depends for its color not on the fact that that was the color that it was but on an association with "the healthy country" from which the daughter has returned. While within the drab color scheme of Lowell's recollections in "Memories of West Street and Lepke," Lowell's daughter's "flame-flamingo children's wear" does more than outdo, with that resplendent epithet, the advertiser's euphorics. This is not to deny Lowell's almost uncanny empathy with the furniture of private and mass living, but also to emphasize his simultaneous degree of controlled remoteness from them.

This feel for secular existence finds its counterpart in the casual movement of the poem itself, hardly insisting on its spatial organization, but appearing to unfold without resistance along the line of relaxed reminiscence. For example, "Memories of West Street and Lepke" seems to accrue section by section, without obvious destination, and, trailing off into space, to lapse trickling out into a ruminative silence, which may at any moment revive and grow audible again. The poem seems to hold off from judgment and conclusion. "Ought I to regret my seedtime?" Lowell asks himself, and the poem comes up with no answer, as though it itself were the flower of that seedtime and as such required no confirmation. Anything like a point of view hardly has time to establish itself before it is undercut. Thus, in the first paragraph:

> . . . even the man
> scavenging filth in the back alley trash cans
> has two children, a beach wagon, helpmate,
> and is a "young Republican."

This looks like pretty mainstream irony, but we are not allowed to indulge it for long: in the very next line Lowell adverts to his own parenthood, the creaturely condition which he shares with the scav-

enger, and wipes the grin at least off his own face. Likewise, the gusty
euphoria of the opening lines rapidly reverses within the perspective of
his reminiscence:

> Only teaching on Tuesdays, book-worming
> in pyjamas fresh from the washer each morning,
> I hog a whole house on Boston's
> "hardly passionate Marlborough Street . . ."

when we are introduced by way of the laundry to

> Czar Lepke
> there piling towels on a rack,
> or dawdling off to his little segregated cell full
> of things forbidden the common man . . .

which forms a grotesque parallel with Lowell's own situation, hogging a
whole house, a thing also forbidden "to the common man." The Lepke
situation throws back a retrospective gloom: the poet's own tranquility
seems a kind of prison, his routines a prison routine. Like Lepke, he is a
prisoner with privileges beyond the common lot. "Hog," of course,
connects with Lepke's flabbiness as it does also with "the man / scavenging filth." We become aware of the reek of depression from beneath the rather manic crisp and jaunty production of image and event.

Lowell's right to his mood of euphoria at the beginning of the poem is
called into question. It has been bought, apparently, at the expense of
a thoroughgoing defensive refusal to make connections. The nine-
months-old daughter rising "like the sun" is not the only—and is perhaps only an irrelevantly posthumous—fruit of his "seedtime." There is
also the connection, disowned, between Lowell's comparative affluence
and "the man / scavenging filth," between his present tranquil—one
might say drug-tranquilized—state and the unprivileged Negro boy with
"curlicues of marijuana in his hair" with whom he had once awaited
sentence. The question arises for the poet whether he had not been in
closer connection all around when in the days of his passionate naiveté
he had gone to prison, and whether the manifest violent horror of the
decades that produced *Murder Incorporated* was not somehow more
hopeful in its openness than "the *tranquilized fifties*."

Is not that tranquility merely a drugged drift toward death, parallel
with Lepke's "concentration on the electric chair"?

> Flabby, bald, lobotomized,
> he drifted in a sheepish calm,
> where no agonizing reappraisal
> jarred his concentration on the electric chair—
> hanging like an oasis in his air
> of lost connections . . .

The poem is a meditation on the edge of middle age. It looks back to a self that is hardly recognizable and—as is to be anticipated on such a theme—forward to death. But the poem also is about the failure to make the middle of a life span connect with and so unify the beginning and the end. The failure is deep and complex: a failure to make the agonizing reappraisal of a state of mind which refuses agonizing reappraisals. The unformed, drifting, apparently randomly wavering lines of the poem is itself an aspect, an expression of this refusal. And yet, despite appearances, this refusal of commitment to a connective structure is turned, against all the odds, itself into a constructive principle. We drift with Lowell's reminiscence as Lepke drifts toward death. And at the moment of the poem's ending, its death, when it runs out upon those eloquent full-stops, we discover the lost connections that Lepke can never find, the analogies and parallelisms and constructive contrasts that have been holding the poem together. The answer to the question is not the poem itself but the alert, militant, and vital chore of unremitting interrogation. The connection in this poem is made through the interrogated fact that everything has come apart and it is made against the defensive grain that would keep it that way. Through this understanding, at the very edge of annihilation, when the poem's sound is about to die away in the air of lost connections, a sense of significance and of coherence is still just able to obtain. So that, after all, the poem survives as a structure which resists the oceanic drift of death of which the mechanical operation of reminiscence is an aspect.

The poem remains an architecture that simulates, anticipates, and thus prevents its own demolition. It is an artfully designed ruin. It only looks like a piece of nature formed haphazardly out of the forces of erosion and accumulation. Secular experience is never, ever, unmediated in Lowell. Not that, in verbal structures, it ever really could be, but, despite appearances, in Lowell's case the ultimate tendency of the poem is to insist upon its structure. Even in this poem, which comes nearer to unmediated existence than any other, in which the poem—the self-substantive, nominative thing—just manages to crystalize out of the stream of poetry—even here there is an appeal to a transcending notion of literature through which this poem takes its place with other poems as part of an order. We are in the presence of a Dejection Ode, of a literary *kind*, and it is that fact which resists the reader's own death-wish; it resists, too, any impulse he might have to drown and be absorbed in the poet's private substance which, until it is owned not as a wholly personal project but as part of a joint human enterprise, must remain part of the chaos out of which order is still to be achieved.

John Berryman: A Question of Imperial Sway

BY JOHN BAYLEY

BERRYMAN, LIKE LOWELL and perhaps more so, is the poet of the time whose size and whose new kind of stylistic being shrugs off any attempt at enclosure. But one thing about both is obviously true. *Life Studies, Notebook,* and *Dream Songs* show that verses, old-fashioned *numbers,* are still capable of being what Byron wanted — "a form that's large enough to swim in and talk on any subject that I please" — and not only the capable but the imperially inevitable form. Compare their talking verse — dense as lead one moment and light as feathers the next — with the brutal monotony of that dimension of talking prose which Hemingway evolved, and which Miller, Mailer, Burroughs, and others have practiced in their various ways. In the *Dream Songs* and *Love and Fame* Berryman makes that kind of prose appear beside his verse not only doltish and limited but incapable even of straight talking.

Formalistically speaking, curiosity has no place in our reception of the Berryman experience. The medium makes the message all too clear. In spite of all the loose ends of talk, the name-dropping and the facts given, we have no urge to find out with whom, when, why, and what; and this is not a bit like Byron. "I perfect my metres," writes Berryman, "until no mosquito can get through." Let's hope he's right. In every context today we sup full of intimacies. The group therapy of our age is its total explicitness; privacy and reticence have lost all artistic function and status: and so a lack of curiosity is not abnormal in the reader or even unusual. But Berryman seals off curiosity with a degree of artistic justification against which there is no *ad hominem* appeal.

The implications of these two phenomena — a new verse and a new self in it — seem to me what discussion of Berryman has to be about. There is no point in prosing along with detailed technical discussion of his verse, for its idioms and techniques are all completely self-justifying and self-illuminating.

"Poetry," said Thoreau, "is a piece of very private history, which unostentatiously lets us into the secret of a man's life." The matter would only have been put thus by a North American, at once orphan and contemporary of romanticism. The triumph of Berryman's poetry is that in becoming itself it has learnt how to undermine the apparent relevance to the poetic art of that niggling adverb: by flinging it suddenly on its back he has revealed that utter and shameless ostentation can become the same thing as total form, and virtually the same thing as the impersonality which our knowledge and love of the traditions of poetry condition us to expect. To let us in unostentatiously usually means today to be *confiding*. Elizabeth Bishop makes her Fish her poem, but is at the same time both confiding and self-justifying, as is such a typical poem of Wallace Stevens' final period as *"The Planet on the Table."* So at the other extreme of length and technique is *Paterson*. These confidences produce the impression that the poet is (to turn Stevens' own words against him) "an obstruction, a man / Too exactly himself." Such confidences cease to be important when they are made by a poet as far back as Wordsworth, but in our own time they are very important because they collapse style, the only thing that enables us to guess at the authority of a modern poet. At the moment they are not "soluble in art" (the phrase from the prologue to *Berryman's Sonnets*) though they may dissolve in time — or the whole poem may.

One thing which that in other respects overrated European author Beckett shares with Berryman and Lowell is the masterly inability to confide. None of them are deadpan: indeed all seem very forthcoming, but what Berryman calls "imperial sway" (Pound was "not fated like his protegé Tom or drunky Jim/or hard-headed Willie for imperial sway") manifests in them as a kind of regal blankness: it is not for them to know or care whether or not their subjects are listening.

Berryman cannot be "exactly himself," for he is so present to us that the thought of the real live Berryman is inconceivable, and scarcely endurable. His poetry creates the poet by a process opposite to that in which a novelist creates a character. We get to know Macbeth, say, or Leopold Bloom, to the point where we enter into him and he becomes a part of us; like Eurydice in Rilke's poem he is *geben aus wie hundertfacher vorrat* — bestowed upon the world as a multitudinous product. Berryman, by contrast, creates himself as an entity so single that we cannot share with or be a part of him. Such an autobiography as his does not make him real in the fictional sense. Everything is there, but so is the poetry, "language / so twisted and posed in a form/that it not only expresses the matter in hand / but adds to the stock of available reality."

That is Blackmur, one of Berryman's heroes: his wisdom put into a lapidary stanza and three quarters, ending with the poet's comment: "I was never altogether the same man after *that*." *That* is after all, though, a conventional formalistic and Mallarméan utterance, and the great apparent size of Berryman and Lowell is that they have achieved a peculiarly American breakthrough: the emancipation of poetry from its European bondage as *chose preservée* and its elevation into a form which can challenge and defeat the authority and easy-goingness of prose at every point. As Valéry perceived when he coined the phrase, Europe can never get over its tradition that poetry occupies a special place, and that prose has grown all round it like some rank and indestructibly vital weed, isolating it in an unmistakable enclave. Wallace Stevens concedes the same thing, in his practice, in his Jamesian persona ("John D. Rockefeller drenched in attar of roses" as Mary McCarthy put it) and in his comment that "French and English constitute a single language" (exclusive of American presumably). Looking back in England we see that Wordsworth, the great seeming liberator, was more subjected than he knew; as he grew older the "poetic" engulfed him; Coleridge's attempts to write a "poetry that affects not to be poetry" renounce all tension, and lack even the circumnambulatory virtues of *Biographia Literaria*. But whatever the difficulties of emancipation American writers had to overcome, this was not one of them. Whitman showed the way. Pound, as he says, "made a pact" with him, and the *Cantos,* no less than *Leaves of Grass,* never strike us as tacitly admitting that the same kind of thing could be or is being said in prose.

For one thing, the "I" is wholly different. Coleridge's and Wordsworth's "I" is usually themselves, the "man speaking to men," in either verse or prose. Even in such a masterpiece as *Resolution and Independence* "I" is not metamorphosed by the medium, by the poetry. Hence, even there, the poetry is not doing its poetic job to the hilt. A prose Wordsworth is, or would be, perfectly acceptable, but a prose Whitman "I" or a prose "Henry" Berryman would be intolerable. To make a poetic "I" as free and even more free, as naturalistic and even more so, than a prose ego, and yet quite quite

different: that is the secret of the American new poetry which appears
to reach its apogee in Lowell and Berryman. By this they show not
only that verse can still do more than prose, but that the more
closely it is involved in the contingent, the more it can manifest
itself as the aesthetically and formalistically absolute.

I must return to this point in a moment, but let us first dispose
of Berryman's own comments about the "I" of the *Dream Songs*.

> Many opinions and errors in the songs are to be referred not to the character
> Henry, still less to the author, but to the title of the work.... The poem
> then, whatever its wide cast of characters, is essentially about an imaginary
> character, (not the poet, not me) named Henry, a white American in early
> middleage in blackface, who has suffered irreversible loss and talks about
> himself sometimes in the first person, sometimes in the third, sometimes even
> in the second; he has a friend, never named, who addresses him as Mr. Bones
> and variants thereof.

This of course is rubbish in one sense, but in another it is a perfectly
salutary and justified reminder by the author that when he puts
himself into a poem he formalizes himself. To labor the point again:
Mailer is always Mailer, but Berryman in verse is Berryman in verse.
That does not mean that he is exaggerated or altered or dramatized:
on the contrary, if he were so the poem would be quite different and
much more conventional. Berryman of course deeply admired and
was much influenced by Yeats, who helped him to acquire the poet's
imperial sway over himself and us, but he is not in the least concerned with Yeats's doctrine of the Masks, and with trying out contrasting dramatic representations of the self; such a cumbrous and
courtly device of European poetry does not go with American directness and the new American expansiveness. Why bother to put on
masks when you can make the total creature writing all the form
that is needed?

Byron and Pushkin also emphasised the formal nature of their
poetic device, often in facetious terms and in the poems themselves —
making characters meet real friends and themselves, etc. — Berryman's
gambit to emphasize a comparable formalism has a long history.
None the less his comments are misleading in so far as they imply
something like a dramatic relation between characters and ideas in
the *Dream Songs*. The hero of Meredith's *Modern Love* would be as
impossible in any other art context as Henry, but he is in a dramatic
situation, and in that situation we can — indeed we are positively
invited to — judge him, as we judge Evgeny Onegin. And to judge
here is to become a part of. The heroes of such poems with dramatic
insides to them are not taken as seriously as heroes in prose; they
are unstable and frenetic, capable of all or nothing, because we do

not get accustomed to them: they appear and vanish in each line and rhyme. None the less they are stable enough to be sat in judgment on, and Berryman's Henry is not. Ultimately, the formal triumph of Henry is that because he is not us and never could be, he has — like our own solitary egos — passed beyond judgment.

The paradox is complete, and completely satisfying. Clearly Berryman knew it. "These songs are not meant to be understood you understand/They are only meant to terrify and comfort" (366). But though it is not dramatic the interior of the *Dream Songs* is grippingly exciting, deep, detailed and spacious. Moreover it is not in the least claustrophobic in the sense in which the world of Sylvia Plath involuntarily constricts and imprisons: on the contrary, like the world of early Auden it is boisterously exhilarating and liberating. It has no corpus of exposition, sententiousness, or pet theory, which is why it is far more like *Modern Love* or *Evgeny Onegin* than the *Cantos* or, say, *The Testament of Beauty*. It never expounds. Another thing in common with the Meredith and Pushkin is the nature of the pattern. Each "Number" is finished, as is each of the intricate stanzas of their long poems, but in reading the whole we go on with curiosity unslaked and growing, as if reading a serial. The separate numbers of the *Dream Songs* published in magazines could not of course indicate this serial significance, which is not sequent, but taken as a whole reveals unity.

The Russian formalists have a term *pruzhina,* referring to the "sprung" interior of a successful poetic narration, the bits under tension which keep the parts apart and the dimensions open and inviting. Thus, in *Evgeny Onegin,* Tatiana is a heroine, a story-book heroine, and a parody of such a heroine; while Evgeny is, conversely, a "romantic" hero for her, a parody of such a hero, and a hero. The spring keeps each separable in the formal art of the poem, and the pair of them in isolation from each other. I am inclined to think that Berryman's quite consciously contrived *pruzhina* in the *Dream Songs* is a very simple and very radical one: to hold in opposed tension and full view the poet at his desk at the moment he was putting down the words, and the words themselves in their arrangement on the page as poetry. When one comes to think of it, it is surprising that no one has thought of exploiting this basic and intimate confrontation before. (The weary old stream of consciousness is something quite other, being composed like any other literature in the author's head, irrespective of where he was and what he was being at the time.)

The extreme analogy of such a confrontation would be Shakespeare
weaving into the words of "To be or not to be," or "Tomorrow and
tomorrow and tomorrow" such instant reactions and reflections as
"Shall I go for a piss now or hold it till I've done a few more lines"
— or — "I wonder what size her clitoris is" — or — "We must be
out of olive oil." Of course there is no effect of interpretation in
Berryman; but the spring does hold apart, and constantly, a terrifying
and comforting image of the poet as *there* — wrestling in his flesh
and in his huddle of needs — while at the same time poetry is engrav-
ing itself permanently on the page. It is this that keeps our awed
and round-eyed attention more than anything else: our simultaneous
sense of the pain of being such a poet, and of the pleasure of being
able to read his poetry.

It is also instrumental in our not judging. The poet is not asking
us to pity his racked state, or to understand and sympathize with
the wild bad obsessed exhibitionist behavior it goes with.   These
things are simply there, as formal achievement, and Henry James,
that great Whitman fan, would oddly enough, I am sure, have understood and been gratified by it. He suggests it in the advice he gave
to the sculptor Andersen about how to convey the tension and the
isolation in an embracing sculptured couple.

> Make the creatures palpitate, and their flesh tingle and flush, and their internal
> economy proceed and their bellies ache and their bladders fill—all in the
> mystery of your art.

"Hard-headed Willie" in his magisterial way, and with his "blood,
imagination, intellect running together," might also have given a
clue; but when he says "I walk through a long school-room questioning" or —

> I count those feathered balls of soot
> The moorhen guides upon the stream
> To silence the envy in my thought.

it is well understood that he is doing no such thing. This is the
rhetoric of the moment, not its apparent actuality; the thought he
is silencing and the questions he asks have all been cooked up in
the study afterward. His air of immediate imperiousness, with
himself and us, is a bit of a fraud, and this seasons our admiration
with an affectionate touch of decision. Yeats is the boss whose little
tricks we can see through and like him the more for: all the same,
we do judge.

And with Berryman we don't; the spring device forbids it. How judge someone who while talking and tormenting himself is also writing a poem about the talk and torment? Except that we know, deeper down, that this effect *is* a formalistic device and that Berryman's control of it is total. And this knowledge makes us watch the taut spring vibrating with even rapter attention. There is a parallel with the formalism so brilliantly pulled off by Lowell in *Life Studies,* where the poetry seemed itself the act of alienation and cancellation, as if poet and subject had died the instant the words hit the paper. The formal device or emblem above the door framing the two collections might be, in Lowell's case, a speech cut off by the moment of death: in Berryman's, a Word condemned to scratch itself eternally, in its chair and at its desk.

Lowell forsook that frame, and in *Notebook* approaches the idiom of the *Dream Songs* (I waive any inquiry, surely bound to be inconclusive, into questions of mutual sympathetic influencing). But in achieving the note of continuing casualness, in contriving to stay alive as it were, *Notebook* remains individual pieces, fascinating in themselves, but lacking the tension that makes *Dream Songs* a clear and quivering serial. The comparison may be unfair, because *Notebook* may not be intended to be a narrative poem, but it shows how much and how successfully *Dream Songs* is one, and *Love and Fame.*

If I am right in thinking that Berryman's aim is to hold in opposed tension and full view the poet and his words, I may also be right in supposing that *Homage to Mistress Bradstreet* was inspired, in the form it took, by the same preoccupation. What seems to have been the donnée for Berryman there was the contrast between the woman as she presumably was, and the poems that she wrote. Berryman's ways of suggesting this are on the whole crude — I do not see they could be anything else; but the idea obviously fascinates him. Why couldn't her poems be *her,* as he wills his to be him? — the poem celebrates a gulf and a contrast.

> When by me in the dusk my child sits down
> I am myself. Simon, if it's that loose,
> Let me wiggle it out.
> You'll get a bigger one there, & bite.
> How they loft, how their sizes delight and grate.
> The proportioned, spiritless poems accumulate.
> And they publish them
> away in brutish London, for a hollow crown.

Homage to Mistress Bradstreet is far from being a masterpiece; it is a very provisional kind of poem. Its virtues grow on one, but so does a sense of the effort Berryman was making to push through a feat of recreation for which a clarified version of the style of Dylan Thomas was — hopefully — appropriate. Had Thomas, instead of lapsing into "Fern Hill," been able to write a long coherent poem on a real subject — the kind of subject touched on in "The Tombstone Told When She Died" — it might have been something like this. But Thomas never got so far. We know from *Love and Fame* that Berryman felt the impact of Thomas early — in Cambridge, England, before the war — found him better than anyone writing in America, and made great use of him, the kind of use a formidably developing poet can make of an arrested one. The superiority of *Mistress Bradstreet* over the poems that are unemancipated from Auden — "World-Telegram", "1 September 1939", "Desire Is a World by Night," etc. — strikingly show how Auden was far too intellectually in shape to be successfully digested by Berryman as Thomas had been.

The feeling imagination, the verbal love, in fact, of *Mistress Bradstreet,* is most moving; and the image of her reading Quarles and Sylvester ("her favorite poets; unfortunately") is, I am convinced, a counter-projection of the image later willed on us by the grand, fully "voiced" Berryman of his own self at his own desk. Finding his own voice is for Berryman a consummation in which his own self and his poetry become one. Nor would it be fanciful to see this as the climax of a historical as well as of a personal process. Poetry, in its old European sense, *was* very largely a matter of getting out of your own perishable tatty self into a timeless metaphysical world of order and beauty. We have only to think of Spenser scribbling in Kilcomman Castle, transforming the horrors of the Irish reality into the beauties of *The Faerie Queen;* while Donne — often taken as "modern" — is no less a transformer of the casual and the promiscuous into metaphysical fantasy and form.

From Bradstreet to "Henry," who is no mask but a nickname in the formal spousals of poet to reader, is therefore a journey of almost symbolic dimensions, and one which only Lowell and Berryman could have successfully accomplished. Whatever their technical interest and merits, all their early poems were strangely clangorous and muffled, as if a new god were trying to climb out from inside the machinery: they needed the machinery to establish but not to *be* themselves. *Berryman's Sonnets* are brilliantly donnish in the way they cavort around the traditions and idioms of the genre, and it is indeed part of that idiom that there is no inside to them, no personal, non-dramatic reality.

> Keep your eyes open when you kiss: do: when
> You kiss. All silly time else, close them to . . .

In combination with such admirable and witty pastiche the gins and limes and so on of the *Sonnets* strike one as mere modern properties, and quite singularly not about what Berryman is. His use of Donne here is more generous than Lowell's grabbings out of the past; yet if Lowell wears his versions more ruthlessly he does it also more comprehensively.

Their absolute need of at last finding, and then being, themselves, could be seen in the light of Auden's comment: "when I read a poem I look first at the contraption and then at the guy inside it." To both Auden and Yeats it would make no sense to be in search of their own voices. They remain what they were from the beginning. When Yeats says — "It is myself that I remake" — he is subsuming guy and contraption under a single flourish, but in fact the continuity between Yeats young and old is unbroken, and so with Auden. There is never any doubt what guy is in the contraption and that he is the same one. I would say, therefore, that there is a radical and important difference, *in this respect,* between the poetry of Auden and Yeats and that of Lowell and Berryman; and, interesting as it is, I would not agree with the conclusion that M. L. Rosenthal comes to in "The Poetry of Confession." * He feels that the Americans "are carrying on where Yeats left off" when he proposed that the time had come to make the literal Self poetry's central redeeming symbol:

> I must lie down where all the ladders start,
> In the foul rag-and-bone shop of the heart.

But that is surely Yeats striking out a new line, apparently turning a somersault but really remaining the same old aesthete and tower-builder who chided the contingencies of this world for "wronging your image that blossoms a rose in the deeps of my heart." Yeats had always affirmed the self: he took it for granted, he did not have to find it: and in "Sailing to Byzantium" he exaggerates almost to the verge of parody the traditional view that seems to start Berryman off in *Mistress Bradstreet*: that "once out of nature" and in the world of art the perishable and tatty self enters a new dimension of

---

The Modern Poets (Oxford University Press). Reprinted in *Robert Lowell: A Portrait of the Artist in His Time,* edited by Michael London and Robert Boyers (New York, David Lewis, 1970).

being, becomes a poet. What is fascinating about Berryman's enterprise is that starting from "the proportioned spiritless poems" he tries to reconstitute, so to speak, the perishable being who so improbably produced them. That seems to me the significant American poetic journey — to discover the living ego as it has to be ("I renounce not even ragged glances, small teeth, nothing") — and it is the exact reverse of Yeats's pilgrimage. In finding themselves Lowell and Berryman must indeed renounce nothing, not a hair of their heads, "forever or / so long as I happen." Such an achievement is a triumph quite new to poetry and confers on it a new and unsuspected authority. Thomas Wolfe said something like: "I believe we are lost in America but I believe we shall be found." Lowell and Berryman could have nothing to do with the lush fervor of the sentiment. None the less, in terms of poetry they embody such a faith and justify it.

2

This is indeed glorious but not necessarily satisfactory. Let us try to see what has been lost as well as gained. My contention would be that the two poets reverse completely one canon of the European aesthetic tradition, as represented by Yeats, and those other European Magi Rilke and Valéry, but in another way they are willy-nilly bound to it.* Their spectacular breakthrough into contingency is only possible because of the other Magi article of belief that things have no existence except in the poet's mind. So that in the iron selfhood the two poets have created, the most apparently feeble, hasty, or obviously untrue comment, sloughed off from day to day, acquires an imperishable existence when it is unsubstantiated on the page. The poems in *Love and Fame,* where even the nickname "Henry" has been dropped between us (as nicknames come to be dropped between old married couples), are apparently bar-room comments on Berryman's past, nothing more, and the people, events, feuds and boastings in them are as commonplace as the lunch-hour. The lines are like a

---

*Berryman's comment on Rilke in the *Dream Songs* is characteristically exhilarating.

> Rilke was a *jerk.*
> I admit his griefs and music
> & title spelled all-disappointed ladies.
> A threshold worse than the circles
> where the vile settle and lurk,
> Rilke's. As I said,—

late Picasso drawing, the realized personality of genius implicit in every flick of the pencil. (One wonders whether Edmund Wilson, who maintained in "Is Verse a Dying Technique?" that modern poetry is the prose of Flaubert, Joyce and Lawrence, had a chance to read them.)

And yet something is missing, the something that might join all these things to life itself. Such a poetry is not "earthed" — cannot be — for it has nothing of the *accidental* and inadvertent in it, no trace of genuine impurity. Art is all trickery, but it is a trickery which can join up with our own lives and dreams, events and responses, our own self-trickery maybe. And can it be that in so meticulously creating the contingent self Lowell and Berryman have had to cut it off from the outside world? That is what I meant by saying that the poet is created here by a process opposite to that in which the novelist creates his characters. The novelist arrives at the reality of the world because his art is not and cannot be fully under his control. He cannot make everything himself: his readers must supply it; and the people and things he writes of will become real not only because his readers are doing a lot of the work themselves but because what he invents will become true by repetition and by being taken for granted; the man he shapes for us on page 2 will have become his own man by page 200. And this is as true of Joyce as of Trollope; it is equally true of much poetry in which "things" and a "world" are created — *Evgeny Onegin* or "The Eve of St. Agnes." But it is not true of Lowell and Berryman, however much they may seem to be putting things and a world before us.

Some time ago, in a book called *The Romantic Survival*, I made a point about the world of Auden's poetry which I still think important, though the rest of the book no longer seems very relevant to me. It is that Auden, following Yeats, had carried the personal and legendary domain of that "Last Romantic" one stage further, creating his characteristically and ominously centripetal world of stylized meaningfulness — derelict factories, semi-detached houses, "the silent comb / Where dogs have worried or a bird was shot." What gave this world its instant authority was its appearance of stern political and social finger-pointing with its actual invitation to conspiracy and relish in the landscape of the evil fairy, the Death Wish. "Auden has followed Yeats," I wrote, "in showing how the intense private world of symbolism can be brought right out into the open, eclectized, and pegged down to every point of interest in contemporary life."

And yet Auden constantly reminded us — his wittiest spokesman was Caliban in "The Sea and The Mirror" — that the realities of such poetry are necessarily mirror realities.

> All the phenomena of an empirically ordered world are given. Extended objects appear to which events happen — old men catch dreadful coughs, little girls get their arms twisted....All the voluntary movements are possible — crawling through flues and old sewers, sauntering past shopfronts, tiptoeing through quicksands and mined areas... all the modes of transport are available, but any sense of direction, any knowledge of where on earth one has come from or where on earth one is going to, is completely absent.

The *bien pensants* of contemporary culture have made so much of the desolating, but also heartening and "compassionate" sense of the pressures of life, of the sheer difficulty of being oneself, which Lowell and Berryman have conveyed in their poetry, that a qualification along these lines may be in order. Auden finds the trick to let out Yeats into a new world of legend: Lowell and Berryman — on a scale and with a virtuosity of which today only American poets are capable — let him out in his turn, into a place where "*all* the phenomena of an empirically ordered world are given," and "*all* the voluntary movements are possible." Its very completeness precludes any attachment to mundane eventfulness — "From a *poet*? Words/to menace action. O I don't think so." Berryman's remark echoes what Auden constantly reiterates. Theirs is a breath-taking achievement, with results not at all like Auden, but I doubt it could have been done without him. As Berryman so engagingly puts it in that superlative *Love and Fame* poem "Two Organs":

> I didn't want my next poem to be *exactly* like Yeats
> or exactly like Auden
> since in that case where the hell was *I*?
> but what instead *did* I want it to sound like?

Temperamentally, one infers, Berryman could hardly be more different from either Yeats or Auden. He was "up against it" in a sense (I take it) unknown to their basically sane and self-centering personalities, but he adapts the mirror world of their invention to sound like what he wants to be. Success is shown by the failure of the alternatives taken by poets in a comparable situation (not of course of Berryman's stature, but that begs the question): the "confidences" of Anne Sexton and the "blown top" meaninglessness of Kenneth Fearing, for example. Berryman takes from Auden not only the mirror world but the wry unswerving knowledge of its use, which adds — as it does in Auden — a further dimension to the meaning of the poem. An instance would be 97 in the *Dream Poems*, which deliberately lapses delicately into gibberish and concludes:

> Front back and backside go bare!
> Cat's blackness, booze, blows, grunts, grand groans.
> Yo-bad yom i-oowaled bo v'ha'l lail awmer h're gawber!
> —Now, now, poor Bones.

This is not like Lear's fool, clowning to hide desolation and fear, though something like his voice can be heard at times in the *Dream Songs*. It is a humorous, rather than a witty, exploitation of the formal idiom; its camp "blackface" touch not unlike Auden's handling of Jewish Rosetta in *The Age of Anxiety*. Both poets know that they can only move us by means of a sort of carnival exploitation of the mirror world: Caliban, with his virtuoso eloquence, and Rosetta with her day dreams, would be equally at home among the exuberance and desperation of the *Dream Songs*. "A man speaking to men" does not say, as Henry does, "He stared at ruin. Ruin stared straight back." The humor of Groucho Marx, even if corny, also belongs to the mirror world.

And so does the straight talk. We can have no objection to sentiments like

> Working & children & pals are the point of the thing for the grand sea awaits us which will then us toss & endlessly us undo.

or

> We will die, & the evidence
> is: nothing after that.
> Honey, we don't rejoin.
> The thing meanwhile, I suppose, is to be courageous and kind.

because they are less earnest than sparkles from the wheel, and have been so wholly cauterized by contrivance. We can have "a human relation," for what that's worth, with poets far less good than Berryman. We can enter into such and share their feelings in a way impossible with him, for all the openness and Olympianly inclusive naturalness of his method. It is strangely unsatisfactory that in his poetry the poet cannot put a foot wrong. He can go off the air (Auden can too) but that is a different thing. If any technological habit has unconsciously influenced this kind of poetry it may be the record player with its click on and off, its hairline acoustics and relentless sensitivity. Both Lowell's and Berryman's poems have the flat finality of something perfectly recorded, and just the right length for perfect transmission. I notice writing down quotations that they do not sound very good, even when I had admired them as part of the poem: for the proper rigorous effect every word of the poem must be there.

This again excludes the accidental. The tone does not change or modulate, does not sag accidentally or rise with deliberate effort; the "supernatural crafter" is too much in charge, as he gives us an inkling in "The Heroes."

> I had, from my beginning, to adore heroes
> & I elected that they witness to,
> show forth, transfigure: life-suffering and pure heart
> & hardly definable but central-weaknesses
>
> for which they were to be enthroned and forgiven by me.
> They had to come on like revolutionaries,
> enemies throughout to accident and chance,
> relentless travellers, long used to failure
>
> in tasks that but for them would sit like hanging judges
> on faithless and by no means up to it Man.
> Humility and complex pride their badges,
> every "third thought" their grave.

Compare and contrast with that the young Stephen Spender's hopefully confiding and altogether by no means up to it poem "I think continually of them that were truly great." Spender gives it away by the touching solemnity of knowing he is writing a poem, a poem about heroes, the truly great. An all too human poem, as human as the embarrassment with and for the author that flushes us as we read it, but at least we know from it what we do *not* feel about those who "left the vivid air signed with their honour," etc. By patronizing it we engage with it: by disliking its sentiment we adjust our own. And we respond to it; it is not a null poem, even though it combines the inadvertent and the contrived in an unstable state.

Great as well as small poets are, or have been, rich with this inadvertence. Keats, writing in halcyon good faith,

> Let the mad poets say whate'er they please
> Of the sweets of peris, fairies, goddesses;
> There is not such a treat among them all,
> Haunters of cavern, lake, and waterfall,
> As a real woman.

seems not to know how it was going to look, or what the reader was going to think, and certainly not how revealing of his genius the lines are. Byron always seems to know, with his posturing and easy anecdotage, and the wholly controlled and calculated swagger of the jotting on the back of *Don Juan*.

> O would to God that I were so much clay
> As I am blood, bone, marrow, passion, feeling,
> Having got drunk exceedingly today
> So that I seem to stand upon the ceiling.

These lines mime a loss of control and a hungover truculence, and
yet every so often he forgets himself genuinely in a way there is no
mistaking, as in the lines written when he heard his wife was ill.
The chagrined pity of its opening seems to try, and fail to be, all
self-pity, until a kind of hangdog solicitude turns to and takes refuge
in the relieved virulence of satiric declamation. There is even an
unexpectedly startled and self-disconcerted note in the famous lines:
"How little know we what we are, how less / What we may be."
Hardy is in this kind of way the most vulnerable of all great poets,
as witness the end of "After a Journey," where the poet revisits the
sea-haunts where he had first fallen in love with a wife long estranged
and now dead.

> Trust me, I mind not, though Life lours,
> The bringing me here; nay, bring me here again!
> I am just the same as when
> Our days were a joy and our paths through flowers.

"I am just the same as when. . .": the reassurance he gives and needs
to give has all the eager clumsiness of life: we can hear the relief
of saying it, a relief all the greater because it can't be true.

I labor this incongruous mixed bag of examples because they all
seem to me to contain something naive and direct that has vanished
or is vanishing from the performance of good poetry. In them we seem
to meet the poet when he doesn't expect it; like Sartre's voyeur he
is looking at something else so intently that he is unaware of the
reader behind him. And can it be that Berryman's preoccupation
— for it appears to be that — with establishing the poet's existence
in all its hopeless contingency ("I renounce not even ragged glances,
small teeth, nothing,") is both an attempt at what earlier poets — and
bad poets today — do without meaning to, and a recognition that
only a formalization of such directness is possible to him? We can
see it in the cunning control of that same poem, "The Heroes," which
slides casually into the subject *a propos* of Pound, a "feline" figure
("zeroing in on feelings,/hovering up to them, putting his tongue in
their ear"); then goes on to distinguish this from the "imperial
sway" exercised by Eliot, Joyce and Yeats; rises to the celebration of
heroism already quoted; and in the last verse shows us where the
first six came from.

> These gathering reflexions, against young women,
> against seven courses in my final term,
> I couldn't sculpt into my helpless verse yet.
> I wrote mostly about death.

The ideas are referred to a pre-poetic stage in the poet, when they were tumbling in the dark together with feelings about girls and resentment against classes. That self could not have written the poem, but it had the ideas, and is coincident with the self that is now sculpting the poetry effectively — perhaps more than coincident, because its topic was the inclusive and unsculpturable one of death. Imperial sway can only be exercised over the words that make up the self.

The last line does not nudge us; it simply looms up — a perspective on the dark contingency of the self that heroes don't have, for they can be sculptured into verse. The self that can't remains pervasively present, disembodied above the poem like a Cheshire cat. There is no question of making or remaking that self in Yeatsian style, nor of making legendary figures out of the poet's *entourage*, as both Yeats and Lowell in their different ways have done. Professor Neff, who gave Berryman a C out of malice at Columbia, in the next poem "Crisis," is paid the subtle compliment of a rapid, unimpartial write-off; there is no attempt to enshrine him in some immortal rogues' gallery, and Mark Van Doren in the poem is also and simply a real person, as in conversation. The poet's mother and father appear in an equally unspectacular way (contrast again with Lowell), figures briefly revealed by night, unless the night, or pre-dawn, time of most pieces, like the seeming traces of drink or drugs, is another convention for conveying the continuity and actuality of the self.

The self can appear in that dark past as in grand guignol, surrounded by ghosts indistinguishable from itself (129: "riots for Henry the unstructured dead") or it can be transposed into a hauntingly meticulous *doppelgänger*, as in 242.

> About that "me." After a lecture once
> came up a lady asking to see me. "Of course.
> When would you like to?"
> Well, *now*, she said.

After a precise, casual, brittle account of the quotidian campus scene — the poet with lunch date, the lady looking distraught — comes the pay-off.

So I rose from the desk & closed it and turning back
found her in tears—apologising—"No,
go right ahead", I assur-
ed her, here's a handkerchief. Cry". She did. I did.
    When she got control, I said "What's the matter—if you want to talk?"
"Nothing. Nothing's the matter." So.
I am her.

Naturally: she could be nobody else. Only through Berryman can
the poem move us, but it does move. The hopelessness, the stasis,
is completely authentic. Not so, I think, those poems in *Love and
Fame* about the others in the mental hospital, Jill and Eddie Jane
and Tyson and Jo. For all their "understanding" "The Hell Poem"
and "*I* know" have something insecure about them, as if threatened
by the presence of other people. The poet was not threatened of
course — we feel his openness, his interest — but the poem is caught
between its equation with contingency and the fact that, as form,
its contingency can only be "me."

The Berryman *pruzhina*, or spring, snaps as the real presence of
these others pulls it too far apart. For the young Berryman, as he
tells us in "Two Organs," the longing was to write "big fat fresh
original & characteristic poems."

> My longing, yes, was a woman's
> She can't know can she *what kind* of a baby
> she's going with all the will in the world to produce?
> I suffered trouble over this.

"I couldn't sleep at night, I attribute my life-long insomnia / to my
uterine struggles." Nothing is more graphic in Berryman than the
sickness and struggle of finding oneself about to become a poet,
lumbered with an unknown fetus that when it arrives will be oneself.
We may note that this is the exact opposite, in this mirror world, of
true childbirth, which produces *another person*. Still, the pains are
real enough, and so is the comedy. Indeed the black comedy of
Beckett again comes to mind, a theater of one. "By virtue of the
aesthetic form," generalizes Marcuse, the "play" creates its own atmosphere of "seriousness" which is *not* that of the given reality, but
rather its "negation." That kind of portentousness is here in a way,
and the theory of the "living theater" has certain affinities with
Berryman's drive — if I am right about it — to coincide poet as man
with poem as thing.

Berryman's fascination with becoming himself as a poet has —
given his genius — an almost equal fascination for us, but it has a
drawback too. We can contemplate it but not share it — it is not

really a part of the universally identifiable human experience, the
experience in Byron or in Gray's "Elegy," to which, as Dru Johnson
observed, every bosom returns an echo. What we have instead is
extreme singularity, the Berrymanness of Berryman, which we and
the poet stare at together: that he absorbs us as much as he absorbs
himself is no mean feat. We want indeed to know "of what heroic
stuff was warlock Henry made" — the American hero whose tale
can be only of himself and who is (unlike Wordsworth) bored by it.

> Life, friends, is boring. We must not say so.
> After all, the sky flashes, the great sea yearns,
> we ourselves flash and yearn,
> and moreover my mother told me as a boy
> (repeatingly) "Ever to confess you're bored
> means you have no
>
> Inner Resources." I conclude now I have no
> inner resources, because I am heavy bored.
> Peoples bore me,
> literature bores me, especially great literature,
> Henry bores me.

Delightful! Our bosoms return an echo to *that,* as to the celebration
of the same mother in 100, and her "two and seventy years of chipped
indignities," but what principally gets to us is the performance of
birth, the pleasure of finding the fetus so triumphantly expelled.
"Le chair est triste, hélas, et j'ai lu tous les livres" — that sensation,
too, for Mallarmé, existed to end up in a book, and so it is with the
perpetual endgame of Berryman — "after all has been said, and all
has been said . . ."

We do miss a *developing* world. Having found himself on the
page the poet has found hell, or God — it is much the same, for in
either case there is nothing further there. Compare with the world of
Hardy, say, who was not bored but went on throughout a long calvary
continuing to *notice* things outside himself, able to bring the outside
world into his poetry while leaving it in its natural place. (Marianne
Moore and Elizabeth Bishop have done the same.) And among
Hardy's preoccupations "the paralysed fear lest one's not one" — a
poet that is — did not, as far as we can see, figure. But it is the
detriment and dynamic of Berryman's book. Hardy had things
easier, for he did not in the least mind writing bad relaxed poems,
and this itself helps to keep him in the outer world, the world of
true contingency. His is the natural contrast to the place discovered
and developed by our two in some ways equally Anglo-Saxon giants.

> I say the paralysed fear that one's not one
> is back with us forever.

So it may be. The struggle to become a great poet, to exercise imperial sway, may indeed be increasingly and ruinously hard, obsessing the poet's whole outlook. But they have shown it can be done.

The novelists of our time have not succeeded in creating a new fictional form as they have created a new poetic one — and that seems to me to have real significance. The bonds that enclosed the novelist and compelled him into his form have up till lately been social as well as aesthetic ones. There was much that he could not say "in so many words," and which therefore had to be said by other means — a style had to be found for creating what society could not tolerate the open expression of: such a style as is created, for example, in the opening lines of *Tristram Shandy*. But in a wholly permissive age the formal bonds of poetry remain drawn taut because they depend on sculpting a voice, graving a shape and pattern. The bonds of fiction slacken into unrecognizability because the pressures of society itself, not of mere craft, which used to enforce them, have withdrawn. The novel form today has no inevitable response to make to its unchartered freedom; it can only concoct unnecessary ones, resurrected devices like those of Barth, Burroughs, Vonnegut and others, which do not impress us with self-evident authority but act as an encumbrance, get in the way. Like the novelist the poet can say anything now, but he must exercise imperial sway as he does so. If he can, poetry has the edge again, and Lowell and Berryman have honed it to a razor sharpness. Despairing art critics, we learn, have been asking not what art is possible today but *is* art possible. As regards poetry, we have our answer. It is still adding to the stock of available reality while expressing the matter in hand.

Between Two Worlds:
The Post-Modernism of Randall Jarrell

BY JEROME MAZZARO

IN HIS LIFETIME, Randall Jarrell found his poetry consistently praised in reviews yet excluded from the powerful Oscar Williams anthologies and ignored by all but a National Book Awards committee in 1961. As a result, it never quite succeeded into popular acceptance or acclaim. The occasional recognition it did get from the *Southern Review* or *Sewanee Review*, the Guggenheim Foundation or *Poetry* merely reinforced the image of a poet with an intense but narrow audience. The presence of *The Complete Poems* (1969) provides a basis for discussions of why this image occurred as well as for discussions of Jarrell's proper place among the poets of his generation. The view that Karl Shapiro expressed in 1966, shortly after Jarrell's death, that he had outpaced all of his contemporaries, seems already overgenerous. Nor does the opinion of Helen Vendler seem more lasting. Her review of the volume leaned heavily on Oscar Wilde to assert that Jarrell "put his genius into his criticism and his criticism and his talent into his poetry." Jarrell's own sense in *A Sad Heart at the Supermarket* (1962) that all poetic audiences were falling before "the habitual readers of Instant Literature" indicates how he might have explained the neglect, but one has the sense, too, in essays like "The End of the Line" (1942), of his "wandering between two worlds, one dead, / The other powerless to be born." Most accurate, it seems, is the metaphor which Jarrell used about Wallace Stevens: "In a lifetime of standing out in thunderstorms," Jarrell managed to be "struck by lightning" enough times to secure himself a notable but not paramount place among those poets who came into their own during and after World War II. Given Jarrell's own need to excel, to go on living life to the fullest, highest reaches and aims of man, this last may seem a harsh judgment, but it is one which in his lifetime Jarrell was willing to make of others and which in his last volume he seems to have understood of his own poetry.

More than any of his contemporaries, Jarrell took seriously Matthew Arnold's hope that a writer should see the world "'with a plainness as near, as flashing' as that with which Moses and Rebekah and the Argonauts saw it" as. well as Arnold's statement in "The Study of Poetry" (1880) that "more and more . . . mankind will have to turn to poetry to interpret life." Most of what his age considered religion and philosophy, Arnold contended, would be replaced by poetry. Without poetry, even science would appear incomplete. Poetry's attachment of emotion to the idea—its refusal to materialize itself in the fact—would allow it to realize for Jarrell the post-Modernist's equivalent to an id's attachment to the superego and the reality of an ego's workaday world. In fact, one difference which Jarrell seems to have from William Carlos Williams and the poets of the previous generation is an uncritical acceptance of Freud's view of the psyche. "The English in England" (1963) hypothesizes of Rudyard Kipling's late stories: "If the reality principle has pruned and clipped them into plausibility, it is the pleasure principle out of which they first rankly and satisfyingly flowered." Similarly, "Stories" (1958) establishes: "the writer is, and is writing for, a doubly- or triply-natured creature, whose needs, understandings and ideals— whether they are called id, ego, and superego, or body, mind, and soul—contradict one another." In the same essay Jarrell asserts: "Reading stories, we cannot help remembering Groddeck's 'We have to reckon with what exists, and dreams, daydreams too, are also fact; if anyone really wants to investigate realities, he cannot do better than to start with such as these. If he neglects them, he will learn little or nothing of the world of life.'" This familiarity with Freud and Georg Groddeck, Jarrell may owe to his attachment to the early poetry of W. H. Auden and Auden's sense of the pair. More even than Arnold's, their visions help to explain Jarrell's own considered "factitiousness" in light of his often unresolved notions of literature as "the union of a wish and a truth" or a "wish modified by a truth."

The previous generation's rejection or neglect of Freud frequently left it without a means for handling the discrepancies between inner and outer experiences except through the terminologies of philosophy and religion and with no language to speak of to handle the area of the age's tendencies toward self-consciousness. Stevens accordingly had erred for Jarrell by "thinking of particulars as primarily illustrations of general truths, or else as aesthetic, abstracted objects, simply there to be contemplated"; he had often treated things or lives so that they seemed "no more than generalizations of an unprecedented low order." Jarrell goes on to insist that "a poet *has* to treat the concrete as primary, as something far more than an instance, a hue to be sensed, a member of a laudable category." In "From the Kingdom of Necessity" (1946), he praises Robert Lowell's "detailed factuality" and "the contrary, persisting, and singular thinginess of every being in the world" which set themselves against the elevation and rhetoric "of much earlier English poetry." Yet, Williams, who does treat particulars as primary in his early poetry, errs by underemphasizing the "organization, logic, narrative, generalization" of poetry, thinking it enough to present merely "data brought back alive." Kipling's description of his writing suffers from a comparable failure in that he, according to Jarrell, "was a professional, but a professional possessed by both the Daemon he tells you about, who writes some of the stories for him, and the demons he doesn't tell you about, who write others." "Nowadays," he continues, reverting to psychoanalytic terminology, "we've learned to call part of the conscious *it* or *id;* Kipling had not, but he called this Personal Daemon of his *it.*"

For Jarrell the expression of all art involved a balance between emotion and idea or id and superego along lines similar to those which Arnold and Freud drew and carrying in their mediation residues of both extremes. "The Age of the Chimpanzee" (1957), for example, presents the hands of a figure in Georges de la Tour's *St. Sebastian Mourned by St. Irene* as resembling "(as so much art resembles) the symptomatic gestures of psychoanalysis, half the expression of a wish and half the defence against the wish," and Jarrell's few comments on music suggest a corresponding emphasis. Jarrell may even have believed that art was a kind of medium to make the forces of the id acceptable to the superego and that, in literature, language worked as wit or dream works in Freud to allow passage through an ontogenetic censor of what Jarrell consistently depicts as dark and phylogenetic feelings. Certainly wit and dream form several of his main stresses when dealing with poetic language. His review of Walter McElroy's translation of Tristian Corbière (1947), for instance, makes "puns, mocking half-dead metaphors, parodied clichés, antitheses, and paradoxes, idioms exploited on every level ... the seven-league crutches on which ... poems bound wildly forward," and, as if to emphasize the connection, Jarrell entitles his own next volume *The Seven-League Crutches* (1951) and includes in it his own version of Corbière's "La Poéte contumace" and four "Rondels pour Après."

Likewise, as early as "Poetry in War and Peace" (1945), Jarrell was investing the previous generation's poetry with Freudian equivalents, dividing it along conscious and unconscious lines, and indicating of Williams that "the tough responsible doctor-half that says and does" and "the violent and delicate free-Freudian half that feels and senses" contribute to one of the "great mythological attitudes" of the country—"the truck-driver looking shyly at the flower." In "The Situation of a Poet" (1952), he notes further of Williams that "he speaks for the Resistance or Underground inside each of us" and of Walter de La Mare (1946) that "from his children and ghosts one learns little about children and nothing about ghosts, but one learns a great deal of the reality of which both his ghosts and his children are projections, of the wishes and lacks and love that have produced their 'unreality.'" Much of the discussion of his "Robert Frost's 'Home Burial'" (1962) is given over to distinguishing the characters' rational and compulsive behavior, and, in "Changes of Attitude and Rhetoric in Auden's Poetry" (1941), he cites the pre-human forms which lurk always behind Auden's individuals in the early poems and concludes: "Many of the early poems seem produced by Auden's whole being, as much unconscious as conscious, necessarily made just as they are; the best of them have shapes (just as driftwood or pebbles do) that seem the direct representation of the forces that produced them." He then generalizes on poetry that it "represents the unconscious (or whatever you want to call it) as well as the conscious, our lives as well as our thoughts; and . . . has its true source in the first and not the second."

The unique character of the ontogenetic half-self assures Jarrell that its presence in the language of art without any additional mannerisms will make that art human and individual. He lauds Frost for "a verse that uses, some-times with absolute mastery, the rhythms of actual speech." In reviews of Auden's later work, Jarrell sees increased mannerisms subverting the unconscious. "Poetry in a Dry Season" (1940) says of *Another Time:* "Auden at the beginning was oracular (obscure, original), bad at organization, neglectful of logic, full of astonishing or magical language, intent on his own world and his own forms; he has changed continuously toward organization, plainness, accessibility, objectivity, social responsibility. . . . Now, in too many of the poems, we see not the will, but the understanding, trying to do the work of the imagination." Jarrell dismisses the volumes as "moral, rational, manufactured, written by the top of the head for the top of the head." He repeats the complaint a year later in a review of *The Double Man:* "Auden's ideas once had an arbitrary *effective* quality, a personality value, almost like the ideas in Lawrence or Ezra Pound. They seem today less colorful but far more correct—and they are derived from, or are conscious of, elements over most of the range of contemporary thought." Thus, it seems that, given a situation where the "thought" of Arnold's overt moral view of art conflicts with an honest resolution of life's "realities," Jarrell chooses Freud and Groddeck, and one gets the first suggestion of the two worlds which his art would wander between.

Later, when Jarrell returns to praise Auden for *The Shield of Achilles*, he does so in *The Yale Review* (1955) with statements that indicate his impatience at Auden's letting art's morality conflict with life: "In many of these last poems the Conscious and Moral Auden is, quite consciously and immorally, coming to terms with the Unconscious Auden by going along with it, letting it have its way—and not just in life, where we can do and gloss over anything, but in poems, which are held against us by us and everyone else." "Perhaps," Jarrell asserts in an effort to keep art moral, "Auden had always made such impossible exacting moral demands on himself and everybody else partly because it kept him from having to worry about more ordinary, moderate demands; perhaps he had preached so loudly, made such extraordinarily sweeping gestures, in order to hide himself from himself in the commotion. But he seems, finally, to have got tired of the whole affair, to have become willing to look at himself *without doing anything about it*, not even shutting his eyes or turning his head away." In *Harper's*, writing of the same volume, Jarrell repeats his reluctance to abandon his belief that moral and artistic senses lie very close together. He attributes their separation in Auden's writing to a lack of Arnoldian high seriousness: "A few of the poems are good, and all of them are brilliant, self-indulgent, marvelously individual: if Auden sometimes loses faith with something as frivolous as poetry, he never loses it in anything as serious as Auden." This last is an allusion to *The Age of Anxiety* (1947), which Jarrell had reviewed, complaining: "One understands what Auden meant when he said, in a recent review, that all art is so essentially frivolous that he prefers it to embody beliefs he thinks false, since its frivolity would degrade those he thinks true. What sounds like an indictment is a confession, and 'The Age of Anxiety' is the evidence that substantiates the confession."

Conversely, "The Age of the Chimpanzee" indicates Jarrell's opposition to a complete submergence of art into the unconscious half-self where it would have at no time the redeeming factors of individuality, Freudian reality, or Arnoldian morality. "Abstract-Expressionism," he writes, "has kept one part [the unconscious] of this process, but has rejected as completely as it could the other part and all the relations that depend on the existence of this other part; it has substituted for a heterogeneous, polyphonic process a homogeneous, homophonic process." This opposition to unconscious art is expanded to include such notions of man as his being an objective, uncensoring recorder. In a review of *Paterson* (1951), Jarrell complains of Williams that he should not have left so much of Book II "real letters from a real woman": "What has been done to them," he asks, "to make them part of the poem *Paterson?* I can think of no answer except: 'They have been copied out on the typewriter.'" Trite and unexamined language come in for similar condemnation. "These Are Not Psalms" (1945) objects that the work of A. M. Klein "has none of the exact immediacy, the particular reality of the language of a successful poem; it has instead the voluntary repetition of the typical mannerisms of poetry in general—mannerisms that become a generalized, lifeless, and magical ritual without the spirit of which they were once the peculiar expression." The redemption of language into this spirit prompts Jarrell to fall back on Goethe's statements concerning technical facility and risk. "Poetry, Unlimited" (1950) asserts: "Goethe said that the worst thing in art is technical facility accompanied by triteness. Many an artist, like God, has never needed to think twice about anything." In "The Profession of Poetry" (1950), Jarrell complains of Howard Nemeroy's timidity: "He knows very well that the poet, as Goethe says, is someone who takes risks (and today most intellectuals take no risks at all—are, from the cradle, critics); but he thinks romantic and old-fashioned, couldn't believe, or hasn't heard of something else Goethe said: that the poet is essentially naive."

This sense of naiveté, which would allow a dark-world layer into the poem, provides the basis on which Jarrell would merge Freud and Arnold so that poetry might outlast religion and philosophy. As he explains in "Ernie Pyle" (1945), "What he cared about was the facts. But the facts are only facts as we see them, as we feel them; and he knew to what a degree experience . . . is 'seeing only faintly and not wanting to see at all.' The exactly incongruous, the crazily prosaic, the finally convincing fact—that must be true because no one could have made it up . . . was his technical obsession." This stress on naiveté—the individually unreflective as opposed to the overly worked—may have led him, as John Berryman's "Randall Jarrell" (1967) would have it, to overvalue Williams considerably. "I'm very fond of Bill Williams' poetry," Berryman writes, "but not as fond as Jarrell was." Moreover, the view would ally Jarrell with John Ruskin, who had written in *Modern Painters*

(1855) of the soul's need "to see something and tell what it saw in a plain way" as "poetry, prophecy, and religion,—all in one." Jarrell's preface to *The Best Short Stories of Rudyard Kipling* (1961) refers to Ruskin's stand on perfectibility in art: "They [Kipling's stories] are not at all the perfect work of art we want—so perhaps Ruskin was right when he said that the person who wants perfection knows nothing about art." A precise lack of naiveté in the overly worked, lifeless perfection of Richard Wilbur's poetry turns Jarrell against it. In "A View of Three Poets" (1952), he accuses Wilbur of being "too poetic," of letting life become an excuse for poetry, and, as Ruskin would have it in the opening volume of *Modern Painters* (1843), of letting art "sink to a mere ornament" and "minister to morbid sensibilities, ticklers and fanners of the soul's sleep."

The strongest indication of the role of language as a mediator between one's senses of art and life and the descending priorities which Jarrell attaches to it as its impulses moved progressively outward come in a review of Rolfe Humphries's *Forbid Thy Ravens* (1948): "What Mr. Humphries's poems say is agreeable, feeling common sense, necessarily a little too easy and superficial, since it has neither the depth of the unconscious, nor that of profound thought, nor that of profound emotion, nor that of the last arbitrary abyss of fact." Under such conditions, poetry in its inmost and purest state would work as Groddeck's It or a Hegelian Geist so that a sequence of its manifestations would provide proof of that motivating inner force adumbrated by psychoanalysis or a history of the highest and noblest thoughts of man similar to the imperfect picture of God that results from a Hegelian survey of history. Jarrell's view in "The Profession of Poetry" that "a poet in the true sense of the word [is] someone who has shown to us one of those worlds which, after we have been shown it, we call the real world" substantiates such a hypothesis. Jarrell proposes what critics typically hold for psychoanalysis. For them, Freud "thought of the artist as an obdurate neurotic who, by his creative work, kept himself from a crack-up but also from any real cure." The artist fashioned his fantasies into a "new kind of reality" that men conceded "justification as valuable reflections of actual life." The context of Jarrell's view which in its desirability embraces Hegelian "highest and noblest thoughts" is the German poet Rainer Maria Rilke: "Rilke, in his wonderful 'Archaic Statue of Apollo,' ends his description of the statue, the poem itself, by saying without transition or explanation: *You must change your life.* He needs no explanation. We know from many experiences we have shared the alien existences both of this world and of that different world to which the work of art alone gives us access—unwillingly accuses our lives."

Jarrell's view also coincides with the starting point of Existential philosophy, that existence precedes essence and that man knows his essence by reflection. As early as "The Dramatic Lyricism of Randall Jarrell" (1952), Parker Tyler hinted at a connection when he framed Jarrell's view of existence and knowledge to echo Jean-Paul Sartre's famous pronunciamento. Tyler wrote, "*Existence* comes before *knowledge* because it retains, even after knowledge has arrived, the unknowable that is so often unpredictable." The Sartrean position which has moved beyond Groddeck has led to the development of an Existential psychoanalysis. As Rollo May's *Existence* (1960) maintains, this psychoanalysis asserts that "what an individual seeks to *become* determines what he remembers of his *has been*. In this sense, the future determines the past"; but the future does so in order to change the present by making the pattern of life it deduces the instrument for one's handling the domains of the past and present. As Hendrik M. Ruitenbeek writes in his introduction to *Psychoanalysis and Existential Philosophy* (1962), "Unlike Freudian analysis, which deals with the *Umwelt* and the *Mitwelt*, the biological and social worlds, but almost ignores the *Eigenwelt*, existential analysis stresses the self and the mode of the patient's relationship to that self." What Existential psychoanalysis offers to the patient is the future directness and choice that the Rilke poem suggests, but its Dasein—unlike Hegel's Geist and Groddeck's It—shows a conscious and willful shaping force which, like his reliance on naiveté rather than consciousness, a need for metaphysical mystery will not let Jarrell accept. As he formulates the present's relation to the future in "A Sad Heart at the Supermarket" (1960), Hegel and Arnold seem most influential: "An artist's work and life presuppose continuing standards, values extended over centuries and millennia, a future that is the continuation and modification of the past, not its contradiction or irrelevant replacement. He is working for the time that wants the best that he can do; the present, he hopes—but if not that, the future."

Upon the sequence of the changes brought about by one's reactions to art, the present world shapes its future along with an evolving new poetry, conceived of for such purposes and, as Arnold believes, in terms "worthily and more highly than it has been the custom to conceive it" and "capable of higher uses, and called to higher destinies, than those which in general men have assigned to it hitherto." Thus, there is a second, more practical disjunction between future and present that arises from Jarrell's efforts to fuse psychoanalysis and Arnold and that his refusal to accept the consciousness of Existential psychoanalysis prevents a resolution of. Throughout his criticism, Jarrell can complain, on the one hand, of living in a time that is worse than Arnold's or Goethe's and, on the other, admit that he is "old-fashioned" enough to believe, like Goethe, in Progress—"the progress I see and the progress I wish for and do not see." The blindness and optimisim of this progress—since for Jarrell only the future can judge the best of the past and that by what it has knowingly incorporated—raises certain questions about the purposefulness of the present which repeatedly, as Arnold before him, Jarrell tries to solve but which, unlike Auden, he is not willing to dismiss by disowning the seriousness of art.

The failure to collapse these visions into one suggests a schematicization of the world—an inner lens—through which one is to see darkly the darkling plain with the "plainness near and flashing" that Arnold called for. Moreover, the failure seems to be built into the vision for as Moses and Rebekah and the Argonauts had cosmic views against which to measure their daily experiences and which never dissolved into an atmosphere of complete immediacy, so, too, in Arnold and Jarrell forces outside their work dictate the selection of words. Goethe's view that the poet must be naive is at least to the extent negated: the "ignorant armies," for instance, which end Arnold's "Dover Beach" are ignorant not because of anything in the poem but because of the world view out of which the poem springs. The same may be said of the emotive language of many Jarrell poems. Delmore Schwartz registers such a complaint in "The Dream from Which No One Wakes" (1945): "In his first two books many of the poems were weakened by a thinness and abstractness of texture and reference; it was as if the poet saw his subjects through opera glasses. . . . For all the genuineness of the poems, the net result resembled the dim and ghastly negative which has to be held up to the light, and not the developed photograph full of daylight and defined objects."

Jarrell's various positions on Auden demonstrate, in addition, an unwillingness to resolve the matter of these disjunctions by focusing necessarily on one persona or about the writings of a single man. This suggests another kind of disjunction hinted at by Shapiro: a yearning for and an opposition to Authority. Shapiro writes of Jarrell's opposition: "It became necessary for everyone my age to attack Auden, as sculptors must attack Mount Rushmore. Nevertheless Auden and Mount Rushmore still stand and probably always will." Nor was Williams a more suitable subject. Jarrell notes of him: "He is a *very* good but *very* limited poet, particularly in vertical range." He adds, "he keeps too much to that tenth of the iceberg that is above water, perhaps." Jarrell is more generous toward Frost: "Frost is that rare thing, a complete or representative poet, and not one of the brilliant partial poets who do justice, far more than justice, to a portion of reality, and leave the rest of things forlorn." And Jarrell says of Whitman, "Of all modern poets he has, quantitatively speaking, 'the most comprehensive soul'—and, qualitatively, a most comprehensive and comprehending one, with charities and concessions and qualifications that are rare in any time." But he reduces his praise by adding, "if we compare this wisdom with, say, that of the last of the Old Ones, Goethe, we were saddened and frightened at how much the poet's scope has narrowed, at how difficult and partial and idiosyncratic the application of his intelligence has become, at what terrible sacrifices he has had to make in order to avoid making others still more terrible."

As an alternative to shaping his views into a single voice, Jarrell seems at times to suggest multiple personae. He champions, for example, anthologies as an ideal critical expression and exposition of an age's taste and laments the fact that Arnold's touchstones "never evolved into an anthology." He also praises individual poets like Williams, Whitman, and Frost for their abilities to get out of themselves, to suggest other voices than their own in their poetry, and he complains of Robert Lowell in "A View of Three Poets" that "you can't tell David from Bathsheba without a program; they both (like the majority of Mr. Lowell's characters) talk just like Mr. Lowell." A decade earlier, "Poets: Old, New, and Aging" (1940) had noted the same of Pound: "Everything is seen through a glass darkly, the glass being Mr. Pound: 1766 B.C. talks exactly like 1735 A.D., and both exactly like Ezra Pound. To the old complaint, 'All Chinamen look alike,' Mr. Pound makes one add, 'And talk alike, and act alike—and always did.'" Jarrell repeatedly insists on dramatic monologue as the poetic vehicle, though, at times, as in the case of Elizabeth Bishop, he is willing to grant morality to description and landscape as had Ruskin.

All three suggestions—anthologies, flexible voices, and the dramatic monologue technique—seem part of a philosophical relativism which Jarrell betrays in statements like "Williams had a real and unusual dislike of, distrust in, Authority; and the Father-surrogate of the average work of art has been banished from his Eden. His ability to rest (or at least to thrash happily about) in contradictions, doubts, and general guesswork, without ever climbing abroad any of the monumental certainties that go perpetually by, perpetually on time—this ability may seem the opposite of Whitman's gift for boarding every certainty and riding off into every infinite, but the spirit behind them is the same." His enlisting of readers to join him on every journey recalls Oswald Spengler's position in *The Decline of the West* (1918). Spengler branded this philosophical relativism the modern counterpart to Classical skepticism which was ahistorical and denied outright. The new skepticism which "is obliged to be historical through and through" gets its solutions "by treating everything as relative, as a historical phenomenon, and its procedure is psychological." It leads to a voice in Jarrell's poetry that is consciously nonauthoritative or whose authoritative tone is undermined by the poem's context in the volume or by other tones within it. Only in his criticism was Jarrell willing to become authoritative, and this may have prompted Helen Vendler's remark that his poetry had talent but his real genius was criticism.

Jarrell's treatment of the childhoods of Auden and Kipling and poems like "A Story" (1939) indicate that there may be added, personal reasons behind his dislike of Authority. The accounts in these works strangely blend into each other and, one suspects, Jarrell's own boyhood. "Freud to Paul: The Stages of Auden's Ideology" (1945) says of Auden's childhood and its part in the creation of "the wicked Uncle": "It is no surprise to learn, in *Letters from Iceland* and other places, that Auden's parents were unusually good ones, very much venerated by the child: Auden moralizes interminably, cannot question or reject Authority except under the aegis of this pathetically invented opposing authority, because the superego (or whatever term we wish to use for the mechanism of conscience and authority) is exceptionally strong in him." Jarrell then cites a statement by Abraham Kardiner that "the superego is based on affection, not hatred." Of Kipling's boyhood, Jarrell notes, "For the first six years of his life the child lived in Paradise, the inordinately loved and reasonably spoiled son of the best of parents; after that he lived in the Hell in which the best of parents put him, and paid to have him kept." After six years, they rescued the boy "and for the rest of their lives they continued to be the best and most loving of parents, blamed by Kipling for nothing, adored by Kipling for everything." Jarrell goes on to conclude: "It is *this* that made Kipling what he was: if they had been the worst of parents, even fairly bad parents, even ordinary parents, it would have all made sense, Kipling himself could have made sense out of it. As it was, his world had been torn in two and he himself torn in two: for under the part of him that extenuated everything, blamed for nothing, there was certainly a part that extenuated nothing, blamed for everything—a part whose existence he never admitted, most especially not to himself."

"A Story" details the same emotions in the son of "the best of parents." The lad eventually extenuates everything and blames his parents for nothing while at the same time he extenuates nothing and blames them for everything. He arrives at the "Hell" of a boarding school whose emptiness is juxtaposed to the "good" mother's concern—even to the point of using the "right" language: "Remember to change your stockings every day— / Socks, I mean." Recollection of the concern changes to resentment as the boy's "mail-box is still empty, / Because they've all forgotten me, they love their / New friends better." The boy plots to punish his parents by disappearing. The same "concern" and "indictment" fill late poems like "Windows" (1954), where the parents who have been accused by their son of being "indifferent" show their concern in noting "you have not slept." For Jarrell, whose parents were divorced, these "parents" are often his paternal grandparents with whom he lived for a while in Hollywood. Significantly the movement in these later poems is ever away from indictment to forgiveness. "In Those Days" (1953) recalls: "How poor and miserable we were. / How seldom together! / And yet after so long one thinks: / In those days everything was better." The sentiment extends to both "The Lost World" and "Thinking of the Lost World" (1963), which concludes that, having spent most of his life learning to forgive his parents for having damaged him, he is left with "nothing" as his reward. The mechanisms by which one's self has been defined, once withered away by forgiveness, leave one nothing by which to define self—a fear implicit in any real skepticism and here expressed "in happiness." Jarrell had come to a similar conclusion twenty-three years before in "For an Emigrant" (1940), and the despair of nothingness, so much complained of by reviewers, runs through the early books. In one of his last poems, "A Man Meets a Woman in the Street" (1967), the narrator gives up identity and the human drive of imagination and contents himself with the wish of the birds' that "this day / Be the same day, the day of my life."

Faced with these various disjunctions, Jarrell's advice in "The Obscurity of the Poet" (1951) is "there is nothing to do different from what we already do: if poets write poems and readers read them, each as best they can—if they try to live not as soldiers or voters or intellectuals or economic men, but as human beings—they are doing all that can be done." Here he falls back on the thesis of Groddeck's *The Book of the It* (1923) that at man's inception he incurs a force that shapes his destiny, and things like breathing which have much to do with the It have little to do with the will. Man may, as Jarrell indicates in "To Fill a Wilderness" (1951), find that the world imaged by poetry is "our nation's life as Yeats saw his own—as a preparation for something that never happened." "A Girl in a Library" (1951), the opening selection of *The Complete Poems*, depicts such conditions. Centering on a girl, a "student of Home Economics and Physical Education, who has fallen asleep in the library of a Southern College," it evolves into a colloquy between the poem's speaker (the present) and Tatyana Larina (the past), who materializes out of Aleksander Pushkin's *Eugen Onegin* (1833). Tatyana wonders at the value of sleep where "the soul has no assignments, neither cooks / Nor referees; it wastes its time." Without ideas against which to shape the present, a person is no more than a "machine-part"; dream and reality are one and homogeneous like the homogeneous Abstract-Expressionism attacked in "The Age of the Chimpanzee." Indulgent with this "machine-part," as often Jarrell's speakers are not, the narrator responds that, since "the ways we miss our lives are life," it is better at death "to squawk like a chicken" and meet Death's challenge "with a last firm strange / Uncomprehending smile" and, then, to see the "blind date that you stood up: your life," than to be aware of the failure beforehand.

Incorporated in this response is Jarrell's somewhat inconsistent view that, whatever the innate or obscure and expanding reaches of excellence, like Rebekah and the Argonauts, people are somehow accountable to strive after them. As with Groddeck's patients, this striving may take the form of a self-examination to make one adjust to the It, but no amount of will can shape an It that is not there. Here knowledge by way of Tatyana emphasizes literature as the source of reform. Jarrell repeats this stress in "The Intellectual in America" (1955) where he speaks of the writer again as "the man who will make us see what we haven't seen, feel what we haven't felt, understand what we haven't understood—he *is* our friend." The student's failure like the failures of the children of "Lady Bates" (1948) and "The Black Swan" (1951) and of the pilot of "The Dead Wingman" (1945) relegates her to the unearned oblivion of "everlasting sleep." In contrast, the "saved"—those whose visions help shape the future—become part of a hovering Spirit which "Burning the Letters" (1945) shows inspiring the present. But even there it must be finally abandoned in order to let new life evolve. In time, as "The Memoirs of Gluckel of Hameln" (1942) asserts, "We take your place as our place will be taken." In both instances, "The Knight, Death, and the Devil" (1951) maintains, man achieves his judgment not by any human design but by doing what he must. Under such nontraditional terms, "The Night before the Night before Christmas" (1949) indicates that "to use God's name" (that is, to imagine him) is "to misuse His name," for what can be imagined, as "In the Ward: The Sacred Wood" (1946) makes clear, can also be unmade. "A Sick Child" (1949) depicts God as "all that I never thought of," and "Eighth Air Force" (1947) shows Christ not as divine but as a "just man" without fault, whom the speaker has tried to imitate. This imitation causes "suffering" and a final self-image as Pontius Pilate, and, in "Seele im Raum" (1950), it produces the "eland," that imaginary creature of the mind which gives life to the soul and humanity to the "machine" and which in German translates as "wretched" (*elend*).

The human designs which result from this wretchedness—often dictated in terms of daydream, wish, fairy tale, make-believe, dream, myth, miracle, and masterwork—are the products, Jarrell insists, only of children and men, and men only insofar as they are childish. In no case are they as idiosyncratic as Heideggerian Daseins. Girls have them until they marry and become women. Then, as "Woman" (1964) states, they become "realists; or a realist might say, / Naturalists," for it is "woman's nature / to want the best, and to be careless how it comes." "Cinderella" (1954) records a coy but significant conversation between a daydreaming girl and her daydream godmother (the Virgin Mary) in the absence of Prince Charming and Christ, who are out childishly imagining. It ends with God's Mother inviting the girl to await inside the return of their men, which might be soon or never. "Mary" herself has taken on the aspects of the Devil's grandmother in Grimm's "The Devil with the Three Golden Hairs." In the light of man's inability to imagine correctly Divine Will, the "wisdom" of their position is obvious, for what they do realize by becoming mothers is a role in Jarrell's almost Darwinian evolution and divinely willed preservation of the species. Here, however the individual may be disregarded, the form or species will be cherished. Yet, as Jarrell seems to say in variations of the "Cinderella" situation such as "The End of the Rainbow" (1954), "Seele im Raum," and "The Woman at the Washington Zoo" (1959), becoming a woman is not very easy. The women of these poems are looked on by their worlds as machine-parts. Only in their imaginations do they preserve their humanity, often by dreaming of fairy-tale and animal creatures in whom to invest their love.

As in Arnold, the cherishing of this species takes the form of the perfection of the state—"the nation in its collective and corporate character"—rather than of the individual. Many of the essays in *A Sad Heart at the Supermarket* are directed toward this end which critics of Jarrell's early poetry mistook for Marxism. Such essays as "The Taste of the Age" (1958), for example, even image Jarrell as a latter-day Arnold or Arnold's favorite, Goethe. The essay opens with a negative reaction to the age: "When we look at the age in which we live—no matter what age it happens to be—it is hard for us not to be depressed by it." Jarrell then goes on to note: "We can see that Goethe's and Arnold's ages weren't as bad as Goethe and Arnold thought them: after all, they produced Goethe and Arnold." The rest of the essay unfolds as an attack on popular culture and an appeal for continuing to upgrade culture, as Arnold had thought to do, through education. Similarly in recommending the second book of Wordsworth's "The Excursion" in *The New York Times's* "Speaking of Books" column (1955), Jarrell writes: "I feel Matthew Arnold's approving breath at my shoulder, and see out before me, smiling bewitchingly, the nations of the not-yet-born." The state thus conceived becomes organic, and war in "The Range in the Desert" (1947) is looked upon as the pitting of one state against another in a struggle for survival much as the lizard of the poem survives by devouring "the shattered membranes of the fly." Caught in a movement from greater to lesser imperfection similar to man's, the state at no time is perfect and incapable of change. Yet, as "The Night before the Night before Christmas" indicates, only a just state may triumph, for the triumph of an unjust state is an indication of an unjust God. The view of this relationship between the state and God is explicitly pronounced in "Kafka's Tragi-Comedy" (1941): "God is the trust, the state, all over again at the next higher level. God's justice and the world's contradict each other; and yet what is God's justice but the world's, raised to the next power, but retaining all the qualities of its original?"

Rather than legally centered upon the protection of the many, the justice of this "just" state is built upon "poetic justice"—the good receiving rewards and the bad, punishments. This central wellspring of art adds a vein of aestheticism which is not obvious in Arnold but which is consistent with nineteenth-century philosophy. It frequently held that the act of poetic creation was closest to the nature of God. Such pieces as "A Sad Heart at the Supermarket" are willing to admit the aestheticism: "To say that Nature imitates Art . . . is literally true. . . . Which of us hasn't found a similar refuge in the 'real,' created world of Cézanne or Goethe or Verdi?" But the aestheticism which Existential psychoanalysis relegates to the past and present by the creation of the Dasein is negated in part by Jarrell's drive toward the future. While granting, as had Wilde, "that the self-conscious aim of Life is to find expression, and that Art offers it certain beautiful forms through which it may realize that energy," Jarrell's location of the real force of art in the realm of the spirit—the phylogenetic or Groddeck's It—gives it a timelessness which transcends, as he supposed Freudian analysis might, the otherwise past-directedness of the recollected childhood.

"The State" (1945) tries to make acceptable through it a state's having killed a child's mother and drafted his sister and cat. Although the acts lead finally to the child's wish to die, they may in the realm of spirit be ultimately right. The deranged nature of the speaker prevents any clear assurance, but Jarrell's concluding remarks in "Auden's Ideology," published in the same year, indicates a willingness to put up with some inconveniences to direct his efforts toward a larger enemy. One senses this "larger enemy" are fears like those expressed in Arthur Miller's *Situation Normal* (1944). Miller defined World War II as a struggle to maintain "the right of each individual to determine his freedom" against "the tyrannic corporate control of the minds and wills of men." A later Jarrell poem, "A Well-to-do Invalid" (1965), tells of a self-interested nurse (the individual?) who tends a self-indulgent invalid (the state?) taking to herself his care so that she feels her justification and her hope of his inheritance in his not being able to get along without her. She dies, and the poem's speaker sees the invalid "well with grief," realizing in the act how easily her vacancy will be filled. The premise of the poem echoes Jarrell's comments on Alex Comfort. Recognizing "that the states themselves are at present the main danger their citizens face," Jarrell adds reluctanty (1945): "It is we who wither away, not the state."

Jarrell comes to these views slowly, and even more slowly is a reader able to put them together. Some are already formed by *The Rage for the Lost Penny* (1940) but their presence is obscured in a more conspicuous admixture of Audenesque phrases. These include "efficiently as a new virus," "the star's distention," and "the actuaries end." They later disappear but their presence here affirms Jarrell's statement in the preface that "Auden is the only poet who has been influential very recently; and this is because, very partially and uncertainly, and often very mechanically, he represents new tendencies, a departure from modernist romanticism." One tendency was the dream poem and its mediation of subconscious and conscious levels, typified by the second poem in Auden's first collection. The poem, which was dropped in subsequent reprintings, forms one reason why Jarrell always cited the 1930 edition of *Poems*, though for convenience he tended to quote from the 1934 edition. A second tendency was Auden's millennialism rooted in "Darwin, Marx, Freud and Co., . . . all characteristically 'scientific' or 'modern' thinkers" about whom the previous generation had "concluded, regretfully: 'If they had not existed, it would not have been necessary to ignore them' (or deplore them)." A third was the power of women to motivate history, as typified by the mothers of Auden's *Paid on Both Sides*. These women keep the feud between their families alive and bloody, and their power, which is present quite often in the backgrounds of these early poems, becomes more apparent as women move into the foreground of Jarrell's poetry with *Losses* (1948).

In *The Rage for the Lost Penny* are located a number of poems which belong to the child's singsong world and whose half-lines and themes occasionally foreshadow lines and themes in Theodore Roethke's *The Lost Son* (1949). The narrator of "A Little Poem" (1940) speaks to his yet-to-be-conceived younger brother in the womb with such Roethkean expressions as "My brother was a fish" and reference to the world as "this sink of time." The opening lines of "The Ways and the Peoples" (1939) add: "What does the storm say? What the trees wish" and "I am the king of the dead." This last assertion finds itself repeated in Berryman's *The Dispossessed* (1948), at the end of the second and psychologically based "Nervous Songs" ("The Song of the Demented Priest"). Jarrell's introduction to *The Golden Bird and Other Fairy Tales* (1962) makes the connection between these poems and Freud apparent: "Reading *Grimm's Tales* tells someone what we're like, inside, just as reading Freud tells him. *The Fisherman and His Wife*—which is one of the best stories anyone ever told, it seems to me—is as truthful and troubling as any newspaper headlines about the new larger sized H-bomb and the new antimissile missile: a country is never satisfied either, but wants to be like the good Lord." Earlier Jarrell's essay on Kafka had described *Amerika* as "a charming and often extremely funny story, as a sort of Candide à la Hans Christian Andersen, with extraordinary overtones": "This world is hardly *judged* at all; its cruelties and barbarities elicit only the blankly anthropological interest we extend to the vagaries of savages or children. The conscientious naiveté, the more-than-scientific suspension or tentativeness of judgment of the later books, are already surprisingly well developed in *Amerika*. In its capacity for generating ambiguity and irony (reinforced in the later books by the similar possibilities of allegory), the attitude resembles that of Socrates, that of the scientist making minimal assumptions, or that of the 'humble observer': child, fairy-tale simpleton or third son, fool."

In addition, Jarrell knows enough about the Arnoldian future of his poetry to begin *The Rage for the Lost Penny* with "On the Railway Platform" (1939). Like the later "A Girl in a Library," it has as its theme the ideas that man travels "by the world's one way" and that his "journeys end in / No destination we meant." What man leaves, he leaves forever. "When You and I Were All" (1939) continues the Arnoldian cast with the lines: "What kiss could wake / whose world and sleep were one embrace?" The influence reappears as well in the telling question of "The Refugees" (1940): "What else are their lives but a journey to the vacant / Satisfaction of death?" "For the Madrid Road" (1940) adds the prospect of people who die to preserve their ideals and who ask continually, "But when were lives men's own? . . . Men die / . . . that men may miss / The essential ills." Malcolm Cowley's review of *Blood for a Stranger* (1942) lists the further echoes of Wilfred Owen's "The Show" in "The Automation" (1937) and of Allen Tate's "Ode to the Confederate Dead" in "A Description of Some Confederate Soldiers" (1936). But the reader's task has been formed: he must reject the surface and work backward from the language of Jarrell's writing not to influences but to the conscious and unconscious impulses which fashioned the work.

Moreover, the views translate into an overall sense of a poetry which, in striving after the noblest thoughts of men and a style which might serve the higher destinies to which poetry has been called, consistently appears unreal and valueless. Often the unreality is necessary, for, by believing that imagination must precede change, Jarrell must stress moments of imagination—daydream, fairy tale, and wish—and minimize the fact. In this, he faces a problem similar to that faced by Dante and Gerard Manley Hopkins: weighing the sensuous beauty of the world which attracts the artist against the idealism which leads him to reject that world for the idea. In reviewing, Jarrell faced the problem by beginning his reviews with his most adverse statements, reversing the usual order of reviewers and prompting Berryman's statement that "Jarrell's reviews did go beyond the limit; they were unbelievably cruel." But their cruelty was often the way Jarrell had for forcing readers out of their complacency into realms where the imagination might function. Since the highest and noblest thoughts of men exclude the ugly, Jarrell tended to exclude it from his poetry or redeem it by means of sentimentalism and romanticism. In a war situation like that opening "Transient Barracks" (1949), the ugly may intrude and allow a sense of life to emerge, but this is rare, and one suspects the additional influence of Pyle. Miller's analysis of Pyle here proves relevant: "Ernie Pyle's thought *was* in his columns. His thought is people. His thought is details about people. War is about people, not ideas. You cannot see ideas bleeding."

More common are the moments in Jarrell's last volume where man is located amid a gross commercialism which hawks its panaceas of Cheer and Joy and All and things are stripped plain. At those moments, as ever where the fact and idea clash, Jarrell's wit intrudes to work, as Freud indicates all wit works, to overcome the valuelessness by letting an unaltered or nonsensical ambiguity of words and multiplicity of thought-relations appear to the consciousness at the same time senseful and admissable as jest. In "A Man Meets a Woman in the Street," Jarrell is willing to forgo such ambiguity by accepting the factitiousness of the world, but the willingness is itself indication that the fact has not occurred. These instants when idea and fact clash are most often the occasions where the purposelessness of the present fades into the brilliance of Jarrell's lines as the concerted direction of his life lay always obscured by the veneer of an incessant instinct of expansion and a refined sensibility. This sensibility, for all its stress on modernism, loved sports cars, bucolic atmospheres, traditional art, good music, poetry, technological advances, and the Russian ballet. Lowell's "Randall Jarrell" (1967) recalls: "His mind, unearthly in its quickness, was a little boyish, disembodied, and brittle. His body was a little ghostly in its immunity to soil, entanglements, and rebellion. As one sat with him in obvious absorption at the campus bar, sucking a fifteen-cent chocolate milk shake and talking eternal things, one felt, beside him, too corrupt and companionable. He had the harsh luminosity of Shelley—like Shelley, every inch a poet, and like Shelley, imperiled perhaps by an arid, abstracting precocity."

Only the imaginary portrait of the poet—akin to the Imaginary Portraits of fin-de-siècle writers—shifting among Goethe, Arnold, and Auden, and formed early by Jarrell—offered him something worldly and static and positive against which to shape his life. That portrait is sketched in the allusions to these writers, the self-comparisons with them, and the appropriations of their tastes that run through all of Jarrell's work. These appropriations go hand in hand with an attack on idiosyncratic individualism which he associated in "The End of the Line" with modernism. This sense led early to a growing drift from the personal that was not reversed until *The Woman at the Washington Zoo* (1960) and *The Lost World* (1965). Here, as M. L. Rosenthal's *The New Poets* (1967) observes, "a change had begun to take place, heralded by three poems in the former book: 'In Those Days,' 'The Elementary Scene,' and 'Windows.' These are poems of private memory—of a time in the past that seemed, often was, 'poor and miserable' (and yet 'everything was better'); of the sadness of what appears, in 'The Elementary Scene,' to have been an unsatisfactory childhood, with a last ironic allusion to the speaker's adult condition ('I, I, the future that mends everything'); and of the impossibility of recovering the dead, simple past of parents who 'have known nothing of today.'" This reversal which brings Jarrell into the Confessional School so much a part of the age was roundly applauded by reviewers who, like Philip Booth, tended to refer to *The Lost World* as a "great new book."

In fact, one might chart the progress of *The Complete Poems* as a succession of efforts by Jarrell to get rid of the "aloneness" which he felt without resorting to the condemnations of his parents which he associates with both Kipling and Auden. Repeatedly one senses what in *The Divided Self* (1960) R. D. Laing calls "ontological insecurity": "The individual in the ordinary circumstances of living may feel more unreal than real; in a literal sense, more dead than alive; precariously differentiated from the rest of the world, so that his identity and autonomy are always in question." Jarrell's personae are always involved with efforts to escape engulfment, implosion, and petrification, by demanding that they somehow be miraculously changed by life and art into people whose ontologies are psychically secure. The changes may allow them then to drop the mechanism by which in their relations they preserve themselves and to feel gratification in relatedness. Laing, who indirectly cites Kafka as a prime example of a writer of ontological insecurity, strikes close to Jarrell's own sensibility. There is something there that along with Rilke's Apollo or Norman O. Brown's *Love's Body* (1966) announces: "Meaning is not in things but in between; in the iridescence, the interplay; in the interconnections; at the intersection, at the crossroads."

For a person with less skill, such purposelessness and militating against the fact might be enough to make his life and poetry unwelcome. Without Williams's rhythms of descent or a comparable instrument of sacramentalization to bridge inner and outer existences, Jarrell's world remains disparate, and he must rely on language as his major means for keeping it together. There is such a reliance running explicitly through much of his criticism and implicit in his poetry; yet, as he perceived in "The Taste of the Age," even language was failing him: "The more words there are, the simpler the words get. The professional users of words process their product as if it were baby food and we babies: all we have to do is open our mouths and swallow." Without a complex language, a language capable of multiplicity, of the ambiguity necessary to wed conscious and unconscious realms, successful poetry would become impossible. Nevertheless, a thingy liveliness might be preserved and, because the future always holds something better, hope as well. Like Arnold who never realized his dream of someday supplanting Tennyson and Browning as the poet of the mid-nineteenth century because of the self-defeating nature of his momentary stays against the confusion of the world, Jarrell seems destined because of his overwhelming reliance on the translucency of language for a secondary role. Readers should not be discouraged, however, from discovering the excellences or the abundances of wisdom, hope, humanity, and despair which the in-betweens of Jarrell's poetry contain, nor from a recognition of his role in bringing psychological concepts to the techniques of American poetry. If, as Shapiro senses, he fails in that role, all the same, he succeeded in making others aware of the course poetry must take. One expects that, as Arnold, Jarrell—though perhaps not as highly ranked as others of his generation—will live as long as any of them.

Roethke: Poet of Transformations

BY STANLEY KUNITZ

IN THE MYTH of Proteus we are told that at midday he rose from the flood and slept in the shadow of the rocks of the coast. Around him lay the monsters of the deep, whom he was charged with tending. He was famous for his gift of prophecy, but it was a painful art, which he was reluctant to employ. The only way anyone could compel him to foretell the future was by pouncing on him while he slept in the open. It was in order to escape the necessity of prophesying that he changed his shape, from lion to serpent to panther to swine to running water to fire to leafy tree—a series of transformations that corresponds with the seasons of the sacred king in his passage from birth to death. If he saw that his struggles were useless, he resumed his ordinary appearance, spoke the truth, and plunged back into the sea.

A lifework that embodied the metamorphic principle was abruptly terminated on August 1, 1963, when Theodore Roethke died, in his fifty-fifth year, while swimming at Bainbridge Island, Washington. He was the first American bardic poet since Whitman who did not spill out in prolix and shapeless vulgarity, for he had cunning to match his daemonic energy and he had schooled himself so well in the formal disciplines that he could turn even his stammerings into art. If the tranformations of his experience resist division into mineral, vegetable, and animal categories, it is because the levels are continually overlapped, intervolved, in the manifold tissue. Roethke's imagination is populated with shapeshifters, who turn into the protagonists of his poems. Most of these protagonists are aspects of the poet's own being, driven to know itself and yet appalled by the terrible necessity of self-knowledge; as-

From *The New Republic*; reprinted by permission of Stanley Kunitz.

suming every possible shape in order to find the self and to escape the
finding; dreading above all the state of annihilation, the threat of
nonbeing; and half-yearning at the last for the oblivion of eternity, the
union of the whole spirit with the spirit of the whole universe.

Roethke's first book, *Open House* (1941), despite its technical re-
sourcefulness in the deft probings for a style, provided only a few
intimations of what was to develop into his characteristic idiom. The
title poem, in its oracular end-stopping and its transparency of language,
can serve as prologue to the entire work:

> My truths are all foreknown,
> This anguish self-revealed. . . .
>
> Myself is what I wear:
> I keep the spirit spare.

Perhaps the finest poem in this first volume is "Night Journey," in
which the poet, telling of a train ride back to his native Michigan,
announces his lifelong loyalty to what he never tired of describing, even
if somewhat sardonically on occasion, as the American heartland. The
poem opens:

> Now as the train bears west,
> Its rhythm rocks the earth . . .

—how important that verb of rocking is to become!—and it ends:

> I stay up half the night
> To see the land I love.

The middle of the poem is occupied by a quatrain that prefigures one of
his typical patterns of response:

> Full on my neck I feel
> The straining at a curve;
> My muscles move with steel,
> I wake in every nerve.

Some thirty years later—he seemed never to forget an experience—in
the first of his *Meditations of an Old Woman,* the old woman being
presumably his mother when she is not Roethke himself, he was to offer,
through the medium of her voice recalling a bus ride through western
country, a recapitulation of that same sensation: "taking the curves."
His imagination was not conceptual, but kinesthetic, stimulated by
nerve ends and muscles, and even in its wildest flights localizing the
tension when the curve is taken. This is precisely what Gerard Manley
Hopkins meant when, in one of his letters, he spoke of the "isolation of

the hip area." The metamorphosis of the body begins in the isolation of the part.

Another poem in *Open House*, entitled "The Bat," concludes:

> For something is amiss or out of place
> When mice with wings can wear a human face.

It took time for Roethke to learn how full the world is of such apparitions . . . and worse!

The confirmation that he was in full possession of his art and of his vision came seven years later, with the publication of *The Lost Son* (1948), whose opening sequence of "greenhouse poems" recaptures a significant portion of his inheritance. Roethke was born, of Teutonic stock, in Saginaw, Michigan, in 1908. The world of his childhood was a world of spacious commercial greenhouses, the capital of his florist father's dominion. Greenhouse: "my symbol for the whole of life, a womb, a heaven-on-earth," was Roethke's revealing later gloss. In its moist fecundity, its rank sweats and enclosure, the greenhouse certainly suggests a womb, an inexhaustible mother. If it stands as well for a heaven-on-earth, it is a strange kind of heaven, with its scums and mildews and smuts, its lewd monkey-tail roots, its snaky shoots. The boy of the poems is both fascinated and repelled by the avidity of the life-principle, by the bulbs that break out of boxes "hunting for chinks in the dark." He himself endures the agony of birth, with "this urge, wrestle, resurrection of dry sticks, cut stems struggling to put down feet." "What saint," he asks, "strained so much, rose on such lopped limbs to a new life?" This transparent womb is a place of adventures, fears, temptations, where the orchids are "so many devouring infants!":

> They lean over the path,
> Adder-mouthed,
> Swaying close to the face,
> Coming out, soft and deceptive,
> Limp and damp, delicate as a young bird's tongue.

When he goes out to the swampland to gather moss for lining cemetery baskets, he learns of the sin committed *contra naturam*, the desecration against the whole scheme of life, as if he had "disturbed some rhythm, old and of vast importance, by pulling off flesh from the living planet"—his own flesh. And he encounters death in a thousand rotting faces—all of them his own—as at the moldy hecatomb he contemplates death crowning death, in a dump of vegetation . . . "over the dying, the newly dead."

The poet's green, rich world of childhood was self-contained, complete in itself. Mother waited there: she was all flowering. When Father entered, that principle of authority, he was announced by pipe-knock and the cry "Ordnung! Ordnung!" So much wilderness! and all of it under glass, organized, controlled. For the rest of his life Roethke was to seek a house for his spirit that would be as green, as various, as ordered. And he was often to despair of finding it. In one of his last poems, "Otto," named after his father, he concludes:

> The long pipes knocked: it was the end of night.
> I'd stand upon my bed, a sleepless child
> Watching the waking of my father's world—
> O world so far way! O my lost world!

Roethke's passionate and near-microscopic scrutiny of the chemistry of growth extended beyond "the lives on a leaf" to the world of what he termed "the minimal," or "the lovely diminutives," the very least of creation, including "beetles in caves, newts, stone-deaf fishes, lice tethered to long limp subterranean weeds, squirmers in bogs, and bacterial creepers." These are creatures still wet with the waters of the beginning. At or below the threshold of the visible they correspond to that darting, multitudinous life of the mind under the floor of the rational, in the wet of the subconscious.

Roethke's immersion in these waters led to his most heroic enterprise, the sequence of interior monologues which he initiated with the title poem of *The Lost Son*, which he continued in *Praise to the End* (1951), and which he persisted up to the last in returning to, through a variety of modifications and developments. "Each poem," he once wrote, "is complete in itself; yet each in a sense is a stage in a kind of struggle out of the slime; part of a slow spiritual progress; an effort to be born, and later, to become something more." The method is associational rather than logical, with frequent time shifts in and out of childhood, in and out of primitive states of consciousness and even the synesthesia of infancy. Motifs are introduced as in music, with the themes often developing contrapuntally. Rhythmically he was after "the spring and rush of the child," he said . . . "and Gammer Gurton's concision: mütterkin's wisdom." There are throwbacks to the literature of the folk, to counting rhymes and play songs, to Mother Goose, to the songs and rants of Elizabethan and Jacobean literature, to the Old Testament, the visions of Blake, and the rhapsodies of Christopher Smart. But the poems, original and incomparable, belong to the poet and not to his sources.

The protagonist, who recurrently undertakes the dark journey into his own underworld, is engaged in a quest for spiritual identity. The quest is simultaneously a flight, for he is being pursued by the man he has become, implacable, lost, soiled, confused. In order to find himself he must lose himself by reexperiencing all the stages of his growth, by reenacting all the transmutations of his being from seed-time to maturity. We must remember that it is the poet himself who plays all the parts. He is Proteus and all the forms of Proteus—flower, fish, reptile, amphibian, bird, dog, etc.—and he is the adversary who hides among the rocks to pounce on Proteus, never letting go his hold, while the old man of the sea writhes through his many shapes until, exhausted by the struggle, he consents to prophesy in the *claritas* of his found identity.

Curiously enough—for I am sure it was not a conscious application—Roethke recapitulated the distinctive elements of this Protean imagery in a prose commentary that appeared in 1950. "Some of these pieces," he wrote in *Mid-Century American Poets*, referring to his sequence of monologues, "begin in the mire; as if man is no more than a shape writhing from the old rock." His annotation of a line of his from "Praise to the End"—"I've crawled from the mire, alert as a saint or a dog"—reads: "Except for the saint, everything else is dog, fish, minnow, bird, etc., and the euphoric ride resolves itself into a death-wish."

Roethke's explanation of his "cyclic" method of narration, a method that depends on periodic recessions of the movement instead of advances in a straight line, seems to me particularly noteworthy. "I believe," he wrote, "that to go forward as a spiritual man it is necessary first to go back. Any history of the psyche (or allegorical journey) is bound to be a succession of experiences, similar yet dissimilar. There is a perpetual slipping-back, then a going forward; but there is *some* 'progress.'"

This comment can be linked with several others by Roethke that I have already quoted: references to "the struggle out of the slime," the beginning "in the mire." I think also of his unforgettably defiant affirmation: "In spite of all the muck and welter, the dark, the *dreck* of these poems, I count myself among the happy poets."

In combination these passages point straight to the door of Dr. Jung or to the door of Jung's disciple Maud Bodkin, whose *Archetypal Patterns in Poetry* was familiar to Roethke. In Jung's discussions of progression and regression as fundamental concepts of the libido theory in his *Contributions to Analytical Psychology*, he describes progression as "the daily advance of the process of psychological adaptation," which at certain times fails. Then "the vital feeling" disappears; there is a damming-up of energy, of libido. At such times neurotic symptoms are observed, and repressed contents appear, of inferior and unadapted character. "Slime out of the depths," he calls such contents—but slime

that contains not only "objectionable animal tendencies, but also germs
of new possibilities of life." Before "a renewal of life" can come about,
there must be an acceptance of the possibilities that lie in the unconscious contents of the mind "activated through regression . . . and disfi-
gured by the slime of the deep."

This principle is reflected in the myth of "the night journey under the
sea," as in the Book of Jonah, or in the voyage of the Ancient Mariner,
and is related to dozens of myths, in the rebirth archetype, that tell of
the descent of the hero into the underworld and of his eventual return
back to the light. The monologues of Roethke follow the pattern of
progression and regression and belong unmistakably to the rebirth
archetype.

In the opening section of "The Lost Son," for example, the hallucinated protagonist, regressing metamorphically, sinks down to an animistic level, begging from the subhuman some clue as to the meaning of
his existence:

> At Woodlawn I heard the dead cry:
> I was lulled by the slamming of iron,
> A slow drip over stones,
> Toads brooding in wells.
> All the leaves stuck out their tongues;
> I shook the softening chalk of my bones,
> Saying,
> Snail, snail glister me forward,
> Bird, soft-sigh me home.
> Worm, be with me.
> This is my hard time.

At the close of the same poem, which remains for me the finest of the
monologues, the protagonist, turned human and adult again, is granted
his moment of epiphany; but he is not ready yet to apprehend it wholly;
he must wait:

> It was beginning winter,
> The light moved slowly over the frozen field,
> Over the dry seed-crowns,
> The beautiful surviving bones
> Swinging in the wind.
>
> Light traveled over the field;
> Stayed.
> The weeds stopped swinging.
> The mind moved, not alone,
> Through the clear air, in the silence.
>
> Was it light?
> Was it light within?
> Was it light within light?
> Stillness becoming alive,
> Yet still?

> A lively understandable spirit
> Once entertained you.
> It will come again.
> Be still.
> Wait.

The love poems that followed early in the 1950's—Roethke was forty-four when he married—were a distinct departure from the painful excavations of the monologues and in some respects a return to the strict stanzaic forms of the earliest work. They were daring and buoyant, not only in their explicit sensuality, their "lewd music," but in the poet's open and arrogant usurpation of the Yeatsian beat and, to a degree, of the Yeatsian mantle:

> I take this cadence from a man named Yeats;
> I take it, and I give it back again. . . .

By this time Roethke had the authority, and self-assurance, indeed the euphoria—"I am most immoderately married"—to carry it off.

Even when he had been involved with the *dreck* of the monologues, he was able, in sudden ecstatic seizures of clarity, to proclaim "a condition of joy." Moreover, he had been delighted at the opportunity that the free and open form gave him to introduce juicy little bits of humor, mostly puns and mangled bawdry and indelicate innuendoes. He had also written some rather ferocious nonsense verse for children. Now he achieved something much more difficult and marvelous: a passionate love poetry that yet included the comic, as in "I Knew a Woman," with its dazzling first stanza:

> I knew a woman, lovely in her bones,
> When small birds sighed, she would sigh back at them;
> Ah, when she moved, she moved more ways than one.
> The shapes a bright container can contain!
> Of her choice virtues only gods should speak,
> Or English poets who grew up on Greek
> (I'd have them sing in chorus, cheek to cheek).

Inevitably the beloved is a shapeshifter, like the poet himself. "Slow, slow as a fish she came." Or again, "She came toward me in the flowing air, a shape of change." "No mineral man," he praises her as dove, as lily, as rose, as leaf, even as "the oyster's weeping foot." And he asks himself, half fearfully: "Is she what I become? Is this my final Face?"

At the human level this tendency of his to become the other is an extension of that Negative Capability, as defined by Keats, which first manifested itself in the Roethke greenhouse. A man of this nature, said Keats, "is capable of being in uncertainties, mysteries, doubt, without any irritable reaching after fact and reason . . . he has no identity—he is continually in for and filling some other body." In "The Dying Man" Roethke assumes the character of the poet Yeats; in *Meditations of an Old Woman*, he writes as though he were his mother; in several late poems he adopts the role and voice of his beloved.

The love poems gradually dissolve into the death poems. Could the flesh be transcended, as he had at first supposed, till passion burned with a spiritual light? Could the several selves perish in love's fire and be reborn as one? Could the dear and beautiful one lead him, as Dante taught, to the very footstool of God? In "The Dying Man" he proposes a dark answer: "All sensual love's but dancing on the grave." Roethke thought of himself as one with the dying Yeats: "I am that final thing, a man learning to sing."

The five-fold *Meditations of an Old Woman* that concludes Roethke's selective volume, *Words for the Wind* (1958), is almost wholly preoccupied with thoughts of death and with the search for God. He had started writing the sequence almost immediately after the death of his mother in 1955. Here he returns to the cyclic method of the earlier monologues. In the First Meditation the Old Woman introduces the theme of journeying. All journeys, she reflects, are the same, a movement forward after a few wavers, and then a slipping backward, "backward in time." Once more we recognize the Jungian pattern of progression and regression embodied in the work. The journeys and the five meditations as a whole are conceived in a kind of rocking motion, and indeed the verb "to rock"—consistently one of the poet's key verbs of motion—figures prominently in the text. The rocking is from the cradle toward death:

> The body, delighting in thresholds,
> Rocks in and out of itself. . . .

An image of transformations. And toward the close:

> To try to become like God
> Is far from becoming God.
> O, but I seek and care!
>
> I rock in my own dark,
> Thinking, God has need of me.
> The dead love the unborn.

A few weeks before his death Roethke completed his arrangement of some fifty new poems, published under the title *The Far Field*. The range and power of this posthumous volume, unquestionably one of the landmarks of the American imagination, have yet to be fully grasped or interpreted. Among its contents are two major sequences, *The North American Sequence*, consisting of six long meditations on the American landscape and on death ... on dying into America, so to speak; and a group of twelve shorter, more formal lyrics, under the generic heading *Sequence, Sometimes Metaphysical*, bearing witness to a state of spiritual crisis, the dance of the soul around the exhausted flesh and toward the divine fire.

"How to transcend this spiritual emptiness?" he cries in "The Longing," which opens the North American sequence. The self, retracing its transformations, seeks refuge in a lower order of being:

> And the spirit fails to move forward,
> But shrinks into a half-life, less than itself,
> Falls back, a slug, a loose worm
> Ready for any crevice,
> An eyeless starer.

He longs "for the imperishable quiet at the heart of form."

In a sense he has completed his dark journey, but he has not yet found either his oblivion or his immortality. He yearns for the past which will also be future. The American earth calls to him, and he responds by struggling out of his lethargy: "I am coming!" he seems to be saying, "but wait a minute. I have something left to do. I belong to the wilderness. I will yet speak in tongues."

> I have left the body of the whale, but the mouth of the night is still wide;
> On the Bullhead, in the Dakotas, where the eagles eat well,
> In the country of few lakes, in the tall buffalo grass at the base of the clay buttes,
> In the summer heat, I can smell the dead buffalo,
> The stench of their damp fur drying in the sun;
> The buffalo chips drying.
>
> Old men should be explorers?
> I'll be an Indian.
> Ogallala?
> Iroquoi.

That diminishing coda is a miracle of compression and connotation.

In "The Far Field," the fifth poem of the North American sequence and the title poem of the collection, Roethke speaks of his journeying, as his mother did in the earlier Meditations.

> I dream of journeys repeatedly:
> Of flying like a bat deep into a narrowing tunnel,
> Of driving alone, without luggage, out a long peninsula,
> The road lined with snow-laden second growth,
> A fine dry snow ticking the windshield,

> Alternate snow and sleet, no on-coming traffic,
> And no lights behind, in the blurred side-mirror.
> The road changing from glazed tar-face to a rubble of stone,
> Ending at last in a hopeless sand-rut,
> Where the car stalls,
> Churning in a snowdrift
> Until the headlights darken.

As always, in these soliloquies, the poet sinks through various levels of time and of existence. There was a field once where he found death in the shape of a rat, along with other creatures shot by the nightwatch-man or mutilated by the mower; but he found life, too, in the spon-taneous agitations of the birds, "a twittering restless cloud." And he tries to relive his selfhood back to its mindless source, so that he may be born again, meanwhile proclaiming his faith in the inexorable wheel of metamorphosis:

> I'll return again,
> As a snake or a raucous bird,
> Or, with luck, as a lion.

Sometimes the faith wavers. In "The Abyss," a poem outside the North American sequence, he inquires, "Do we move toward God, or merely another condition?" . . . "I rock between dark and dark."

An even deeper anguish saturates the verses of the *Sequence, Some-times Metaphysical*:

> Dark, dark my light, and darker my desire.
> My soul, like some heat-maddened summer fly,
> Keeps buzzing at the sill. Which I is *I*?

But if the shapeshifter for a moment despairs of his identity, he still has strength and will enough to drag himself over the threshold of annihi-lation:

> A fallen man, I climb out of my fear,
> The mind enters itself, and God the mind,
> And one is One, free in the tearing wind.

I do not always believe in these ecstatic resolutions—they sometimes seem a cry of need rather than of revelation—but I am always moved by the presence of the need and by the desperation of the voice.

"Brooding on God, I may become a man," writes Roethke in "The Marrow," out of the same sequence—one of the great poems of the century, a poem at once dreadful and profound, electric and shudder-ing:

Godhead above my God, are you there still?
To sleep is all my life. In sleep's half-death,
My body alters, altering the soul
That once could melt the dark with its small breath.
Lord, hear me out, and hear me out this day:
From me to Thee's a long and terrible way.

I was flung back from suffering and love
When light divided on a storm-tossed tree;
Yea, I have slain my will, and still I live:
I would be near; I shut my eyes to see;
I bleed my bones, their marrow to bestow
Upon that God who knows what I would know.

Such furious intensity exacts a price. The selves of the poet could be fused only by the exertion of a tremendous pressure. If only he could be content to name the objects that he loved and not be driven to convert them into symbols—that painful ritual.

In "The Far Field," where he evokes his own valedictory image, Whitman is with him, and Prospero, and—in the shifting light —Proteus, the old man of the sea fatigued by his changes:

An old man with his feet before the fire,
In robes of green, in garments of adieu.

The lines that follow have a touch of prophecy in them as the poet, renewed by the thought of death, leaving his skins behind him, moves out into the life-giving and obliterating waters:

A man faced with his own immensity
Wakes all the waves, all their loose wandering fire.
The murmur of the absolute, the why
Of being born falls on his naked ears.
His spirit moves like monumental wind
That gentles on a sunny blue plateau.
He is the end of things, the final man.

All finite things reveal infinitude:
The mountain with its singular bright shade
Like the blue shine on freshly frozen snow,
The after-light upon ice-burdened pines;
Odor of basswood on a mountain slope,
A scent beloved of bees;
Silence of water above a sunken tree:
The pure serene of memory in one man,—
A ripple widening from a single stone
Winding around the waters of the world.

John Ashbery: The Charity of the Hard Moments

BY HAROLD BLOOM

OF THE AMERICAN POETS now in mid-career, those born in the decade 1925-1935, John Ashbery and A. R. Ammons seem to me the strongest. This essay, an overview of Ashbery's published work to date, is meant as a companion-piece to the essay on Ammons printed in my book of studies in Romantic tradition, *The Ringers in the Tower* (University of Chicago Press, 1971). Ashbery goes back through Stevens to Whitman, even as Ammons is a more direct descendant of American Romanticism in its major formulation, which remains Emerson's. Otherwise, these two superb poets have nothing in common except their authentic difficulty. Ammons belongs to no school, while Ashbery can be regarded either as the best poet by far of the "New York School" or — as I would argue — so unique a figure that only confusion is engendered by associating him with Koch, O'Hara, Schuyler and their friends and disciples.

I remember purchasing *Some Trees,* Ashbery's first commercially published volume (Yale Press, 1956, Introduction by Auden) in December, 1956, after reading the first poem ("Two Scenes") in a bookstore. The poem begins: "We see us as we truly behave" and concludes with "In the evening / Everything has a schedule, if you can find out what it is." A skeptical honesty, self-reflexive, and an odd faith in a near-inscrutable order remain characteristic of Ashbery's work after sixteen years. Also still characteristic is the abiding influence of Stevens. I remember being fascinated by the swerve away from Stevens' *Credences of Summer* in "Two Scenes":

> This is perhaps a day of general honesty
> Without example in the world's history
> Though the fumes are not of a singular authority
> And indeed are dry as poverty.

Where Stevens, in a moment of precarious satisfaction, entertained the possibility of overcoming "poverty," imaginative need, the young Ashbery identified self-knowledge with such need. Auden, hardly an admirer of Stevens, introduced Ashbery as an ephebe of Rimbaud, seer "of sacred images and ritual acts." But, actual disciple of Stevens (in his most Whitmanian aspect) and of Whitman ultimately, Ashbery necessarily began in a poetic world emptied of magical images and acts. The highly Stevensian "The Mythological Poet" opposed "a new / Music, innocent and monstrous / As the ocean's bright display of teeth" to "the toothless murmuring / Of ancient willows," sacred images for outworn seers. In the title-poem, clearly the book's best, Ashbery had found already his largest aesthetic principle, the notion that every day the world consented to be shaped into a poem. "Not every day," Stevens warns in his "Adagia," which Ashbery couldn't have read then, but Stevens' point was that on some days it could happen. The point is Emersonian or Whitmanian, and though Ashbery antithetically completes Stevens in this principle, he is ultimately, like Whitman and Stevens, a descendant of Emerson's *Nature,* though at the start a wry one:

> . . . you and I
> Are suddenly what the trees try
>
> To tell us we are:
> That their merely being there
> Means something; that soon
> We may touch, love, explain.
>
> And glad not to have invented
> Such comeliness, we are surrounded . . .

The Not-Me, as Emerson said, is nature and my body together, as well as art and all other men. Such a conviction leads Ashbery, even as it impelled Whitman and Stevens, to a desperate quest that masks as an ease with things. The poem is to be discovered in the Not-Me, out in the world that includes the poet's body. Rhetorically, this tends to mean that every proverbial cliché must be recovered, which becomes almost a rage in Ashbery's *Three Poems.* Where the middle Ashbery, the poet of the outrageously disjunctive volume, *The Tennis Court Oath,* attempted too massive a swerve away from the ruminative continuities of Stevens and Whitman, recent Ashbery goes to the dialectical extreme of what seems at first like a barrage of bland commonplaces. Emerson, in *Nature,* anticipated Ashbery with his characteristic sense that parts of a world and parts of speech are alike emblematic, so that either, however worn out, could yet be an epiphany, though the world *seemed* so post-magical:

> . . . the memorable words of history and the proverbs of nations
> consist usually of a natural fact, selected as a picture or parable
> of a moral truth. Thus; a rolling stone gathers no moss; a bird
> in the hand is worth two in the bush; a cripple in the right way
> will beat a racer in the wrong; make hay while the sun shines;
> 'tis hard to carry a full cup even; vinegar is the son of wine;
> the last ounce broke the camel's back; long-lived trees make roots
> first . . .

Emerson insisted each worn proverb could become *transparent.* In
his rare startlements into happiness, Ashbery knows this transparency,
but generally his hopes are more modest. He is, in temperament,
more like Whitman than like Emerson or Stevens. Even the French
poet he truly resembles is the curiously Whitmanian Apollinaire,
rather than Reverdy:

> Et ce serait sans doute bien plus beau
> Si je pouvaise supposer que toutes ces choses dans lesquelles je suis partout
> Pouvaient m'occuper aussi
> Mais dans ce sens il n'y a rien de fait
> Car si je suis partout a cette heure il n'y a cependant que moi qui suis en moi

Let us, swerving away from Apollinaire, call these Ashbery's two
contradictory spiritual temptations, to believe that one's own self,
like the poem, can be found in "all the things everywhere," or to
believe that "there is still only I who can be in me." The first temptation will be productive of a rhetoric that puts it all in, and so must
try to revitalize every relevant cliché. The second temptation rhetorically is gratified by ellipsis, thus leaving it all out. I suppose that
Ashbery's masterpiece in this mode is the long spiel called "Europe"
in *The Tennis Court Oath,* which seems to me a fearful disaster. In
Stevens, this first way is the path of Whitmanian expansiveness,
which partly failed the not always exuberant burgher of Hartford,
while the second is the way of reductiveness, too great a temptation
for him, as Stevens came to realize. The road through to poetry for
Stevens was a middle path of invention that he called "discovery,"
the finding rather than the imposition of an order. Though there
are at least three rhetorics in Stevens, matching these three modes of
self-apprehension, none of the three risks Ashbery's disasters, whether
of apparently joining together bland truisms or of almost total disjunctiveness. But I think that is close to the sorrow of influence in
Ashbery, which is the necessary anxiety induced in him by the siren
song of Stevens' rhetorics. Ashbery (who is not likely to be pleased
by this observation) is at his best when he is neither revitalizing
proverbial wisdom nor barely evading an ellipsis, but when he dares
to write most directly in the idiom of Stevens. This point, and Ash-

bery's dazzling deflection of it, will be my concern when I arrive at *The Double Dream of Spring.*

My own melancholy, confronting Ashbery, is provoked by his second public volume, *The Tennis Court Oath* (Wesleyan University Press, 1962). Coming to this eagerly as an admirer of *Some Trees,* I remember my outrage and disbelief at what I found:

> for that we turn around
> experiencing it is not to go into
> the epileptic prank forcing bar
> to borrow out onto tide-exposed fells
> over her morsel, she chasing you
> and the revenge he'd get
> establishing the vultural over
> rural area cough protection
> murdering quintet. . . .

This is from the piece called "Leaving The Atocha Station," which (I am told) has a certain reputation among the rabblement of poetasters who proclaim themselves anti-academic while preaching in the academies, and who lack consciousness sufficient to feel the genuine (because necessary) heaviness of the poetic past's burden of richness. *The Tennis Court Oath* has only one good poem, "A Last World." Otherwise, its interest is now entirely retrospective; how could Ashbery collapse into such a bog by just six years after *Some Trees,* and how did he climb out of it again to write *Rivers and Mountains,* and then touch a true greatness in *The Double Dream of Spring* and *Three Poems?*

Poets, who congenitally lie about so many matters, *never* tell the truth about poetic influence. To address an audience sprinkled with poets, on the subject of poetic influence, is to risk a *sparagmos* in which the unhappy critic may be mistaken for Orpheus. Poets want to believe, with Nietzsche, that "forgetfulness is a property of all action," and action for them is writing a poem. Also, no one can write a poem without remembering another poem, even as no one loves without remembering, though dimly or subconsciously, a former beloved, however much that came under a taboo. Every poet is forced to say, as Hart Crane did in an early poem: "I can remember much forgetfulness." To live as a poet, a poet needs the illusive mist about him that shields him from the light that first kindled him. This mist is the nimbus (however false) of what the prophets would have called his own *kabod,* the supposed radiance of his own glory.

In *Some Trees,* Ashbery was a relatively joyous ephebe of Stevens, who evidently proved to be too good a father. Nietzsche suggested

that "if one has not had a good father, it is necessary to invent one."
Yes, and for a poet, if one's father was too good, it becomes necessary
to re-invent one's father's sorrows, so as to balance his glory. This
necessity, which Ashbery met in all his subsequent work, is merely
evaded throughout *The Tennis Court Oath,* where a great mass of
egregious disjunctiveness is accumulated to very little effect. Apollinaire had counseled *surprise* for the modern poet's art, but what is
surprising about a group of poems that will never yield to any reading
or sustained re-reading? Poems may be like pictures, or like music,
or like what you will, but if they *are* paintings or musical works, they
will not be poems. The Ashbery of *The Tennis Court Oath* may have
been moved by De Kooning and Kline, Webern and Cage, but he
was not moved to the writing of poems. Nor can I accept the notion
that this was a necessary phase in the poet's development, for who
can hope to find any necessity in this calculated incoherence? Yet
the volume matters, and still upsets me because it is Ashbery's, the
work of a man who has written poems like "Evening in the Country,"
"Parergon," the astonishingly poignant and wise "Soonest Mended,"
and "Fragment," probably the best longer poem by an American
poet of my own generation, and unmatched, I believe, by anything
in the generation of Lowell.

Isolated amid the curiosities of *The Tennis Court Oath* is the
beautiful "A Last World," which in its limpidity and splendor would
fit well into one of Ashbery's later volumes. The poem prophesies
the restorative aesthetic turn that Ashbery was to take, and reveals
also what has become his central subject and resource, the imagination
of a later self questing for accommodation not so much with an earlier
glory (as in Wordsworth) but with a possible sublimity that can
never be borne, if it should yet arrive. Stevens more than Whitman
is again the precursor, and the greatness of Ashbery begins to emerge
when the anxiety of influence is wrestled with, and at least held to a
stand-off.

"A Last World," like any true poem, has the necessity of reminding
us that the meaning of one poem can only be another poem, a poem
not itself, and probably not even one by its own author. Ashbery
emerges into a total coherence when he compels himself to know that
every imagining is a misprision, a taking amiss or twisting askew of
the poetic *given.* Mature creation, for a poet, rises directly from an
error about poetry rather than an error, however profound, about
life. Only a willful *misinterpretation* of a poetry already known too

well, loved too well, understood too well, frees a maturing maker's mind from the compulsion to repeat, and more vitally from the fear of that compulsion. This is not what "A Last World" *thinks* it is about, but the poem so presents itself as to compel us to read it as an allegory of this poet's struggle to win free of his own evasions, and not the aesthetic evasions alone, but of everything that is elliptical in the self.

The Stevensian "he" of "A Last World" becomes a constant presence in the next two volumes, modulating from Ashbery as a self-deceiver to a perpetually late learner who is educated with the reader, so as to become a convincing "we":

> Everything is being blown away;
> A little horse trots up with a letter in its mouth,
>   which is read with eagerness
> As we gallop into the flame.

This, the poem's conclusion, is the ostensible focus of "A Last World"; the present is the flame, things vanish perpetually as we come up to them, and we are — at best — romance questers made pathetic as we read the message so charmingly delivered to us, which is hardly going to save us from joining a general state of absence. The poem seems to end dispassionately in loss, yet its tone is serene, and its atmosphere suffused with a curious radiance. This radiance is a revisionary completion of the difficult serenity of late Stevens, a completion that is also antithetical to Stevens' rockier composure, or as his "Lebenweisheitspielerei" calls it, his sense of "stellar pallor":

> Little by little, the poverty
> Of autumnal space becomes
> A look, a few words spoken.
>
> Each person completely touches us
> With what he is and as he is,
> In the stale grandeur of annihilation.

Stevens, contemplating the departure of the proud and the strong, bleakly celebrated those left as "the unaccomplished, / The finally human, / Natives of a dwindled sphere." Ashbery, counterpointing his vision against that of Stevens' *The Rock*, celebrates loss as an accomplishment, a treasure, a mint flavoring in Stevens' land of hay, which was too ripe for such enigmas:

> Once a happy old man
> One can never change the core of things, and light burns
>   you the harder for it,
> Glad of the changes already and if there are more it will
>   never be you that minds

> Since it will not be you to be changed, but in the evening
>   in the severe lamplight doubts come
> From many scattered distances, and do not come too near.
> As it falls along the house, your treasure
> Cries to the other men; the darkness will have none of you,
>   and you are folded into it like mint into the sound
>   of haying

Loss is not gain here, and yet Ashbery takes Stevens' vision back
from the last world of *The Rock* to "A Postcard from the Volcano"
of 1936, where at least we leave behind us "what still is/The Look
of things." Absence or denudation is the common perception of the
two poets, but Ashbery, though always anxious, is too gentle for
bitterness, and rhetorically most himself where least ironic. Stevens'
"qualified assertions" (Helen Vendler's apt phrase) become in Ashbery
a series of progressively more beautiful examples of what we might
call "qualified epiphanies," the qualifications coming partly from
Ashbery's zeal in tacitly rejecting a poetry of privileged moments or
privileged phrases. But this zeal is misplaced, and almost impossible
to sustain, as will be seen in his later development.

Rivers and Mountains (Holt, Rinehart & Winston, 1966) is a
partial recovery from *The Tennis Court Oath*, though only one poem
in it, "The Skaters," seems to me major Ashbery when compared to
what comes after. But then, "The Skaters" is nearly half the volume,
and its most luminous passages are of the same poetic ambience as the
work beyond. With *Rivers and Mountains*, Ashbery began to win
back the dismayed admirers of his earliest work, myself included. The
curious poem called "The Recent Past," whatever its intentions, seems
to be precisely addressed to just such readers, in very high good
humor:

> You were my quintuplets when I decided to leave you
> Opening a picture book the pictures were all of grass
> Slowly the book was on fire, you the reader
> Sitting with specs full of smoke exclaimed
> How it was a rhyme for "brick" or "redder."
> The next chapter told all about a brook.
> You were beginning to see the relation when a tidal wave
> Arrived with sinking ships that spelled out "Aladdin."
> I thought about the Arab boy in his cave
> But the thoughts came faster than advice.
> If you knew that snow was a still toboggan in space
> The print could rhyme with "fallen star."

As far as intention matters, the "you" here is another Ashbery, to
whom almost the entire book is directed, as will be the recent *Three
Poems*. "These Lacustrine Cities" sets the book's project:

> Much of your time has been occupied by creative games
> Until now, but we have all-inclusive plans for you . . .

"Clepsydra," the longer poem just preceding "The Skaters," is printed as the first attempt at the project's realization, and is a beautiful failure, outweighing most contemporary poetic successes. The water-clock of the title is ultimately Ashbery himself, akin to the sun-flower of Blake's frighteningly wistful lyric. A history-in-little of Ashbery's poethood, "Clepsydra" is Ashbery's gentle equivalent of Stevens' surpassingly bitter "The Comedian as the Letter C," and is as dazzling an apparent dead end. I judge it a failure not because its exuberance is so negative, in contrast to the Whitmanian "The Skaters," but because its solipsism, like the "Comedian," is too perfect. Though splendidly coherent, "Clepsydra" gives the uncanny effect of being a poem that neither wants nor needs readers. It sits on the page as a forbiddingly solid wall of print, about as far from the *look* of Apollinaire as any verse could be. From its superbly opaque opening ("Hasn't the sky?") to its ominous closing ("while morning is still and before the body/Is changed by the faces of evening") the poem works at turning a Shelleyan-Stevensian self-referential quality into an absolute impasse. Perhaps here, more than in "The Skaters" even, or in his masterpiece, "Fragment," Ashbery tries to write the last poem about itself and about poetry, last by rendering the mode redundant:

> . . . Each moment
> Of utterance is the true one; likewise none are true,
> Only is the bounding from air to air, a serpentine
> Gesture which hides the truth behind a congruent
> Message, the way air hides the sky, is, in fact,
> Tearing it limb from limb this very moment: but
> The sky has pleaded already and this is about
> As graceful a kind of non-absence as either
> Has a right to expect: whether it's the form of
> Some creator who has momentarily turned away,
> Marrying detachment with respect . . .

"Detachment with respect" is Ashbery's attitude toward transcendental experience, for which he tends to use the image of transparence, as Whitman and Stevens, following Emerson, did also. Stevens, as Helen Vendler notes, tends to *sound* religious when his poems discourse upon themselves, and "Clepsydra," like much of the *Three Poems,* similarly has an oddly religious tone. All of Ashbery (I am puzzled as to why Richard Howard thinks Ashbery an "anti-psychological" poet), including "Clepsydra," is profound self-revelation. Ashbery — like Wordsworth, Whitman, Stevens, Hart Crane — writes out of so profound a subjectivity as to make "confessional" verse seem as self-defeating as that mode truly has been, from Coleridge (its inventor) down to Lowell and his disciples. "Clepsydra," so wholly self-enclosed, is an oblique lament rising "amid despair and isolation/ of the chance to know you, to sing of me/Which are you." The poem's subject overtly is Ashbery's entrapped subjectivity, objectified in the pathetic emblem of the water-clock, and represented in large by the outrageously even tone that forbids any gathering of climaxes. This refusal to vary his intensities is one of Ashbery's defense mechanisms against his anxiety of poetic influences. I can think of no poet in English, earlier or now at work, who listens upon so subtly unemphatic a pervasive tone. As a revisionary ratio, this tone intends to distance Ashbery from Whitman and from Stevens, and is a kind of *kenosis,* a self-emptying that yields up any evident afflatus:

> . . . Perhaps you are being kept here
> Only so that somewhere else the peculiar light of someone's
> Purpose can blaze unexpectedly in the acute
> Angles of the rooms. It is not a question, then,
> Of having not lived in vain . . .

The *kenosis* is too complete in "Clepsydra"; the tone, however miraculously sustained, too wearying for even so intelligent a poet rightly to earn. With relief, I move on to "The Skaters," Ashbery's most energetic poem, the largest instance in him of the revisionary movement of *daemonization,* or the onset of his personalized Counter-Sublime, as against the American Sublime of Whitman and Stevens. Yet, "The Skaters" is almost outrageously Whitmanian, far more legitimately in his mode than Ginsberg manages to be:

> Old heavens, you used to tweak above us,
> Standing like rain whenever a salvo . . . Old heavens,
> You lying there above the old, but not ruined, fort,
> Can you hear, there, what I am saying?

"The Skaters" is not a parody, however involuntary, of *Song of Myself,* though sometimes it gives that impression. *Song of Myself* begins where the British Romantic quest-poem is sensible enough to end: with an internal romance, of self and soul, attaining its consummation. Whitman, having married himself, goes forth as an Emersonian liberating god, to preside over the nuptials of the universe. The daemonic parodies of this going forth stand between Whitman and Ashbery: *Paterson,* the *Cantos, The Bridge, Notes toward a Supreme Fiction, Preludes to Attitude, The Far Field.* What remains for Ashbery, in "The Skaters," is a kind of Counter-Sublime that accepts a reduction of Whitmanian ecstasy, while reaffirming it nevertheless, as in the vision early in the poem, when the poet's whole soul is stirred into activity, flagellated by the decibels of the "excited call" of the skaters:

> The answer is that it is novelty
> That guides these swift blades o'er the ice
> Projects into a finer expression (but at the expense
> Of energy) the profile I cannot remember.
> Colors slip away from and chide us. The human mind
> Cannot retain anything except perhaps the dismal two-note theme
> Of some sodden "dump" or lament.

One can contrast the magnificent skating episode in Book I of *The Prelude*, where colors have not slipped away, and the mind has retained its power over outer sense. The contrast, though unfair to Ashbery, still shows that there is a substance in us that prevails, though Ashbery tends to know it only by knowing also his absence from it. His poem celebrates "the intensity of minor acts," including his self-conscious mode of making-by-ellipsis, or as he calls it: "this leaving-out business." Putting off (until *Three Poems*) "the costly stuff of explanation," he movingly offers a minimal apologia:

> . . . Except to say that the carnivorous
> Way of these lines is to devour their own nature, leaving
> Nothing but a bitter impression of absence, which as we know involves presence,
> but still.
> Nevertheless these are fundamental absences, struggling to get up and be off
> themselves.

"The Skaters," admitting that "mild effects are the result," labors still "to hold the candle up to the album," which is Ashbery's minimalist version of Stevens' "How high that highest candle lights the dark." In the poem's second part, Ashbery sets forth on a Romantic voyage, but like Crispin sees every vision-of-the-voyage fade slowly away. The long third movement, a quasi-autobiographical panorama of this poet's various exiles, needs careful examination, which I cannot give here, for nothing else in Ashbery succeeds nearly so well at the effect of the great improviser, an excellence shared by Whitman and by the Stevens of the blue guitar. With the fourth and final section, partly spoken by the persona of a Chinese scholar-administrator, the poem circles to a serene resolution, precisely prophetic of the Ashbery to come. "The whole brilliant mass comes spattering down," and an extraordinary simplicity takes its place. After so many leavings-out, the natural particulars are seen as being wonderfully sufficient:

The apples are all getting tinted
In the cool light of autumn.

The constellations are rising
In perfect order: Taurus, Leo, Gemini.

Everything promised by "The Skaters," Ashbery has performed, in the very different greatnesses of *The Double Dream of Spring* (Dutton, 1970) and *Three Poems* (Viking, 1972). The first of these is so rich a book that I will confine myself to only a handful of poems, each so wonderful as to survive close comparison with Whitman and Stevens at almost their strongest: "Soonest Mended," "Evening in the Country," "Sunrise in Suburbia," "Parergon" and the long poem "Fragment." Before ruminating on these representative poems, a general meditation on Ashbery's progress seems necessary to me, as I am going on to make very large claims for his more recent work.

Though the leap in manner between *Rivers and Mountains* and *The Double Dream of Spring* is less prodigious than the gap between *The Tennis Court Oath* and *Rivers and Mountains,* there is a more crucial change in the later transition. Ashbery at last says farewell to ellipsis, a farewell confirmed by *Three Poems,* which relies upon "putting it all in," indeed upon the discursiveness of a still-demanding prose. The abandonment of Ashbery's rhetorical evasiveness is a self-curtailment on his part, a purgation that imparts simplicity through intensity, but at the price of returning him to the rhetorical world of Stevens and of the American tradition that led to Stevens. It is rather as if Browning had gone from his grotesque power backward to the Shelleyan phase of his work. Perhaps Browning should have, since his last decades were mostly barren. As a strong poet, Ashbery has matured almost as slowly as his master Stevens did, though unlike Stevens he has matured in public. Even as Stevens provoked a critical nonsense, only now vanishing, of somehow being a French poet writing in English, so Ashbery still provokes such nonsense. Both are massive sufferers from the anxiety-of-influence, and both developed only when they directly engaged their American precursors. In Ashbery, the struggle with influence, though more open, is also more difficult, since Ashbery desperately engages also the demon of discursiveness, as Hart Crane differently did (for the last stand of Crane's mode, see the one superb volume of Alvin Feinman, *Preambles and Other Poems,* 1964). This hopeless engagement, endemic in all Western poetries in our century, is a generalized variety of the melancholy of poetic influence. It is not problematic form, nor repressed allusiveness, nor recondite matter, that makes much modern verse difficult. Nor, except rarely, is it conceptual profundity, or sustained mythical invention. Ellipsis, the art of omission, almost always a central device in poetry, has been abused into the dominant rhetorical element of our time. Yet no modern poet has employed it so effectively as Dickinson did, probably because for her it was a deep symptom of everything else that belonged to the male tradition that she was leaving out. I cannot involve myself here in the whole argument that I have set forth in a little book, *The Anxiety of Influence: A Theory of Poetry* (1972; see the discussion of Ashbery in the section called *"Apophrades: or the Return of the Dead"*), but I cite it as presenting evidence for the judgment that influence becomes progressively more of a burden for poets from the Enlightenment to this moment. Poets, defending poetry, are adept at idealizing their relation to one another, and the magical Idealists among critics have followed them in this saving self-deception. Here is Northrop Frye, greatest of the idealizers:

> Once the artist thinks in terms of influence rather than of clarity of form, the effort of the imagination becomes an effort of will, and art is perverted into tyranny, the application of the principle of magic or mysterious compulsion to society.

Against this I cite Coleridge's remark that the power of originating *is* the will, our means of escaping from nature or repetition-compulsion, and I add that no one needs to pervert art in this respect, since the Post-Enlightenment poetic imagination is necessarily quite perverse enough in the perpetual battle against influence. Wordsworth *is* a misinterpretation of Milton (as is Blake), Shelley *is* a misinterpretation of Wordsworth, Browning and Yeats *are* misinterpretations of Shelley. Or, in the native strain, Whitman perverts or twists askew Emerson, Stevens is guilty of misprision toward both, and Ashbery attempts a profound and beautiful misinterpretation of all his precursors, *in his own best poetry*. What the elliptical mode truly seeks to omit is the overt continuity with ancestors, and the mysterious compulsion operative here is a displacement of what Freud charmingly called "the family romance."

Ashbery's own family romance hovers uneasily in all-but-repressed memories of childhood; his family-romance-as-poet attains a momentarily happy resolution in *The Double Dream of Spring*, but returns darkly in *Three Poems*. Ashbery is a splendid instance of the redemptive aspect of influence-anxiety, for his best work shows how the relation to the precursor is humanized into the greater themes of all human influence-relations which, after all, include lust, envy, sexual jealousy, the horror of families, friendship, and the poet's reciprocal relation to his contemporaries, ultimately to all of his readers.

I begin again, after this anxious digression, with "Soonest Mended," and begin also the litany of praise and advocacy, of what Pater called "appreciation," that the later work of Ashbery inspires in me. The promise of *Some Trees* was a long time realizing itself, but the realization came, and Ashbery is now something close to a great poet. It is inconvenient to quote all of "Soonest Mended," but I will discuss it as though my reader is staring at pages 17 through 19 of *The Double Dream of Spring*. The poem speaks for the artistic life of Ashbery's generation, but more for the general sense of awakening to the haphazardness and danger of one's marginal situation in early middle age:

> To step free at last, miniscule on the gigantic plateau—
> This was our ambition: to be small and clear and free.
> Alas, the summer's energy wanes quickly,
> A moment and it is gone. And no longer
> May we make the necessary arrangements, simple as they are.
> Our star was brighter perhaps when it had water in it.
> Now there is no question even of that, but only
> Of holding on to the hard earth so as not to get thrown off,
> With an occasional dream, a vision . . .

Dr. Johnson, still the most useful critic in the language, taught us to value highly any original expression of common or universal experience. "Has he any fresh matter to disclose?" is the question Johnson would have us ask of any new poet whose work seems to demand our deep consideration. The Ashbery of his two most recent volumes passes this test triumphantly. "Soonest Mended," from its rightly proverbial title through every line of its evenly distributed rumination, examines freshly that bafflement of the twice-born life that has been a major theme from Rousseau and Wordsworth to Flaubert and Stevens. This is the sense of awakening, past the middle of the journey, to the truth that *"they* were the players, and we who had struggled at the game/Were merely spectators. . . ." Uniquely Ashbery's contribution is the wisdom of a wiser passivity:

> . . . learning to accept
> The charity of the hard moments as they are doled out,
> For this is action, this not being sure, this careless
> Preparing, sowing the seeds crooked in the furrow,
> Making ready to forget, and always coming back
> To the mooring of starting out, that day so long ago.

Action, Wordsworth said, was momentary, only a step or blow, but suffering was permanent, obscure, dark and shared the nature of infinity. Ashbery's action is Wordsworth's suffering; the way through to it, Ashbery says, is "a kind of fence-sitting/Raised to the level of an esthetic ideal." If time indeed is an emulsion, as this poem asserts, then wisdom is to find the mercy of eternity in the charity of the hard moments. Shelley, forgiving his precursors, said that they had been washed in the blood of the redeemer and mediator, time. Ashbery domesticates this fierce idealism; "conforming to the rules and living/Around the home" mediate his vision, and redemption is the indefinite extension of the learning process, even if the extension depends upon conscious fantasy. The achievement of "Soonest Mended" is to have told a reductive truth, yet to have raised it out of reductiveness by a persistence masked as the commonal, an urgency made noble by art.

The implicit argument of "Soonest Mended" is adumbrated in "Evening in the Country," a reverie rising out of a kind of Orphic convalescence, as another spent seer consigns order to a vehicle of change. "I am still completely happy," Ashbery characteristically begins, having thrown out his "resolve to win further." Yet, this is not the "false happiness" that Stevens condemned, for it is being rather than consciousness, cat more than rabbit. The shadow of Stevens hovers overtly in this poem, the poet of the never-satisfied mind:

> . . . He wanted that,
> To face the weather and be unable to tell
> How much of it was light and how much thought,
> In these Elysia, these origins,
> This single place in which we are and stay,
> Except for the images we make of it,
> And for it, and by which we think the way,
> And, being unhappy, talk of happiness
> And, talking of happiness, know that it means
> That the mind is the end and must be satisfied.

Away from this Ashbery executes what Coleridge (in *Aids to Reflection*) calls a "*lene clinamen,* the gentle bias," for Ashbery's inclination is to yield to a realization that the mind had better be satisfied. Somewhere else, Coleridge speaks of making "a *clinamen* to the ideal," which is more in Stevens' mode, despite Stevens' qualifications. Ashbery, in his maturity, tries to be content not to originate an act or a state, though his achievement is to have done so anyway. "Evening in the Country" persuades that Ashbery has "begun to be in the context you feel," which is the context of the mind's surrender to visionary frustration. I quote at length from the poem's marvelous conclusion:

> Light falls on your shoulders, as is its way,
> And the process of purification continues happily,
> Unimpeded, but has the motion started
> That is to quiver your head, send anxious beams
> Into the dusty corners of the rooms
> Eventually shoot out over the landscape
> In stars and bursts? For other than this we know nothing
> And space is a coffin, and the sky will put out the light.
> I see you eager in your wishing it the way
> We may join it, if it passes close enough:
> This sets the seal of distinction on the success or failure of your attempt.
> There is growing in that knowledge
> We may perhaps remain here, cautious yet free
> On the edge, as it rolls its unblinking chariot
> Into the vast open, the incredible violence and yielding
> Turmoil that is to be our route.

Purification here is a kind of Orphic *askesis,* another revisionary movement away from the fathers. The gods of Orphism, at least of that variety which is the natural religion of the native strain in American poetry, are Dionysus, Eros and Ananke. Ashbery's Dionysiac worship, in his recent work, is mostly directed to absence. Eros, always hovering in Ashbery, is more of a presence in "Fragment." Ananke, the Beautiful Necessity worshiped by the later Emerson and all his poetic children, is the governing deity of "Evening in the Country" as of "Soonest Mended" and the *Three Poems.* Purgation "continues happily," while the poet asks the open question as to whether the motion of a new transcendental influx has started. Ashbery's genuine uncertainty is no longer the choice of poetic subject, as it was in *The Tennis Court Oath,* but concerns his relation to his own subject, which is the new birth or fresh being he has discovered in himself, yet which sets its own timing for manifestation.

Nothing is more difficult for me, as a reader of poetry, than to describe *why* I am moved when a poem attains a certain intensity of quietness, when it seems to wait. Keats, very early in his work, described this as power half-slumbering on its own right arm. I find this quality in only a few contemporary poets — Ashbery, Ammons, Strand, Merwin, James Wright, among others. Recent Ashbery has more of this deep potential, this quietness that is neither quietism nor repression, than any American poet since the last poems of Stevens. Webern is the nearest musical analogue I know, but analogues are hard to find for a poem like "Evening in the Country."

For, though the poem is so chastened, it remains an Orphic celebration, as much so as Hart Crane at his most ecstatic.

Ashbery's ambitions as a mature poet, rising out of this still Orphic convalescence, are subtly presented in "Sunrise in Suburbia." Ashbery, never bitter, always charged by the thrill of the sun coming up, nevertheless suggests here an initial burden too complex for the poem to bear away from him. This burden is eloquently summed up in a line from "Parergon": "That the continuity was fierce beyond all dream of enduring." Repetition is the antagonist in "Sunrise in Suburbia," which quests for discontinuity or, as the poem calls it, "nuance":

> And then some morning there is a nuance:
> Suddenly in the city dirt and varied
> Ideas of rubbish, the blue day stands and
> A sudden interest is there:
> Lying on the cot, near the tree-shadow,
> Out of the thirties having news of the true source:
> Face to kiss and the wonderful hair curling down
> Into margins that care and are swept up again like branches
> Into actual closeness
> And the little things that lighten the day
> The kindness of acts long forgotten
> Which gives us history and faith
> And parting at night, next to ocean, like the collapse of dying.

An earlier passage in the poem juxtaposes the "flatness of what remains" to the "modelling of what fled," setting the poem in the large tradition that goes from "Tintern Abbey" to "The Course of a Particular." The difficulty, for Ashbery as for his readers, is how to construct something upon which to rejoice when you are the heir of this tradition, yet reject both privileged moments of vision and any privileged heightenings of rhetoric in the deliberately subdued and even tone of your work. Stevens is difficult enough in this kind of poem, yet for him there are times of unusual excellence, and he momentarily will yield to his version of the high style in presenting them. For Ashbery, the privileged moments, like their images, are on the dump, and he wants to purify them by clearly placing them there. Say of what you see in the dark, Stevens urges, that it is this or that it is that, but do not use the rotted names. Use the rotted names, Ashbery urges, but cleanse them by seeing that you cannot be apart from them, and are partly redeemed by consciously suffering with them. Stevens worked to make the visible a little hard to see; Ashbery faces "a blank chart of each day moving into the premise of difficult visibility." The sounds of nature on this suburban sunrise have a hard tone: "this deaf rasping of branch against branch." These too are the cries of branches that do not transcend themselves, yet they do concern us:

> They are empty beyond consternation because
> These are the droppings of all our lives
> And they recall no past de luxe quarters
> Only a last cube.
> The thieves were not breaking in, the castle was not being stormed.
> It was the holiness of the day that fed our notions
> And released them, sly breath of Eros,
> Anniversary on the woven city lament, that assures our arriving
> In hours, seconds, breath, watching our salary
> In the morning holocaust become one vast furnace, engaging all tears.

Where "The Course of a Particular" rejects Ruskin's Pathetic Fallacy or the imputation of life to the object world, Ashbery uncannily labors to make the fallacy more pathetic, the object world another failed version of the questing self. Yet each day, his poem nobly insists, is holy and releases an Orphic "sly breath of Eros," to be defeated, and yet "engaging all tears." If a poem like this remains difficult, its difficulty arises legitimately from the valuable complexity of its vision, and not from the partial discontinuity of its rhetoric.

The thematic diffidence of "Sunrise in Suburbia" is transformed in the superb short poem "Parergon," which gives us Ashbery's version of pure Shelleyan quest, "Alastor" rather than its parody in "The Comedian as the Letter C." As in "Evening in the Country," Ashbery begins by affirming, without irony, a kind of domestic happiness in his artist's life of sitting about, reading, being restless. In a dream-vision, he utters the prophecy of the life he has become: "we need the tether/of entering each other's lives, eyes wide apart, crying." Having done so, he becomes "the stranger," the perpetual uncompromising quester on the model of the Poet in Shelley's "Alastor":

> As one who moves forward from a dream
> The stranger left that house on hastening feet
> Leaving behind the woman with the face shaped like an arrowhead,
> And all who gazed upon him wondered at
> The strange activity around him.
> How fast the faces kindled as he passed!
> It was a marvel that no one spoke
> To stem the river of his passing
> Now grown to flood proportions, as on the sunlit mall
> Or in the enclosure of some court
> He took his pleasure, savage
> And mild with the contemplating.
> Yet each knew he saw only aspects,
> That the continuity was fierce beyond all dream of enduring,
> And turned his head away, and so
> The lesson eddied far into the night:
> Joyful its beams, and in the blackness blacker still,
> Though undying joyousness, caught in that trap.

Even as the remorseless Poet of "Alastor" imperishably caught up the element in Shelley that was to culminate in "Adonais" and "The Triumph of Life," so "Parergon" portrays the doomed-poet aspect of Ashbery, of whom presumably we will hear more in his later life. One of the few ironies in Ashbery is the title, which I assume is being used in the sense it has in painting, something subsidiary to the main subject. Yet the poem is anything but bywork or ornamentation. As beautiful as nearly anything in Ashbery, it is central to his dilemma, his sorrow and his solace.

With reverence and some uneasiness, I pass to "Fragment," the crown of *The Double Dream of Spring* and, for me, Ashbery's finest work. Enigmatically autobiographical, even if it were entirely fantasy, the poem's fifty stately ten-line stanzas, orotundly Stevensian in their rhetoric, comment obliquely upon a story never told, a relationship never quite a courtship, and now a nostalgia. Studying this nostalgia, in his most formal and traditional poem, more so than anything even in *Some Trees*, Ashbery presents his readers, however faithful, with his most difficult rumination. But this is a wholly Stevensian difficulty, neither elliptical nor obscure, but a ravishing simplicity that seems largely lacking in any referential quality. I have discussed the poem with excellent and sympathetic students who continue to ask: "But what is the poem *about*?" The obvious answer, that to some extent it is "about" itself, they rightly reject, since whether we are discussing Shelley, Stevens, or Ashbery, this merely distances the same question to one remove. But though repeated readings open up the referential aspect of "Fragment," the poem will continue to inspire our uneasiness, for it is profoundly evasive.

What the all-but-perfect solipsist *means* cannot be right, not until he becomes perfect in his solipsism, and so stands forth as a phantasmagoric realist (one could cite Mark Strand, a superb poet, as a recent example). "Fragment," I take it, is the elegy for the self of the imperfect solipsist, who wavered before the reality of another self, and then withdrew back into an interior world. The poem being beautifully rounded, the title evidently refers not to an aesthetic incompleteness, but to this work's design, that tells us only part of a story, and to its resigned conclusion, for the protagonist remains alone, an "anomaly" as he calls himself in the penultimate line.

The motto to "Fragment" might be from Ashbery's early "Le Livre est sur la table" where much of the enigma of the poet's mature work is prophesied. Playing against the mode of "The Man with the

Blue Guitar," Ashberry made a Stevensian parable of his own sorrows, stating a tentative poetic and a dark version of romance. The overwhelming last stanza of "Fragment" comes full circle to this:

> The young man places a bird-house
> Against the blue sea. He walks away
> And it remains. Now other
>
> Men appear, but they live in boxes.
> The sea protects them like a wall.
> The gods worship a line-drawing
>
> Of a woman, in the shadow of the sea
> Which goes on writing. Are there
> Collisions, communications on the shore
>
> Or did all secrets vanish when
> The woman left? Is the bird mentioned
> In the waves' minutes, or did the land advance?

As the table supports the book, this poem tells us, so deprivation supports "all beauty, resonance, integrity," our poverty being our imaginative need. The young poet, deprived of a world he can only imagine, and which he is constrained to identify with "the woman," learns that the sea, Stevensian emblem for all merely given reality, must triumph. Yet, if he is to have any secrets worth learning in his womanless world, it must come from "collisions, communications on the shore," where his imagination and the given meet. "Collisions, communications" is a fearfully reductive way of describing whatever sustenance Eros grants him to live, and is part of an open question. The final question can be read more as a rhetorical one, since the poems got written, and the later work of Ashbery proves that the land did advance.

We need to read this against the splendid final stanza of "Fragment":

> But what could I make of this? Glaze
> Of many identical foreclosures wrested from
> The operative hand, like a judgment but still
> The atmosphere of seeing? That two people could
> Collide in this dusk means that the time of
> Shapelessly foraging had come undone: the space was
> Magnificent and dry. On flat evenings
> In the months ahead, she would remember that that
> Anomaly had spoken to her, words like disjointed beaches
> Brown under the advancing signs of the air.

He has learned that there are indeed "collisions, communications on the shore," but this apparently crucial or unique instance saw two people "collide in this dusk." Yet this was not failure; rather, the advent of a new time. The stanza's balance is precarious, and its answer to the crucial earlier question, "Did the land advance?" is double. The brown, disjointed beaches seem a negative reply, and "the advancing signs of the air" a positive one.

In the context of Ashbery's development, "Fragment" is his central poem, coming about a year after "The Skaters" and just preceding "Clepsydra," his last major poem written abroad. "Sunrise in Suburbia" and the powerful shorter poems in *The Double Dream of Spring* came later, after the poet's return to this country in the autumn of 1966. My own intoxication with the poem, when I first read it in *Poetry* magazine, led me on to the two recent volumes, and my sense of the enormous importance of this poet. Though I lack space here for any extended account of "Fragment" before I go on to *Three Poems* I want to give an encapsulated sense of some of its meanings, and the start of the appreciation it deserves, as perhaps the first successful poem of its kind in English since Swinburne's "The Triumph of Time."

The poem opens, as it will close, with the unnamed woman of "a moment's commandment," whom Ashbery sometimes addresses, and sometimes describes in the third person. After a vision of April's decline, "of older / Permissiveness which dies in the / Falling back toward recondite ends, / The sympathy of yellow flowers," the poet commences upon one of these recondite ends, an elegy for "the suppressed lovers," whose ambiguous time together seems to have been only a matter of weeks.

Much of the difficulty, and the poignance, of "Fragment" is generated by Ashbery's quasi-metaphysical dilemma. Committed, like the later Stevens, to the belief that poetry and *materia poetica* are the same thing, and struggling always against the aesthetic of the epiphany or privileged moment, with its consequent devaluation of other experience, Ashbery nevertheless makes his poem to memorialize an intense experience, brief in deviation. This accounts probably for the vacillation and evasiveness of "Fragment," which tries to render an experience that belongs to the dialectic of gain and loss, yet insists the experience was neither. There are passages of regret, and of joy, scattered through the poem, but they do little to alter the calm, almost marmoreal beauty of the general tone of rapt meditation. Even the apparent reference to the death of a paternal figure, in the forty-seventh stanza, hardly changes Ashbery's almost Spenserian pace. The thirtieth stanza sums up Ashbery's inclination against the Stevensian tendency to move from a present intensity to a "That's

it" of celebration, "to catch from that / Irrational moment its unreasoning." The strength of Ashbery's denial of "that Irrational
moment" comes from its undersong of repressed desire:

> But why should the present seem so particularly urgent?
> A time of spotted lakes and the whippoorwill
> Sounding over everything? To release the importance
> Of what will always remain invisible?
> In spite of near and distant events, gladly
> Built? To speak the plaits of argument,
> Loosened? Vast shadows are pushed down toward
> The hour. It is ideation, incrimination
> Proceeding from necessity to find it at
> A time of day, beside the creek, uncounted stars and buttons.

Of story, "Fragment" gives almost nothing, yet it finds oblique
means of showing us "the way love in short periods / Puts everything out of focus, coming and going." Variations upon this theme
constitute almost the whole of the poem's substance, and also its
extraordinary strength, as Ashbery's insights in this area of perception seem endless. In its vision of love, "Fragment" hymns only the
bleak truth of the triumph of absence:

> Thus your only world is an inside one
> Ironically fashioned out of external phenomena
> Having no rhyme or reason, and yet neither
> An existence independent of foreboding and sly grief.
> Nothing anybody says can make a difference; inversely
> You are a victim of their lack of consequence
> Buffeted by invisible winds, or yet a flame yourself
> Without meaning, yet drawing satisfaction
> From the crevices of that wind, living
> In that flame's idealized shape and duration.

This eloquent despair, Shelleyan in its paradoxical affirmation of
love yet acknowledgment of love's delusiveness, ends precisely in
Shelley's image of the coming and going of the Intellectual Beauty,
"like darkness to a dying flame." Uniquely Ashberian is the emphasis on *satisfaction*, despite the transitoriness of "living" in so purely
"idealized" a shape and duration. "Fragment" alternately explores
the saving crevices and the shape of love's flame. Progression in this
almost static poem is so subtle as to be almost indiscernible until the
reader looks back at the opening from the closing stanzas, realizing
then that:

> . . . This time
> You get over the threshold of so much unmeaning, so much
> Being, prepared for its event, the active memorial.

The reader's gain is an intensified sense of "time lost and won," never more strongly felt than in the poem's erotic culmination, stanzas 13-20, where Ashbery seeks "to isolate the kernel of / Our imbalance." In stanza 16, Ashbery finds no satisfaction in satisfaction anyway, in the only stanza of the poem that breaks the baroque stateliness and artful rhetorical repetitiveness of its form:

> The volcanic entrance to an antechamber
> Was not what either of us meant.
> More outside than before, but what is worse, outside
> Within the periphery, we are confronted
> With one another, and our meeting escapes through the dark
> Like a well.
> Our habits ask us for instructions.
> The news is to return by stages
> Of certainty, too early or too late. It is the invisible
> Shapes, the bed's confusion and prattling. The late quiet,
> This is how it feels.

"The volcanic entrance to an antechamber," as a dismissal of the inadequacy of phallic heterosexuality to the love meant, is a kind of elegant younger brother to Hart Crane's bitter characterization of this means of love as "a burnt match skating in a urinal." Ashbery wisely does not pause to argue preferences, but accomplishes his poem's most surprising yet inevitable transition by directly following "This is how it feels" with a return to childhood visions: "The pictures were really pictures / Of loving and small things." As the interchange of interior worlds continues, Ashbery attains a point of survey in stanza 36 where he can assert: "You see, it is / Not wrong to have nothing." Four years later, writing "Soonest Mended," this joined an echo of Lear's speech to Cordelia to become: "both of us were right, though nothing / Has somehow come to nothing." Expectation without desire is henceforth Ashbery's difficult, more-than-Keatsian attitude, not a disinterestedness nor any longer a renunciation, but a kind of visionary sublimation. This self-curtailing poetic *askesis* is performed as I think the dialectic of poetic influence compels it to be performed by a strong poet, as Ashbery has now become. That is, it is a revisionary movement in regard to the prime precursor, Stevens, who blends with what seems to be the dying figure of Ashbery's own father in the dense and exciting sequence of stanzas 38 through 49. These stanzas are Ashbery's version of Stevens' "Farewell to Florida" and recall its Spenserian image of the high ship of the poet's career being urged upon its more dangerous and mature course. Though Ashbery will back away from this ominous freedom in his final stanza (which I quoted earlier), the quest aspect of his career attains a wonderful culmination in stanza 49:

One swallow does not make a summer, but are
What's called an opposite: a whole of raveling discontent,
The sum of all that will ever be deciphered
On this side of that vast drop of water.
They let you sleep without pain, having all that
Not in the lesson, not in the special way of telling
But back to one side of life, not especially
Immune to it, in the secret of what goes on:
The words sung in the next room are unavoidable
But their passionate intelligence will be studied in you.

Here, as in so many passages having a similar quality, Ashbery reaches his own recognizable greatness, and gives us his variety of the American Sublime. The "parental concern" of Stevens' "midnight interpretation" (stanza 38) produced the grand myth of the Canon Aspirin in *Notes toward a Supreme Fiction*, where Stevens at last, detaching himself from the Canon, could affirm: "I have not but I am and as I am, I am." Ashbery, in his moment akin to Stevens' sublime self-revelation, affirms not the Emersonian-Whitmanian Transcendental Self, as Stevens most certainly (and heroically) does, but rather "the secret of what goes on." This is not, like Stevens' massive declaration, something that dwells in the orator's "special way of telling," but inheres painfully in Ashbery's vulnerability. As a self-declared "anomaly," Ashbery abides in the most self-revelatory and noble lines he has yet written:

The words sung in the next room are unavoidable
But their passionate intelligence will be studied in you.

That the pathos of "Fragment," a poem of the unlived life, of life refusing revenge upon its evaders, could lead to so lucid a realization, is a vital part of Ashbery's triumph over his earlier opacities. In the recent *Three Poems*, written in a prose apparently without precursors, this triumph expands, though again large demands are made upon the reader. But this I think is part of Ashbery's true value; only he and Ammons among poets since Stevens compel me to reread so often, and then reward such labor.

Though "The New Spirit," first of the *Three Poems*, was begun in November, 1969, most of it was written January to April, 1970. In a kind of cyclic repetition, the second prose poem, "The System," was composed from January to March 1971, with the much shorter "The Recital" added as a coda in April. This double movement from winter vision to spring's reimaginings is crucial in *Three Poems*, which is Ashbery's prose equivalent of *Notes toward a Supreme Fiction*, and which has the same relation as *Notes* to *Song of Myself*. Where

Stevens reduces to the First Idea, which is "an imagined thing," and then equates the poet's act of the mind with the reimagining of the First Idea, Ashbery reduces to a First Idea of himself, and then reimagines himself. I am aware that these are difficult formulae, to be explored elsewhere, and turn to a commentary upon *Three Poems*, though necessarily a brief and tentative one.

I described "Evening in the Country" as a "convalescent's" displacement of American Orphism, the natural religion of our poetry. *Three Poems* might be called the masterpieces of an invalid of the Native Strain, even a kind of invalid's version of *Song of Myself*, as though Whitman had written that poem in 1865, rather than 1855. Ashbery's work could be called *Ruminations of Myself* or *Notes toward a Saving but Subordinate Fiction*. Whitman's poem frequently is address of I, Walt Whitman, to you or my soul. Ashbery's *Three Poems* are addressed by *I*, John Ashbery writing, to *You*, Ashbery as he is in process of becoming. *I*, as in Whitman, Pater, Yeats, is personality or self or the *antithetical*; *You*, as in the same visionaries, is character or soul or the *primary*. Ashbery's swerve away from tradition here is that his *You* is the reimagining, while his *I* is a reduction.

"The New Spirit," the first poem's title, refers to a rebirth that takes place after the middle-of-the-journey crisis, here in one's late thirties or early forties:

> . . . It is never too late to mend. When one is in one's late thirties, ordinary things—like a pebble or a glass of water— take on an expressive sheen. One wants to know more about them, and one is in turn lived by them. . . .

This "new time of being born" Ashbery calls also "the new casualness," and he writes of it in a prose that goes back to his old rhetorical dialectic of alternating ellipsis and the restored cliché. Indeed, "The New Spirit" opens by overtly giving "examples of leaving out," but Ashbery then mostly chooses to stand himself in place of these examples. Why does he choose prose, after "The Skaters" had shown how well he could absorb prose into verse at length? It may be a mistake, as one advantage, in my experience, of "The New Spirit" over "The System" and "The Recital," is that it crosses over to verse half a dozen times, while they are wholly in prose. I suppose that the desire to tell a truth that "could still put everything in" made Ashbery wary of verse now, for fear that he should not be as comprehensive as possible. Speaking again as the poet of "Fragment" he defines his predicament: "In you I fall apart, and outwardly am a

single fragment, a puzzle to itself." To redress his situation, the
New Spirit has come upon him, to renovate a poet who confesses he
has lost all initiative:

> . . . It has been replaced by a strange kind of happiness
> within the limitations. The way is narrow but it is not hard, it
> seems almost to propel or push one along. One gets the narrow-
> ness into one's seeing, which also seems an inducement to moving
> forward into what one has already caught a glimpse of and which
> quickly becomes vision, in the visionary sense, except that in
> place of the panorama that used to be our customary setting and
> which we never made much use of, a limited but infinitely free
> space has established itself, useful as everyday life but trans-
> figured so that its signs of wear no longer appear as a reproach
> but as indications of how beautiful a thing must have been to
> have been so much prized, and its noble aspect which must have
> been irksome before has now become interesting, you are fascin-
> ated and keep on studying it. . . .

This, despite its diffidence, declares what Emerson called Newness
or Influx, following Sampson Reed and other Swedenborgians.
Sometimes the *Three Poems*, particularly "The System," sound like
a heightened version of the senior Henry James. But mostly Ashbery,
particularly in "The New Spirit," adds his own kind of newness to
his American tradition. At first reading of "The New Spirit," I felt
considerable bafflement, not at the subject-matter, immediately clear
to any exegete aged forty-two, but at the procedure, for it was
difficult to see how Ashbery got from point to point, or even to
determine if there were points. But repeated reading uncovers a
beautiful and simple design: first, self-acceptance of the minimal
anomalies we have become, "the color of the filter of the opinions
and ideas everyone has ever entertained about us. And in this form
we must prepare, now, to try to live." Second, the wintry reduction
of that conferred self is necessary: "And you lacerate yourself so
as to say, These wounds are me." Next, a movement to the *you* and
to reimagining of the *I,* with a realization that the *you* has been
transformed already, through the soul's experience as a builder of
the art of love. With this realization, the consciousness of the New
Spirit comes upon the *I,* and self and soul begin to draw closer in a
fine lyric beginning: "Little by little / You are the mascot of that
time" (pp. 33-34). An event of love, perhaps the one elegized in
"Fragment," intervenes, illuminates, and then recedes, but in its
afterglow the New Spirit gives a deeper significance to the object-
world. After this seeing into the life of things, the growth of the
mind quickens. But the transparency attained through the new

sense of wholeness "was the same as emptiness," and the sense of individual culmination serves only to alienate the poet further from the whole of mankind, which "lay stupefied in dreams of toil and drudgery." It is at this point of realization that the long and beautiful final paragraph comes (pp. 50-51), ending "The New Spirit" with a deliberate reminiscence of the end of "The Skaters." Two visions come to Ashbery, to make him understand that there is still freedom, still the wildness of time that may allow the highest form of love to come. One is "the completed Tower of Babel," of all busyness, a terror that could be shut out just by turning away from it. The other is of the constellations that the tower threatened, but only seemed to threaten. They beckon now to "a new journey" certain to be benign, to answer "the major question that revolves around you, your being here." The journey is a choice of forms for answering, which means both Ashbery's quest for poetic form, and his continued acceptance of an "impressive grammar of cosmic unravelings of all kinds, to be proposed but never formulated."

I think that is an accurate account of the design of "The New Spirit," but I am aware such an account gives little sense of how Ashbery has added strangeness to beauty in thus finding himself there more truly and more strange. The transcendental reawakening of anyone, even of an excellent poet, hardly seems *materia poetica* anymore, and perhaps only Ashbery would attempt to make a poem of it at this time, since his aesthetic follows Stevens by discovering the poem already formed in the world. His true and large achievement in "The New Spirit" is to have taken the theme of "Le Monocle de Mon Oncle," already developed in "Fragment," and to have extended this theme to larger problems of the aging and widening consciousness. Men at 40, Stevens says, can go on painting lakes only if they can apprehend "the universal hue." They must cease to be dark rabbis, and yield up their lordly studies of the nature of man. "The New Spirit" is Ashbery's exorcism of the dark rabbi in his own nature. Its achievement is the rare one of having found a radiant way of describing a process that goes on in many of us, the crisis of vision in an imaginative person's middle age, without resorting to psychosexual or social reductiveness.

"The System" is Ashbery's venture into quest-romance, his pursuit as rose rabbi, of "the origin and course / Of love," the origin and course together making up the System, which is thus a purposive wandering. Since the poem opens with the statement that "the system was breaking down," the reader is prepared for the prose-poem's penultimate paragraph, that tells us "we are rescued by what we cannot imagine: it is what finally takes us up and shuts our story."

The account of the System begins in a charming vision too genial for irony, as though Aristophanes had mellowed wholly:

> From the outset it was apparent that someone had played a colossal trick on something. The switches had been tripped, as it were; the entire world or one's limited but accurate idea of it was bathed in glowing love, of a sort that need never have come into being but was now indispensable as air is to living creatures . . . if only, as Pascal says, we had the sense to stay in our room, but the individual will condemns this notion and sallies forth full of ardor and *hubris*, bent on self-discovery in the guise of an attractive partner who is *the* heaven-sent one, the convex one with whom he has had the urge to mate all these seasons without realizing it. . . .

This "glowing love" inevitably is soon enough seen as "muddle," and the first phase of quest fails: "Thus it was that a kind of blight fell on these early forms of going forth and being together, an anarchy of the affections sprung from too much universal cohesion." Rather than despair, or yield to apocalyptic yearnings, Ashbery consolidates upon his curious and effective passivity, his own kind of negative capability, becoming "a pillar of waiting," but Quixotic waiting upon a dream. As he waits, he meditates on "twin notions of growth" and on two kinds of happiness. One growth theory is of the great career: "a slow burst that narrows to a final release, pointed but not acute, a life of suffering redeemed and annihilated at the end, and for what?" This High Romanticism moves Ashbery, but he rejects it. Yet the alternative way, a Paterian "life-as-ritual" concept, the *locus classicus* of which we could find in the magnificent "Conclusion" to *The Renaissance*, he also turns from, or asserts he does, though I think he is more a part of this vision than he realizes. He fears the speed with which the soul moves away from others: "This very speed becomes a source of intoxication and of more gradually accruing speed; in the end the soul cannot recognize itself and is as one lost, though it imagines it has found eternal rest."

By evading both notions of growth, Ashbery rather desperately evades growth itself. Confronting two kinds of happiness, "the frontal and the latent," he is again more evasive than he may intend to be. The first is a sudden glory, related to the epiphany or Paterian "privileged moment," and Ashbery backs away from it, as by now we must expect, because of its elitism, he says, but rather, we can surmise, for defensive reasons, involving both the anxiety of influence and more primordial Oedipal anxieties. The latent and dormant kind he seeks to possess, but his long espousal of it (pp. 73-86) seems to me the weakest sequence in *Three Poems*, despite a poignant culmination in the great question: "When will you realize that your dreams have eternal life?" I suspect that these are, *for Ashbery*, the most important pages in his book, but except for the lovely pathos of a dreamer's defense, they are too much the work of a poet who wishes to be more of an anomaly than he is, rather than the "central" kind of a poet he is fated to become, in the line of Emerson, Whitman, Stevens.

This "central" quality returns wonderfully in the last 20 pages of "The System," as the quest for love begins again. A passage of exquisite personal comedy, Chaplinesque in its profundity, climaxes in the poet's defense of his mask: "your pitiable waif's stance, that inquiring look that darts uneasily from side to side as though to ward off a blow—." Ashbery assimilates himself to the crucial Late Romantic image of the failed quester, Browning's Childe Roland, for the author of *Three Poems* now approaches his own Dark Tower, to be confronted there by every anxiety, as human and as poet, that he has evaded:

> . . . It is only that you happened to be wearing this look as you arrived at the end of your perusal of the way left open to you, and it "froze" on you, just as your mother warned you it would when you were little. And now it is the face you show to the world, the face of expectancy, strange as it seems. Perhaps Childe Roland wore such a look as he drew nearer to the Dark Tower, every energy concentrated toward the encounter with the King of Elfland, reasonably certain of the victorious outcome, yet not so much as to erase the premature lines of care from his pale and tear-stained face. Maybe it is just that you don't want to outrage anyone, especially now that the moment of your own encounter seems to be getting closer.

This version of Childe Roland's ordeal is an Ashberian transformation or wish-fulfillment, as we can be reasonably certain that Browning's quester neither wants nor expects a "victorious outcome." But Ashbery feels raised from a first death, unlike Childe Roland, who longs for any end, and lacks a "quiet acceptance of experience in its revitalizing tide." Very gently, Ashbery accomplishes a Transcendental and open ending to "The System," complete with an Emersonian "transparent axle" and even an equivalent to the closing of Emerson's Orphic Poet in *Nature*, though Ashbery's guardian bard speaks to him in a "dry but deep accent," promising mastery (p. 99).

Insisting that he has healed the sadness of childhood, Ashbery declares his System-wanderings are completed, the right balance attained in "what we have carefully put in and kept out," though a "lyric crash" may impend in which all this will be lost again. But, for now:

> The allegory is ended, its coils absorbed into the past, and this afternoon is as wide as an ocean. It is the time we have now, and all our wasted time sinks into the sea and is swallowed up without a trace. The past is dust and ashes, and this incommensurably wide way leads to the pragmatic and kinetic future.

This Shelleyan conclusion, akin to Demogorgon's dialectical vision, offers hope in "the pragmatic" yet menaces a return of the serpent-allegory (whose name is Ananke, in Ashbery as in Stevens or Shelley) in the still "kinetic" future.

The Coda of "The Recital" is a wholly personal apologia, with many Whitmanian and Stevensian echoes, some of them involuntary. "We cannot interpret everything, we must be selective," Ashbery protests, "nor can we leave off singing" which would return the poet to the living death of an unhappy childhood. Against the enemy (p. 111), who is an amalgam of time and selfishness, Ashbery struggles to get beyond his own solipsism, and the limits of his art. On the final page, an Emersonian-Stevensian image of saving transparence serves to amalgamate the new changes Ashbery meets and welcomes. This transparence movingly is provided by a Whitmanian vision of an audience for Ashbery's art: "There were new people watching and waiting, conjugating in this way the distance and emptiness, transforming the scarcely noticeable bleakness into something both intimate and noble." So they have and will, judging by the response of my students and other friends, with whom I've discussed Ashbery's work. By more than 15 years of high vision and persistence he has clarified the initial prophecy of his work, until peering into it we can say: "We see us as we truly behave" and, as we can see, we can think: "These accents seem their own defense."

The Death Throes of Romanticism:
The Poems of Sylvia Plath

BY JOYCE CAROL OATES

> I am not cruel, only truthful—
> The eye of the god. . . .
>
> —"Mirror"

TRAGEDY IS NOT A WOMAN, however gifted, dragging her shadow around in a circle or analyzing with dazzling scrupulosity the stale, boring inertia of the circle; tragedy is cultural, mysteriously enlarging the individual so that what he has experienced is both what we have experienced and what we need not experience—because of his, or her, private agony. It is proper to say that Sylvia Plath represents for us a tragic figure involved in a tragic action, and that her tragedy is offered to us as a near-perfect work of art in her books *The Colossus* (1960), *The Bell Jar* (1963), *Ariel* (1965), and the posthumous volumes published in 1971, *Crossing the Water* and *Winter Trees*. This essay is an attempt to analyze Miss Plath in terms of her cultural significance, to diagnose through her poetry the pathological aspects of our era which make a death of the spirit inevitable—for that era and for all who believe in its assumptions. It is also based upon the certainty that Miss Plath's era is concluded and that we may consider it with the sympathetic detachment with which we consider any era that has gone before us and makes our own possible: the cult of Sylvia Plath insists that she is a saintly martyr, but of course she is something less dramatic than that, though more valuable. The "I" of the poems is an artful construction, a tragic figure whose tragedy is classical, the result of a limited vision that believed itself the mirror held up to nature—as in the poem "Mirror," the eye of a little god that imagines itself without preconceptions, "unmisted by love or dislike." This is the audacious hubris of tragedy, the inevitable reality-challenging statement of the participant in a dramatic action which he does not know is "tragic." He dies, and only we can see the purpose of his death—to illustrate the error of a personality that believed itself godlike.

The assumptions of this essay are several: that the artist both creates and is created by his art and that the self—especially the "I" of lyric poetry—is a personality that achieves a kind of autonomy, free not only of the personal life of the artist but of the part-by-part progression of individual poems as well; that the autobiographical personality is presented by the artist as a testing of reality and that its success or failure or bewilderment will ultimately condition the artist's personal life; that the degree to which an audience accepts or rejects or sympathetically detaches itself from a given tragic action will ultimately condition the collective life of an era; and that the function of literary criticism is not simply to dissect either cruelly or reverentially, to attack or to glorify, but to illustrate how the work of a significant artist helps to explain his era and our own. The significance of Sylvia Plath's art is assumed. Her significance as a cultural phenomenon is assumed. What needs desperately to be seen is how she performed for us, and perhaps in place of some of us, the concluding scenes in the fifth act of a tragedy whose first act began centuries ago.

D. H. Lawrence said in *Apocalypse* that when he heard people complain of being lonely he knew their affliction: "they have lost the Cosmos." It is easy to agree with Lawrence, but less easy to understand what he means. Yet if there is a way of approaching Sylvia Plath's tragedy it is only through an analysis of what Miss Plath has lost and what she is half-conscious of having lost:

> I am solitary as grass. What is it I miss?
> Shall I ever find it, whatever it is?
>
> —"Three Women"

We must take this loss as a real one, not a rhetorical echoing of other poets' cries; not a yearning that can be dismissed by the robust and simple-minded among us who are like that formidably healthy and impossible Emerson who sought to dismiss the young people of his day, "diseased" with problems of original sin, evil, predestination, and the like, by contemptuously diagnosing their worries as "the soul's mumps, and measles, and whooping-coughs" ("Spiritual Laws"). Emerson possessed a consciousness of such fluidity and explorative intelligence that any loss of the Cosmos for him could seem nothing more serious than an adolescent's perverse rebelliousness, at its most profound a doubt to be answered with a few words.

These "few words" in our era are multiplied endlessly—all the books, the tradition at our disposal, the example of a perpetually renewed and self-renewing nature—and yet they are not convincing to the Sylvia Plaths of our time. For those who imagine themselves as filled with emptiness, as wounds "walking out of hospitals," the pronouncements of a practical-minded, combative, "healthy" society of organized individuals are meaningless. Society, seen from the solitary individual's viewpoint, is simply an organization of the solitary linked together materially—perhaps in fact crowded together but not "together," not vitally related. One of Miss Plath's few observations about larger units of human beings is appropriately cynical:

> And then there were other faces. The faces of nations,
> Governments, parliaments, societies,
> The faceless faces of important men.
>
> It is these men I mind:
> They are so jealous of anything that is not flat! They are jealous gods
> They would have the whole world flat because they are.

And, in a rapid associative leap that is typical of her poetry—and typical of a certain type of frightened imagination—Miss Plath expands her sociological observation to include the mythical figures of "Father" and "Son," who conspire together to make a heaven of flatness: "Let us flatten and launder the grossness from these souls" ("Three Women"). The symbolic figures of "Father" and "Son" do not belong to a dimension of the mind exclusive, let alone transcendent, of society; and if they embody the jealous assumptions of an imagined family of "parent" and "child" they are more immediate, more terrifyingly present, than either.

"Nations, governments, parliaments, societies" conspire only in lies and cannot be trusted. Moreover, they are male in their aggression and their cynical employment of rhetoric; their counterparts cannot be women like Sylvia Plath, but the creatures of "Heavy Women," who smile to themselves above their "weighty stomachs" and meditate "devoutly as the Dutch bulb," absolutely mute, "among the archetypes." Between the archetypes of jealous, ruthless power represented by the Father/Son of religious and social tradition, and the archetype of moronic fleshly beauty represented by these smug mothers, there is a very small space for the creative intellect, for the employment and expansion of a consciousness that tries to transcend such limits. Before we reject

Sylvia Plath's definition of the artistic self as unreasonably passive, even as infantile, we should inquire why so intelligent a woman should assume these limitations, why she should not declare war against the holders of power and of the "mysteries" of the flesh—why her poetry approaches but never crosses over the threshold of an active, healthy attack upon obvious evils and injustices. The solitary ego in its prison cell is there by its own desire, its own admission of guilt in the face of even the most crazily ignorant of accusors. Like Eugene O'Neill, who lived into his sixties with this bewildering obsession of the self-annihilated-by-others, Miss Plath exhibits only the most remote (and rhetorical) sympathy with other people. If she tells us she may be a bit of a "Jew," it is only to define herself, her sorrows, and not to involve our sympathies for the Jews of recent European history.

Of course, the answer is that Sylvia Plath did not like other people; like many who are persecuted, she identified in a perverse way with her own persecutors and not with those who, along with her, were victims. But she did not "like" other people because she did not essentially believe that they existed; she knew intellectually that they existed, of course, since they had the power to injure her, but she did not believe they existed in the way she did, as pulsating, breathing, suffering individuals. Even her own children were objects of her perception, there for the restless scrutiny of her image-making mind and not there as human beings with a potentiality that would someday take them beyond their immediate dependency upon her, which she sometimes enjoyed and sometimes dreaded.

The moral assumptions behind Sylvia Plath's poetry condemned her to death, just as she, in creating this body of poems, condemned it to death. But her moral predicament is not so pathological as one might think, if conformity to an essentially sick society is taken to be—as many traditional moralists and psychologists take it—a sign of normality. Miss Plath speaks very clearly a language we can understand. She is saying what men have been saying for many centuries, though they have not been so frank as she and, being less sensitive as well, they have not sickened upon their own hatred for humanity—they have thrived upon it, in fact, "sublimating" it into wondrous achievements of material and mechanical splendor. Let us assume that Sylvia Plath acted out in her poetry and in her private life the deathliness of an old consciousness, the old corrupting hell of the Renaissance ideal and its "I"-ness separate and distinct from all other fields of consciousness, which exist only to be conquered or to inflict pain upon the "I." Where at one point in civilization this very masculine, combative ideal of an "I" set against all other "I's"—and against nature as well—was necessary in order to wrench man from the hermetic contemplation of a God-centered universe and get him into action, it is no longer necessary; its health has become a pathology and whoever clings to its outmoded concepts will die. If Romanticism and its gradually accelerating hysteria is taken as the ultimate end of a once-vital Renaissance ideal of subject/object antagonism, then Miss Plath must be diagnosed as one of the last Romantics; and already her poetry seems to us a poetry of the past, swiftly receding into history.

The "I" that is declared an enemy of all others cannot identify with anyone or anything, since even nature—or especially nature—is antagonistic to it. Man is spirit/body, but as in the poem "Last Things," Sylvia Plath states her distrust of the spirit which "escapes like steam / In dreams, through the mouth-hole or eye-hole. I can't stop it." Spirit is also intellect, but the "intellect" exists uneasily inside a prison house of the flesh, a small, desperate calculating process (like the ego in Freud's psychology) that achieves only spasmodic powers of identity in the constant struggle between the id and the superego or between the bestial world of fleshly female "archetypes" and hypocritical, deathly male authorities. This intellect does not belong naturally in the universe and feels guilt and apprehension at all times. It does not belong in nature; nature is "outside" man, superior in brute power to man though admittedly inferior in the possibilities of imagination. When this intellect attempts its own kind of creation, it cannot be judged as transcendent to the biological processes of change and decay but as somehow conditioned by these processes and, of course, found inferior. Why else would Miss Plath call a poem about her own poetry "Stillborn" and lament the deadness of her poems, forcing them to compete with low but living creatures?—"They are not pigs, they are not even fish. . . ." It is one of the truly pathological habits of this old consciousness that it puts all things into immediate *competition*; erecting Aristotelian categories of X and non-X, assuming that the distinction between two totally unconnected phases of life demands a kind of war, a superior / inferior grading.

For instance, let us examine one of Sylvia Plath's lighter and more "positive" poems. This is "Magi," included in the posthumous *Crossing the Water*. It summons up literary affiliations with Eliot and Yeats, but its vision is exclusively Miss Plath's and, in a horrifying way, very female. Here, the poet is contemplating her six-month-old daughter, who smiles "into thin air" and rocks on all fours "like a padded hammock." Imagined as hovering above the child, like "dull angels," are the Magi of Abstraction—the intellectual, philosophical concepts of Good, True, Evil, and Love, the products of "some lamp-headed Plato." Miss Plath dismisses the Magi by asking, "What girl ever flourished in such company?" Her attitude is one of absolute contentment with the physical, charming simplicities of her infant daughter; she seems to want none of that "multiplication table" of the intellect. If this poem had not been written by Sylvia Plath, who drew such attention to her poetry by her suicide, one would read it and immediately agree with its familiar assumptions—how many times we've read this poem, by so many different poets! But Miss Plath's significance now forces us to examine her work very carefully, and in this case the poem reveals itself as a vision as tragic as her more famous, more obviously troubled poems.

It is, in effect, a death sentence passed by Sylvia Plath on her own use of language, on the "abstractions" of culture, or the literary as opposed to the physical immediacy of a baby's existence. The world of language is condemned as only "ethereal" and "blank"—obviously inferior to the world of brute, undeveloped nature. Miss Plath is saying here, in this agreeably mannered poem, that because "Good" and "Evil" have no meaning to a six-month-old infant beyond the facts of mother's milk and a bellyache, they have no essential meaning at all—to anyone—and the world of all adult values, the world of complex linguistic structures, the world in which Sylvia Plath herself lives as a normal expression of her superior intellect, is as "loveless" as the multiplication table and therefore must be rejected. It is extraordinary that the original Romantic impulse to honor and appreciate nature, especially mute nature, should dwindle in our time to this: a Sylvia Plath willfully admitting to herself and to us that she is inferior to her own infant. The regressive fantasies here are too pathetic to bear examination, but it is worth suggesting that this attitude is not unique at all. It reveals much that is wrong with contemporary intellectuals' assessment of themselves: a total failure to consider that the undeveloped (whether people or nations) are *not* sacred because they are undeveloped, but sacred because they are part of nature; and the role of the superior intellect is not to honor incompletion, in itself or in anything, but to help bring about the fulfillment of potentialities. Miss Plath tells us that a six-month-old infant shall pass judgment on Plato; and in the poem "Candles" she asks, "How shall I tell anything at all / To this infant still in a birth-drowse?" It is impossible, of course, for her to tell the infant anything if she assumes that the infant possesses an intuitive knowledge superior to her own. And yet she does desire to "tell" the infant and us. But her "telling" cannot be anything more than a half-guilty assertion of her own impotence, and she will ultimately condemn it as wasteful. The honoring of mute nature above man's ability to make and use language will naturally result in muteness; this muteness will force the individual into death, for the denial of language is a suicidal one and we pay for it with our lives.

Back from the maternity ward, resting after her painful experience, the most "positive" of Sylvia Plath's three women is reassured when she looks out her window, at dawn, to see the narcissi opening their white faces in the orchard. And now she feels uncomplex again; she is relieved of the miraculous pain and mystery of childbirth, and wants only for herself and for her child "the clear bright colors of the nursery, / The talking ducks, the happy lambs." She meditates:

> I do not will [my baby] to be exceptional.
> It is the exception that interests the devil.
> . . . .
> I will him to be common.

It seems to us pitiful that Miss Plath should desire the "common"—should imagine that her loving words for her infant are anything less than a curse. But her conviction that "the exception interests the devil" is very familiar to us, an expression of our era's basic fear of the intellect; the centuries-old division between "intellect" and "instinct" has resulted in a suicidal refusal to understand that man's intelligence *is* instinctive in his species, simply an instinct for survival and for the creation of civilization. Yet the "loving of muteness" we find in Sylvia Plath is understandable if it is seen as a sensitive revulsion against the world of strife, the ceaseless battle of the letter "I" to make victories and extend its territory. Even the highest intelligence, linked to an ego that is self-despising, will utter curses in the apparent rhythms of love:

> . . . right now you are dumb.
> And I love your stupidity,
> The blind mirror of it. I look in
> And find no face but my own. . . .
>
> —"For a Fatherless Son"

The narcissi of the isolated ego are not really "quick" and "white" as children (see "Among the Narcissi"), but victimized, trampled, and bitter unto death. Miss Plath's attitude in these gentler poems about her motherhood is, at best, a temporary denial of her truly savage feelings—we are shocked to discover her celebration of hatred in "Lesbos" and similar poems, where she tells us what she really thinks about the "stink of fat and baby crap" that is forcing her into silence, "hate up to my neck."

The poems of hatred seem to us very contemporary, in their jagged rhythms and surreal yoking together of images, and in their defiant expression of a rejection of love, of motherhood, of men, of the "Good, the True, the Beautiful. . . ." If life really is a struggle for survival, even in a relatively advanced civilization, then very few individuals will win; most will lose (and nearly all women are fated to lose); something is rotten in the very fabric of the universe. All this appears to be contemporary, but Sylvia Plath's poems are in fact the clearest, most precise (because most private) expression of an old moral predicament that has become unbearable now in the mid-twentieth century. And its poignant genesis is very old indeed:

> And now I was sorry that God had made me a man. The beasts, birds, fishes, etc., I blessed their condition, for they had not a sinful nature; they were not obnoxious to the wrath of God; they were not to go to hell after death. . . .
>
> —John Bunyan,
> *Grace Abounding*

All this involves a variety of responses, though behind them is a single metaphysical belief. The passive, paralyzed, continually surfacing and fading consciousness of Sylvia Plath in her poems is disturbing to us because it seems to summon forth, to articulate with deadly accuracy, the regressive fantasies we have rejected—and want to forget. The experience of reading her poems deeply is a frightening one: it is like walking to discover one's adult self, grown to full height, crouched in some long-forgotten childhood hiding place, one's heart pounding senselessly, all the old, rejected transparent beasts and monsters crawling out of the wallpaper. So much for Plato! So much for adulthood! Yet I cannot emphasize strongly enough how valuable the experience of reading Miss Plath can be, for it is a kind of elegant "dreaming-back," a cathartic experience that not only cleanses us of our personal and cultural desires for regression, but explains by way of its deadly accuracy what was wrong with such desires.

The same can be said for the reading of much of contemporary poetry and fiction, fixated as it is upon the childhood fears of annihilation and persecution, the helplessness we have all experienced when we are, for one reason or another, denied an intellectual awareness of what is happening. For instance, the novels of Robbe-Grillet and his imitators emphasize the hypnotized passivity of the "I" in a world of dense and apparently autonomous things; one must never ask, "Who manufactured these things? Who brought them home? who arranged them?"—for such questions destroy the novels. Similarly, the highly praised works of Pynchon, Barthelme, Barth (the Barth of the minimal stories, not the earlier Barth), and countless others are verbalized screams and shudders to express the confusion of the ego that believes—perhaps because it has been told so often—itself somehow out of place in the universe, a mechanized creature if foolish enough to venture into Nature; a too-natural creature for the mechanical urban paradise he has inherited but has had no part in designing. The "I" generated by these writers is typically a transparent, near-nameless personality; in the nightmarish works of William Burroughs, the central consciousness does not explore a world so much as submit pathetically to the exploration of himself by a comically hostile world, all cartoons and surprising metamorphoses. Sylvia Plath's tentative identity in such poems as "Winter Trees," "Tulips," and even the robustly defiant "Daddy" is a child's consciousness, essentially, seizing upon a symbolic particularity (tulips, for instance) and then shrinking from its primary noon, so that the poems—like the fiction we read so often today—demonstrate a dissolution of personality. As Jan B. Gordon has remarked in a review of *Winter Trees* (*Modern Poetry Studies*, II, 6, p. 282), Miss Plath's landscapes become pictorial without any intermediate stage, so that we discover ourselves "in 'una selva oscura' where associations multiply endlessly, but where each tree looks like every other one. . . ." That is the danger risked by those minimal artists of our time whose subject is solely the agony of the locked-in ego: their agonies, like Miss Plath's landscapes, begin to look alike.

But if we turn from the weak and submissive ego to one more traditionally masculine, activated by the desire to *name* and to *place* and to *conquer*, we discover a consciousness that appears superficially antithetical: "Average reality begins to rot and stink as soon as the act of individual creation ceases to animate a subjectively perceived texture" (Nabokov).

Wallace Stevens:

> The obscure moon lighting an obscure world
> Of things that would never be quite expressed,
> Where you yourself were never quite yourself
> And did not want nor have to be,

Desiring the exhilarations of changes:
The motive for metaphor, shrinking from
The weight of primary noon,
The A B C of being. . . .

Where in Sylvia Plath (and in countless of our contemporaries) the ego suffers dissolution in the face of even the most banal of enemies, in such writers as Nabokov and Stevens the ego emerges as confident and victorious. Yet we see that it is the same metaphysics—the same automatic assumption that there is an "average" reality somehow distinct from us, either superior (and therefore terrifying) or inferior (and therefore saved from "rot" and "stink" only by our godly subjective blessing). This is still the old Romantic bias, the opposition between self and object, "I" and non-"I," man and nature. Nabokov and Stevens have mastered art forms in which language is arranged and rearranged in such a manner as to give pleasure to the artist and his readers, excluding any referent to an available exterior world. Their work frees the ego to devise and defend a sealed-off universe, inhabited chiefly by the self-as-artist, so that it is quite natural to assume that Nabokov's writing is about the art of writing, and Stevens's poems about the art of writing, that the work gives us the *process* of creativity which is its chief interest. Again, as in Sylvia Plath, the work may approach the threshold of an awareness of other inhabitants of the human universe, but it never crosses over because, basically, it cannot guarantee the existence of other human beings: its own autonomy might be threatened or at least questioned. The mirror and never the window is the stimulus for this art which, far from being overwhelmed by nature, turns from it impatiently, in order to construct the claustrophobic *Ada* or the difficult later poems of Stevens, in which metaphors inhabit metaphors and the "weight of primary noon" is hardly more than a memory. The consciousness discernible behind the works of Nabokov and Stevens is like that totally autonomous ego imagined—but only imagined—by Sartre, which is self-created, self-named, untouched by parental or social or cultural or even biological determinants.

Since so refined an art willfully excludes the emotional context of its own creation, personality is minimal; art is all. It is not surprising that the harsh, hooking images of Miss Plath's poetry should excite more interest, since Sylvia Plath is always honest, perhaps more honest than we would like, and her awareness of a lost Cosmos involves her in a perpetual questioning of what nature is, what the Other is, what does it want to do to her, with her, in spite of her . . . ? Nabokov and Stevens receive only the most incidental stimuli from their "average reality" and "obscure world," but Miss Plath is an identity reduced to desperate statements about her dilemma as a passive witness to a turbulent natural world:

> There is no life higher than the grasstops
> Or the hearts of sheep, and the wind
> Pours by like destiny, bending
> Everything in one direction. . . .
>
> The sheep know where they are,
> Browsing in their dirty wool-clouds,
> Grey as the weather.
> The black slots of their pupils take me in.
> It is like being mailed into space,
> A thin, silly message.
>
> —"Wuthering Heights"

And, in "Two Campers in Cloud Country," the poet and her companion experience a kind of comfort up in Rock Lake, Canada, where they "mean so little" and where they will wake "blank-brained as water in the dawn." If the self is set in opposition to everything that excludes it, then the distant horizons of the wilderness will be as terrible as the kitchen walls and the viciousness of hissing fat. There is never any integrating of the self and its experience, the self and its field of perception. Human consciousness, to Sylvia Plath, is always an intruder in the natural universe.

This distrust of the intellect in certain poets can result in lyric-meditative poetry of an almost ecstatic beauty, when the poet acknowledges his separateness from nature but seems not to despise or fear it:

> O swallows, swallows, poems are not
> The point. Finding again the world,
> That is the point, where loveliness
> Adorns intelligible things
> Because the mind's eye lit the sun.
>
> —Howard Nemerov,
> "The Blue Swallows"

Nemerov shares with Stevens and Miss Plath certain basic assumptions: that poems are "not the point" in the natural universe; and that the poet, therefore, is not in the same field of experience as the swallows. Poetry, coming from the mind of man, not from the objects of the mind's perception, is somehow a self-conscious, uneasy activity, which must apologize for itself. In this same poem, the title poem of Nemerov's excellent collection *The Blue Swallows*, the poet opposes the "real world" and the "spelling mind" that attempts to impose its "unreal

relations on the blue swallows." But, despite Nemerov's tone of acquiescence and affirmation, this is a tragic assumption in that it certainly banishes the poet himself from the world: only if he will give up
poetry and "find again the world" has he a chance of being saved. It is a
paradox that the poet believes he will honor the objects of his perception—whether swallows, trees, sheep, bees, or infants—only by with-
drawing from them. Why does it never occur to Romantic poets that
they exist as much by right in the universe as any other creature, and
that their function as poets is a natural function—that the human
imagination is, to put it bluntly, superior to the imagination of birds
and infants?

In art this can lead to silence; in life, to suicide.

Among the lesser known of Theodore Roethke's poems is "Lines
upon Leaving a Sanitarium," in which the poet makes certain sobering,
unambiguous statements:

> Self-contemplation is a curse
> That makes an old confusion worse.
> .   .   .   .   .   .
> The mirror tells some truth, but not
> Enough to merit constant thought..

Perhaps it is not just Sylvia Plath's position at the end of a once-
energetic tradition, and the circumstances of her own unhappy life, that
doomed her and her poetry to premature dissolution, but something in
the very nature of lyric poetry itself. What of this curious art form
which, when not liberated by music, tends to turn inward upon the
singer, folding and folding again upon the poet? If he is immature to
begin with, of what can he sing except his own self's immaturity, and to
what task can his imagination put itself except the selection of ingenious images to illustrate this immaturity? Few lyric poets beginning as
shakily as the young Yeats will continue to write and rewrite, to imagine
and reimagine, in a heroic evolution of the self from one kind of
personality to another; and the distance from the technical virtuosity of
Sylvia Plath's best poems to the technical virtuosity of Lorca's can be
measured in light-years. They did not inhabit the same universe. The
risk of lyric poetry is its availability to the precocious imagination, its
immediate rewards in terms of technical skill, which then hypnotize the
poet into believing that he has achieved all there is to achieve in life as
well as in his art. How quickly these six-inch masterpieces betray their
creators! The early successes, predicated upon ruthless self-examination,

demand a repeating of their skills even when the original psychological dramas have been outgrown or exhausted, since the lyric poet is instructed to look into his heart and write, and by tradition he has only himself to write about. But poetry—like all art—demands that its subject be made sacred. Art *is* the sacralizing of its subject. The problem, then, is a nearly impossible one: How can the poet make himself sacred? Once he has exposed himself, revealed himself, dramatized his fantasies and terrors, what can he do next? Most of modern poetry is scornful, cynical, contemptuous of its subject (whether self or others), bitter or amused or coldly detached. It shrinks from the activity of making the profane world sacred, because it can approach the world only *through* the self-as-subject; and the prospect of glorifying oneself is an impossible one. Therefore, the ironic mode. Therefore, silence. It is rare to encounter a poet like Robert Lowell who, beginning with the stunning virtuosity of his early poems, can move through a period of intense preoccupation with self (*Life Studies*), into a period of exploratory maneuvers into the personalities of poets quite unlike him (*Imitations*), and though a shy, ungregarious man, write plays and participate in their productions (*The Old Glory*), and move into a kind of existential political-historical poetry in which the self is central but unobtrusive (*Notebook*). Most lyric poets explore themselves endlessly, like patients involved in a permanent psychoanalysis, reporting back for each session determined to discover, to drag out of hiding, the essential problem of their personalities—when perhaps there is no problem *in* their personalities at all, except this insane preoccupation with the self and its moods and doubts, while much of the human universe struggles simply for survival. If the lyric poet believes—as most people do—that the "I" he inhabits is not integrated with the entire stream of life, let alone with other human beings, he is doomed to a solipsistic and ironic and self-pitying art in which metaphors for his own predicament are snatched from newspaper headlines. The small, enclosed form of the typical lyric poem seems to preclude an active sanctifying of other people; it is much easier, certainly, for a novelist to investigate and rejoice in the foreign /intimate nature of other people, regardless of his maturity or immaturity. When the novel is not addressed to the same self-analysis as the lyric poem, it demands that one look out the window and not into the mirror; it demands an active involvement with time, place, personality, pasts and futures, and a dramatizing of emotions. The novel allows for a sanctification of any number of people, and if the novelist pits his "I" against others he will have to construct that "I" with care and love; technical virtuosity is so hard to come by—had Dostoevski the virtuosity of Nabokov?—that it begins to seem irrelevant. The novelist's obligation is to do no less than attempt the sanctification of the world, which will take him a lifetime and more—while the lyric poet, if he is stuck in a limited emotional cul-de-sac, will circle endlessly inside the bell jar of his own world, and only by tremendous strength can he break free.

The implications of this essay are not that a highly self-conscious art is inferior by nature to a more socially committed, mature art—on the contrary, it is usually the case that the drama of the self is very exciting. What is a risk for the poet is often a delight for his reader; controlled hysteria is more compelling than statements of Spinozian calm. When Thomas Merton cautioned the mystic against writing poems, believing that the "poet" and the "mystic" must never be joined, he knew that a possession of any truth, especially an irrefutable truth, cannot excite drama. It may be a joy to possess wisdom, but how to communicate it? If you see unity beneath the parts, bits, and cogs of the phenomenal world, this does not mean you can make poetry out of it:

> All leaves are this leaf,
> all petals, this flower
> in a lie of abundance.
> All fruit is the same,
> the trees are only one tree
> and one flower sustains all the earth.
>
> —"Unity,"
> from *Manual Metaphysics*
> by Pablo Neruda;
> trans. by Ben Belitt

This is not Neruda's best poetry.

By contrast, Sylvia Plath's poems convince us when they are most troubled, most murderous, most unfair—as in "Daddy," where we listen in amazement to a child's voice cursing and re-killing a dead man in a distorted rhythmic version of what would be, in an easier world, a nursery tune. An unforgettable poem, surely. The "parts, bits, cogs, the shining multiples" ("Three Women") constitute hallucinations that involve us because they stir in us memories of our own infantile pasts and do not provoke us into a contemplation of the difficult and less dramatic future of our adulthood. The intensity of "Lesbos" grows out of an adult woman denying her adulthood, her motherhood, lashing out spitefully at all objects—babies or husbands or sick kittens—with a strident, self-mocking energy that is quite different from the Sylvia Plath of the more depressed poems:

> And I, love, am a pathological liar,
> And my child—look at her, face down on the floor,
> Little unstrung puppet, kicking to disappear—
> Why, she is schizophrenic,
> Her face red and white, a panic. . . .
> .   .   .   .
> You say I should drown my girl.
> She'll cut her throat at ten if she's mad at two.
> The baby smiles, fat snail,
> From the polished lozenges of orange linoleum.
> You could eat him. He's a boy. . . .

Though Miss Plath and her friend, another unhappy mother, obviously share the same smoggy hell, they cannot communicate, and Miss Plath ends the poem with her insistence upon their separateness: "Even in your Zen heaven we shan't meet."

A woman who despises herself as a woman obviously cannot feel sympathy with any other woman; her passionate love/hate is for the aggressors, the absent husbands or the dead fathers who have absorbed all evil. But because these male figures are not present, whatever revenge is possible must be exacted upon their offspring. The poem "For a Fatherless Son" is more chilling than the cheerful anger of "Daddy," because it is so relentless a curse. And if it hints of Miss Plath's own impending absence, by way of suicide, it is a remarkably cruel poem indeed. Here, the mother tells her son that he will be aware of an absence, presently, growing beside him like "a death tree . . . an illusion / And a sky like a pig's backside. . . ." The child is temporarily too young to realize that his father has abandoned him, but "one day you may touch what's wrong / The small skulls, the smashed blue hills, the godawful hush." This is one of the few poems of Sylvia Plath in which the future is imagined, but it is imagined passively, helplessly; the mother evidently has no intention of rearranging her life and establishing a household free of the father or of his absence. She does not state her hatred for the absent father, but she reveals herself as a victim, bitter and spiteful, and unwilling to spare her son these emotions. Again, mother and child are roughly equivalent; the mother is not an adult, not a participant in the world of "archetypes."

So unquestioningly is the division between selves accepted, and so relentless the pursuit of the solitary isolated self by way of the form of this poetry, that stasis and ultimate silence seem inevitable. Again, lyric poetry is a risk because it rarely seems to open into a future: the time of lyric poetry is usually the present or the past. "This is a disease I carry home, this is a death," Miss Plath says in "Three Women," and, indeed, this characterizes most of her lines. All is brute process, without a future; the past is recalled only with bitterness, a stimulus for present dismay.

When the epic promise of "One's-self I sing" is mistaken as the singing of a separate self, and not the universal self, the results can only be tragic.

Sylvia Plath's essential innocence, her victimization by the pressures of an old, dying, ungenerous conception of man and his relationship to nature, must be made clear; this essay is not an attack upon her. She understood well the hellish fate of being Swift's true counterpart, the woman who agrees that the physical side of life is a horror, an ungainly synthesis of flesh and spirit—the disappointment of all the Romantic love poems and the nightmare of the monkish soul. Since one cannot make this existence sacred, one may as well dream of "massacres" or, like the Third Voice in the play "Three Women," express regret that she had not arranged to have an abortion: "I should have murdered this," she says in a Shakespearean echo, "that murders me." "Crossing the water"—crossing over into another dimension of experience—cannot be a liberation, an exploration of another being, but only a quiet movement into death for two "black, cut-paper people":

> Cold worlds shake from the oar.
> The spirit of blackness is in us, it is in the fishes
> .   .   .   .   .   .
> Are you not blinded by such expressionless sirens?
> This is the silence of astounded souls.

> —"Crossing the Water"

In most of the poems, and very noticeably in *The Bell Jar,* Sylvia Plath exhibits a recurring tendency to dehumanize people, to flatten everyone into "cut-paper people," most of all herself. She performs a kind of reversed magic, a de-sacralizing ritual for which psychologists have terms—reification, rubricization. Absolute, dramatic boundaries are set up between the "I" and all others, and there is a peculiar refusal to distinguish among those who mean well, those who mean ill, and those who are neutral. Thus, one is shocked to discover in *The Bell Jar* that Esther, the intelligent young narrator, is as callous toward her mother as the psychiatrist is to her, and that she sets about an awkward seduction with the chilling precision of a machine—hardly aware of the man involved, telling us very little about him as an existing human being. He does not really *exist,* he has no personality worth mentioning. Only Esther exists.

"Lady Lazarus," risen once again from the dead, does not expect a sympathetic response from the mob of spectators that crowd in to view her, a mock phoenix rising from another failed suicide attempt: to Sylvia Plath there cannot be any connection between people, between the "I" that performs and the crowd that stares. All deaths are separate, and do not evoke human responses. To be really safe, one must be like the young man of "Gigolo," who has eluded the "bright fish hooks, the smiles of women," and who will never age because—like Miss Plath's ideal self—he is a perfect narcissus, self-gratified. He has successfully dehumanized himself.

The Cosmos is indeed lost to Sylvia Plath and her era, and even a tentative exploration of a possible "God" is viewed in the old terms, in the old images of dread and terror. "Mystic" is an interesting poem, on a subject rare indeed in Miss Plath, and seems to indicate that her uneasiness with the "mill of hooks" of the air—"questions without answer"—had led her briefly to thoughts of God. Yet whoever or whatever this "God" is, no comfort is possible because the ego cannot experience any interest or desire without being engulfed:

> Once one has seen God, what is the remedy?
> One one has been seized up
>
> Without a part left over,
> Not a toe, not a finger, and used,
> Used utterly. . . .
> What is the remedy?

"Used": the mystic will be exploited, victimized, hurt. He can expect no liberation or joy from God, but only another form of dehumanizing brutality. Sylvia Plath has made beautiful poetry out of the paranoia sometimes expressed by a certain kind of emotionally disturbed person, who imagines that any relationship with anyone will overwhelm him, engulf and destroy his soul. (For a brilliant poem about the savagery of erotic love between lovers who cannot quite achieve adult autonomy or the generosity of granting humanity to each other, see Ted Hughes's "Lovesong," in *Crow*, not inappropriate in this context.)

The dread of being possessed by the Other results in the individual's failure to distinguish between real and illusory enemies. What must be in the human species a talent for discerning legitimate threats to personal survival evidently never developed in Miss Plath—this helps to explain why she could so gracefully fuse the "evil" of her father with the historical outrages of the Nazis, unashamedly declare herself a "Jew" because the memory of her father persecuted her, and in other vivid poems, sense enemies in tulips (oxygen-sucking tulips?—surely they are human!), or sheep (which possess the un-sheep-like power of murdering a human being), or in the true blankness of a mirror which cannot be seen as recording the natural maturation process of a young woman but must be reinterpreted as drawing the woman toward the "terrible fish" of her future self. Sylvia Plath's inability to grade the possibilities of danger is reflected generally in our society, and helps to account for peculiar admissions of helplessness and confusion in adults who should be informing their children: if everything unusual or foreign is an evil, if everything *new* is an evil, then the individual is lost. The political equivalent of childlike paranoia is too obvious to need restating, but we have a cultural equivalent as well which seems to pass unnoticed. Surely the sinister immorality of films like *A Clockwork Orange* (though not the original, English version of the Burgess novel) lies in their excited focus upon small, isolated, glamourized acts of violence by nonrepresentative individuals, so that the unfathomable violence of governments is totally ignored or misapprehended. Delmore Schwartz said that even the paranoid has enemies—yes, indeed he has enemies, and we all do—but paranoia does not allow us to distinguish them from friends.

In the summer of 1972 I attended a dramatic reading of Sylvia Plath's "Three Women," given by three actresses as part of the International Poetry Conference in London. The reading was given in a crowded room and, unfortunately, the very professional performance was repeatedly interrupted by a baby's crying from another part of the building. Yet here was—quite accidentally—a powerful and perhaps even poetic counterpoint to Sylvia Plath's moving poem. For there, in the baby's cries from another room, was what Miss Plath had left out: the reason for the maternity ward, the reason for childbirth and suffering and motherhood and poetry itself.

What may come to seem obvious to people in the future—that unique personality does not necessitate isolation, that the "I" of the poet belongs as naturally in the universe as any other aspect of its fluid totality, above all that this "I" exists in a field of living spirit of which it is one aspect—was tragically unknown to Miss Plath, as it has been unknown or denied by most men. Hopefully, a world of totality awaits us, not a played-out world of fragments; but Sylvia Plath acted out a tragically isolated existence, synthesizing for her survivors so many of the sorrows of that dying age—Romanticism in its death throes, the self's ship, *Ariel*, prematurely drowned.

> It is so beautiful, to have no attachments!
> I am solitary as grass. What is it I miss?
> Shall I ever find it, whatever it is?
>
> —"Three Women"

On Adrienne Rich: Intelligence and Will

BY ROBERT BOYERS

THE TITLE OF Adrienne Rich's sixth and most recent book of poems is *The Will to Change*. As a title it declares emphatically the centrality of that will in the poet's life and work, and indeed, it has provided an unmistakable thrust in the poems she has written since 1958 or so. Now it seems to me that most of our contemporaries value this will to change all too much, not because they are politically radical or personally nimble and adventurous in any striking way, but because such a will has taken on the qualities of an ideological fashion. To be sure, fashions in the realm of intellect do necessarily bespeak particular emotional commitments and frames of mind, and may not therefore be reduced to the status of intellectual phenomena pure and simple. But we know that ideological fashions frequently detach themselves from underlying emotional factors and assume in time a life and momentum of their own. So important is the will to change in Adrienne Rich's mature work that it may well serve as primary focus in any consideration of her poetry, for it is her understanding and treatment of the ideological dynamics involved that will have much to say about the kind of intelligence we respond to as we read the successive volumes. At the same time, we must try to do justice to the wide range of insights, indeed to the variety of wills, represented in this very singular poetry.

The poet has had an abiding sense of her life and work as split in a decidedly simple and predictable way. As a young woman she had thought of herself as neat and decorous, cultivating a solid look, "Neither with rancor at the past/ Nor to upbraid the coming time," as she described it wistfully in "At Majority" (1954). In those years, things had a certain weight and poems could express them in all their apparent accustomedness and density. It was not as though the young poet were entirely unaware of the abyss of uncertainty, but she had a confident way of holding it off, of handling it elegantly so that it seemed at most a mildly threatening idea. Her poetic skills, lavishly praised in the early '50's by Auden and Jarrell among others, seemed altogether a match for any difficult notions or untoward sensations that might have disturbed that wonderful poise and control, whether of self or of the aesthetic medium. All at once, though, in the poems of the late '50's, a more embattled and urgent air began to creep in, and the poet discovered that she had been covering up, not controlling merely, but willfully evading. There is a certain tidiness in the discovery as she seeks to evoke it in the volume *Snapshots of a Daughter-in-Law* (1963), but we know in the perspective of subsequent volumes that the experience was in fact deeply important to the poet. Where in 1954 she could announce: "Now knowledge finds me out;/ in all its risible untidiness / it traces me to each address, / dragging in things I never thought about" ("From Mourning Glory to Petersburg"), she handles her material much more substantively, if still a bit programmatically, in "The Roofwalker" (1961):

> Was it worthwhile to lay—
> with infinite exertion—
> a roof I can't live under?
> —All those blueprints,
> closings of gaps,
> measurings, calculations?
> A life I didn't choose
> chose me: even
> my tools are the wrong ones
> for what I have to do.

The single, controlling image demanding control of all particulars in a given poem is perhaps the most consistent element in the volume *Snapshots,* and accounts for the still formal quality we sense in the various poems. They deliver up their treasures rather too explicitly, we feel, and the note of discovery becomes so pointed and anticipated that we are grateful even for outbursts of spite or anger that break the pattern. But best of all are the rare introductions of specific tensions the poet wishes to work through rather than to resolve. In the ten-part title poem (1958-1960) she asks of herself, of women generally, "Pinned down / by love, for you the only natural action,/ are you edged more keen / to prise the secrets of the vault? has Nature shown/ her household books to you, daughter-in-law, /that her sons never saw?" There is no clamoring here for definitive answers, no triumphant declarations of the courage to change as though change were all one could conceivably ask of anyone truly human. The poet's self-concern here is seemly and reasonable. She wants to know about herself, her secrets, her gifts. She does not speak yet as though perpetual motion were the ideal state, the will to change the index of perfect maturity. Her business, to the degree that she can make it out, is to feel herself, to think beyond formal categories, to reject whatever is merely habitual on behalf of what she can discover as potentially to be won. Most important of all, she does not blithely reject the past as though it had nothing to tell, nor dismiss orderliness and the clean lines of a modest behavior for undifferentiated passion. The lust to be wholly contemporary has not yet become dangerously compelling.

In what is surely her best book to date, *Necessities of Life* (1966), Adrienne Rich moves steadily to inhabit the world and to make contact with that self she had thought largely repressed and almost forgotten. It is a volume not so much of youthful discovery as of sobering expansiveness, a coming out into a challenging universe armed with all the gifts of steady vision and confident warmth we associate only with a very mature person. Adrienne Rich achieves in the poems of this volume a dignity and casual elevation that are altogether rare in the poetry of any period. Imagination here is in the service of intelligence in a way that might well dampen the poetic ardor of most poets, more committed as they are to the sheer vagrancies of creative inspiration. The remarkable thing about the poems in *Necessities*, though, is that they betray no decline of invention, no thinning of poetic texture, nothing in the way of mere reasonable constraint. They are rich in a quality I can only call character. They bear, everywhere, the marks of a rare and distinguished personhood which we take as at least an implicit celebration of our being. But the poems themselves can say ever so much better what I mean to describe. Here is "After Dark" (1964), of which it would be unfair to quote less than the full text:

> I
>
> You are falling asleep and I sit looking at you
> old tree of life
> old man whose death I wanted
> I can't stir you up now.
>
> Faintly a phonograph needle
> whirs round in the last groove
> eating my heart to dust.
> That terrible record! how it played
>
> down years, wherever I was
> in foreign languages even
> over and over, *I know you better*
> *than you know yourself   I know*

you better than you know
yourself   I know
you   until, self-maimed,
I limped off, torn at the roots,

stopped singing a whole year,
got a new body, new breath,
got children, croaked for words,
forgot to listen

or read your *mene tekel* fading on the wall,
woke up one morning
and knew myself your daughter.
Blood is a sacred poison.

Now, unasked, you give ground.
We only want to stifle
what's stifling us already.
Alive now, root to crown, I'd give

—oh,—something—not to know
our struggles now are ended.
I seem to hold you, cupped
in my hands, and disappearing.

When your memory fails—
no more to scourge my inconsistencies—
the sashcords of the world fly loose.
A window crashes

suddenly down. I go to the woodbox
and take a stick of kindling
to prop the sash again.
I grow protective toward the world.

II

Now let's away from prison—
Underground seizures!
I used to huddle in the grave
I'd dug for you and bite

my tongue for fear it would babble
—Darling—
I thought they'd find me there
someday, sitting upright, shrunken,

my hair like roots and in my lap
a mess of broken pottery—
wasted libation—
and you embalmed beside me.

No, let's away. Even now
there's a walk between doomed elms
(whose like we shall not see much longer)
and something—grass and water—

and old dream-photograph.
I'll sit with you there and tease you
for wisdom, if you like,
waiting till the blunt barge

bumps along the shore.
Poppies burn in the twilight

like smudge pots.
I think you hardly see m

but—this is the dream now—
your fears blow out,
off, over the water.
At the last, your hand feels steady.

The echoes in such a poem serve only to enhance one's sense of its largeness, its breadth of vision and informed intelligence. Nothing in the way of irrelevant local texture removes our concern from the very grave and beautiful relation that is evoked, a relation that is as much a communing of a soul with itself as it is the working out of affections between the generations. The tension here is not between idea and image, between abstraction and concretion, but between what we know and what we feel. It is the business of the poem to do justice to both, to see to it that the one is at least to some degree informed by the other. There is no pristine self here, no absolutely authentic being the discovery of which is exclusively potentiated by a cutting loose from all that is customary and embedded. How gratifying that the father's actual or imagined "*I know you better /than you know yourself*" should be dealt with not by way of severe rejection or denial, but in the context of the words, "woke up one morning / and knew myself your daughter. / Blood is a sacred poison." Relation is something we make, to be sure, but it may be conferred as well, and this the poet gracefully acknowledges in the poem as a way of coming to terms with her own inclinations. As she ponders the relationship, projects for herself a consoling vision of it that is at once conclusive and fragrantly evocative, her associations become progressively literary, but there is no ounce in them of the inauthentic. The poetic echoes refresh the context by reminding us of comparably moving treatments of similar themes. At one point she exclaims, "no more to scourge my inconsistencies —" and we think of Lowell's farewell to his grandfather in *Life Studies*. Or, as we read the first three stanzas of part two, we think of Sylvia Plath's ritualistic efforts to make contact with her father. Or we call to mind Lear's farewell to Cordelia as we ponder such lines as "I'll sit with you there and tease you / for wisdom, if you like," and so on. This is a poetry that can afford such echoes, for as it is generous with its emotions without railing or ranting, so can it securely draw upon an entire tradition to substantiate its sincerity. In a work less open, less generous, the associations might seem insufficiently modulated or assimilated, perhaps even calculated. Here they strike us as fine.

I have chosen to look at "After Dark" because it is a wonderful poem and because it illuminates by contrast what has lately happened in Adrienne Rich's work. We notice in this poem that the speaker is not pleased that "the sashcords of the world fly loose." Though she struggles to win her own sense of self, she yet feels the need to be known, to be seen if not quite seen through. How beautifully she puts her impulse in the line "I grow protective toward the world," for we understand that the impulse of which she speaks is nothing less than the mature desire to resume coherence in the face of progressive assaults on those stable props that constitute our necessity and at least part of our definition. That "blunt barge" is more than the vehicle of death here. It is, in fact, an emblem of that coming home to which each of us must incline, not in the sense that we simply resign ourselves to things as they are or to our eventual demise, but in the sense that we acknowledge what belongs, inescapably, to each of us. As the poet recalls the murderous fantasies of childhood she senses — as she sensed when still a child — the degree of her participation in her father's death, and we are impressed with the profound ambivalence of most such relationships. The poem's conclusion in no sense banishes this ambivalence, or resolves it, but it allows for a final expression of affection that further validates the sincerity of that ambivalence.

Not all of the poems in *Necessities*, superb as most of them are, have quite that air of intense sentiment, so bittersweet in "After Dark." In "Side by Side" (1965), for example, the poet gives us something considerably more fragile, more suffused with that silken ethereality we conventionally associate with woman's poetry. No doubt about it, it is a woman's poem, but to say so in this case is not so much to describe its limitations as to do homage to its fragrance:

> Ho! in the dawn
> how light we lie
>
> stirring faintly as laundry
> left all night on the lines.
>
> You, a lemon-gold pyjama,
> I, a trousseau-sheet, fine
>
> linen worn paper-thin in places,
> worked with the maiden monogram.
>
> Lassitude drapes our folds.
> We're slowly bleaching
>
> with the days, the hours, and the years.
> We are getting finer than ever,

time is wearing us to silk,
to sheer spiderweb.

The eye of the sun, rising, looks in
to ascertain how we are coming on.

We may think, upon first encountering such a poem, that it demonstrates the gift of a certain style without any corresponding gift of thought. And surely, "Side by Side" is not a poem rich in ideas. What it has is a flexible central image the exploration of whose nuances constitutes the heart of the matter. We feel about the poem that it has, if not strength, then a kind of tenacity, a tenacity that is a function of persisting focus. "The eye of the sun," explicitly evoked in the final stanza, is the dominant presence throughout, we feel, and we are not a little struck by the seeming benevolence of its steady illumination. "We are getting finer than ever," the poet announces, "time is wearing us to silk, / to sheer spiderweb." How fortunate, we are tempted to exclaim, how lovely that we should be "getting finer than ever" with the passage of time, that our lot should be refinement rather than impairment. The element of passivity, though frequently unwholesome elsewhere, is in this poem so lightly evoked that it comes to seem a positive strength. No doubt, the mildly ironic domestic image of laundry hanging out to dry in the opening stanzas at once establishes the basically congenial nature of the vision, so that we are prepared to accept what we read as at least partially fanciful. This initial sense is surely confirmed at the poem's conclusion in the image, simultaneously wry and hoary, of the sun as proprietary eye looking in at his tender morsels, the suggestion of delicious consumption surely playing in the margins. I do not want to make more of the poem than it deserves, but surely it records with a fidelity both grave and delighting the trancelike sense of life's passage, the experience of confronting less, where once there lay ahead only more. What we miss in the poem is that exquisite particularity Adrienne Rich is so skilled in embodying in her major work, but we are pleased all the same with what we have, in all its quiet ambivalence.

If we ask what are the sources of such ambivalence, what allows the poet to be so unflinching while yet so pleasant, so generous, we should have to speak again of character, but also and more precisely of the poet's sense of the rhythms of experience, the necessary alternations of dream and reality in the life of the spirit, the cultivated tension between knowing and feeling. In the poem "Not Like That" (1965) the speaker woos a picturesque extinction, a deliberate for-

getfulness that prepares one for nullity of a most encompassing sort.
She envisions herself in a domesticated cemetery — "The turf is a
bedroom carpet" — and muses: "To come and sit here forever, / a
cup of tea on one's lap / and one's eyes closed lightly, lightly / perfectly still / in a nineteenth century sleep! / it seems so normal to die."
As she works the shadows of the portrait, probing its secrets, she
concludes that it is not extinction she wants, but some soothing vision
of ultimacy such as we find perpetually available to us as children.
Perhaps it is the very availability of childish consolation that announces to the older poet the insufficiency of those earlier visions.
This has nothing to do with simply growing up and accepting the
fact that we can no longer delude ourselves with childish fancies.
What the mature poet determines to banish is the tendency to drift.
She refuses to allow imagination to go its own way, to seek its objects
in any guise. Not just the fantasies, the easy consolations, but the
very time of childhood "was a dream too, even the oatmeal / under
its silver lid, dream-cereal / spooned out in forests of spruce." In the
remarkable image of dream-cereal the poet tells us she refuses to be
nourished by anything patently insubstantial, rejects easy regressions
as the means to any satisfying identity. Such symbolic returns have
about them a death-like air when too regularly or lavishly indulged,
and the static portraiture of the seated figure, "eyes closed lightly,
lightly," surely stands in this regard as starkly emblematic warning.
Things are not still, not permanent, not easy, though we are sometimes tempted by "the warm trickle of dream / staining the thick
quiet" — a dazzling image bespeaking at once the coziness and pueril-
ity of the all too available. The final lines are bracing: "The drawers
of this trunk are empty. / They are all out of sleep up here."

The rejection of the dream-life, the emergence into clarified perception and knowing interaction with the things of this world, is
central to the poems of *Necessities.* The will to change is considered
within a relatively stable context, for the poet here presupposes a way
of life. It is nothing so exalted and distinctive as the old high way
Yeats wistfully remembers in the poems of Coole Park or in the
"Prayer" for his daughter, but it has its decided features. Chiefly
these features have to do with a decision to work through one's
problems, to be attentive to one's needs and to the shifting demands
of one's environment and companions, to work always at breeding
flowers from the refuse heap of the contemporary situation. Involved
as well is a growing commitment to what might be called social

reality, as though one could not legitimately expect to know oneself or to deal with one's personal limitations without considering the degree to which they are conditioned by external actualities. What we have quite frequently in these poems, and to a much greater extent in the later work, is the spectacle of a vivid intelligence working to avoid being overwhelmed by brute matter. In "Open-Air Museum" (1964) the poet wonders at frail flowers sprouting in the town dump, and feels she has been brought "face to face with the flag of our true country: / violet-yellow, black-violet, / its heart sucked by slow fire." Fragments of shattered dreams lie about, "the rose-rust carcass of a slaughtered Chevrolet," scraps of a photo-album, a three-wheeled baby carriage. But it is not the poet's function simply to mourn what is past, or to shake her fist at a civilization that betrays its best hopes. The emphasis of her poem lies in the lines "those trucked-off bad dreams / outside the city limits / crawl back in search of you." Her heart counsels that she listen carefully for the intermittent "Cry of truth among so many lies." There is no stratification of meaning here, no loose weaving together of various levels of intention that yet remain distinct, but a total human situation truly observed. The poem creates an enduring illusion of virtual experience, in Susanne Langer's terms. Our sense of the poem is of having entered a world that is whole and clearly related to the world we customarily inhabit, though not literally coextensive with it. What we recognize, are never permitted to forget in Adrienne Rich's poems, is that the materials we are shown constitute events in the poet's mental and emotional life. We do not expect, and never feel that we get, transcriptions of reality such as a theory of verisimilitude might enjoin upon the artist. Nor do we get, or expect, discursive argument of a philosophical nature. All we are shown carries with it that peculiar baggage of associations and tensions that the poet customarily lugs around, as though it were strapped forever to her back. She may shift the weight from time to time, may dance about to lighten the load, may even, temporarily, forget her burden, but it is there, and she will acknowledge it in time.

In "Like This Together" (1963), the poet's understanding of her work as in some basic way a clarification of life, her own and others', is verified in a whole range of particulars. She informs us in a recent interview (*The Ohio Review*, 1972) that "what it means to be a man, what it means to be a woman . . . is perhaps the major subject of poetry from here on." But such an approach seems almost parochial set against the more embracing drive of "Like This To-gether" and comparable pieces. Not "what it means to be a woman" but how to preserve one's essential humanity is the underlying thrust of her poem. What threatens is the disintegration of the immediate physical landscape, an erosion of stable landmarks that leaves us without concrete roots, "sitting like drugged birds / in a glass case," unable to break out for want of identifiable objects toward which we may press ourselves to struggle. So the civic disaster, the blight of perpetual and empty urban renewals is a reminder of the hollow-ness of most other renewals undertaken in the spirit of escape. "They're tearing down the houses /we met and lived in," she cries. ". . . soon our two bodies will be all/ left standing from that era." And on. It is a miserable scene, dank and impoverished, and it leaves the lonely soul with no recourse but to "old detailed griefs / [that] twitch at my dreams," an aftermath of "miscarried knowledge." But it is not victimization that Adrienne Rich courts, despite her obvious affinities with the victims of recent confessional verse. She takes what we may call a more active approach to the body of her fate most of the time. The marvelous final stanza, part five of her poem, puts the case as follows:

> Dead winter doesn't die,
> it wears away, a piece of carrion
> picked clean at last,
> rained away or burnt dry.
> Our desiring does this,
> make no mistake, I'm speaking
> of fact: through mere indifference
> we could prevent it.
> Only our fierce attention
> gets hyacinths out of those
> hard cerebral lumps,
> unwraps the wet buds down
> the whole length of a stem.

To read such a stanza is to have rather a sharp sense of how the world appears to a woman of intelligence and purpose, who is yet capable of considerable pain. It is a sequence of lines that impresses much more than affirmation, more than the blithe overcoming to which so many of our poets since Emerson have directed their ener-gies. And, as an important aspect of its message is the exalting of "fierce attention," just so does the poem ask us for careful scrutiny if we would glean its fullness. In particular we shall need to address cautiously the lines: "Our desiring does this, / make no mistake, I'm speaking/of fact: through mere indifference / we could prevent it."

Prevent what? we may at first wonder. Prevent "dead winter"? "Our desiring"? Actually, of course, the poet refers to something we may call the impaling past, the past imperfectly apprehended that locks us into sterile patterns, rehearsed postures, that blocks our way when we would step out and experience ourselves as creatures of quite remarkable extension. Shall we be anything but creatures of "fierce attention," the poet wants to know, and she is well advised to ask, for indifference, a function of cultural disorder and the breakdown of established authority, is surely among the central blights of our period.

The 1969 volume *Leaflets* seems to me to mark a decline in the poet's career. There are some brilliant things in the volume, patches of exquisite writing, several perfectly achieved poems, but the sense one takes from the volume is of things coming apart, not the texture of the universe merely, but the fiber of the poet's attention. She seems, if I may say so, less careful about what she says. She says, in fact, silly things, of a sort we cannot easily ignore or attribute to passing inattention, while moving on to the nearest reassuring sentiment. When a mature and accomplished poet writes ("In the Evening," 1966): "The old masters, the old sources, haven't a clue what we're about, / shivering here in the half-dark 'sixties," we are forced to stop and vent serious doubts about the entire enterprise. What is the poet after? She seems too shrewd for us to say it is simply rage or utter desperation that prompts her to declare the perfect uniqueness of her own burdened moment. Is human experience in general so radically disparate that even the old masters could fail to intimate our problems, provide us with a clue? Apparently the poet believes in the specialness of her experience, though frankly nothing she tells us seems to me in the least astonishing. But that is not really so important. What matters is why she feels compelled to make us feel we have no clues. She apparently does not wish to play the role of victim to the hilt, so that vulnerability is but one of the notes she regularly sounds. And even when indulging such a posture, she resists the temptation to wring it for all it's worth, so that she appears at once vulnerable and wryly ironic. In "Flesh and Blood" (1965) she begins with "A cracked walk in the garden, / white violets choking in the ivy," and we anticipate a slightly off-beat but gruesome cataloguing of small disasters. We get instead some mild reminiscence and a line like "Nobody's seen the trouble I've seen / but you." The play on the song title is casual and flat and encourages a kind of pleasurable if silently knowing, collaborative wink between poet and reader. The tone is similarly right and more or less satisfying in "Holding Out" (1965) with its flavor of Frost or David Wagoner, the word "maybe" hovering over every insight: "Maybe the stovepipe is sound, / maybe the smoke will do us in / at first — no matter." Why, then, the insistence upon the radical unfamiliarity of our vulnerability in poems like "In the Evening," a poem by the way, that bears more than slight resemblance to "Dover Beach," both in the dire situation it posits and in the persistent clinging together of the two central figures.

In *Leaflets* and in *The Will to Change*, Adrienne Rich labors, it would seem, under the notion that we are inevitably period-creatures, that to deny the fact is to deny our very being. She tells us in "The Demon Lover" (1966) that "A new / era is coming in. / Gauche as we are, it seems / we have to play our part." Taken by themselves, such lines surely point in but one direction. The fact is, though, that they may not be taken in isolation from a great many other lines which not only qualify but openly contradict them. What I conclude is that Adrienne Rich wishes with all her strength to be other than a period-creature. She wishes, that is, to retain that sense of self displayed so handsomely in *Necessities of Life*. The problem is that progressively she falls prey to ideological fashions like the will to change, so that, though she is too intelligent ever to mouth petty slogans, she allows herself to be violated by them. They touch her verse with an almost programmatic wand. The underlying energy and tension remain, but they grow less and less visible as the set assertions come staggering forward:

> The friend I can' trust is the one who will let me have my death.
> The rest are actors who want me to stay and further the plot.
> . . . .
> If the mind of the teacher is not in love with the mind of the student,
> he is simply practising rape, and deserves at best our pity.
> . . . .
> Leroi! Eldridge! Listen to us, we are ghosts
> condemned to haunt the cities where you want
> to be at home.
> . . . .
> I have learned to smell a *conservateur* a mile away:
> they carry illustrated catalogues of all that there is to lose.

(quotations from "Ghazals," 1968)

To think that the poet who could write so persuasively of her father's loss, of her own hard-earned, satisfying growth, should be so snide about having something to lose. What can she be thinking when she writes of smelling "a *conservateur*"? Does the poet imagine that men who have something to lose are necessarily blind reactionaries? Does she hold at no value the fruits of a man's labors when he is able to taste and savor those fruits? I ask such questions not to suggest that the poet has lost her senses — far from that — but to suggest how charged she has become with the nauseous propaganda of the advance-guard cultural radicals. Such sentiments as I've quoted from Adrienne Rich's poems are not, I insist, serious expressions of her intelligence but reflections of a will to be contemporary, to please those who are nothing but contemporary, and who therefore can have little sense of the proper gravity of the poetic act. Sincere they may well be, some of them, but the density of language, the gravity of the word well chosen and scrupulously employed are surely considerations beyond their characteristic sense of things. That Adrienne Rich should have "fallen in" with such models is greatly to be lamented, for her development as a poet cannot be a happy one under such an influence.

I say this recognizing full well that one is not supposed to confuse the content of poems with their specific value as poems. The idea does seem to me a little ridiculous, taken generally, but I can see the point of such an objection where the works of certain other poets are at issue. If a poet is a radical innovator who brings experimental resources to his craft that may alter the direction of poetry in his time, he is surely entitled to be examined in a special way. Or if the poet is possessed of a voice so grandly authoritative that it strikes us as in some sense the expression of an entire age, so again will we need to deal with it in a special way. Adrienne Rich is neither a radical innovator nor the voice of an age. We think of intelligence when we read her best work, and we miss that intelligence when we examine much of her recent verse. It is no use pretending that what she says does not matter, or oughtn't to, or is marginal, by comparison with the brightness and energy of her line or the sharpness of her diction. It matters to us as readers that she should speak of practicing rape when "the mind of the teacher is not in love with the mind of the student." How many students have minds, we should wonder when confronted with such a line, that any sensitive and intelligent person could love? How many of us can love what we at best but barely know? When I repeat such questions to myself, particularly in connection with the work of someone I admire as much as Adrienne Rich, I try to recall other lines, better urgings from the same body of verse. I remember, for example, "How did we get caught up fighting the forest fire, / we, who were only looking for a still place in the woods?" The quality of such a line is more than plaintive. It is touched, perhaps, by a certain pride, but it is not altogether misplaced, at least. The suggestion is that we could not but take our place fighting the blaze, and this is no doubt what many serious people feel. Such sentiments, as the heart of a poet's work, are surely acceptable provided that they are meaningfully hedged, provided that they are accompanied by other sentiments that sufficiently undercut or challenge them, so that readers are called upon for participation rather than unambiguous assent. Only in scattered poems do we feel the presence of this fruitful tension as we go though the last two volumes. One slight poem in *Leaflets* called "The Observer" (1968) quietly establishes the tension of which we speak, a tension that abides as much in the poet as in the poem. What impresses me about this poem as well is the measured coherence of the vision, a coherence no doubt impossible for the poet trying to capture the unstable rhythms of the contemporary Western scene. Where most often in *Leaflets* we have fragmentary observations, notations jotted in the tumult of manning the front-lines, here we have a sense of something approaching duration, the picture to be pondered in place of the frantic words trailing beyond our grasp:

> Completely protected on all sides
> by volcanoes
> a woman, darkhaired, in stained jeans
> sleeps in central Africa.
> In her dreams, her notebooks, still
> private as maiden diaries,
> the mountain gorillas move through their life term;
> their gentleness survives
> observation. Six bands of them
> inhabit, with her, the wooded highland.
> When I lay me down to sleep
> unsheltered by any natural guardians
> from the panicky life-cycle of my tribe
> I wake in the old cellblock
> observing the daily executions,
> rehearsing the laws
> I cannot subscribe to,
> envying the pale gorilla-scented dawn
> she wakes into, the stream where she washes her hair,
> the camera-flash of her quiet
> eye.

Other poems in *Leaflets* one ought to read, for pleasure and provocation, include "5:30 A. M.," "The Key," "Abnegation," and "Nightbreak."

We began by speaking of the centrality of the will to change in Adrienne Rich's mature verse, and surely it is time we turned to that subject as a central focus in what remains to be said here. It is difficult to avoid such a turning in looking at the volume *The Will to Change,* of course, but few are the readers who seem ready to front the subject directly. A reviewer for *The New York Times Book Review* spoke of the volume's ". . . tough distrust of completion," and declared that "the poems are about departures, about the pain of breaking away from lovers and from an old sense of self." The observations seem accurate enough, but they do not tell us much. The poems in this recent volume are about more than departures. They are about the will to be both self and other, to embody at once both presence and possibility. They are, in fact, about the will not to be left behind, not to be deluded, not to rest with one's achievements or comforts. "A man isn't what he seems but what he desires:/ gaieties of anarchy drumming at the base of the skull," she tells us in one of *The Blue Ghazals* (1968). A familiar enough idea, looked at casually, but why the insistence upon anarchy, we should like to know. Why such further lines as "Disorder is natural, these leaves absently blowing." Absence, disorder as natural: and only a few years earlier she had spoken so fiercely of the blight that is rampant disorder, of the indifference and inattention that permit the wasting of our endowments. In another of *The Blue Ghazals* the poet writes: "Everything is yielding toward a foregone conclusion, / only we are rash enough to go on changing our lives. / An Ashanti woman tilts the flattened basin on her head / to let the water slide downward: I am that woman and that / water." The terrible downward glide is evoked in these poems as an inevitability to which we lend ourselves as a mark of honor, of lucidity. But to describe our drift as in some sense honorable is not to see how terrible it is, I'm afraid, and I doubt the poet has lately stepped out of the current long enough to attend to this problem. In "I Dream I'm the Death of Orpheus" (1968) she presents "A woman feeling the fullness of her powers / at the precise moment when she must not use them / a woman sworn to lucidity." What is this terrible lucidity, we wonder, that it should prevent us from using our powers: some such thing occurs to us to ask as we move through any number of poems here.

As earlier intimated, the will to change is at the heart of Adrienne Rich's thought and work, and it has much to do with this terrible lucidity. For what the poet insists upon is nothing less than full

revelation of every motive, every shabby instinct and cheap thrill
that drives her on. Now it is customary today to applaud a whole
host of writers, prophets and other culture-heroes for their frankness,
and surely we do not need to be reminded of the degree to which
frankness has become a salable commodity. There is nothing offensive
or commercial in Adrienne Rich's poetry, but it shares with other
contemporary work a quality of impatience and of rashness that is a
little disappointing. She is too ready in her poems to see the "Meanings burnt-off like paint / under the blow-torch" ("Our Whole Life,"
1969). Oh, she knows the toll the blow-torch will take, writhes a
good deal under its too steady heat and glare. What disturbs us is
that she should have so little faith in the usefulness of resistance.
For the *conservateurs* she had ready contempt, but for the anxious
wielders of the blow-torch, for the more openly murderous of her
own intellectual instincts, she has no strength to resist. She laments
that we are "Always falling and ending / because this world gives
no room/ to be what we dreamt of being," but she mistrusts the very
idea of being anything solid and loyal. How often does she tell us
that change and the will to change are all. More and more I think
of Adrienne Rich's recent project as a kind of perpetual hungering
relieved by nothing at all, for nothing we take in can satisfy this
hunger to know, to devour, to transform, to move on. In "Images
for Godard" (1970) we read: "the notes for the poem are the only
poem / the mind collecting, devouring / all these destructibles," and
later, "free in the dusty beam of the projector / the mind of the poet
is changing / the moment of change is the only poem." And is the
only reality worth knowing about, apparently.

The effect of all this on Adrienne Rich's writing has not been
good, for though the poet need not manifest the organic wholeness
of the traditional novelistic vision, obviously, she is responsible for
more than a series of intensely noted fragments. There is some
pleasure in watching her manage her combination of intimate detail
and abstract rumination, in pondering her attempt to forge an authentic language deserving of the name dialogue, but we are impressed
by the absence of that steady largeness of vision, those marked traits
of character formed and expanding, that we marveled at in her
earlier writing. The will to change has turned the poet from wholeness to analytic lucidity. Or perhaps it would be more appropriate to
say that, unable to live according to those calmly alternating rhythms
we think of as the emblem of a poised maturity, the poet has had to

turn to the will to change to validate her hungers, to provide the stamp of authenticity she sought. I don't know for certain. What seems to me clear is that a point has been passed beyond which the poet has ceased to be herself, that blend of instinct and learned wisdom, innocent eye and educated adult, who knew there was a limit to will, and worth in steadfastness. Now that she has begun to speak of nature, of doing her thing, giving herself to the perform-ance of "something very common, in my own way," I don't know that we may hope for very much from her verse beyond striking fragments. I shall have to hope for a resumption of that other tough-ness so well expressed in "Snapshots of a Daughter-in-Law." It may be fitting to conclude with a few lines from that poem, to remind ourselves of the course we have traveled:

> mere talent was enough for us—
> glitter in fragments and rough drafts . . .
> .   .   .   .
> our mediocrities over-praised,
> indolence read as abnegation,
> slattern thought styled intuition,
> every lapse forgiven . . .

Those of us who believe in the altogether special and distinguished qualities of Adrienne Rich's best work will not, I hope, forgive lightly her recent lapses, nor praise overmuch her more indulgent intuitions.

W. D. Snodgrass: An Interview *

INTERVIEWER: ROBERT BOYERS

Q: *All sorts of recent poets, from Jarrell to Lowell, have complained about the climate of the culture and the relationship between the poet and his audience. I was wondering, is there bound to be a weakening of the forcefulness and authority of the work of art when the poet no longer feels close to his audience, when he feels that there is no longer a constituency for which he speaks?*

SNODGRASS: I don't really know — of course, I've only lived under these conditions and I don't know what it would be like living some other way. Different conditions do prevail in other parts of the world; we know that people in Bulgaria and Rumania and Hungary find it impossible to imagine being a writer generally opposed to the culture. They simply can't think of enduring this, and you know, there are great gains and losses involved in such a situation. It means that, for instance, when a young poet puts out a book of poetry, he may expect to sell more than anyone here does. In Bulgaria, a little country about as big as half of Saratoga, their first edition will be 10,000 copies for a beginning poet, where nobody here ever gets beyond 500 at the most, and even they won't all sell. We all want 5000 people to come to our readings, like Yevtushenko, but at the same time I think I'm just about as glad not to have it. It doesn't seem to me there ever are 5000 people in any area really interested in poetry. They can be interested in a kind of state occasion or a kind of communal piety like going to church or something like that, that you do as a member of a group, but this doesn't have anything to do, really, with poetry. And surely that's the case with a lot of what happens to Yevtushenko or Voznesensky. Such poets aren't in the very special position of poets here, they needn't take it as their business to see what nobody else sees. That responsibility

---

*This is an edited transcript of a public interview held at Skidmore College in December, 1971.

can have peculiar consequences in our time, so that one day you kick the society in the teeth and the next day it awards you a fellowship. Elsewhere, when you decide to kick, you go to jail. Which rather helps enforce upon you the seriousness of what you're doing. But for most poets such results will best be avoided — at least they'll see it that way.

Q.: *Do you feel any compulsion these days to get more of the political and cultural life of the country into your verse? I had a sense that some of your poems were taking a direction of that sort in a very vague sort of way in* After Experience, *though the direction was never really sufficiently developed in that volume to constitute a real departure.*

SNODGRASS: I sometimes feel a pressure in that direction, although frankly social and political things seem to me of very second-rate importance. I'm just not very interested in them. I'm really much more interested in how fathers work than in how presidents work or how diplomats work, simply because that's much more intimately a part of my experience. And I confess also that it seems to me all kinds of poets and others talk about this because they would like to be interested in it and they've been told that this is a thing to be interested in — if they can't think of what else they're interested in, they get interested in this. But you know, it doesn't seem a very real interest. A psychoanalyst a couple of years ago said, someplace or other, that family trouble, troubles in your love life, has caused people a hundred times more real agony than all the wars, famines, oppressions and the other stuff that gets in the history books. If those were your only troubles, boy would you be lucky. No, it's the fact that you keep devouring the person you love, that you keep throwing people away and sitting there saying "Where'd everybody go?" And you can't help it. And you just keep doing it. These are agonies much more important, and it seems to me that they are the agonies out of which we create our other agonies: that's one of the things I try to say in my poems, that it is out of the pattern of the life you know, with the people you love, that you create these larger patterns. It seems to me that Freud would have seen it that way entirely, and I must say that I do, but I don't think I get that from him, I hope I don't. One would hate to be a little Freud, to be thinking his thoughts rather than one's own. But no, that seems to me how it is. I remember when I was in school, we were all taught to write obscure, brilliant, highly symbolized poems about the loss of myth in our time, and, you know, it suddenly began to occur to me that I didn't care about the loss of myth in our time; frankly, I was glad to be rid of the stuff, and if I wanted it, it was easy enough to go get some — I mean, that stuff wasn't scarce. If I didn't have it, it was because I didn't believe in it and I didn't want it and could only have it by killing part of my mind. But we were all writing poems about what we thought "The Wasteland" was about. None of us had bothered to find out that "The Wasteland" isn't about that at all. We thought it was about that because you could make doctoral dissertations by talking about all the learned allusions in "The Wasteland" and how it was about, you know, the need for a "meaningful myth" in our lives; nobody had noticed it was about Eliot's insane wife and his frozen sex life. He had helped disguise this, with Pound's assistance, by his editing of the poem. We believed people's doctoral statements about the poem. We believed Frost and Eliot when they said their poems were about other things than their own sex lives, and we can now look at the poems and see that that just isn't so at all. We know, for instance, that a poem like "Home Burial" is about a specific child that Frost lost at a certain specific time and that the loss of that child simply destroyed the family, that he wrote poem after poem about that child and his sense of guilt for that child's death. But at the time, nobody recognized that. At one point I just began to notice I didn't really care about what those poems were supposed to discover. What I care about is, ah, where's Agnes? Where'd all the girls go? I realized I had to write about such things because, even if the poems weren't going to be any good, at least I'd have written about what I cared about, at least I'd have made a big mistake. I wasn't going to go on making the same small mistakes. Then later I found I didn't want to write that kind of very personal poem, and I certainly don't want to anymore. The poems about my sister I read last night at Skidmore are the last poems of that sort I will write, I know, and most of those are quite old. . . . Well, to return to your question, I would like in a way to talk about social issues. But I tend to do that more in prose and it seems to me that I don't really feel that much about it. I'm not really much interested in the state. I've got a certain number of things to say about the nature of the society and they're somewhat different from what anyone's saying. But I'm not really concerned about them. I'm much more concerned about my son.

Q.: *Have there been, do you think, genuinely new directions in*

American and British poetry over the last 30 or 40 years? Do you see your own work and the work of Robert Lowell, for example, as a significant formal departure from the work of the modernist poets, from the generation of Eliot, Pound, and Stevens?

SNODGRASS: I don't think about this very much, so I don't really know about it. In many ways that would seem to be true: for instance, in writing the kind of poetry that I first began to write, a very personal lyric often in a kind of close metric, it would look like I was going against, say, Eliot and Pound, going in the direction of, oh, if you like, Hardy and Frost. Actually, my models there were often songs, German lyrics from the early 19th century, or certain earlier models. From these I learned you could do very personal things, very direct, strident statements about your own feelings, about some specific person. But I must say that gradually since that time my work has become more and more experimental and I write more and more free verse now. For one thing, at that time it seemed to me that there was an awful lot of stuff which called itself experimental and which was just as predictable and as much like every other experimental poem being written as it could possibly be. Poets seemed bent on producing a distortion of reality without facilitating any real insight through it.... Rimbaud did it and it was absolutely new and strange and different; but we have got so many little Rimbauds deliberately inverting reality, in a certain sense putting the symbolic elements on the surface simply to have them in there. Most of us, when we imitated Rimbaud, just weren't making any discoveries, and it made no sense to go on pretending you were doing something different. As to really new, no, I don't think I've seen that many new things.

There are very few real inventors around. The best American poetry that I know of in the last ten years surely are the first book of Berryman's *Dreamsongs*, the first 44, which absolutely kill me. But they don't seem to me ... they couldn't have existed without Cummings, for one. They don't seem to me a new direction, any more than most of the stuff that claims to be new which, in one way or another, follows thoroughly established traditions.

Q.: *In connection with that, I wanted to ask you a bit about the whole notion of the poet's unique or original voice. In contemporary poetry we have all sorts of fine poets, even someone like Theodore Roethke, for example, who spend a good deal of their lifetimes worrying about the heavy hand of one predecessor or another on the page.*

Roethke, even in his major period, worried about Yeats and other figures in the background of his verse. Now just recently a new volume of Sylvia Plath's poems was published (Crossing the Water) and in it there's a whole sequence of poems printed together in the volume, which sound very much as if they were written by Theodore Roethke — really very polished works. There's some sense of Sylvia Plath in the poems themselves, and yet one feels, reading them, that they could have been written by Roethke. Is this the sort of thing that a poet ought to be bothered about, that his poems somehow have the ring of a predecessor's work, even when they are polished and complete?

SNODGRASS: Well, it's very hard for me even to talk about what a poet ought to do because, you know, each one ought to do something different from what anyone else has ever done. I suppose it's at least theoretically possible that you can in some way inherit someone else's voice and be fully creative with it. I mean, I don't like to rule out any possibility, though I've never seen it happen, and almost always somebody, when he is talking in someone else's voice, is in some very important way sort of refusing his own voice — that certainly was the case with Roethke when he wrote like Yeats. At least, so it seems to me, Roethke more than any other poet of his generation was offered the chance of true greatness. He invented a language, very really, and it wasn't like anyone else's. I don't begin to understand the "Lost Son" poems, and others written in that incredible whip-cracking language. I don't understand them, but I know they aren't like anyone else's, and they create a world and that it is a terribly vital creation. Roethke was the man that would have been as big as Whitman — well, maybe not that big, but almost. He was offered a virtual continent of language and fled from it, fled from doing the great work into the voice of Yeats. Then again, toward the end of his life, he created another and different language, not as drastically inventive, one derived from Eliot, and I don't mind that so much because those poems of Eliot never really satisfied me, those late "Quartets" just didn't do it, no matter what my friends told me. So I don't mind somebody taking their voice and doing, well, I think, some very great poems, and again Roethke was on the edge of making a great discovery, a great book, and fled from it by adopting a set of foolish beliefs and finally by killing himself. Anything to get out of greatness, anything to destroy the voice he could create. As to Sylvia Plath, I can't talk about her as well as I'd like, for I haven't read the recently published stuff you mention, and don't in general read much new verse. But it seems to me to be very interesting that she would take Roethke's voice, because I think very much of her work was determined by her hatred of her husband, by her detestation of the man who is the greatest living English poet, an incredibly powerful man, and one who often takes much the same subject matter that Roethke takes, but is better at it. You read Roethke's poems, and as marvelous as they are you feel something akin to his refusal of his own voice, that he in some desperate way never grew up, that he is a self-pitying little boy. That great, monstrous powerful man, the tennis coach who could drink any twenty people under the table, had something buried under there saying "I'm so little, love me" and many of his poems are about that. His love of the minimal, his refusal of the bigness he might have had, all this I think you feel in his animal poems, as in others, whereas in Ted Hughes's poems you don't feel that, you feel, that's a man. And he knows every bit as much as Roethke ever thought of knowing how rough the world is, but he never pities himself about it, he just feels this is the world and it's absolutely made out of granite, and how are you going to cope with it? There's an old story about the different ways that different congregations come to deal with the fact that the flood is coming, I forget the details — the Catholic priest says, "We all have to go to confession for the next two weeks because we're . . ." I forget what the Protestant guy says, but the Jewish guy says, "In three weeks the Flood is coming — you've got three weeks to learn to breathe underwater." Hughes is like that: "The Flood's coming, get to work, learn to breathe underwater!" and in a way he does. He's really tough, and remarkable to have survived Plath's attempts, by her death, among other things, to destroy him . . . she was a really powerful woman, and an American woman if there ever was one, who simply wouldn't endure him for being a better poet than she was. And he's marvelous, he's marvelous. If Plath has picked up the voice of Roethke it seems to me especially interesting because I look upon Hughes and Roethke as poets who take very much the same subject matter, though Hughes is better at it. He makes up his own language too, in poems like the one about the pike, a very rough, harsh language that isn't like anyone else's. As to his new crow poems, I don't understand them, but clearly they're something different, they're something all his own.

Q.: *Do you think that there is too much concentration in the*

Academy even today on the question of how a poem is made, how it is put together? All sorts of poets and critics speak about the fact that the technique in American poetry has become almost suffocatingly careful, making poems artificial and abstract. They claim there are so many competent craftsmen around that spirit is being driven out.

SNODGRASS: Well, no, I don't really think so. I mean, to me that's a very fertile kind of atmosphere, and one in which something really exciting can happen. You've got to have a lot of competent people around in order that the guy who then can really do something different can have a background to rebel against, to fight against — you can't do great and different things without great competition; I mean, you can't run a mile by yourself. You can run a mile, but you can't run a good mile, you must have somebody push you; I always used to love those guys who ran second and who made it possible for the other guy to get his name in the headlines. Think of the fat little guy who pushed Bannister and Landes over for the first four-minute mile — Chris Chattaway — and who used to train by drinking all the beer he could. He was marvelous — without him, Bannister and Landes never could have done the mile they did. You've got to have someone to push you, and the competition has got to be good. If they're not good enough, you're not going to be able to do it, and that's all. Among people who do this there comes to be a very loving kind of competition and a respect for the other guy. When I was in Iowa, for instance, there were a lot of guys you knew wouldn't make it, but they were very valuable — in a way they were like a green crop that's grown to be plowed under, but they really fertilized the field. The poet who has the guts to go ahead and do the real thing may have to do it by opposing them, but that's all right. They're part of the process, too. Also it seems to me that if you are analyzing poems in such a way that you think you'll be able to take their technique and use it for your poem, then you're missing the whole point. You want to understand how works of art work, but when you make a new work of art it's got to be different from any that were ever made before, and if you're not getting to that, you haven't really studied earlier works to find out how they were different from what went before. I mean, one of the things you have to know when you listen to Beethoven is what chords stood people's hair on end when they were first played, though they don't do it any more — it all sounds pleasant to us. But that just means that we've heard so many imitations that we can't really hear the work of art. If you're not recreating in your mind what in the earlier work was mean and rough and nasty and hard to get along with, you're not getting the work of art. It's like when I was a boy I used to read my father's chess books. He was a very good chess player. He almost got a draw with Sammy Reshevsky. And there were lots of chess books around and some of them were very wonderful. And I would read these, and saw my father sitting around playing games of chess out of the book, so I started playing games of chess out of the book. And then I would go play with my friends and wait for them to come up with that game, but of course they never did, and — well, I figured if I memorized more games, sooner or later I'd have them all. It sort of seemed to me that that was what my father was doing, you know, and one day he finally took me aside and said, "It ain't like that. What I'm trying to figure out are what are the principles behind the games these guys are playing. I'll never be able to use their moves precisely." And surely it's that way with the writing of poems.

Q.: *Have you learned anything substantial, do you think, from William Carlos Williams? A great many poets, contemporary poets, claim that they've been heavily influenced by Williams though I confess my own inability to see the influence at work in their poems. I speak of people like Elizabeth Bishop, for instance, and Lowell too, who speak very highly of Williams and his impact. I'm just wondering if you felt him comparably.*

SNODGRASS: I don't know. I find myself very impressed with a lot of Williams although it doesn't seem to me that I sound like him, or that I use what is the really impressive thing about him — I speak of the way he fractures the sentence by means of the line break, so that you have to fight for the sense constantly and once you get it you feel that it's something you've purchased because you had to battle for it. It somehow means much more to you because you had to fight the line. I admire that, but I don't think I tend to do it. I'm much more interested in a kind of music that he rarely achieved; I want a much more musical kind of structure because I want to get to something much more unconscious. Most of the people who say they are influenced by Williams, and who in some way are, seem to me in many ways overconscious poets, and although they talk about the freedom of the unconscious a lot, their talk doesn't prove it's there. It seems to me that one of the ways above all that you get to something deeper than the conscious meaning of your poem is by the poem's music which is something so deep that almost no one ever knows what it means. What in the world does the rhythm of "Out of the cradle/Endlessly rocking" say? You know, the way Whitman sets up that rhythm that so dominates the whole first stanza, and then brings it back at the end of the poem: "(Or like some old crone (rocking the cradle,) swathed in sweet garments, bending aside),/The sea whisper'd me." You know, it absolutely makes your hair stand on end when that comes back at the end of the poem. Well, who knows what that means? I mean, I don't have any idea. But it certainly means that above all things Whitman was a creator at the deepest level, he created new rhythms — nobody'd ever heard a sound quite like that. And in some way I guess it has something to do with the mother's heartbeat. It's a ⅞ rhythm, oddly enough. My brother's a drummer, just as I used to be, and once we were working out a program of Whitman readings with drums. Boy, were we having fun with that. We were trying to notate the poem, when all of a sudden it hit us — it's a ⅞! And where would Whitman ever have heard a ⅞? You know, he loved music, all kinds of performances, went to operas, concerts, band concerts, and loved all that kind of stuff. But he never would have heard a ⅞ rhythm in his whole career. You'd hear it in belly dance joints and places like that, it would be very common. But we oversimplified the rhythms in Western music right during that period in such a way that a guy like Whitman would have had to go someplace very deep inside to hear that rhythm, someplace way below the conscious level. By comparison Williams is a poet who interests me, but I don't love him as a poet whose music says something to me, deeper than what his dictionary sense says to me. In, say, a poem like "The Yachts" you do get a kind of music created and it's something special and something his own. Also in that very late poem, written to his wife, "Asphodel," which is just terribly beautiful. You know, he came in that poem to see something very strange. All those years he had been saying over and over again, so you absolutely wanted to belt him in the mouth, "Don't write English, write American" on and on and on. And he wrote American in poem after poem, and the poems were sort of allright, but then, for God's sake, after he'd had about his third heart attack, I think, he wrote "Of Asphodel," a poem where he stopped mouthing all that "Hey, you ought to get out and lie around with a lot of girls" and "Live it up" and "That's freedom and real life." All of a sudden he realized that he was going to die and he'd better say something to the woman he really cared about, who was Flossie, and get it said before he didn't say anything more. And that poem to her is just a heartbreaker, and sounds like Tennyson.

Q.: *Some years ago you wrote a rather extraordinary essay, for the volume* The Contemporary Poet as Artist and Critic. *And in this piece you say a number of things about poetry, and in particular about the life of the poet, which I find extremely striking and interesting. You say, for example, "we have exciting enough works from contemporary poets, . . . splendid last works, but little work of maturity." And you say, "In their middle years our poets can often not write at all." I was wondering if you could elaborate for us why you think this should be.*

SNODGRASS: First of all, it seems to me that it is related to a simple failure of maturity in our culture. Look around you at most of the parents that you see and notice how childish they are, how above all things they're trying to get their children to run them. It surely is related to the fact that in our culture we can afford a great deal of mediocrity. I mean, we're in a luxury situation that can afford to be mediocre, and so encourages every kind of mediocrity. We encourage every kind of sameness because difference threatens us. And of course one of the things that above all says that you're different is to be able to write a poem, to be able to really say in what way you're different from everybody else, in what way your world really looks different and feels different. But that puts you in a very suspect situation in this culture where we have done everything to discourage that. Most people don't want to put their abilities on the line. They'd rather not know that some people have got it and some people haven't, some can do it and some can't. So, you know, we do everything we can to chop the strong men down to be the equals of the weak, to drop the able men down to be the same as the comfortable. And it runs through our whole lives: Everybody, you know, trying desperately to look like everybody else, to get rid of sexual differences as much as they can, to get rid of differences in power, to get rid of differences in age, because it threatens everyone. You hate the people you fear have more than you have. You've offered your curses against the guy who's stronger than you are, too. Suddenly if it becomes apparent that you are maybe stronger, one of the stronger ones, you hear your own past curses ready to strike you down any minute. You feel your whole culture closing down on you. Who goes to an analyst? Who do you see there? It isn't the failures. Here you can be a failure just great. Everyone will love you. The government will put you on the dole, your wife will adore you, think how long Sylvia Plath would have lived happily with Ted Hughes if he had been a rotten poet, or if he'd frozen up and couldn't write. That's a dirty thing to say, and I'm not glad I said it, but it's true. And I don't mean that only other people are responsible for this, you've got to get yourself down, you've got to castrate yourself. It's you that does it more than anyone else, but you do it because you really feel that you can't be where there's real competition. It also relates to something very deep in your love life. I mean, one of the things obviously we don't care for is masculine power. And obviously we couldn't have a society if we hadn't in part cut down on the male's desire for dominance, his desire to get all the girls, to kill all the men within sight, and so forth — those energies have to be channeled in other directions. Get rid of too much of it and you have everyone looking like milk cows. All right, if you were in the middle of a big herd of cattle somewhere and suddenly discovered that you were a gazelle, it would worry you blue and you'd end up in the analyst's office. You know, it's the guy who's just made a killing and to whom it's been suggested "Yeah, you've got power enough to knock the world down" who's absolutely scared blue, frozen up. You really become unable to operate. And I do not speak from a position of superior exceptionality. No sir, as soon as it becomes obvious to you that you could do some good work, and you receive recognition, you've got trouble. All right, who ever did a better first work than *The Naked and the Dead*? Or *The Glass Menagerie*? Those are magnificent and immediate success came to their authors, but neither one has done a respectable piece of work since, except one essay about how success destroyed them. Very fine little essays about how they simply couldn't endure that. If they could have got on with failure they could have gone on writing all their lives. Who wants to be anything but the starving artist in the garret? As my analyst said, "There's one thing your money won't buy you — poverty." Boy, you thought, wait till I get my first fellowship and I can write the Great American Novel and astonish all of my friends. The first things you did, though, was put on the hair shirts and start shooting your veins full of all kinds of things you weren't allowed to shoot your veins full of, going to bed with everything in sight, anything to ruin your life so you wouldn't have to write the Great American Novel.

You know, I said "That won't happen to me, I'm prepared." Ho ho ho, hair shirt, here I come. It really floors you. Because suddenly you do have to become mature. You've got to quit going around saying, "I'm poor, help me." Because all of a sudden you're not that poor and everybody wants you to help him. They all want you to grow up so they can be the baby. Also all the friends that you ever had suddenly can't stand you because they think it's better being successful, and they're mad at you 'cause you've got it, and you're mad at you 'cause you've got it. You're partly on their side — all the people that you've loved won't touch you, they detest you, and in place of friends or loved ones you have people who want to mark you up on their score card. You know, you like to think, as long as you're protected by unavailability or impotence or something of the sort, poverty, that it'd be great to have a lot of girls. All of a sudden you can sort of start chalking things up like pool players do on a score card somewhere. That does it. All of a sudden all your deepest fears of your own energies get you. You know, you get terrified that you could kill your father, you could get your mother in a corner. You could do any of the horrible things that you fear you might. And you get so busy trying to hold yourself down from doing those awful things that you can't do anything. It has the effect upon you that a great rage always had: you become so terrified that you'll kill everyone in sight, that you become totally unable to write anything. Well, this happens to us, and it seems to me that, if you looked at our poets' careers, you'd see that again and again. Cummings, who wrote almost all of his good poems before he was twenty-three, after a while hardened into a few easy attitudes, so that at the age of sixty he was going around saying, "Say, sex is great, ain't it?" Oh, go away. I never would have heard that if you hadn't come and told me. And he never came back to life, really. John Crowe Ransom was lucky — he came back to life after the menopause, when many poets do come back to life. Look at Stevens, after all those years of writing that philosophical glop, all of it a desert to me. His first poems are magnificent, but then you will get all that philosophy: you know, I feel that when philosophy comes in, humanity goes out the window. I'm not interested in anybody's ideas, or at least not more than once in a while, when you find some new ones. It didn't seem to me Stevens had any that were very interesting or very different from what you read in other places. Now after the first marvelous book, and the slop, you got the last book; again, it was the presence of the threat of death that scared him out of the philosophizing and made him say what really counted. "The Rock" is a beautiful work, just full of magnificent poems. But there you seem to me to have the typical American poet's career — he simply doesn't have a mature period.

Q.: *I'm sure you've heard the charge which has been leveled regularly over the last 15 years or so at you and other so-called confessional poets, to the effect that you offend what's been called aesthetic distance. I wanted to ask you about your view of emotion recollected in tranquillity — to what degree would you have naked emotion present in the reader's immediate experience of the poem? Are there certain emotions which are somehow better for poetry than others?*

SNODGRASS: No, no, I don't think so at all. After all, I have to write about the emotions that I feel. The important thing, though, is that above everything else, art is about emotion, with ideas at best secondary. Lucretius was a poet of ideas, I suppose, maybe the best. And really and truly, Lucretius is as great as they say he is. But what's that beside the *Iliad*? I would hate to lose Lucretius, but I'd throw away ten of him for half an *Iliad* any day. Mostly your ideas are excuses for what you're gonna do anyway. They don't really control anything, it's your feelings that control you, that really run your life. Your ideas are normally just the way you disguise your feelings so that you can do what you want without admitting you're doing it. All right, so our disguises are a part of us. I'm not interested in, if you like, Naked Poetry, frankly because I'm not interested in naked people very much, at least except under specific circumstances. Most people, by taking off their clothes, don't demonstrate much except that they aren't very interesting. . . . I'm much more interested in the kinds of disguises we put on all the time. Our disguises can reveal a lot more about the way we feel.

Q.: *I wanted to switch for a moment to something very different. I'm interested in getting some idea of how you teach poetry writing in workshop classes. Do you insist that writing students master basic poetic forms, that they learn to write sonnets, or couplets, or master Alexandrines and so on before they may be liberated to do their thing poetically?*

SNODGRASS: Sometimes I do and sometimes I don't. I think they should have done this in high school and if they haven't done it by the time I get them, well, I'm not always happy about it. Some of them will actually want this sort of training very much, and other times I give it to them even if they don't want it because I figure that if I'm taking a kind of paternal position to them, it's my business to be hated. I mean, that's the father's business. Gives you somebody to focus it on so it doesn't go floating around and getting lost. "Okay, hate me, go home and write a sonnet. Or else." And I think that helps. I don't like to do that, I don't like to teach that way. I prefer to teach the other way. In many ways we have an ideal situation at Syracuse where Philip Booth and I often exchange students, and he always has them work very closely and with tremendous intensity on line breaks and things like that, even though he may not assign that specifically. Well, then he sends his best students to me, and it always makes me mad because I only come up with three or so. And I always want to pick them. So I get furious and he comes to me and says "You got to take this kid, believe me, he's great." And I say, "What do you mean, I got to take this kid? I want to pick my own!" But they come, these students of his, and they're like people who've been caged and they're just raging to get out, so I sit there limply saying "write a bunch of poems." And they go home and write poems like fury. I suppose I ought to do this for Phil Booth more. But I don't. As to how you teach, maybe you should do it the way César Franck taught composition — he just sat there at the organ, apparently never left the organ loft. He just sat there playing morning, noon and night. And his students were Vincent Dandee, Ernest Chasson; and all those other people would come to him and they would bring him their latest composition and he'd put it up on the rack and sit down and play it, and he'd turn around and say "I don't like it." Then he'd play it again and say "Hm, I don't like it." Then he'd play it again and say "I'm going to play it again." Then he'd play it again and turn around and say "I like it." Oh, I don't know, you read this stuff and you read it out loud and above all you try to get the kids talking to each other. You get two or three of the best you can find and you try to set a very high standard of criticism, really high. "I want to criticize you on this level. Get brilliant." Then you say, "Okay, that'll be good enough." And they get brilliant because you told them you expected them to and you showed them you thought they were able to. So they get able to. And also they're going to need criticism when they leave you, and if they've made friends they'll be able to do that. They'll send their poems back and forth to each other. You read the stuff out loud and you talk about it, tell what you like and what you don't about it the same way you teach them to paint or write music or anything else. Ah, yes, common sense. But above all, as I learned from the teachers at Iowa I really revere very much, you give them something worth fighting against. Those men were marvelous teachers, though at a certain point, I felt that they were teaching me to write learned, symbol-laden poems that any good modern poetry committee could write. They all thought I was wrong, and were really concerned for me. And they said, "You mustn't do this, you got a brain, you can't write this kind of tear-jerking stuff." But above all they had really taught me how to pack a poem with meaning, and from that it's a fairly easy jump to how to pack a poem with feeling, which to me tells a lot more. They were worth opposing, and they were strong enough so that you could oppose them without being fearful that you'd destroy them. You know, I had people like Robert Lowell, Berryman, all those people came there to teach, and they were worth fighting, too. They were all like a good father. They really gave you substance and they stood for something and you knew they did. You knew that they were putting their lives, their careers on the line. And if they were wrong it was a real loss. And also you knew, when they told you to stop writing "that kind" of poem, it was because they cared for you. The regulars at Iowa were really concerned for me when I started writing the kind of poems that later I got known for writing. You know, I never felt scornful of them for that at all. Of course, who knows but that they were right. We'll know about that in 300 years. I just figured I'd rather make a big mistake than be right in a small way. The teachers kept it so it didn't get into little picky competitions. If we fought we were going to fight about whether there was a God or not, about something that mattered. Just so, I would want my students to think I really believed in something. The good student is the one that is finally going to have to decide I'm wrong and go some other way and fight me. I want to think I'm tough enough that he can do that.

Melville: To Him, Olson

BY MARTIN L. POPS

1

CALL ME ISHMAEL (1947) is a book in name only. It is print rendered aural and haptic, a metaphor for manuscript and collage. That is why its sound and shape are so startling. As Charles Olson says of *Billy Budd:* "It all finally has to do with the throat, SPEECH."[1] And therefore, with the breath.

In "Projective Verse" (1950), Olson argued that the projective poet starts "down through the workings of his own throat to that place where breath . . . has its beginnings," where language possesses bodily resonance, "drama has to come from," and "all act springs" (*HU*, 61); conversely, the nonprojective poet is *"print bred"* and, insofar as he stays "where the ear and the mind are," is print-bound. Olson, who charts the history of verse as McLuhan the history of media, contends that Anglo-American poetry, with few exceptions, is nonprojective from the post-Elizabethans to Ezra Pound, the methodology of whose *Cantos* "points a way" toward the redramatization of language (*HU*, 51, 61). *Call Me Ishmael*, a consummate instance of aurality and hapticity in modern literature, is a redramatization of language. For although it is (often brillant) scholarship and criticism, it is also something much more ambitious, an extrapolation of *Moby-Dick* as a species of Projective Verse.

"I still have this enormous conviction," Olson told Ann Charters in July, 1968, "that I knew what went on inside that cat. I haven't had that feeling for anyone else, not even my own father" (*OM*, 64).* Henry James may have possessed Hawthorne but Olson was possessed by

Reprinted from *Modern Poetry Studies*, by permission of the Editor.
* Notes appear at the end of this selection.

Melville as, in fact, Melville was possessed by Shakespeare. Yet Shakespeare's possession of Melville was not absolute because Melville saw (or claimed to see) the incompleteness of his master: "And if I magnify Shakespeare, it is not so much for what he did do as for what he did not do, or refrained from doing." [2] Melville's possession of Olson was not complete for the same reason and was expressed in similar words: "I had the feeling for what he [Melville] did do, and didn't do. And that's important—what he *didn't do*" (*OM*, 64). *Moby-Dick* is Olson's point of departure, Melville his accomplice, and *Call Me Ishmael* his prophecy of what Melville might have written a hundred years later.

Breath is to act as manuscript is to collage, and Olson advised Cid Corman, the editor of *Origin*, in May, 1951,

> to push
> what you have already started (as to the devices of presentation) even further
> —that is, the one man, the book, the juxtaposition of varying materials, or varying
> devices, thicken, thicken, PACK, in order to set aside any lingering results of "literary" or "aesthetics" or "professional" orderings. . . .
>
> [*LO*, 76] [3]

Olson set the typography for *Call Me Ishmael* himself (*OM*, 11) according to the above prescription and, for the purpose of thickening and packing his text, juxtaposed many ingenious "devices of presentation." For example, the last lines of "What lies under" are printed like this:

> Quote.   The American Whaling era—in contrast to the
>   Basque, French, Dutch and English—
>   developed independently
>   concentrated on different species of whale
>   covered all seas including the Arctic
>   yielded on a larger scale than in any other coun-
>   try or group of countries before.
>   Unquote.
>
> [*CMI*, 25]

As McLuhan has made abundantly clear, book technology—and this is particularly true in the production of critical and scholarly books—has arrogated to itself the values visuality fosters—what, after several centuries, we have come to experience as the conventions of lineality, sequentiality, and regularity. By merely subverting a typographical convention, Olson rescues into earshot two nouns from an ossified sign language (". . ."), breathes speech force into the quoted passage by metaphrasing it, and he evidently understood that, as he distorted the naturalism of the book, his text would more nearly resemble a manuscript (a page to be read aloud, product of an aural culture) and a collage (a thickened object, product of a haptic one). Between the medieval manuscript which educes speech and the modern collage which educes touch falls the book which educes neither. A book holds its reader at arm's length, but *Call Me Ishmael* demands his unexpected participation.

The distorted naturalism of which I speak is easiest to understand in terms of painting and is one of the legacies of the first modern painters, the Impressionists and post-Impressionists. In the polarities of painting style, visual and haptic are opposed—Bouguereau, let us say, as opposed to Cézanne (though Cézanne is not his absolute opposite). The problem with Bouguereau—I have chosen an artist of extreme visual bias, one whom only a camp sensibility can redeem—is that, in obsessively converting all paint to texture, he withdraws all human feeling from the art of picture-making, bequeaths a grotesque impersonalism to ostensibly holy and sentimental subjects, and borrows from his predecessors that visual space, presumably normative, which functions as a preexistent envelope for action. In his late landscapes, on the other hand, Cézanne confronts the world as with a revirginized eye, seizes it until it germinates within. Then re-creating his sensations of it in partially unconverted paint strokes, he projects the shallowed space those sensations inhabit and those strokes create, implicating the viewer in his shimmering substances.

Like two-dimensional book print, Bouguereau's purely visual bias excludes the spectator from sensual participation. The dead end of visuality is where Modern Painting begins, and during the last hundred years we have witnessed an ever-increasing auralization and hapticization: from the Impressionists and post-Impressionists with their symphonies and nocturnes and improvisations, their doctrines of uninterpreted sensation and the painting as object, to the Tachistes with their gesture-language and gigantic viscosities; from the Cubists who constructed the collage to the painters who sculpted the Shaped Canvas; from the master of the incorporative *Water Lilies* to those contemporary environmentalists who encircle and assault their audience (Bouguereau eccentrically reversed, the dead end of hapticity). Olson rescues *Call Me Ishmael* from the abstractions of the eye, and one remembers the delight with which he acknowledged receipt of his first volume of poems, *In Cold Hell, In Thicket* (1953), printed by Robert Creeley:

and the type, and the page, reads like cream (i think
Robt is rite, when he sez, it's human, that book, feels
like humans made it

[LO, 206]

But the presence of the "human" and the "humans [who] made it" is
much more evident in *Call Me Ishmael.*

Olson introduces his text with a poem in a variation of seventeenth-
century English (thereby distorting the linguistic "space" of modern
English) and calls Melville a "scald" (though he is the poet of Scan-
dinavian origin and oral delivery). Thereafter, with the exception of
Moby-Dick, Olson is not principally concerned with the novels but with
original manuscripts, some of which he publishes for the first time, most
of which lead us not to Melville's literary manner but to his private
voice. For example, Olson prints a scrap which Melville had entitled:
"What became of the ship's company of the whaleship 'Acushnet,'
according to Hubbard who came home in her (more than a four years'
voyage) and who visited me at Pittsfield in 1850" (*CMI*, 22). We
remember with embarrassment that sentimental yearning for shipmates
dead and gone in Melville's late poetry, and we appreciate how unsen-
timental his remembrance of them here is, how authentic his voice, that
we hear it undisguised. It is one way—Olson has many ways—of forcing
language into our ears and out of our throats, of forcing us to respond at
that physiological place where breath has its beginning.

He will use arcane words like usufruct, variant spellings like hurrick-
ans, and abbreviations like N.G., all of which are sufficiently strange to
the eye so that one is impelled to sound them on the tongue. And there
are other such "devices of presentation" as well. More important, Olson, like Whitman, is fond of slang, because it has not yet shed the
impress of speech and become "literary": "You can approach BIG
America and spread yourself like a pancake, sing her stretch as Whitman did, be puffed up as we are over PRODUCTION" (*CMI*, 69). In
like manner Olson willingly distorts the naturalism of the English sentence (a complete thought rendered) and the paragraph (the topic
sentence developed). His model for such distortion was D. H. Lawrence's *Studies in Classic American Literature*, and his theoretical justification Pound's edition of Fenollosa's " The Chinese Written Character as a Medium for Poetry," an essay which silently undergirds
"Projective Verse." Thus, the first two "paragraphs," part one of *Call
Me Ishmael*, read as follows, and they are not atypical:

> I take SPACE to be the central fact to man born in America, from Folsom cave to now. I spell it large because it comes large here. Large, and without mercy.
> It is geography at bottom, a hell of wide land from the beginning. That made the first American story (Parkman's): exploration.

> [*CMI*, 11]

Most important of all, Olson does not merely describe—he enacts—his vision of Melville's space: action criticism like action painting; criticism as enactment. "The cadences and acclivities of Melville's prose change," he writes. "The long ease and sea swell of Ishmael's narrative prose contrasts [the] short, rent language of Ahab" (*CMI*, 68). This observation is true, but Olson deliberately exaggerates Melville's contrast between protagonists: not primarily by what his prose says but by what it does to the reader. The "parts" of *Call Me Ishmael* are shards of language and rapid-fire discourse in Olson's version of Ahab's cadence—staccato, metaphoric, apocalyptic, nervous, lofty. The three intercalated FACTS in slow and countermotion are exquisite elongations in his version of Ishmael's. "FACT 2," for instance, is in a plain style so gentle that, though it is composed of a single sentence of 175 words, nowhere in the lull of its ease and swell is that remarkable fact declared. (Similarly, the "LAST FACT" is an uninterrupted sentence of 116 words.) These intercalations—whose genesis is surely the intercalated cetology of *Moby-Dick*—are so conspicuous that even the least perceptive will not only hear but, as of the cetological passages, will experience their greater specific gravity, the sense of the fault-lines they create, opening spaces. The distinction between "part" and "FACT," in other words, strikes us not merely in a verbal but also in a physiological way, as Robert Duncan understands the way in which *The Maximus Poems* strike him.[4] The weights of Melville's prose are as irregular as the spaces in Cézanne's landscapes are discontinuous.

"FACT 2," "the longest sentence Olson ever wrote," is called "dromenon." Ann Charters quotes Olson who quotes Jane Harrison's *Ancient Art and Ritual*: "The Greek word for a *rite* as already noted is *dromenon*, 'a thing done'—and the word is full of instruction. The Greeks had realized that to perform a rite you must *do* something, that is, you must not only feel something but express it in action, or, to put it psychologically, you must not only receive an impulse, you must react to it. The word for rite, *dromenon*, 'thing done,' arose, of course, not from any psychological analysis, but from the simple fact that rites among the primitive Greeks were *things done*, mimetic dances and the like" (*OM*,

56). I am suggesting that, as nearly as literature can come, *Call Me Ishmael* is the performing of a rite, and it shares with much Abstract Expressionist painting and sculpture the character of a gnosis which, as the critical reception of *Call Me Ishmael* indicates, attracts those who are privy to its uses and repels those who are not. The dust wrapper for the original edition claims that it is "that rare and perfect thing—a work of scholarship that is full both stylistically and conceptually of the greatest excitement and movement" (*OM*, quoted on page facing Table of Contents), and although one suspects that Olson, again like Whitman, had a supervisory hand in his press notices, one nevertheless agrees with this judgment. Evidently heeding the notion he would later formulate in "Projective Verse," that "ONE PERCEPTION MUST IMMEDIATELY AND DIRECTLY LEAD TO A FURTHER PERCEPTION" (*HU*, 52), Olson did this thing at great speed in less than four months.

Olson finished the 400-page first draft of *Call Me Ishmael* in 1940, but his mentor, Edward Dahlberg, found the "Hebraic, Biblical Old Testament" style inappropriate, and Olson never revised his manuscript. He wrote the much shortened version we now have "at a clip" between April 13, 1945, and the first week of August, 1945 (*OM*, 9).[5] He was thirty-four years old. Like the Abstract Expressionists painters (Jackson Pollock, for example, who began his drip-paintings in 1947 at the age of thirty-three), Olson came relatively late to his artistic maturity. The early work of the Abstract Expressionists (Pollock in particular) is often a disguised representation of mythical subjects, and, although I have not seen the first draft of *Call Me Ishmael*, I would guess that its archaic manner bespeaks an equivalent representationality. These artists mature late not merely because they must overthrow this earlier mode but because they must learn a radically new technique for the presentation of myth: the technique of freely associating, a systematic, controlled undercutting of consciousness in the act of creating. Olson describes it in "Projective Verse" as the "process" of poem making: "get on with it, keep moving, keep in, speed, the nerves, their speed, the perceptions, theirs, the acts, the split second acts, the whole business, keep it moving as fast as you can, citizen" (*HU*, 53). DeKooning, it used to be said jokingly, could paint at ninety-eight miles per hour, and that is no time for a novice to make split-second decisions. At most, a plasmatic figuration remains in Pollock's high-speed drip-paintings, and what becomes highly visible is not the representation of myth but the enactment of process, not a myth of creation but the uncreated Word of creation itself. Pollock and Olson create sacred texts in "the context of / Now!" the mythological present, for mythology "is literally the activeness, the possible activeness and personalness of experiencing it as such" (*M*, 22; *CM*, 9). Needless to say, figuration is more easily and willingly erased by the painter than the poet, and from this point of view Olson and Pollock are not strictly comparable. But I have been arguing their relationship in the context of their larger inventions.

Olson invariably uses blank and nearly blank pages whenever he shifts from part to FACT and vice versa as a way of endorsing his stylistic distinction. He always places the title of each part or FACT in thickened capitals and approximately a fourth of the way down from the top of the page and always begins his text approximately a third of the way up from the bottom; at least in part for the sake of breath. Again we are reminded of his advice to Cid Corman:

> give the 1st piece in any issue
> an open page ahead of itself: not necessarily a whole
> white page, in fact, on the contrary, i think not: but
> give it some breath, the reader, to, start anew with,
> the material, after, the intros

> [*LO*, 65]

But elsewhere Olson tells Corman that "graphics was, once, a little bit my profession: Ben Shahn and I were, once, a 'team' " at the Office of War Information during the Second World War (*LO*, 52). The design of each title page—the relation of type and typeface to space—suggests the asymmetrical ordering of Constructivist art and Bauhaus design just as the emphasis on speed, instantaneity, and the "human" suggest its aesthetic opposite, the Abstract Expressionism of Pollock and DeKooning. We may describe the first page of each section in words Olson used to advise Corman about the cover of *Origin*: "a simple straight space, presenting itself in one glance, gains . . . by severity & formality" (*LO*, 67). In fact, one is constantly discovering interesting indentational patterns, oddly shaped "paragraphs," arguments by design, outline, and formula which present themselves, like geometric abstractions, in a single glance. To capitalize all the letters of an important word is a painter's device, not a writer's—to match the scale of the word's significance with an equivalent physicality.

The first page of each section is itself an abstraction whose aesthetic properties are twofold: first, in its configuration, its concretion as design, the tension of its asymmetry; and second—insofar as we recognize this aesthetic ordering—our realization that the white page is integral to the shape, that it has real existence as a complement of the design, as created space. A conventional book does not exist in such space, and *Call Me Ishmael*, which does, means not to be a book but an object. Formally, it is a fiction, and perhaps that is why it is the only scholarship and/or criticism I know which is convertible into another art, in this case film. As a start, I can easily imagine the FACTS narrated (as Orson Welles used to introduce his films with a narration) as the events described therein are enacted in a grainy gray, in slow motion, and in silence.

As speech is the "solid of verse"—the aural become palpable—*Call Me Ishmael* is a metaphoric collage composed of various intercalated planes small and large: syllables, words, fragments, a prefatory poem, a note of thanks (on the fortieth page), a dedication on the eighty-eighth (against the syntax of the book broken open), a table of "CONTENTS," blank pages, pages asymmetrically ordered, FACTS, and parts—just as in some not strictly comparable sense *Moby-Dick* is a collation of genres—sermon, poem, dictionary, affadavit, encyclopedia, epic, drama, short story. In Olson and Melville (though more consciously in Olson), these solids are of varying textures, sizes, weights, intensities, speeds of motion and direction in space, and degrees of transparency and verisimilitude; their interrelations, like the interrelations of objects in projective verse, "are to be seen as creating the tension of [the work of art] just as totally as do those other objects create what we know as the world" (*HU*, 56). A conventionally organized book, like a painting by, say, Raphael, means to be, whatever else, the representation of a symbolic structure: *Call Me Ishmael*, like a painting by, say, Pollock, means to be, whatever else, the presentation of a physical object, and one is particularly aware of it as a series of pages one physically turns.

Though Olson himself slides into the language of modern art criticism with his talk of tension among objects and "planes of expression" and though in *Call Me Ishmael* he incorporates a certain amount of syntactic and typographic distortion—I think of certain collages by such other Americans as Arthur B. Dove and Robert Motherwell—Olson neither treats Melville as a subject for sheer verbal abstraction (as Gertrude Stein treats Cézanne) nor fractions objects into the sometimes indistinguishable planes of Analytical Cubism. *Call Me Ishmael* always remains literature for use, a verbal and visual object possessing both speech force and significant form. It is not like that modern hybrid of language and design, the painting poem (vide Frank O'Hara and Jasper Johns) or the calligramme of Guillaume Apollinaire, but like that ancient aural-haptic compound, the ideograph (vide Pound) and the calligraph (vide Franz Kline). *Call Me Ishmael* means to be a hieroglyph. But what does a hieroglyph mean?

2

If Nature is a book, as Sir Francis Bacon averred, then reading her letters will win her secrets. There will be a conjunction between the two, the reader will be able to "match" them, and book knowledge will be power. Reading the book of Nature, the supreme act of visuality, will become and remain the means of controlling her until the nineteenth century discovered that the letters and the secrets were no longer matchable. It is appropriate that I quote Melville on this discovery: "Say what some poets will, Nature is not so much her own ever-sweet interpreter, as the mere supplier of that cunning alphabet, whereby selecting and combining as he pleases, each man reads his own peculiar lesson according to his own peculiar mind and mood." [6] Similarly, painters in the Renaissance inaugurated a full-scale effort to "match" Nature on canvas. But to reduce a three-dimensional reality to a two-dimensional surface is an illusionist act, the conversion of a haptic reality into a visual one, a means of depotentiating Nature. Mimetic art, like reading, is an act of overlordship, a stance taken toward reality (whatever the local differences) adopted by virtually every important painter from Raphael to Courbet—until the Impressionists realized that "making" not "matching" (invention, as Emerson said, not imitation) was the key to the new art, that a painting was not, in the first instance, an act of mimesis.

Olson introduces this argument into *Call Me Ishmael* (and elaborates upon it in successive essays): "As an artist Melville chafed at representation. His work up to *Moby-Dick* was a progress toward the concrete and after *Moby-Dick* a breaking away" (*CMI*, 42–43). The alphabet of Nature, in other words, had become indecipherable hieroglyphs—things in themselves—like those markings on the bodies of Queequeg and the Whale. The matcher Ahab, irritably reaching after fact and reason, tries to decipher the markings and dies crying his blindness; the maker Ishmael, adopting a different stance, exhibits

Negative Capability, squeezes sperm and the hands of his fellow sea-
men, and lives in the final reciprocity of Nature. Melville's heroes
incarnate the two kinds of will (stance or posture) Olson discerned in
history, and we must understand them if we would understand the
context in which *Moby-Dick* is located in his intellectual and spiritual
life.

In the beginning,

> from 3378 BC (date man's 1st city, name and face of creator also known) in unbroken
> series first at Uruk, then from the seaport Lagash out into colonies in the Indus
> Valley and, circa 2500, the Nile, until date 1200 BC or thereabouts, civilization had
> ONE CENTER, Sumer, in all directions, that this one people held such exact and
> superior force that all peoples around them were sustained by it, nourished,
> increased, advanced, that a city was a coherence which, for the first time since the ice,
> gave man the chance to join knowledge to culture and, with this weapon, shape
> dignities of economics and value sufficient to make daily life itself a dignity and a
> sufficiency.
>
> [HU, 19]

This is the "FIRST WILL" of Neolithic man, whose shadow Olson
recognized in Yucatán where he lived from December, 1950, to July,
1951, and where he daily experienced the descendants of the Maya
(themselves, he speculates, descended from the Sumerians) and the
ancient Mayan hieroglyphs. The experience of Mexico, the primer and
trigger of primitivity, evidently produced as great a "culture shock" in
Olson as the descent into Polynesia produced in Melville—though, like
the corrupted islanders of *Omoo*, the contemporary Maya are, to a
necessary extent, fallen: "They are poor failures of the modern world,
incompetent even to arrange that, in the month of June, when the rains
have not come far enough forward to fill the wells, they have water to
wash in or to drink. They have lost the capacity of their predecessors to
do anything in common" (HU, 6).

What the Maya, those extraordinary people who domesticated
maize, once possessed in the spirit of the First Will was "the management of external nature so that none of its virtue is lost, in vegetables or
in art" (HU, 8). In that unfallen time, according to Olson, that management "kept attention so poised that . . . men were able to stay so
interested in the expression and gesture of all creatures, including at
least three planets in addition to the human face, eyes and hands, that
they invented a system of written record, now called hieroglyphs, which,
on its very face, is verse, the signs were so clearly and densely chosen
that, cut in stone, they retain the power of the objects of which they are
the images" (HU, 7). In Sumer, "just about 1200 BC . . . something

broke ... a bowl went smash" (*HU*, 19); so, in Mexico, the Fall is into incoherence:

> When the attentions change / the jungle
> leaps in
> > even the stones are split
> > > they rive

The unsplit stones are exercises in hieroglyph, a jugglery of ideographic and phonetic, a compound of alternate systems of communication raised to a higher third, which skirt alternate risks: on one hand, "the danger, the stereotype, of the very formalism of which the maya were masters [i.e., abstraction]" and, on the other, the risk which "never got out of hand (out of media) as did the architecture & the pots, [the] running, to naturalism" (*SW*, 110). Or as Olson writes in "Mayan Heads": "In the Mayan case, as in the Chinese, was, by intenseness of objectness able to be formal with that abstracting." [7]

The Fall is into the specialism of alphabet: "Logos, or discourse, for example, has ... [since 450 BC] so worked its abstractions into our concept and use of language that language's other function, speech, seems so in need of restoration that several of us go back to hieroglyphs or to ideograms to right the balance. (The distinction here is between language as the act of the instant and language as the act of thought about the instant.)" (*HU*, 3-4). This distinction corresponds to the one between enactive and representational forms of art. Glyphs enact the objects of the world, and the poem which follows means to be such an enactment:

What continues to hold me, is, the tremendous levy on all objects as they present themselves to human sense, in this [ancient Mayan] glyph-world. And the proportion, the distribution of weight given same parts of all, seems, exceptionally, distributed & accurate, that is that
> sun
> > moon
> > > venus
> > > > other constellations & zodiac
>
> snakes
> > ticks
> > > vultures
>
> jaguar
> > owl
> > > frog
>
> feathers
> > peyote
> > > water-lily

```
                         not to speak of
                         fish
                                carocol
                                        tortoise
                         &, above all,
                         human eyes
                                       hands
                                                limbs
```

(PLUS EXCEEDINGLY CAREFUL OBSERVATION
OF ALL POSSIBLE INTERVALS OF SAME,
as well as ALL ABOVE (to precise dimension of
eclipses, say, & time of, same etc. etc.)

And the weights of same, each to the other, is immaculate (as well as, full) That is, the
gate to the center was, here, as accurate as what you & i have been (all along) talking
about—viz., man as object in field or force declaring self as force because is force in
exactly such relation & can accomplish expression of self as force by conjecture [i.e.
throwing disparates together], & displacement in a context best, now, seen as space
more than a time such. . . .

                                                                        [SW, 111-12]

The Fall is into disobedience of Nature, overlordship; and Olson's
notion of the prelapsarian primitive—before the Sumerian bowl went
smash and the Mayan stones split—describes the ecological poise of
objects and forces (including man as object and force unobstructed by
ego), their interrelation, interval and distribution, in that space-field of
forces which is, in Dylan Thomas's phrase, "below a time." As Olson
told Cid Corman: at "each of its extremes, time takes on more the
nature of space" (LO, 92), the primitive time of the hieroglyphs or this
moment of instantaneity in projective verse. That is why Olson speaks
of space as if it were time in Call Me Ishmael: "from Folson cave to
now." The primitivist re-creates an original (i.e., "sacred" or haptic)
space below a time; the projectivist restores the original relation among
objects in this space above a time. As a primitivist, "Melville had a way
of reaching back through time until he got history pushed back so far he
turned time into space" (CMI, 14). "Melville wanted a god. Space was
the First. . . . Space was the paradise Melville was exile of. When he
made his whale he made his god" (CMI, 82). In "Letter for Melville
1951" Olson argues the manner in which Melville reached forward into
projectivist space, and in a lecture at Black Mountain College in 1953
he recalled that his intention in Call Me Ishmael was "to give space . . .
the mass and motion I take it to have, the air that it is and the lungs we
are to live in it as our element"—though this reminiscence sounds as if it
might have been colored by Olson's own subsequent practice of projective verse.

In "The Materials and Weights of Herman Melville" (1952), Olson asserted that "We know the literal space there is inside a microcosm, the nature of the motion hidden in any mass. Yet I do not know another writer except Homer who achieves by words so much of the actual experiencing of this *dimension* as Melville does" (*HU*, 113-14). And yet even the work of blind and aural Homer "is not good enough (ditto only modern example I know, one melville), simply because humanism is (homer) coming in, and (melville), going out" (*SW*, 112). "Homer was an end of the myth world from which the Mediterranean began" (*CMI*, 117). The *Odyssey*, at the edge of the world fallen from FIRST WILL, is not good enough because its protagonist, Odysseus, is complected according to that "second will" which supersedes the FIRST, what we commonly call "humanism," *the will to "search, the individual responsible to himself"* (*HU*, 20; *CMI*, 118), the heroic and originally necessary quest which in its ultimate perversion is Ahab's madness. This is the will of power "in which the will collapses back to the subjective understanding—tries to make it by asserting the self as character" (*SVH*, 45). "The egocentric concept, a man himself as, and only contemporary to himself, the PROOF of anything, himself responsible only to himself by the exhibition of his energy, AHAB, end" (*HU*, 20-21).

And yet Ahab's vaulting egotism is renewed with some success in Olson's vision of Ezra Pound (though, as far as I know, Olson never consciously draws the connection):

> Ez's epic solves problem by his ego: his single emotion breaks all down to his equals or inferiors (so far as I can see only two, possibly, are admitted, by him, to be his betters—Confucius, & Dante. Which assumption, that there are intelligent men whom he can outtalk, is beautiful because it destroys historical time, and thus creates the methodology of the Cantos, viz; a space-field where, by inversion, though the material is all time material, he has driven through it so sharply by the beak of his ego, that, he has turned time into what we must now have, space & its live air . . . .

> [*SW*, 81-82]

But Ahab himself, a hero born centuries out of his time, subscribes to an invalid metaphysic for action, is a technocrat who cannot turn time into space. Though he has "all space concentrated into the form of a whale" before him, he cannot penetrate Moby Dick with the only weapon at his command, "the only master of space" (*CMI*, 12) he knows, himself as machine, his soul grooved to run in tracks. Melville "mounted" space, but Ahab is locked out of the Grand Armada of "Leviathan amours," the sacred space where Ishmael discovers his untornadoed center. Ahab is confined to a prison (as he says), the whale-wall shoved near to him, and that is half the Oedipal struggle he loses. The other half is failing to kill the antemosaic Father—Moby Dick, the "king of natural force, resource"—for killing him means transcending historical time, in which transcendance "man acquires the lost dimension of space" (CMI, 12, 85). According to Olson, Melville intuited the secret of Freud's Moses, the fatal warfare between the brothers and the father, "the great deed and misdeed of primitive time" (CMI, 85). To slay the father is to become the father, and Olson's prefatory poem to Call Me Ishmael, addressed to his dead father, is a poem of depotentiation both poignant and celebratory. Written in a primitive American dialect, it signifies, among other things, that the writing of Call Me Ishmael redeems a lost space, is a religious event:

> O fahter, fahter
> gone amoong
>
> O eeys that loke
>
> Loke, fahter:
> your sone!

The blurb—Olson's own, I believe—on the original dust wrapper of Call Me Ishmael begins: "Charles Olson has devoted thirteen years to the study of Melville—his is a work of understanding and of a well-nigh religious devotion." It is as if he were saying in his poem: I have finally created this object, this Call Me Ishmael after these many years' labor. I have done it with the kind of attention you displayed in your fishing and care of gear (see Olson's prose sketch "Stocking Cap" about fishing expeditions with his father).[8] You were proud of your accuracies, and I was proud of you. And now I am one with you and now you may know my worth, our equality.

Fishing for trout or hunting whales "the truth is, that the management of external nature so that none of its virtue is lost . . . is as much a delicate juggling of her content as is the same juggling by any one of us on our own. And when men are not such jugglers, are not able to manage a means of expression the equal of their own or nature's intricacy, the flesh does choke" (HU, 8). As intricate Ahab, attempting to "dominate external reality," fails to manage himself and Nature, chokes, the line tightening around his neck. As Ishmael does not. As Billy suffocates. As the Maya do not: "The individual who peers out from that flesh is precisely himself, is a curious wandering animal like me—it is so very beautiful how animal human eyes are when the flesh is not worn so close it chokes, how human and individuated the look comes out of a human eye when the house of it is not exaggerated" (*HU*, 7).

After Pound the struggle for an existential space (the "arena" of the abstract Expressionists, the "field" of the Projective Poets) is renewed in Jackson Pollock—though not mentioned by name, another of the "space cadets" (*LO*, 231) in Olson's twitting phrase—hurling paint, cutting each new instant open the subject of his art, discovering his authenticity in acts of violence, as Ahab does. And Projective Verse issues from the tip of Ahab's lance. Its three characteristics which Olson arrays against the "NON-Projective" are "projectile" (i.e., harpoonlike), "percussive" (i.e., in collision with the Whale, naked slidings), and "prospective" (for Ahab, too, is a "Figure of Outward") (*HU*, 51). The "glyph" on the title page of *The Maximus Poems*, Olson's "Figure" striding forth, is particularly reminiscent of the semi-abstract *Monoceros* and other figural open-forms sculpted by Ibram Lassaw in the 1950's, which are the nearest three-dimensional equivalents I know to Pollock's drip-paintings. Ahab's heroic confrontation with Moby Dick is precisely the kind of confrontation Olson explicitly urges upon Cid Corman in editing *Origin* and upon himself implicitly in writing *Call Me Ishmael "fronting* to the *whole* front of reality *as it now presents itself"* (*LO*, 7).

And yet, for purposes of heroic action, "the EGO AS BEAK"— Ahab's and Pound's—"is bent and busted." Which way to turn?

> the primary contrast, for our purposes is BILL: his Pat is, exact opposite of Ez's, that is, BILL HAS an emotional system which is capable of extensions & comprehensions the ego-system . . . is not. Yet
>
> by making his substance historical of one city (the Joyce deal), Bill completely licks himself, lets time roll him under as Ez does not, and thus, so far as what is the more important, methodology, contributes nothing. . . .
>
> [*SW*, 82–83]

I do not mean to evaluate the rigor of Olson's remarks about his elder contemporaries, merely to establish the cultural roles he, all unawares, asks them to play. If Pound is Ahabic, Williams is Queequeg-like: Queequeg, for instance, has an emotional system capable of extensions toward Ishmael that egotistical Ahab is not capable of toward Pip; Queequeg, as passive as Paterson in the river, lets the sea and the sea of "time roll him under," and, unlike Ahab who fights to the end, contributes nothing to the methodology of survival. In short, "the lethargic vs violence as alternatives of each other for los americanos" (*AM*, 118).

Like Ahab and Queequeg, the *Cantos* and *Paterson*. These "jobs are HALVES," protests Olson, and neither has "been able to bring any time so abreast of us that we are in this present air, going straight out, of our selves, into it" (*SW*, 83).

Olson describes his dilemma in the *Mayan Letters*: "I am trying to see how to throw the materials I am interested in so that they take, with all impact of a correct methodology AND WITH THE ALTERNA-TIVE TO THE EGO-POSITION" (*SW*, 83). *The Maximus Poems*, like the painting of Pollock, DeKooning, and Kline, presume to bring time so abreast of us that we are in this present air, that we have entered space, that egotism has been confuted by its only viable alternative, obedience (which is not the same as passivity). The stance of obedience, however, is very difficult to achieve, and in "Maximus to himself" [Letter 12] (1953), Olson admits his business is as yet undone and explains why:

> I have had to learn the simplest things
> last. Which made for difficulties.
> Even at sea I was slow, to get the hand out, or to cross
> as wet deck.
>   The sea was not, finally, my trade.
> But even my trade, at it, I stood estranged
> from that which was most familiar. Was delayed,
> and not content with the man's argument
> that such postponement
> is now the nature of
> obedience,
>   that we are all late
>   in a slow time,
>   that we grow up many
>   And the single
>   is not easily
>   known
>
> I could be, though the sharpness (the *achiote*)
> I note in others,
> makes more sense
> than my own distances. . . .
>
> It is undone business
> I speak of, this morning,
> with the sea
> stretching out
> from my feet

                                                                    [M, 52–53]

In *The Special View of History*, Olson quotes Heraclitus: "*Man is estranged from that which he is most familiar*" (*SVH*, 14). That is, "man is estranged from himself as man" (*SVH*, 32). And why? Because his second will, his imperialist "stance toward reality disengages him from the familiar" (*SVH*, 29). In the development of logic, classification, and Ideal Categories, Socrates, Aristotle, and Plato performed "a removal from the particular," and since the particular "is the absolute, because it is in fact the way absolute energy asserts itself" (*SVH*, 27), that removal distances man from his universe and estranges him from himself. We grow up many in accordance with the second will, a "rash of multiples which that wish to disperse causeth to break out" (*HU*, 20). In our time this second will incarnates disease, sickness, monomania.

Where then is the man who obeys dictates deeper than appetite and obsession, the man of obedience? Olson writes: "He who possesses rhythm possesses the universe" (*HU*, 10). *Moby-Dick* "has a deeply imagined systolic and diastolic pulsation, as though of the universe itself." [9] Ishmael obeys the alternating rhythm of his blood, the Ahab and Queequeg, quester and non-quester, world without end. Ishmael practices an ecology of spirit, possesses a methodology of management toward the Whale and himself. Ishmael—the "homo maximus" of *Moby-Dick*,[10] as far as there is one—possesses the universe. At the still point of the circumambient Whale Armada, at the World Navel, amid images of gestation and birth, Ishmael rediscovers the inner impermeable space of the individual man; he has regained "touch with the primordial & phallic energies & methodologies which . . . make it possible for man, that participant thing, to take up, straight, nature's, live nature's force" (*HU*, 23). It is worth remembering that, in a lifelong devotion to Melville, Olson's first important work is called *Call Me Ishmael* and that the last line of *Maximus VI* (1968)—in which Maximus tells of his setting forth—is one Melville himself could have used to describe Ishmael's transit on the coffin buoy at the end of *Moby-Dick*; the trade from which, at least temporarily, he is not estranged: "I set out now / in a box upon the sea. . . ." So Olson described the birth of *Call Me Ishmael*, in 1953, of the poet in obedience to his trade: "It started, for me, from a sensing of something I found myself obeying for some time before. . . . It got itself put down as *space*, a factor of experience I took as of such depth, width, and intensity that, unwittingly, I insisted upon it as fact. . . . The mark of life is that what we do obey is who and what we are" (*OM*, 83–84).

"The riddle is that the true self is not the asserting function [i.e., Ahab] but an obeying one [i.e., Ishmael], that the actionable is *larger* than the individual and so can be obeyed to" (*SVH*, 45). As Ishmael lies without anxiety in the arms of the maternal sea waiting to be rescued. As a woman waits for a child to be born. As a cook waits for a pot to boil. As a poet, like Whitman, waits for a style to crystallize ("I was simmering, simmering, simmering, and Emerson brought me to a boil"). As a man, like Melville, waits fifty years, from 1840 to 1890, as his works reveal, for a personality to be individuated. The image of the sea stretching out from Olson's feet reminds me of Melville's late protagonist Daniel Orme (i.e., or me), sitting at the sea, his pipe fully smoked, now dying peacefully, his business among lions done and well. The adoption of a new stance, obedience in the lions' cage, is hardest of all and worthiest. "You might say that I teach posture" (OM, 84), Olson replied when asked what he taught at Black Mountain. The new stance, as object among objects, will bridge the distances of which Olson speaks. And the stance is dance, even sitting at the sea: "how dance / sitting down" (M, 35). The hieroglyph, as we shall see, is a world in dance; the man of obedience accepts the unintelligibility of the hieroglyph, and learns to dance.

Ishmael is the higher third the hieroglyph is, larger than the sum of forces he embodies, and a foreordination that, as Olson has it, "now, only, once again, and only a second time, is the FIRST WILL back in business" (HU, 21). Because the time is ripe. In the tide of ebb and tumescence, "what shall be / already is within the moonward sea" (SW, 159). "The will to cohere in both [the Sumerians and the Mayans] is what I see in us, in now," Olson wrote in 1960 (cover of The Distances). "We have come full circle" (SW, 159). The world is once again a hieroglyph, whose condition, as Olson glosses Keats, Is the Penetralium. There is a metaphor for psychic growth, rebirth, in Melville's "Mosses" essay which Olson uses on several occasions (for example, in "Lear and Moby Dick," Call Me Ishmael, and "Some Good News") which seems particularly appropriate to Ishmael: "I somehow cling to the strange fancy that, in all men, hiddenly reside certain wondrous, occult properties—as in some plants and minerals—which by some happy but very rare accident (as bronze was discovered by the melting of the iron and brass at the burning of Corinth) may chance to be called forth here on earth." [11] Such growth never simply depends upon an act of will but upon the staking of one's life, upon an absolute respect for that wondrous occult urge toward individuation some men feel and some do not. In a slow time such growth takes a long time; one must learn to wait, but also always and unremittingly to manage the world and oneself with one's highest effort, in obedience to the First Will. As, according to Olson, the Corinth of Melville and Shakespeare makes the bronze of *Moby-Dick*, the higher third (*CMI*, 40), so FACTS and parts, Matter and the Imagination, make *Call Me Ishmael*, ideographs and phonemes make hieroglyphs, Queequeg and Ahab make Ishmael. (The opposites of "La Chute," the last poem of *In Cold Hell, In Thicket*, are drum and lute.) The projectivist burden of the "Letter for Melville 1951" is that as opposites intersect, they create a space above time, the space of Melville's temporary renewal, the interface of a higher third.

Like several of Olson's other productions—for example "Anecdotes of the Late War," "Y & X," and "The Sutter-Marshall Lease"—the "Letter" is literally spatial: originally printed as a broadside for oral delivery, it is a foldout, hard-covered, multicolored object filled with voice and tone, masculinity and mascularity, a marvelous performance of wit, love, and malice. It was published in approximately fifty copies—a production quota nearer that of a manuscript than a book (which, economics aside, is the point)—and like the other examples I have cited and others I haven't, the "Letter" is, to a visible extent, hand-produced, as if it were a preindustrial artifact. As in "The Materials and Weights of Herman Melville" (1952) and "Equal, That Is, to the Real Itself" (1957), so in this "Letter" Olson makes mash of those critics whom he feels have done Melville a disservice, but in particular those who have not understood his prophetic, projectivist, achievement; for example,

> this brightest of these mischievous men
> who does not know that it is not the point
> either of the hook or the plume which lies
> cut on the brave man's grave
> —on all of us—
> but that where they cross is motion,
> where they constantly moving cross anew, cut
> this new instant open—

According to Olson, this is the knowledge that Melville did have, who knew

> that knowledge
> is only what makes a ship shape, takes care
> of the precision of the crossed sign, the feather
> and the anchor, the thing
> which is not the head but is
> where they cross, the edge
> the moving edge of force, the wed
> of sea and sky (or land & sky), the Egyptian
> the American backwards

The plume and the hook, the feather and the anchor, the sky and the sea: as of the broken tabletop planes of Cézanne, where they cross is motion; as in his late landscapes where crossing planes cut this new instant open, cutting open a timeless space. Man and the universe: "where they cross, the edge / the moving edge of force" is the knowledge of his "Human Universe" (1951) which Olson attributes to Melville: "The meeting edge of man and the world is also his cutting edge. If man is active, it is exactly here where experience comes in that it is delivered back [as Cézanne sat in the fields for hours before his *motif*, incorporating the world within himself, waiting with his highest effort, before making a stroke], and if he stays fresh at the coming in he will be fresh at his going out" (*HU*, 11).

So we must speak of Melville's confrontation with the particulars of the world, "not the thing's 'class,' any hierarchy, of quality or quantity, but the thing itself" (*HU*, 6). Though Olson is overhard on Melville critics, he is ironically, quite soft on Melville scholars, applauding the discovery of data, however trivial; they are, for Olson, the objects of a world. In *A Bibliography on America* (1964), he cites the precedents of Melville—"how to cook a whale," "how a whale uses his flukes" (*BOA*, 8, 9)—and in a book review about Billy the Kid (1953), he observes that "if you have ever cut behind any American event or any presentation of them, to the primary documents, you will know the diminishment . . . that only Melville escapes" (*HU*, 137). Olson, of course, was an important archaeologist of Melville documents, and he advises Dorn in the *Bibliography* to do what he himself had done: "*dig one thing or place or man until you yourself know more abt that man than is possible to any other man*"; "you'll have to dig *mss.*" (*BOA*, 13). Which is, in fact, what Ishmael, Melville's own greatest archaeologist, has done, for is not Queequeg, whom he discovers, a living manuscript of hieroglyphs? "Actuality [is] in its essence a process," and "a carpenter *doing it* is the same thing, or a sailor, or anyone who really knows what he is doing doing it" (*BOA*, 9). The latest Maximus is a poet; before him—though Olson never says so—was Ishmael the sailor. The first Maximus (among the original settlers) was a carpenter: "he was the first to make things, / not just live off nature" (*M*, 31). He must have been like that early explorer of America, Captain John Smith, another "stater of / quantity and / precision," who

> sucks
> down, into the terrible
>
> inert of
> nature (the Divine
> Inert, the literary man
> of these men
> of the West,

                        who knew private
                        passivity as these
                        quartermasters knew
                        supplies, said
                        it has to be

                        if princes
                        of the husting
                        are to issue from

                        the collapse
                        of the previous

                        soul:
                            [M, 122]

In "The Specksynder" chapter of *Moby-Dick*, from which this passage largely derives, Melville observes that "God's true princes," "the Divine Inert," refusing to avail themselves "of external arts and entrenchments," forever exclude themselves "from the world's hustings." [12] Bartlebly, I suppose, is Melville's truest unelected prince, but so to an extent is Ishmael who chooses to sail neither as Commodore, Captain, nor Cook, who "abandon[s] the glory and distinction of such offices to those who like them" and goes to sea as a simple sailor, right before the mast.

The sucking down into the Divine Inert must precede the issuance, for only then, as the outworn soul of an epoch collapses, is Ishmael, prince of the hustings, reborn to tell his tale. "From passive places," says Olson of Melville, "his imagination sprang a harpoon" (*CMI*, 15), and this is how the drama of *Moby-Dick* ends and begins again—sucking down, collapsing and springing forth: "when the half-spent *suction* of the sunk ship reached me, I was then, but slowly, drawn towards the closing vortex. When I reached it, it had subsided to a creamy pool. Round and round then, and ever contracting towards the button-like black bubble at the axis of that slowly wheeling circle, like another Ixion I did revolve. Till, gaining that vital centre, the black bubble upward burst; and now, liberated by reason of its cunning *spring*" (*MD*, 724, italics removed). Melville's archetypal text of death and rebirth corresponds to the phylogenetic reemergence of First Will and the hero obedient to it. Ishmael the bookman is a connoisseur of information: unlike the crew of the *Pequod*, allegorists trapped in fixities and definites, he stands before the doubloon and concedes just this much: "some certain significance lurks in all things" (*MD*, 549). Ahab's tragedy, if you like, is that he can neither accept Ishmael's concession nor Pip's more radical formulation. "I look, you look, he looks; we look, you look, they look." Which is the wisdom of Maximus:

> There are no hierarchies, no infinite, no such many as mass,
>   [there are only
> eyes in all heads,
> to be looked out of
>
>   [M, 29]

"The Materials and Weights of Herman Melville" argues Melville's ability to go inside a thing in order to explore its spatial particularity, to experience not merely its essence but its dimension, "that part of a thing which ideality . . . tended to diminish."

> There is no where else to go but in and through; there is no longer any least piece of pie in the sky. With Melville's non-Euclidean penetrations of physical reality ignored or avoided, all the important gains he made in expressing the dimension possible to man and to story are also washed out.
>
>   [HU, 113–14]

In "Equal, That Is, to the Real Itself," Olson further claims that man in the nineteenth century "was suddenly possessed or repossessed of a character of being, a thing among things . . . his physicality. It made a re-entry of or to the universe" and led Melville to endow the prose of *Moby-Dick*—but only of *Moby-Dick*—with "such physical quantities as velocity, force and field strength" (the attributes, in painting, quintessentially expressed by the Abstract Expressionists) (*HU*, 118, 120).

For Olson, then, Melville's triumph devolves upon one book, not upon an *oeuvre*. Although he wrote Cid Corman in 1953 that "Melville & Homer & Shakespeare have been my masters," [13] Olson believed that, as Judeo-Christian mythographers, Melville and Shakespeare finally offer the redemption of First Will only at the unacceptable price of a maimed human sexuality; that, seduced as he has been by the God of his tradition, Western man has denied his manhood in quest of transcendence ("ideality"); that he has come to regard woman not as the completion of his being but as the obstacle to that completion. No Penelope waits for Prospero and Vere, and neither would say with Odysseus, whom the gods visit and who, in consequence, properly situates his humanness,

> There is no boon in life more sweet, I say,
> than when a summer joy holds all the realm,
> and banqueters sit listening to a harper
> in a great hall, by rows of tables heaped
> with bread and roast meat, while a steward goes
> to dip up wine and brim your cups again.[14]

Like Homeric Greeks, the ancient Celts of "The Laughing Ones"

(1950) also possess an unashamed exuberance of the senses: for woman, sport, hunting, dance, food.

> Women
> are delights, things to run with, equals
> —small game they slay....
>
> [They]
> want to dance, only to dance
> & slay. They
> are without suspicion, stupid, gay, think
> the world is a banquet....
>
> [*AM*, 39]

In Melville, sensual exuberance is invariably misplaced: those who most fully possess the "low enjoying power" turn out to be halfmen like Master Betty the Fiddler or the Bachelors of Paradise whose life is an escapist round of banqueting and song. In Olson, the exuberance is genuine though ascetic in a desiccate time; though no Greek or Celt, Maximus knows that

> there is no other issue than
> the moment
>   the pleasure of
>   this plum,
> these things
> which don't carry their end any further than
> their reality in
> themselves
>
> [*M*,42]

To argue the physicality of a thing is to argue its objecthood, itself as hieroglyph. And if the object is a hieroglyph, so art, the only twin life has, as Olson says, must also assume that shape and definition. "Art does not seek to describe but to enact" (*HU*, 10, 127). But as for "non-Euclidian penetrations of physical reality"—and, in general, Olson's use of scientific terminology to define aesthetic experience—I am more than doubtful. I prefer the wit by which he expresses John Smith's "penetrations": "And its that, that gets me, about Smith—how he bites into, the thing" (*HU*, 132). But Olson was determined to validate the "truth" about Melville's objects and their space in the language of the new mathematics and physics, and this is what "Equal, That Is, to the Real Itself" is about, his last essay on Melville, the essay he came to regard as the true last chapter of *Call Me Ishmael,* a definitive, formulaic rendition of his most recent ideas (*OM*, 13).

Olson seems to have derived much of his scientific language from Hermann Weyl's *Philosophy of Mathematics and Natural Science*

(1949), and although he never cites that book (any more than he cites Fenollosa in "Projective Verse"), it is certain that what he regards as the most "relevant single fact to the experience of *Moby-Dick* and its writer" is a nearly exact quotation, word for italicized word, from Weyl: *"The inertial structure of the world is a real thing which not only exerts effects upon matter but in turn suffers such effects."* [15] According to Weyl, the mathematician Riemann made this discovery regarding "the metrical structure of space" in the middle of the nineteenth century and Einstein independently rediscovered it at the beginning of the twentieth. I doubt Olson was (I know I am not) competent to analyze this discovery in mathematical terms or apply it to *Moby-Dick* insofar as it is a mathematical formulation. But if we lift the remark from its context—demathematicize it into metaphor—I think we can understand why Olson was so struck by it. It allows him to rediscover the psychic ecology of opposites, their reciprocal relation, in the macro-universe where, as he notes, Melville joins "the feeling or necessity of the inert, or of passivity as a position of rest . . . to the most instant and powerful actions" (*HU*, 122). "From passive places his imagination sprang a harpoon" implies an interchange analogous (and not just metaphorically either) to what Olson presumes to find in the micro-universe of modern physics: "the structures of the real are flexible, quanta do dissolve into vibrations, all does flow, and yet is there, to be made permanent, if the means are equal" (*HU*, 122).

3

But how does one make vibrations permanent and yet retain the flexibility of the structure of the real? How, in other words, does one make a hieroglyph? In 1929, under the tutelage of Constance Taylor, Olson took lessons in the proto-dance of posture exercise [16] and tells us about his experience in "Maximus, to Gloucester," "Letter 14" (1953) of *The Maximus Poems*, under the heading "on how men do use / their lives":

> "to tend to move
> as though drawn",
> it also says
>
> Or might it read
> "compare
> the ripe sun-flower"?

The old charts
are not so wrong
which added Adam
to the world's directions

which showed any of us
the center of a circle
our finger
and our toes describe

(one taught us
how to stand in crowds
there we were, three actors,
in a loft above Tarr's Railway
in shorts, in front of her,
doing,
her bidding: "Buttocks
in & under, buttocks"

seeking,
like Euclid,
the ape's line, the stance
fit for crowds, to watch
parades, never
to tire

It was in our minds
What she put there,
to get the posture
to pass from the neck of,
to get it down,
to get the knees bent

not as he was shown, arms out, legs out, leaping

another Adam, a nether
man

It does stem. And the joker
that the sense is
of a sash-weight,
after the head is clear,
after the burst
a sash-weight does hang
from between the legs
if you are drawn,
if you do unite,
if you do be
pithecanthropus

[M, 60–61]

Dance is the art of obedience: to tend to move as though drawn. Dance is the insignia of wholeness: the mandala of the ripe sunflower, Adam configured as a perfect circle. Dance is the discovery of stance, of posture. If these conditions are realized, then a sash-weight does hang from between the legs: man, "that participant thing," is reunited with "primordial & phallic energies & methodologies ... nature's, live nature's force" (*HU*, 23). Melville says as much in the "Midnight, Forecastle" chapter of *Moby-Dick:* "There's naught so sweet on earth— heaven may not match it!—as those swift glances of warm, wild bosoms in the dance, when the overarboring arms hide such ripe, bursting grapes." Dance as the stance of process sexualizes the world in perpetual enactment, like Keats's unburst grape upon his palate fine. Dance provides final knowledges in the body—the sense of a sash-weight— knowledges that poetry can never provide. The stance of dance is obedience to First Will, to the restoration of a field of force which includes you ("unite") as a force poised, suspended like a sash-weight ("as drawn"), among others.

Olson knew on his pulses the exhilaration of dance, its primordiality, expressivity, and value:

> I believe, for example, that all men and women can dance—and this alone is enough to establish expression—that all other expression is only up from this base; and that to dance is enough to make a whole day have glory, granting that work is called for of each of us. The hook is that work will always make sense if dancing is understood to be—expression is—the other issue of a day.
>
> [*LO*, 172]

Not just a balletomane (one mad about ballet), Olson struck up a friendship in the mid-thirties with the famous dancer and choreographer Leonid Massine, who evidently obliged Olson by giving him a big part in the Ballets Russes de Monte Carlo production of *Bacchanale*. Olson's colleague in balletomania, John Finch, recounted the event in a recent memoir:

> He was to amble on, taller than a dream giant [Olson was six feet eight inches], and lie down full length on the stage for a time, while tiny ballerinas in Dali costumes swirled and swarmed above him. Then slowly, dreamlike, he was to rise and amble off. All this he did. All this I saw. Where they found tights to fit him, I never learned. And the ballerinas must have been warned about him, for prone and vast, he blocked off most of down-stage left and they detoured around him. But Charlie was very good, calm and poised, a dreaming presence. Motionless, he danced his best dance.[17]

Olson's "Syllabary for a Dancer" (a Black Mountain document though not published until 1971) contains material which he later reworked in "Tyrian Business" (Letter 8 of *The Maximus Poems*). The "Syllabary" is dedicated to an Indian dancer "whose people did not have to lose coherence as much as we of the west did who were led to disperse." Olson asks her to "teach us what you know about sitting," to teach us who "don't even yet know how to sit down, how to dance sitting down!" So Finch's praise is perhaps not beside the point—that "motionless, [Olson] danced his best dance"—and we may compare such praise with Olson's own rude assault on the unnamed Martha Graham in "Tyrian Business," an assault even more rudely cast in the "Syllabary," where she exemplifies those who cannot sit:

> such monsters of the old [i.e., the second] will like a creature such as Martha Graham (who is so far back she craves to be scalped and dragged over the ground and so, because nobody has dragged her, she has everybody do it, she does it, she makes dance an enemy!)[18]

Olson evidently wanted an intellectual analysis of dance more complete than his "Syllabary" and urged Corman to publish "an investigation into, the whole question of, where dance is, as an *art*, now," and offered him the benefit of several dicta. For example, "any player is (has to be) 1st dancer." Why? Because dance is the *"graphic of drama"* and below it expressively, because the voice and verse of an actor work out of and against motion. With "the body as instrument," Olson recommends an "investigation of dance as [a] problem of space (not, time & not all act)"(*LO*, 82). Why space? Because dance is the primary artistic means for dissolving unreal boundaries between self and other, opening an existential space. Dance is the metaphor for the management of self suspended in the world. Dance returns man to egoless reciprocity, to the condition of Ishmael in the sea at the end of *Moby-Dick*. A man who dances lives like a part of the poem of the world. For Olson the dancer's life-become-art is managed for use ("to watch / parades, never / to tire") not beauty, the vernacular aesthetic of New England. The man who dances is always space-creating and glyph-enacting, and Olson marvels in a letter to Corman: "you should see what movements, gestures, investigations of nature these [Mayan] glyphs, contain" (*LO*, 82). A hieroglyph is a world in dance.

>   the art of the language of glyphs
> IS
>   motion is [space-] time on stone
>   [*LO*, 85]

The editor of *Origin* is supposed to choreograph a "dance of mss" with each issue. When he succeeds, he earns Olson's highest praise:

>   If you ain't *the god damn best*
>   *editor* since when
>   (since ever such leading on a dance

> of mss, such a man
> to compose a collective? where, has there been such
> a man as Cid
> corman—core-
> man (chore-
> agos)?

[LO, 102]

But if Corman is chore-agos, what of Olson who tutored him? And if *Origin*, predicated on Olsonian principles, may be a dance, then what of *Call Me Ishmael*, "that thing . . . of the greatest excitement and movement"?

In 1951 Olson wrote the scenario "Apollonius of Tyana," "A Dance, with Some Words, for Two Actors." Apollonius, a near contemporary of Christ, is a dancer in Olson's version; Tyana, the city, the woman, from whose arms he literally emerges and into whose arms he ultimately returns. Apollonius is bound to the city of his birth in rebirth: he comes back voluntarily as he is pulled back, as he obeys, because he and Tyana are, in Olson's metaphor, like magnets in a field of force. Their relation, Olson specifies, is one of health not sickness, and I must note that in my book *The Melville Archetype* I try to graph Melville's unconscious symbols of a similar relation, of his transit in health from the mother to the mother, individualism to individuation, second will to First.[19] As works of art the *Odyssey* and *Moby-Dick* are "act[s] of anticipation" which prophesy the psychic development of Western man (*CMI*, 118): Odysseus breaks through the uroboros of First Will, the primal round, into the exercise of the second, the exploration of outer space, the necessary potentiation of consciousness. Olson's mythologem is neither psychologically nor historically fanciful: "Toward the close of the Age of Iron (c. 1250 B.C. in the Levant), the old cosmology and mythologies of the goddess mother were radically transformed, reinterpreted, and in large measure even suppressed, by those suddenly intrusive patriarchal warrior tribesmen whose traditions have come down to us chiefly in the Old and New Testaments and in the myths of Greece." [20]

By the nineteenth century, however, our psychic well-being depended not on the development of this separatist consciousness, as exemplified by Ahab, but on the reintegration of consciousness into the unconscious, as exemplified by Ishmael, whose destiny is to return at will and in obedience to the circumambient mandala of the vortex. From Coleridge, Goethe, and Melville to such major contemporary artists as Frank Lloyd Wright, D. H. Lawrence, Henry Moore, and

Jackson Pollock there has been, in our patriarchal and fiercely techno-
logic time, a powerful reexpression of maternal primitivist imagery, but
whether it augurs new birth (is credible evidence that "the FIRST
WILL [is] back in business") or whether it merely represents a nostalgic
wish-fulfillment (a cry for coherence which can never again be answered), I cannot say. Olson's position is a little like Melville's at the
end of *Billy Budd*: Billy will triumph in eternity but Claggart is
triumphing in time, in the news media. Olson's enthusiasm, in other
words, is tempered by the existent culture. "Pejorocracy is here," he says
in *The Maximus Poems*, addressing those Melvillean "Isolatos," "Isolated persons in Gloucester, Massachusetts," in the country Melville
called Anathema (*M*, 3, 12). Olson's indictment is lengthy and scathing,
and I will confine myself to one pertinent illustration, this from "The
Morning News" (1950):

> IN ADDITION, AT THIS WAKE-UP HOUR,
>
> WE BRING YOU—
> THE HANDSOME SAILOR!
>
> (Crowd noises: "sesquipedentifrice
> sesquipedentifrice sesquipedentifrice"
>
> and shouts of: "Fer cryssake, he
> won't TALK!"
> "Look! the dope, he
> STUTTERS!"
>
> and all: "KILL 'im, KILL 'IM"
>
> no, citizens,
> no
> (musical bridge, in, & over:
> "This is
> th-is is,
> the NEWooo
> DA-YYYYY!"

Like Ishmael, like Maximus, Apollonius is a measurer and is also
configured in a Leonardan mandala. A traveler through all the compass
points of the world, he is a missionary for First Will whose quandry is
ours: how to redeem a world which has lost coherence, squandered the
knowledges of primitive man, forgotten an organic operationalism, debased the identity of objects: "*his* job, at least, is to find out how to
inform all people how best they can stick to the instant, which is both
temporal and intense, which is both shape and law" (*HU*, 34). The
dance of Apollonius "is a wide investigation into the local, the occasional"; his problem as dancer, "how to extricate what he wants from

the mess he is surrounded by, how to manage to locate what he himself
feels: that life as spirit is in the thing, in this man" (*HU*, 35). In these
men dancing.

> they dance
> what it is   what it is to say wherein it lies
> where beauty lies
>   that men containeth
>   at this hour
>   [*AM*, 8]

To dance is to discover "the thrust / of what you are," "the hidden
constance of which all the rest / is awkward variation" (*AM*, 79). The
dancer em-bodies his particularity, the nourishment of his beauty. Nor
is there dance without love: "no dance / outside the modes and figures
of that trance" (*AM*, 3). Because love is the trance, the ring dance whose
leader is Christ. The wisest man, like Apollonius, is the dancer who
obeys the dance. So *The Maximus Poems* begin:

> Off-shore, by islands hidden in the blood
> jewels & miracles, I, Maximus
> a metal hot from boiling water, tell you
> what is a lance, who obeys the figures of
> the present dance

Maximus, a baptized and tempered lance like Ahab, is obedient like
Ishmael. Obedient to what? To the present dance of syllables. "For
from the root out, from all over the place, the syllable comes, the figures
of, the dance" (*HU*, 54). In "Projective Verse," Olson argues the necessity of listening to the syllables forty hours a day, constantly and
scrupulously; Maximus is a man of aesthetic action, like that first Maximus, the carpenter, who undoubtedly also knew that in the making of a
thing his instrument was magical and alive. In "the obedience of his ear
to the syllables," "the dance of the [poet's] intellect is" revealed.

> So, is it not the PLAY of a mind we are after, is not that that shows whether a mind
> is there at all?
>   And the threshing floor for the dance? Is it anything but the LINE?
>
>   .   .   .   .
>
> And the line comes . . . from the breath, from the breathing of the man who writes, at
> the moment that he writes, and thus is, it is here that, the daily work, the WORK,
> gets in. . . .
>   [*HU*, 53–55 passim]

The syllable is of the ear, in dance; the line is of the breath, in work.

Together they perfect a poet's life and the life of Maximus, the Anthropos: "to dance is enough to make a whole day have glory, granting that work is called for of each of us."

NOTES

1. Charles Olson, *Call Me Ishmael* (New York, 1958), p. 104; hereafter referred to as *CMI* and page number. The following texts of Olson's work have been used in this essay. Each is accompanied by the abbreviation which will be employed in citations: *HU—Human Universe and Other Essays*, ed. Donald Allen (New York, 1967); *OM—Olson/Melville*, by Ann Charters (Berkeley, 1968); *SW—Selected Writings*, ed. Robert Creeley (New York, 1966); *AM—Archeologist of Morning* (London, 1970), no pagination; *M—The Maximus Poems* (New York, 1960); *CM—Causal Mythology*; *BOA—A Bibliography on America for Ed Dorn* (San Francisco, 1964).
2. Herman Melville, "Hawthorne and His *Mosses*," reprinted in *The Shock of Recognition*, ed. Edmund Wilson (New York, 1943), I, pp. 193–94.
3. *Letters for Origin*, ed. Albert Glover (SUNY-Buffalo, unpublished doctoral dissertation, 1968), p. 76. I have tried to reproduce or, at least, approximate wherever relevant Olson's typography, spacing, and punctuation—"the spatial proportions of the original letters" in Glover's phrase. I have drawn my quotations from this manuscript because the published edition is a selection which does not always include the letters or parts thereof I quote.
4. Robert Duncan, "Notes on Poetics Regarding Olson's *Maximus*," *Black Mountain Review*, No. 6 (1956), p. 202
5. Olson's first efforts at Melville criticism were academic; his master's essay at Wesleyan University, "The Growth of Herman Melville, Prose Writer and Poetic Thinker" (1933), and "Lear and *Moby Dick*," *Twice a Year*, I (Fall-Winter, 1938), pp. 165–89. The first draft of *Call Me Ishmael* remains as yet unpublished as does two thirds of his *oeuvre*, according to the estimate of Charles Boer, Olson's literary executor. How much of it annotates Melville—aside from fugitive references which we may suppose are scattered through—I cannot say. We do know that Olson wrote "another long Melville poem" in addition to the "Letter for Melville 1951," for in one of his letters to Corman he refers to its title as "THE COLLECTED POEMS OF" (1953) (*Letters for Origin*, 194). I presume it is extant. *The Collected Poems of Herman Melville* (1947) was edited by Howard Vincent, and one may suppose that Olson renewed an attack on Vincent who namelessly appears in the earlier poem as one whose "edition of this here celebrated man's verse . . . has so many carelessnesses in it that, as of this date, it is quite necessary to do it over." There is strong reason, however, to doubt that Professor Vincent was responsible for the final "carelessnesses" of the edition.
6. Herman Melville, *Pierre* (New York, 1957), p. 476.
7. "Mayan Heads," *Black Mountain Review*, No. 2 (Summer, 1954), p. 27.
8. "Stocking Cap," *Montevallo Review*, I, No. 2 (Summer, 1951), pp. 16–21.
9. "Lear and *Moby-Dick*," p. 185.
10. The "homo maximus" is Jung's Anthropos, individuated man, he who has realized his Self. In the sea at the end of *Moby-Dick*, Ishmael experiences a temporary individuation.
11. "Hawthorne and His *Mosses*," p. 204.
12. Herman Melville, *Moby Dick* (New York, 1964), p. 198; hereafter referred to as *MD* and page number.
13. *Origin: Third Series*, No. 20 (January, 1971), p. 45.
14. *The Odyssey*, tr. Robert Fitzgerald (New York, 1963), p. 145.
15. Hermann Weyl, *Philosophy of Mathematics and Natural Science* (Princeton, 1946), p. 105. See also *HU*, 122.

16. George Butterick, "An Annotated Guide to the Maximus Poems of Charles Olson" (SUNY-at Buffalo, unpublished doctoral dissertation, 1970), p. 54.
17. John Finch, "Dancer and Clerk," *Massachusetts Review* (Winter, 1971), pp. 34–40.
18. "A Syllabary for a Dancer," *Maps*, No. 4 (1971), pp. 9–15.
19. Martin L. Pops, *The Melville Archetype* (Kent, 1970).
20. Joseph Campbell, *The Masks of God* (New York, 1964), III, p. 7.

A "Wild Severity": Toward a Reading of Ben Belitt

BY JOAN HUTTON LANDIS

WILLIAM JAMES, WHOSE INFLUENCE on Ben Belitt's work seems almost tutelary, once reflected on Tolstoi as follows: "His crisis was the getting of his soul in order, the discovery of its genuine habitat and vocation, the escape from falsehoods into what, for him, were ways of truth." Certainly, in a cohesive body of written work, particularly poetry, a reader ought to be able not only to glean some notion of what the crises were, or what the "ways of truth" might constitute, but to participate in the very process through which the "habitats" and "vocations" are yearned for, entertained, invented, rejected and sometimes accepted. In "reading toward" the poetry of Ben Belitt, I should like to examine some of the central themes and preoccupations of a poet whose very human yearning for the things of this world, as well as things ascribable to other worlds "intact and unseen, like the orange's scent in the orange tree," have too often been obscured by the scope of his erudition or the elliptical brilliancies of his tactics. I should like to concern myself with the mind of a poet, his sense of self and event as it is revealed through the poem, and the teleologies implied: the "getting of the soul in order" with its attendant need for "habitats," the desire that life might somehow be, in Milton's sense, a "true poem," and the poetics to which it gives rise — the life lived and its fictive equivalence in the art of a poet.

Belitt's early work, roughly that of his first two volumes, *The Five-Fold Mesh* (1938) and *Wilderness Stair* (1955), establishes the primary facts and figures of his world. It is a place closely attended by the qualities of betrayal and loss, a world in which he is both literally and figuratively "orphaned." If, as he writes, "The quieter god comes early to the childhood/that is unhappy," it is equally true that neither the protective figure of this god nor the paternalism of orthodoxy can long maintain reality. "I had not stirred a limb/To turn from Him./I saw His vast loins girt, and He was gone from me:/And so, when help was very far,/Past the clasping of hands or the heart's call,/I hid my head/And wept for the betrayed, infatuate dead./That is the truth and the whole truth and is all." That he weeps for himself is rare, but that he does so for others who have suffered similar ordeals of trust and desertion is characteristic — for although many of these poems are tempered by isolation, anguish and despair, the poet has never been partial to the confessional or to the open-heart surgery of the self. Although he may understandably have yearned for such solipsistic indulgences, a basic severity of taste and, perhaps, an Eliotian sense of the rightness of the impersonal have served to keep his truths "slant" in precisely the way Emily Dickinson meant when she advised, "Tell all the truth, but tell it slant."

In an extraordinary poem, "Charwoman," the poet appropriates the figure of a charwoman at her repetitive and lonely task and finds it the perfect analogue for his own sense of waste and impotence in the world, of life as "a rote erasure in the night." How unredeemable things seem is underscored by light which falls and a stairwell which falls. All either waits "on the shaftway for my own descent" or flings "the day's drowned faces out" in a disequilibrium of despair occasioned not only by the pathos of human wretchedness but by an implicit comparison between the trembling and waning arcs of the scrubwoman's ineffectual rite of purification and those of poetry itself. The poem gives us the first in a series of "sorrowing women" (see "Another Sorrowing Woman," "The Lives of Mrs. Gale," "The Orphaning"), exploring an almost obsessive imagery of stairways, precipices, gorges, elevators, wells, ladders, pits, to delineate ascents and descents of mood in a perspective that underlies not only very recent poems like "Soundings," but an older necessity to praise in the face of what he calls "a causeless occasion." This desire, not only to penetrate the causes of "the innocent anguish in the heel," but to find release from it is strangely and movingly enacted in the youthful "Festival," where Belitt writes: "When the spirit could not bear/ The desperate season of the snare,/It dropped the indifferent body there." At the end of the poem, which works itself out in the rhythms of the primitive, dedicatory dance, we have "Till, where the sinister wonder trod,/Falcon-footed, feather-shod, Body found itself a god." Body and spirit: the poet early foresees these as divisive, the profane engaging the sacred in a habitual "contest of angels," tempting the man from the "wilderness stair" to serve some high and arduous calling in a dedication both to the "sinister wonder" of which the wild spirit of poetry is made, and severities of form which shape the ritual poem itself.

If loss, and particularly loss of love, is a constant motif in the early poems, a poignant alliance with mythic or spiritual fathers is another. Presumably, all young poets ally themselves imaginatively with older poets for the grace, luck and hope such linkings offer. One of Belitt's "fathers" and myth-makers is Dostoevski, whose imagination and work he enters with the same familiarity and gusto that Milton reserved for the landscape of Genesis. In a poem such as "Smerdyakov with a Guitar," which takes its title from a chapter heading in *The Brothers Karamazov*, the poet as epilept turns against his own father, evoking him in all the details of his corruptibility, and expresses a conspiratorial wish to murder him, a wish that is both actual and mythic as the epigraph, "Who doesn't wish his father dead?" suggests. He would murder him as sire, as haunter of memory, as symbol of the inherited nature of his own imperfections. However, the mother, who is surely his own as well as Dostoevski's Stinking Lizaveta or the poet's Muse, forbids parricide and enjoins honor. It is in this sense that the poet can obey and attempt to celebrate life even in its most fallen state and reverse the murderousness and obscenity of the world. Inhabiting the epilept's dream, using the parable as a crystal through which to look into the abysses of his past, employing the only means at his disposal, a "jawbone on a melon rind," the poet can "bow to his father and sing."

Another of Belitt's myth-makers, certainly, is Keats. At the risk of devoting too much space to these early poems, I should like to look briefly at "John Keats: Surgeon." It is, in ways which I shall try to indicate, an ancestral poem.

> "No, no; go not to Lethe . . ."
> Is not the level shine of steel
> Honed to the littleness of hair
> Sufficient implement to deal
> A stroke to lay the spirit bare?
>
> The hurt lies not so recondite
> As point may drive, or probe explore—
> Yet, though the blade drink long or light,
> The fever kindles as before.
>
> It nothing augurs that the hand
> Hew the division deep enough:

The sutures, though they tremble, stand,
And cast the kindly unguent off.

Mere were a juggler's fraud, at best:
To mitigate the lesser ill
And leave, like an unriddled jest,
The ruined heartbeat ailing still.

Is there a stranger provender
To get the ravaged part its peace—
Wolfsbane, aloe? Mandrake? Myrrh?

No, no; not these . . .

At the level of a first reading, this promises to be a simple poem; simple in the sense that if one is familiar with the life of Keats — knows that he studied surgery before dedicating himself to poetry — if one recognizes the epigraph as the opening line of the "Ode on Melancholy," one feels the necessary history and field of allusion lie readily at hand. Yet, further readings force one to readjust one's purchase and multiply the contexts uneasily. Who is speaking? When? Presumably, the poem stands as a fictive preface to the whole body of poetry of both John Keats and Ben Belitt. The first stanza is framed as a question to which the response of the reader, like that of the persona of the poem and his imaginer, is negative. (Belitt's interest in metal "honed to the littleness of hair," in instruments capable of meticulous distinction and penetration, will reappear continuously in his later work.) Abruptly, the tone shifts from one of reflection to one of bitterness. The mode of approach is reassessed as "a juggler's fraud" and the poet wonders, prophetically, if there might be a "stranger provender" than surgery. Like Keats, he rejects the poisonous balms and mithridates traditionally associated with death and healing; these are not applicable to the disease in question which is nothing less than the malaise of poetry itself, whose way is to intensify rather than to soothe or anesthetize. The real answer lies, by extension, in Keats's own ode, not only in the general sense that poetry itself is the proper instrument to "lay the spirit bare" but in the particular insight it offers to "get the ravaged part its peace." The tone there is diagnostic. It is a prescription for the location of true melancholy, a description of how to behave in its presence and a prognosis of its cause and effect. For both poets, the states of joy and the abnegation of joy are simultaneous as well as sequential. The effect of such an insight is profoundly consoling; not only does it make of the poetic sensibility something elevated, something to be "among her cloudy trophies hung"; it offers a mode of balance to the mind preoccupied both by beauty and its own dis-ease in a world where beauty is apprehended mainly through its quality of desolating transcience. Keats's paradox will remain to become the organizing center of Belitt's work. The "enemy" is indeed joy because it bears within itself its inimical opposite.

If these early poems are dark, sometimes plaintive, sometimes too hermetic for unriddling, almost always close to the fearful, the poems of Belitt's next two books, *The Enemy Joy* (1964) and *Nowhere But Light* (1970), constitute a fascinating journey both further in and further out. They move upward in paradoxical circuition, if not vertically away from the awesome "void at the sheer of the stair," at least to a distance that puts the dark side of things into new perspective; which is merely another way of saying that Belitt becomes a weightier and more various poet.

The newer poems are everywhere marked by the tangible presence of the spirit of place. Place names serve to set a scene; they invest the subject matter with the sort of specificity a traveler feels who may be unfamiliar with the architecture he is seeing but who knows, at least, that he is in Italy. If places to which we go are often colored by preconception, they also engage our expectation, acumen and surprise in new ways. Thus, during the course of an interview, Belitt remarked of his poem, "Court of the Lions: Alhambra": "I suppose one of my reasons for going to Spain was a search for what, in the poem, I call simplicity. . . . I certainly felt the aloneness of the hermetic writer and I expected that in Spain there would be such a profusion of the rococo that I'd experience surfeit, and there would be some kind of cathartic value in confronting myself with all the intense life of externalized detail." The idea is a moving one: it comes out of a commitment so total that the aesthetics of architecture and ambience directly affect the writer's whole style and poetics; it touches on that mysterious nexus where life and art are one.

Places have transforming as well as locative properties. We go to them for excitement, solace, remembrance. One says, "I am more myself here." The psychology of place is inexhaustible and Belitt feels this with all the yearning and attention of a man and poet who has known alienation and deracination intimately. The more intimately he can imagine a place, be it house, bog, graveyard, pond, the more deeply he is embodied in the world, its artifacts and processes. This is not to imply that he pictures them in any naturalistic or representational manner; rather, he draws on them to open up and corporealize ideas and thrusts of thought that might otherwise seem abstract. He also turns places into antagonists or makes of them a kind of geographical oxymoron. A location to Belitt is definable not only in terms of itself and all the approximations it offers, but in contrast with other places, usually different, distant, capable of drawing the sensibility toward speculations that are somehow generic. The "heres and theres" of Belitt's cosmology are multiple. Thus, Mexico and Vermont stand as two distinct compass points on the poet's map. One is northern, cold, austere, pure; the other is southern, hot, primitive, luxuriant, erotic. If the southern latitude often represents all that might be connected with the "wild," the northern speaks of everything "severe." (Such a delineation is more expedient than substantive, of course; the Mexican poems are autonomous and rely for structure on a spatial metaphor akin to Dante's, with a nether, middle and upper world which Belitt employs brilliantly to scaffold the descents and ascents he makes from one ground level to the next.)

What I mean by a geographical oxymoron is illustrated surreally in "Siesta: Mexico/Vermont." It is both about place and about stance. Through dream, which "delivers us blindfold to our upper and nether senses," the poet turns into an antipodal man whose divine power is that of synthesis. "While the antipodal man/turns heavily in mid-air,/locking his flying footsoles above and below,/ enters the horizon's double ring, the tropic/and polar fires — an icicle in Vermont/rayed like Guadalupe's mantle, the frost/on the machete's edge — head downward and head/upward, king of the playing-cards,/ who sleeps in the slalom's angle with the Mexican." A strategy for making one place or one stance out of opposites has been ingeniously imagined. Indeed, one senses throughout these poems a search for some perfection of place, some destination so total that all places might become one. This almost cartographical triangulation of desire is another aspect of the quest for simplicity and integrity; yet, the impossibility of such a quest is already projected in an earlier poem, "Cricket Hill," with its terrifying epigraph, "Place there is none; we go backwards and forwards and there is no place." A decade later, as if in unwilling admission of the heart's placelessness, Belitt entitles his fourth book *Nowhere But Light.*

As any reader may note,* Belitt is not only compelled by the min-

*See Howard Nemerov's fine essay on Belitt, "The Fascination of What's Difficult" in *Reflections on Poetry and Poetics* (Rutgers, 1972).

erals and rocks which make up the earth's substratum and those rockish qualities of hardness, obduracy, opacity, endurance; he is uniquely in love with light. Verbs like dazzle, burn, glint, blaze, everywhere illuminate this love. All poems, of course, are attempts at clarification. However, Belitt's obsession is that of the camera man who calls persistently for "more light" to blacken the negative of a film on the subject of radiation. It is the source and emblem of energy in precisely the sense in which Blake, another of Belitt's myth-makers, used it. In one of his finest and starkest poems, "The Light-ning Rod Man," lightning is the focus and organizing principle; it penetrates through layers of time and memory, uniting act with act, like some explosive Proustian madeleine. What we have here is no series of chronological additions that build vertically; it is a series of exposures engendered by lightning in the act of striking. Striking has always been one of Belitt's metaphors for the way the mind and heart are acted upon, the way in which the imagination is quite literally galvanized into perception. Here, it forces him back to a catastrophic point in his childhood where he must confront the guilt of a sexual encounter between man and boy to find the image of his father seen "smashing clothes in a pressing machine." While the reappearance of the father remains mysterious, if not actually incestuous, it is as inevitable as the meeting with the lions at the center of the labyrinth in the poet's vision of the Alhambra and stands as some initial and monumental cause of all his own vulnerability. The final section, entitled "A View of Toledo," I quote in full:

What does the lightning intend?
                    The wish is beneficent, surely,
that bends toward such brightness to show us the shape of our terror
or works in a cloud on a city's unpeopled perspectives—
not with the dark and the light of a sun-dial's graduations, but purely,
in pumice and hurricane, all at once, like a landscape of knives.
As once in Toledo:
                    a Greek at a burial, coming nearer,
struck at the shroud of Count Orgaz, found the eschatalogical greens
in the rust of a cardinal's cape, the gold of the surplice's
threads, rolled back the stone of his eyeballs
in place of the skulls, and shewed us the bread of our lives.

Here, clarity is equated with purity—whatever it is that permits us to place our terrors in perspective, beyond all distortions of moral-ity, as once El Greco's eye penetrated the burial of Count Orgaz (and what a stunning coincidence that name must have offered the poet) and created something vital out of death. Like light, the artist's vision "strikes through the mask" and clarifies not only what it beholds but the very process of the making of meaning.

In singling out *Nowhere But Light* to see how its poems might resemble or differ from earlier work, I am immediately aware of a new set of inflections in the poet's voice. The voice expresses itself in two modes: the first and more familiar is essentially epithalamial, elegiac; the second and unfamiliar is marked by a new black humor which might be called, with a not-appropriate wildness, the Locoesque, or absurd, as though the pathological madness of Smerdyakov had found shelter at last in the "abjectly ridiculous." Both approaches conduce to a serenity and an acceptance of things manifest in the poet's repeated assertions, "All is well with me, Mother"; or "Love is content with that"; or "The spirit is willing"; or "It is well; it is well." Both "bow to the father and sing."

This is not to suggest that Belitt has stumbled on any easy answers to the questions that have continuously beset him. Like Pablo Neruda, he is a poet who purports to shrug off all fictions of solution. Also, like Machado, to whom he dedicates "Fat Tuesday," he prides himself on celebrating the "stubborn heterogeneity of things" — which is to say that he is a devout pluralist, interested always in the diversity and disjunction of things. Of course, to say that any poet is a pluralist is a contradiction in terms, for by the very nature of the form they espouse, all accomplished poems serve the cause of monism. However, formal resolution and positional solutions are not necessarily synonymous.

One way to approach the problem unproblematically (a way prefigured by the "antipodal man") would be to recall Keats's definition of Negative Capability; "that is, when man is capable of being in uncertainties, Mysteries, doubts without any irritable reaching after fact and Reason." Another would be to take a page out of William James's diary, where, after musing on the question of good and evil, he asks: "Can one with full knowledge and sincerity ever bring himself so to sympathize with the total process of the universe as to heartily assent to the evils that seem inherent in its details? If so, optimism is possible." He goes on to speculate that if one cannot assent to such a diminishing of evil, the only possibility left one is pessimism. Thirdly, he continues, "if a divided universe be a conception possible for his intellect to rest in, and at the same time he have the vigor of will to look universal death in the face without blinking, he can live the life of meliorism." That notion — of the ability to achieve rest or poise in the midst of tense and unresolvable fact — is not dissimilar to the effect produced by a close reading of these poems. The epigraph of "The Gorge," "Out of this nettle, danger, we pluck this flower, safety," describes exactly the psychological direction of the whole book. A brief look at parts three and five of the poem will elucidate both the presence and the humors of what I have called "the Loco-esque."

The Loco-bird, "the bird of the abjectly ridiculous," enters our awareness like a clown stumbled into the solemnities of a mass. A raspberry-blowing Woody Woodpecker, he sails over the Gorge with its established "kingdoms of ordure," its purgatorial middle, its twin peaks where "the condor imagines perfection," but he does not see them humanly. To imagine his unimaginable, uncaring point of view is enough to make the poet admit that such a stance undoes his own habitual attention to "portents and sounds from down under." Because "unawed by obliquity" (a Belittian synonym for reality), "all's one to him." A dewdrop equals a turd. The Loco-bird is indeed a very anti-self for this poet and one's delight in the presence of outrageous humor stems partially from a novelty so unexpected. The "portents," of course, are *there,* and suggest that we live in a world where nothing means or conduces to meaning; it is the existential view which treats life itself as absurd: "the bird in the tulipan tree has no answers." Perhaps the comic deflection of the tragic is the only possible equation for balance left us, a modern version of despairing meliorism.

The same risky, cartoon-haunted tone announces the final poem in the series, "Gayosso Ambulance Service: Emergency." "Feet last,/ on Gayosso's tea-caddy for corpses/and convalescents/all seemed an / 'Emergency.'" The quality of danger is comically underlined in the parable of a traveler's frantic ride toward the hospital. "The idea of non-being" impels his imagination, makes itself an attractive destination, and all takes on the flickering histrionics of a race against time. The moment is externalized in Belitt's favorite cinematographic manner: "All tripped like a lens and a shutter/on the flare of a moment and spoke for the traveler;/'Urgent'!" Then, in a shift like a turn for the better, he asks himself, "Urgent?/ And what of the fraud of that 'safety'?" If the propulsion toward death is fraudulent, so is the race toward salvation. Urgency implies vital importance. Just as the search becomes one for a less melodramatic perspective, the poet marvelously evokes a figure reminiscent of Harold Lloyd in a movie that might well have supplied the basic metaphor of this poem: "Safety Last." "One walks as one can/on the vertical/planes of the windows like ties on a trestle,/looking fifty flights down to a dumb-show of/Stock Exchange runners; one slips/toward the tooth of the buzz-saw/while the freight cars bear downward from Toonerville,/sparkling with danger." To take on the viewpoint of the clown, to draw the scene in the imagery of the cartoon and the comedy is a mode of diminishing hazard and panic. Then, as if the comic view were no longer viable, as if fever had returned to normal, the poet returns to his rented "cut in the gorge" to testify that "one endures the precarious." Belitt's insight here is reminiscent of Yeats's in "Lapis Lazuli"where he asserts that even if Hamlet and Lear know the curtain will fall, that they are playing in a tragedy, the total effect must be a comic one: they must act with the gaiety of those not in the know. That is the stance the poet accepts here, seriously, I think, at the same time that he admits that "Always,/Gayosso's 'emergency' rides on the scream/of a moment:" that the "equilibrist falters,/shocked by his personal hazard." If hazard is necessary to our sense of vitality, to keeping ourselves alive in all senses of that word, its mutual term, safety, inheres in distance, in tricks of per-spective, in proper metaphors, in an artistry of balance which may well be synonymous with our own sanity. At the same time as one attends to the personal, the ear must hear "an equivocal thrashing of bamboo and manure and papyrus,/neither pure nor impure; the spirit/that works in the middle/stark under the sun-stone/in the mash of the upper and nether." That simultaneous taking in of the personal and impersonal, of the subjective and the objective and the acceptance of the mysterious or "equivocal," is what permits the voice to affirm, "It is well. It is well." We have, then, both the Jamesian stance and another version of the Keatsian insight — that mutuality and co-existence of opposites which do not abrogate the rightness of either but allow a certain, if momentary, coming to rest.

As I have said, the lyric mode is sung in two keys, that of the elegy and that of the epithalamium. The elegiac tone is hardly new to Belitt, but here it is employed with specific consciousness, as in "Papermill Graveyard" and "The Stone Mason's Funeral." Although too long to examine in the detail which it deserves, Belitt's extra-ordinary poem, "The Orphaning," is the inevitable exemplum of the commemorative and combines a funeral and marriage song in one. An avowedly autobiographical piece, it records the historical and ontological journey into and out of the stages in his rebellion against and acceptance of an "orphaning." Through its process, he understands and celebrates not only the death of someone he has loved, his mother, but of someone he has obsessively blamed and hated, his father. By placing him in the docks of his poems, accusing him, wooing him, vilifying him, symbolically baiting and murdering him, he can finally forgive him posthumously — "A stone in the grave of his mouth moves/and he cries from the grave-clout: *Father!*/and forgives him his dying, who knew not what he did " — and elevate him through identification with mythic fathers such as Karamazov and God himself. The reader both watches and becomes the poet who takes to himself gladly the conditions of his own past and contrives, through all the subterfuges of art yet without guilt or self-interest, to make peace with his own identity. The poem stands in Belitt's work as a kind of Wordsworthian *Prelude* in which trauma and self-doubt take the place of the beautiful or noble forms of nature and enacts that difficult and restorative emergence "out of the ways of falsehood, into what, for him, were the ways of truth."

I had intended to call Belitt's "The Orange Tree" a pure example of the epithalamium. Yet, that term is inexact. Perhaps it can only be called a prayer. If many of his poems attract us as elegant problems, "The Orange Tree" must be approached in altogether different terms.*

> To be
> intact and unseen,
> like the orange's scent
> in the orange tree:
>
> a pod of aroma
> on the orange's ogive of green
> or a phosphorus voice
> in the storm of the forge and the hammer:
>
> to climb up a ladder of leaven
> and salt, and work in the lump
> of the mass, upward and down
> in the volatile oils of a wilderness heaven:
>
> to sleep, like the karat,
> in the void of the jeweler's glass,
> yet strike with the weight of the diamond—
> perhaps that is to live in the spirit.

*For a fine, detailed analysis of "The Orange Tree," see Robert Boyers's "To Confront Nullity: The Poetry of Ben Belitt," *Sewanee Review,* Fall, 1973.

So the orange tree
waits on its stump as the wood of its armature
multiplies: first, the branch, then the twig in the thicket
of leafage, then the sunburst of white in the leaves, the odor's epiphany.

All burns with a mineral
heat, all hones an invisible edge on the noonday, while the orange's scent
speaks from the tree in the tree to declare what the holocaust meant:
to be minimal,

minimal: to diminish excess, to pare it
as a child pares an orange, moving the knife through the peel
in a spiral's unbroken descent, till only the orange's sweat,
a bead of acidulous essence, divides the rind from the steel:

perhaps that is to live in the spirit.

One is advisedly reticent to use the rhetoric of religion to describe poetry; yet here, one witnesses what can only be called an act of consecration. While the poem is certainly an *ars poetica,* a description not only of how the artist aspires to his art, about how poems grow and aspire to speak of their meaning, it is, if inadvertently, more universal and hortatory than that. It recreates, I think, the religious attitude we all have at some time in our lives to the object of our love, a love that is necessarily distant, above one and difficult to aspire to, be it deity, human or the heart's irreversible desire. When that object has attained the magnitude of an all-consuming teleology, our mode of approach is singularly and exactingly simplified, just as the penitential strategy is to the supplicant or the rigors of chivalry to the knight. So, here, the language and style are charged with the piety appropriate to the devout prefigurations of the poet. From its inception, the poem compounds its tensions, not with the dramatics of a sudden "strike" and an answering revelation or release, but in the unobtrusive architecture of a prayer in which no word or modulation of feeling can be spared. James describes his own halting sense of what it is to be in the presence of some mystical significance in similar terms: "The keynote of it is invariably *reconciliation.* It is as if the opposites of the world, whose contradictoriness and conflict make all our difficulties and troubles, were melted into unity. Not only do they, as contrasted species, belong to one and the same genus, but one of the species, the nobler and better one, is itself the genus and so soaks up and absorbs its opposite into itself."

That quest for unity, simplicity and purity which we have noted throughout is re-enacted here in an all-encompassing paradox: through growth, through the process of some mysterious flowering out, one can be "minimal," can "dimish excess" and "pare it." It was

the whim of Pablo Neruda, who said, "The poet's heart is an inter-
minable artichoke"; it was the wish of Thoreau who would keep his
whole record of Walden on his thumbnail; it was the need of the
medieval monk, Guigo, whose prayers were filled with the resolve to
peel away from himself all his skins, like those of an onion, in the
hope that he might eventually reach some essence that was finally
irreducible. That longing, to weld our divided selves into one, to be
joined with our highest self, is the search for the integrity of poet with
poem of which Milton spoke. It is the artist's viaticum for the
journey into and dream of reconciliation with art. If such a thing
as pure poetry exists, we are in its presence here.

In the light of my own predilection for the transcendental, "The
Orange Tree" offers a convenient termination to these reflections.
However, there is an epilog demanded by the chronology which has
overseen them. I should like to examine a long poem, written approximately two years ago, and published in *The New Yorker* a year later.
If the direction of *Nowhere But Light* tended toward a reconciliation
with past, present and future, to find consolations in the face of
nullity, "Soundings: Block Island" recoils from and contradicts that
drift, as if prophetically fulfilling the figure of ascent and descent
which obsessed the earlier work. Beatific visions are brief, and if they
constitute the "joy" of which Keats speaks, their evanescence leaves
a deeper sense of its having bid the beholder "adieu." It is that depth
which this poem explores.

SOUNDINGS: BLOCK ISLAND
(For Pablo Neruda)

1

The sea closes like a plum
on its stone. It will presently fall.
Halfway toward Newton's head,

it shows a nap of numbers,
rosettes for the navigator
under the mariner's glass, a gooseflesh of soundings—

a flat map where gulls enter
reading the fine print in tawny aquarelle. Later,
that ripping of edges

at the Lighthouse's base, a pounding
of tumblers and bells in the coarse salt,
the reef in its necklace of skulls.

2

Whales work. A swan leading its cindery cygnets
sees transparently down
to the center: Alice's tears, the nausea of Rimbaud,

green gall and spittle
to pucker the sea floor, constellate
polyps in the flinty asparagus,

the unsuffocating flora
where the diver's heart explodes
in cross-threads of mica and the sardine throbs like a hummingbird—

all the bright business of darkness
I would read in the charred scrolls, the double pillars
of vellum, crossing with chariots, like Torah.

3

The parachutists lie where they have fallen
on mandalas of terry cloth. The sea has cast
them up like anemones, split prismatic canvas

in spinnakers of beach umbrellas. A sound
of drowned transistors, gull's claws in the froth,
a lifeguard's whistle, the breathing of pontoons,

hisses through the noon's bicarbonation.
Light hardens the facets; but there in the sleeper's
eye, the glacial emulsions of a camera,

sight keeps its core of darkness—
an apple halved, and, in the satin pockets, point
touching point, like Indian paisley, the seed-shaped tears.

4

What holds the eye to its salt, Orphean
lookers-back, Sodomites, ruminants
licking a briny meniscus—

what? The pastures of plankton,
coffined nerve gas, sarcophagi
lifted like thistle three miles under,

are not as inland meadows are. There,
green goes aerial, drives star over star through the chicory,
stays nowhere, asks nothing of the malcontent—but here?

Something unappeasable
in the blond marination of whips, melancholy
bearing night in its bile: an expectation of black.

5

Failures! The thunderheads of bracken
rise over minefields, the sea burns
like a slum, sends arabesques of oil

on all my summer salvage:
young losses, nightmares, a kneecap smashed
or a back, forfeiture of sons,

the wild severity of poems,
the mouth's sanctuary, the Mona Lisa smile
of adolescent bellies sloping toward their sex,

drowned fathers, photographs, translations
in the middle kingdom of the languages—
fog, foam, hallucinated form.

6

Noah's drunken dream: the animals in twos,
delineated water, rainbows. Fog works in the mummy cloths;
the sandspit goes, in its spiral nebulae of boulders,

the millrace of the upper air, flying
iodine, the binnacle's
mathematics, battlefields of bathers,

the Pharaonic sun that calcifies the beaches
and cuts the swimmer's diamond in the sand,
the light dividing water from the land,

matter, motion, mind—all goes to bandages,
equinoctial steam. The floating bobbins empty,
bearing the corpse of darkness toward the ocean.

7

Block Island, Black Island; Pablo, Prospero—
how utterly the landmarks tarnish!
Our "residence on earth" shows spiracles,

watery torches, sharks' fins, the purgatorial jaw
of Jonah's disobedience. It is time
for the breaking of wands and books.

The rose-hip looses
its petal on the blackberry's dagger
under the certain apparition of a ship,

and I enter the desolating soda
again, taking the whole weight of the sun upon my skin
to drive the darkness in.

To effect maximum depth, poets require an abyss; we have that
here in the sea, plus an island and a sky. As his unfathomably beautiful and disturbing chapter on the whiteness of the whale was Melville's ground for meditation on the absences that occasion dread,
so Belitt's poem approaches that condition through scrupulous attention to surfaces, darkness and depths. The intention seems not so
much to discover particularities as those analogies and resonances
which surface when the memory and imagination are fortuitously
and mysteriously yoked and startled into motion by a landscape that
is itself like another level of language.

The first stanza involves a crossing, a literal one in a boat, and the
reading of a map, flat and tangible as the sea is deep and intangible,
on which navigators confront themselves with signals which stand
for danger; "a gooseflesh of soundings." That "whales work" under
the surfaces, tugs our awareness toward that Biblical or Melvillian
world of subterranean perspective, of the transparencies of art, in
which literary allusions will work as directly as personal experience
itself. The poet is led to remember that after her trip down the

rabbit-hole, Alice fell into a pool of her own tears; that in "Bateau Ivre," Rimbaud represented the sea as the "Poème de la Mer" in which one encountered one's own drunken nausea. Through these images rise visions of the sea's depths seen, like Gethsemane, as both a garden of death and a place of equivocal transformations. Both sea and map are likened to a Dead Sea Scroll which might be parted to illumine the past, to show us those who are to be delivered and those who are to be overwhelmed.

The subsequent shift is to the beach, that latter-day "temple of delight" for vacationers where, in spite of all the paraphernalia of holiday and innocent good weather, the barometer continues to fall. All hisses with the sibilance of warning and inside the sleeper's eye, literally blackened by the sun, darkness of sight is pictured in one of the most astonishing and perfect metaphors of which I know: "An apple halved, and, in the satin pockets, point/touching point, like Indian paisley, the seed-shaped tears." As the sea closed "a plum on its stone," sight is likened to that first forbidden fruit whose fall has traditionally represented to the mind the cause of its own Edenic rejection, and is thereafter translated by Belitt into the mathematics of Newtonian physics.

The memory, as if in some mythic flashback, seeks out images of other tragic "lookers-back": Orpheus and Lot. That all such meditators are named "ruminants," suggests that there is something as biologically necessitous in the process as that which compels the animal to the salt-lick. Why do we turn back to look at past anguish? The answer, distilled like salt itself, is marinated out of a comparison between the sunken pastures (and *past* is certainly an intended inflection here) of the sea with its "coffined nerve gas," where all is imagined "as through a glass, darkly," and inland pastures which ask "nothing of the malcontent." As the pastoral mode has been used to witness what is gay, natural, innocent, so the "pastures of plankton" of the underwater scene is the appropriate one for the sounding of desolation. There, as the poet recognizes, exists "something unappeasable." One is somehow brought to a remembrance of Keats's "Sonnet to Homer." As if in some imperative denial of the lines, "Aye, on the shore of darkness there is light/and precipices show untrodden green;/There is a budding morrow in midnight, —/There is a triple sight in blindness keen ", Belitt can only attest that he sees "melancholy bearing night in its bile: an expectation of black."

Stanza five is the true nadir of the poem. Here, the poet finds his own equivalences for the location of melancholy. They consist of his "failures," or, as Georges Guy has wittily translated that word into French, "Echec!": the master-chessman's term for the move which compels absolute forfeit. The poet names them explicitly. They are the ones which readers of Belitt's poetry will recognize with that shock that makes the "strange familiar, the familiar strange." They are the reasons of the artist who has been driven to retreat from the violations of life into the presumably inviolate exile of his art, who then turns on his own asceticism as if it were only one more imperfect subterfuge. There is an oblique progression linking wound with cure. From his "young losses" followed "nightmare," or the mind's cunning reordering of experience; as if from actual physical wounds came his own "forfeiture of sons"; both the "mouth's sanctuary" and "the wild severity of poems" seem sublimations of energy rather than creative acts, just as do the repeated drownings of his fathers, whereby they suffer the redeeming sea-change of art. His concern with photographs and translations is viewed as yet another instance of tricky subversion, of interest in the imitation rather than the reality. Such a perspective looks down on and into art and treats it as "hallucinated form." In this stanza, we have not only the actual autobiographical matters that "work" in the poet but those that have been worked by him obsessively into his poetry. Our terror comes not only from the ruthless telling of such human truths but in beholding the artist brought to bay by his art. One thinks of Rimbaud's historic repudiation of poetry and wonders if one is witnessing a similar intent here.

The final stanzas, while they are as enciphered as any, cast up enough clues for the reader not to be left totally at sea. As if reaching for some solid, the poet recalls order as it was envisioned by another drunken sailor of the world's deluge: Noah. Perhaps it is only in such dreams, in intoxicated fictions, in the wholeness of beliefs no longer believable, that order can exist. Fog works in the poem to suggest both the literal blurring and the ambiguity and inchoateness of all things. It is the same fog which will turn all recollection of hard, delineated forms into "equinoctial steam." That it bears the "corpse of darkness toward the ocean," rather than pledging a return to clarity or any restorative solution, only maximizes the mystery and majesty of original Darkness or the disappearance of all knowable things. All comes to what, in another late poem, Belitt will call "the salt comedy of unknowing."

Finally, the poem addresses itself to Pablo Neruda, the poet whose work Belitt has so finely translated. Neruda, too, inhabits an island refuge — Isla Negra — and has submerged himself in the same watery brooding enacted here; has found that the sea, rather than the land, was the right place to search for ways to read the ineffable. Block Island and Black Island become one. Like Pablo, like Prospero whose farewell to "rough magic" reads, "I'll break my staff/Bury it certain fathoms in the earth/And deeper than did ever plummet sound/I'll drown my book," Belitt takes to himself not only the end of the illusion of form but surrenders the very premise of meaning itself. The modern consciousness which has heard so much and, perhaps, felt so profoundly that despair against which no stance is ever proof, takes the insight in, just as the poet will "drive the darkness in."

Yet, inevitably, the final stanza acts to gather up, antipodally, the floating oppositions of the poem; hence, the "certain apparition of a ship," which, like the poet, will enter "the desolating soda," that encaustic element basic to tears and salt in which the poem is immersed. The final lines take one back again to the "Ode on Melancholy." As Keats insists that it is in the "very temple of Delight/Veil'd Melancholy has her sovran shrine," so this poem is conceived at midday in an atmosphere of maximum clarity and "bicarbonation" and so this poet takes "the whole weight of the sun," the full awareness of clarity, energy and joy upon his skin in order to drive the darkness not out, but in.

This is certainly the most unflinching and powerful poem in Belitt's whole work. It is a voyage into darkness and failure but, of course, whatever the poet intends, it is a voyage out of it too. The very act of poetic imagination embodied in the poem itself transcends its self-denials and triumphs over them. Although one cannot overlook the distance between "The Orange Tree" and "Soundings" — one turns prayerfully toward art while the other seems on the verge of abandoning it — "Soundings" constructs something on which to rejoice and leaves us with that beauty which Kenneth Burke defines as "the term we apply to the poet's success in evoking our emotion," and that ultimately unrefractable delight in the assembling genius and integrity of the poetic mind.

Similarly, Belitt has forged, out of his own sense of the contradictory and unresolvable, a cosmology and its attendant iconography.

The poet's longing for purity and perfection involves itself providentially in what has traditionally been called impure, the excremental, the erotic; his sense of betrayal and alienation in a complex creation of fathers, mothers and sons; his radical displacement in the loving construction of place. His acute awareness of hazard directs him into strategical modes of balance and self-preservation, and his disbelief in the possibilities of solutions is consistently undone by the upsurge of disparate detail into one design. The permutations are manifold and they work, like Penelope at her vital weaving, both away from and toward fruition. Her act, like that of all poets, is performed in the trust and the hope that it will put off danger in the imminence of some dreamed-of return and reconciliation. In that same hope, Belitt achieves the goal of the poet who "ought himselfe to bee a true Poem."

To the Roots:
An Interview with Galway Kinnell

INTERVIEWER: JAMES J. MCKENZIE

Q: *This is your sixth poetry reading in as many days, and you have three more to go. In spite of the obvious rigors of such an experience, do you enjoy reading on a poetry circuit?*

KINNELL: Well, I enjoy it if I'm feeling well and feeling up to reading. I have learned to be careful on these trips — I go to bed early, don't drink, play tennis when I can, and don't eat much. I bring work with me and try to get in two or three hours of work each day. And then, somehow — it seems O.K. to read. I used to get exhausted on tours, and sometimes I'd loathe the prospect of reading poems, get sick of the poems, feel indifferent to the people I was reading to.

Q: *Do you feel that reading poetry in public helps you with your poetry in any way?*

KINNELL: I'm not sure. I notice when I'm reading that there are certain lines I don't feel like reading; something is wrong with them that I hadn't realized until I had to say them aloud. But that happens so seldom it hardly justifies wandering over the country for a long time. There's something else, though. Writing poems is a solitary occupation. You send poems out and maybe they appear in a magazine or in a book, and that's all you know about them. A poetry reading is the one time that you come face to face with people who respond to them.

Q: *Do you ever get feed-back from someone in the audience, or maybe talk to someone afterward who helps you to change a poem? Or don't you pay any attention to such things?*

KINNELL: No, that doesn't make me change a poem. But it might affect the way I feel about my poetry. Sometimes it happens — last night it happened after the Moorhead reading — a girl came up choked with emotion and just put her arms around me and hugged me, then she burst into tears and fled.

Q: *Would you say there is something different, then, between reading it aloud to a couple of friends, perhaps even poets, whom you normally read things to, and reading it to an audience?*

KINNELL: Yes. Your friends, after all, know you, and know your previous work. They wouldn't be asking you to read the poems unless they already liked the poems. It's a little different to touch a stranger.

Q: *Do you often send poems off to friends around the country for criticisms and suggestions before you reach the final version of the poem?*

KINNELL: Yes, often; though I do it less now. There are three or four people I send poems to. Sometimes they make suggestions for cutting out things. I've never found my alter ego, however, the person I could absolutely rely on. I guess nobody does. But often the suggestions help.

Q: *Do you write, then, for an ideal reader, for an alter ego?*

KINNELL: Well, yes, I write for an alter ego — for myself, I suppose.

Q: *Are there people to whom you send your poems sometimes who are not themselves successful poets?*

KINNELL: Yes.

Q: *Would they be friends?*

KINNELL: Friends.

Q: *Are they people who don't even try to write poetry but whose suggestions you nevertheless value and that are helpful to you?*

KINNELL: Well, I don't know that there's any friend I send poems to like that other than my wife. She has never put pen to paper except for practical purposes, but she often has valuable reactions.

Q.: *Do you pay attention to written responses to your books, such as reviews of them as they come out?*

KINNELL: I would *like* to pay attention to them. Unfortunately, in the space of a review it's hard for anyone to say anything truly helpful. The few long articles that have been published on my poems — while they have been interesting, haven't approached the poems in the way that I approach them, so that whatever they have said hasn't helped much either.

Q: *Would you care to cite any examples of articles that approach your poetry in such a different way that it's of little use to you?*

KINNELL: Well, Richard Howard has an article in *Alone with*

America. It is a rather eloquent article about the use of fire imagery in my poetry, but there's no way that I can use that perception — I can't think, "Well, now I'm going to put in more flames. . . ."

Q: *Or less flames.*

KINNELL: Or "less flames," on account of it.

Q: *You see your poems in a totally different way than he does. Could you talk a little about how a poem typically begins with you — or isn't there any typical beginning?*

KINNELL: There isn't any typical way. There are at least three ways that I can at the moment think that poems have started. One is through some experience from which I found words suddenly coming to my tongue. Another is when words appear without forewarning. And another is when I've conceived of a poem without any words at all — just the idea of what it might be.

Q: *Could you talk about the genesis of a specific poem; perhaps how, say, the poem "The Bear" or "Another Night in the Ruins" began?*

KINNELL: "The Bear" had a prolonged history. Somebody once told me the story of how Eskimos hunted for bears. I guess he had read it in a book, but over the course of a few months I forgot who had told me and I imagined it was told me by someone who had actually hunted with the Eskimos. In any case the story stuck with me for a long time, particularly because of that detail, that the hunter was obliged to eat the bear's turds, to be nourished by the blood in them, as he pursued the bear. It stuck with me (I generally forget most stories). Perhaps a year later, I was in Alabama and heard some rather shattering news and was rather broken up personally. Also, I was staying with some black people and felt all the more keenly the crude and racist world they confronted. The combination, anyway, caused me to be unable to sleep. I went all around asking "Does anyone have a sleeping pill?" No one had a sleeping pill. I tried to sleep and I couldn't. So I got up and suddenly the story of the bear hunt came to my mind. I wrote off the poem that night.

Q: *The whole poem?*

KINNELL: The whole poem. However, the last part of it was different from the way it turned out to be, finally. I ran into a typist a few weeks ago who had worked for me about that time. She showed me a copy of the manuscript of *Body Rags* she had typed up. I looked at "The Bear" and I could not recognize the last third of it. I spent a lot of time revising that poem.

Q: *Could you tell us about the genesis of a poem that's quite differ-*

ent from "The Bear" in that it doesn't seem to have a narrative sequence, "Another Night in the Ruins."

KINNELL: Well, I had bought an old ruined house in Vermont. It didn't have any windows or doors and the roof was falling in. I went up there in winter once—went in on skis, boarded up some windows and I stayed there awhile. One night I stayed up all night and wrote—I wrote rather disconnected little fragments. The seven fragments that finally came together in that poem were among those I wrote in the course of that night. There were others that I discarded.

Q: *But did it begin with a notion of the whole poem?*

KINNELL: No, it didn't begin as a single poem. It just began as pieces.

Q: *Did that poem reach its final stages in that one night?*

KINNELL: No, again I think it was the seventh section which later on I worked on a great deal. It was at least a year later that I finished it.

Q: *I wonder if maybe you could talk a little about the genesis of* The Book of Nightmares. *At what point in your writing with that sequence did you know you were going to do a whole book-length poem? Did you begin with a few poems or did you have a conception of the whole thing from the beginning?*

KINNELL: I began that poem as one whole ten-part sequence. I had been reading the *Duino Elegies* quite a lot. In the Ninth Elegy, Rilke says, in effect: "Don't try to tell the angels about the glory of your feelings, or how splendid your soul is, they know all about that. Tell them something they're more fascinated by, something that you know better than they; tell them about the things of the world." So it came to me to write a poem called "The Things" which would have as its preceptor as well as its model, its historical ancestor, the *Duino Elegies*—a ten-part poem without plot and yet with a close relationship of part to part, and if possible a development from beginning to end. I did write that entire poem while I was living in Seattle. I didn't like it much and threw away probably over half of it. I kept, for example, a part of the poem which is now the third section called "The Shoes of Wandering," and almost all of the "Hen Flower." Then I started again with those fragments to write a new poem, one which moved away from its original conception to be merely about things, and which in fact now probably does try to tell the angels about the glory of my feelings.

Q: *But it started out from the initial conception as a ten-part long poem. Did you have the seven-part divisions of each poem from the beginning also?*

KINNELL: No. But the sections seemed to be coming out that way, so I made them all come out that way. It's clear that some of those poems could have been divided into eight or six parts quite as easily.

Q: *Did you have to labor to finish the ten-part sequence or did it come pretty easily?*

KINNELL: Not easily at all. I worked a long, long time on that poem; four years in all. A lot of time during that four years I worked on it six or eight or ten hours a day, day after day; particularly the year I spent in Spain I worked every day for at least six hours, not writing, of course, all that time, but nevertheless working on it.

Q: *Do you feel that* The Book of Nightmares *represents some kind of a break-through for you, some discovery of a new method or form in which you will now write? Do you think you may, for example, write mostly in long sequences now?*

KINNELL: From the beginning the long poem has always been more interesting to me than the short poem. Even when I was in college I was writing long poems. While this is certainly longer than anything I ever wrote, in length at least it's not really different from the others — from the "Avenue C" poem, for example. And yet it was a breakthrough of another kind — I felt in this poem free to say *everything*, to relate all areas of my life. As for its being the kind of poem I shall write in the future, I don't know, I doubt it, I just have to see what happens. Since writing *The Book of Nightmares* I have written very little — just a few very short poems, though I have in my mind another long poem.

Q: *This is a conception that you haven't started to flesh out yet?*

KINNELL: Yes.

Q: *Would you care to talk about that at all?*

KINNELL: I don't think so, no.

Q: *There's one thing about* The Book of Nightmares *that may be a very minor question but it has intrigued me since I first saw the volume, and that is the illustrations. I wonder if maybe you did them yourself?*

KINNELL: I wish I had. No, they're taken mostly from various 17th-century books.

Q: *Did you select them yourself?*

KINNELL: Yes. The cover illustration I saw reproduced rather poorly in some book — and I knew that it was the illustration I wanted on the cover. To find out where I could obtain a good copy I wrote to the Library of Congress and asked them if there existed in this country a copy of the original book. I was living in Iowa City at the time. They wrote back that the one copy of the book in this country — one of the two or three existing in the world — was in the Medical Library of the University of Iowa in Iowa City. So I just went next door.

Q: *Changing the subject a bit then, can you recall any particular time when you knew you wanted to be a poet? Or have you been writing for such a long time that you can't remember any special time when you really began?*

KINNELL: In high school I knew that I wanted to write poetry and to do nothing else, but it wasn't until years later that I actually wrote anything that appeared to me to be a poem. It was a strange feeling: long before I wrote a poem I knew that was all I wanted to do.

Q: *Was there any particular person or source that helped you in the beginning to keep going on with your poetry?*

KINNELL: In college I had the good fortune to get to know a teacher and poet, Charles Bell. I liked him and trusted him, and one day I showed him some of my poems. To my surprise he liked them. That was the first time that it came to me that this desire to write poems of mine might not, after all, be an adolescent delusion which would condemn me to a meaningless life, but a true possibility. It was therefore an enormously important moment for me to meet Bell and to have his encouragement; it remains the moment which makes me know that teaching is a useful profession.

Q.: *What poem was the first poem that you wrote that you felt was a poem, and secondly, did other people think it was?*

KINNELL: Well, I think it was a sonnet "When to the foam of those Galetian shores my scallop shell I threw. . . ." I don't know. Well, that was the poem I showed to Charles Bell. I never published it.

Q: *After you had gathered some confidence that you were not, as you say, deluding yourself and started writing and publishing, did you pay attention to any older poets, and the things they were doing, or did you try to block out all such influences?*

KINNELL: I didn't try to block out any influences, yet I didn't find any living poets whose work I greatly admired until I ran across Theodore Roethke's poems. I was around 26 years old when I first saw his poems.

Q: *Can you say what it was about those poems that struck you as being poems of someone whose voice you could admire?*

KINNELL: Well, for one thing, they touched my own experience. I found it hard to understand the poems of John Berryman and John Crowe Ransom and R. P. Blackmur, people like that. Their poems seemed far-fetched and ornate and intellectual and learned and polite, and not really like anything that I really wanted to do. Roethke's poetry seemed direct and forthright and full of real things. He was the only person I had encountered who seemed to relate to Whitman instead of going back to English models from the 17th-century.

Q: *When you say "Roethke is related to Whitman," do you mean his form or the whole poetic, or what?*

KINNELL: Less his form than his feeling for reality, and his urgent need to express it. The other poets loved making complicated poems but had in fact no pressing weight to get out something.

Q: *Do you remember which volume of Roethke's it was that you first discovered?*

KINNELL: Well, it was those Greenhouse Poems, I don't know what volume it was. What would that have been?

Q: *They're in* The Lost Son. *Did you also take any inspiration from the long Roethke sequences?*

KINNELL: I guess the longer things didn't strike me quite so much as those shorter ones with their slimy things.

Q: *I sometimes feel I hear an echo, in the rhythms of your poetry, of T. S. Eliot. Do you feel that he was any sort of influence at all?*

KINNELL: I'm surprised that you find that echo. But it could be. I did like parts of "The Wasteland," and "Gerontion" and "Prufrock." But I have always felt that there was something withheld in his voice compared with Whitman, for example. And yet I did steep myself in Eliot. It could be I drew something from him.

Q: *What about* The Quartets? *Did you read them?*

KINNELL: Yes, but I didn't like them very much.

Q: *Is that mostly because of the sense that he's "withholding something," as you put it?*

KINNELL: Partly that he's withholding, and partly that the poems are very dry and abstract. The physical world doesn't enter them. The abstract ideology is a retreat which may be what saved Eliot, but it offered little to me. In some way *The Quartets* are more personal than Eliot's earlier poems, he's saying what he himself deeply believes as faithfully as he can say it; yet the poetry keeps ascending to the airiness of a sermon.

Q: *Have you seen the facsimile edition of "The Wasteland" that came out? Are you at all interested in seeing it?*

KINNELL: I would love to see it. Has it been published?

Q: *Yes. It's interesting to see the things that Pound helped Eliot with in the poem, what he took out, and so forth. Some of the deletions do seem to be more personal references.*

KINNELL: That's interesting. I imagine that one day when the copyrights run out someone else will edit "The Wasteland" instead of Pound and make a different poem from it.

Q: *One last thing about Roethke — you may remember James Dickey's essay in* The Atlantic *about four years ago in which he called Roethke "the greatest American poet." Do you think that was rather extreme on Dickey's part?*

KINNELL: He meant the greatest of all American poets?

Q: *Yes.*

KINNELL: I don't think that's true. If we must use the term "greatest" it seems to me beyond question that Whitman is our greatest poet. Everybody else is on a different level. I guess Roethke is at that first level below Whitman. Whitman was a special creature and doesn't accept comparison. Among the sons of Whitman, Roethke is splendid.

Q: *Whitman is certainly someone that sooner or later almost every American poet feels that he has to come to terms with.*

KINNELL: Yes, though of course very few have done so. It's the great disgrace of American poetry that we had a supreme poet and nobody until recently paid any attention to him, not even the poets. The only one was Hart Crane, and even he learned very little from Whitman. The Whitmanesque line which is so naturally beautiful, Crane didn't take up. He, too, refused it in favor of a counted metric. Allen Tate rebuked Crane for his interest in Whitman; and Crane's defense was so guarded it was as though Crane, too, accepted that it was scandalous and regressive to really like Whitman.

Q: *Do you then accept the notion that there are two main strands of American poetry: the academic and the non-academic; or as some people call them, "pale face and redskin," Whitman being among the latter?*

KINNELL: Well, I think it's not very useful to talk about American poetry in terms of two kinds. People who use those terms, academic and non-academic, think of the Black Mountain Poets, for example, as being non-academic, yet they have no connection with Whitman either, even less than someone like Robert Lowell who, I guess, would be an academic. The "schools" of poetry in this country are more complicated because we have always drawn on foreign poetry and spiritual sources. The whole Transcendentalist movement had roots outside this country, and this has been true ever since. French poetry, by contrast, relates primarily to itself. The history of French poetry can be written almost entirely without mentioning any poet who isn't French or any tradition that isn't French.

Q: *Robert Bly and some of his associates have been talking a lot about bringing the surrealist tradition within the American tradition. He speaks, for example of Pablo Neruda and René Char and others. Do you think that's a healthy influence for American poets or is it another instance of American poets turning to outside sources?*

KINNELL: Yes, the New York School of Koch and Ashbery has brought French Dadaism and surrealism into our poetry, and Robert Bly has brought in Spanish surrealism. I think Spanish surrealism is more useful to us. French surrealism has a certain mechanical quality, written off the top of the head rather than from the unconscious. I would not call Neruda a surrealist; Neruda experienced but passed beyond the surrealist movement. He remains in love with the real. I think what Bly has done in his magazine, as well as with his poems and translations, his bringing of the Spanish tradition into this country, has been one of the most fruitful things that's happened.

Q: *But you think the New York School's kind of surrealism is a less fruitful influence on American poetry?*

KINNELL: Yes. French surrealism draws from the thinking part of the brain whereas the Spanish poets affected by surrealism wrote poems that flowed from deep within them. What surrealism had given them was the license to let come out all those strange inner images and to let them come out in their own form.

Q: *Do you consider yourself in any way to be a surrealist?*

KINNELL: No.

Q: *Do you see any connection between this Spanish tradition you were just talking about and Whitman? Is Whitman in any way a surrealist as you have been defining it?*

KINNELL: No. He comes out with a few things that you might think of as surreal but not characteristically. He is interested in what Rilke called, if I can remember his phrase, "the purely mundane, the deeply mundane, the spiritually mundane." Everything in Whitman is related to the visible. At the end of "Crossing Brooklyn Ferry" he has that wonderful apostrophe to visible things. I can't remember it. . . .

Q: *Read it if you want.*

KINNELL: Yes, here it is. "You have waited, you always wait, you dumb, beautiful ministers . . . /Not you anymore shall be able to foil us, or withhold yourselves from us,/We use you and do not cast you aside—/we plant you permanently within us." That, of course, is what Rilke was interested in: transforming the world within one's self. Whitman took the surfaces of things, the faces of things, brought them into himself and resurrected them within himself. His imagery is the kind of imagery that makes sense to an ordinary person.

Q: *It sounds like what you were describing awhile back when you were explaining your initial conception of* The Book of Nightmares, *and how you were trying to deal with "things" as Rilke did.*

KINNELL: Yes, something like that. Ponge has done that in *"Le Parti Pris des choses,"* and Neruda's "Elemental Odes" do just that.

Q: *Another American poet that comes to my mind when you talk about the way one uses the surface of things is William Carlos Williams. Do you think that he's in the Whitman tradition as you have been describing it?*

KINNELL: I don't think he is. You'd think he would be. But for most of his life he tended to be photographic. Whitman uses the surfaces of things but he is not photographic. Whitman's adjective doesn't remain at the surface, it enters the thing and feels out some inner quality. Williams tended to use the straight adjective. In his little poem, "So much depends/upon/a red wheelbarrow, . . ." we can see the scene vividly, but it's a photographic scene. None of the adjectives enters the things, or makes them live, or relates their lives to ours. The things remain, therefore, in the service of the idea he wished to express. His phrase, "No ideas but in things," is therefore reversible, "No things but in ideas." Later in his life, when he got over his need to develop a theory of metrics, when he started writing in something close to the Whitmanesque line, though with more of an iambic beat, and especially in that great poem, "Asphodel That Greeny Flower," Williams comes close to joining Whitman.

Q: *It's become very fashionable for American poets to cite Williams and Pound as their mentors though I feel a lot of them haven't really read these poets with a whole lot of care, and I take it that regardless of that you wouldn't cite them, but go back instead to Whitman.*

KINNELL: Yes, I think there are great, immortal passages in the *Cantos* but immortal in the sense that Keats is immortal and that older writers are immortal. Whereas I feel that Whitman is not only contemporary but somewhat ahead of us. We haven't caught up with him yet. Pound's language, for example, often strikes me as already archaic, and sometimes dry and professorial in tone, with little human presence. The disembodied voice is characteristic of the followers of Pound. For example, Charles Olson seldom put his voice into his poetry. Also Pound's followers focus on technique. Even Williams does, Williams who felt so uneasy in the company of learned people like Pound and Eliot. He felt that he, too, had to develop a theory. I find it a rather opaque theory. I don't think it did him any harm, but it perhaps had harmful consequences for others. It got American poets thinking in ways that have led us to use slash marks in poems, and to preoccupation with the visual disposition of a poem on the page, rhythmic controls which are damaging because they don't arise from the words themselves, but are imposed by the typewriter. One often finds poetry today which doesn't look as if it should be read out loud. It doesn't have a verbal life or a voice present in the words. It could as well be read like prose.

Q: *The other poet that comes to mind automatically then, when you talk about the Whitman tradition, is Allen Ginsberg. What do you think of his attempts to use the Whitman line?*

KINNELL: Ginsberg is a true son of Whitman. In several of the poems in *Howl,* including the title poem, we have for the first time a poetry which revives the Whitman tradition in all its splendor. I think of "Sunflower Sutra" and "Howl" particularly.

Q: *I'd like to ask about something that came up when Denise Levertov was here. In talking about her writing methods she cited you as someone whose methods were quite different from hers.*

KINNELL: Yes, quite different.

Q: *She said that you seem to labor over poems and throw out a great deal, whereas she thought that she herself didn't revise as much as you do and didn't tend to cut out as much. Do you care to talk about this?*

KINNELL: I don't know that I can say very much. She's told me that when she's going to write a poem she lets it exist within her for a while until it's fully formed, then she writes it down. She may change only a few words afterward. This has happened to me on a few occasions, but on the whole I struggle a great deal. Perhaps it has something to do with the clarity of one's life. Her life, her feelings, her ideas, are clearer than mine. I often find myself floundering. My poems are attempts to find myself again. So I start off but I don't know where I'm going; I try this avenue and that avenue, that turns out to be a dead end, this is a dead end, and so on. The search takes a long time and I have to back-track often.

Q: *Do you feel that you, or for that matter, poets in general today have any special problems that might make poetry almost impossible to write at times? Is there anything about the events of the 20th-century that present peculiar problems such as, say, someone like Whitman did not have to contend with? I am thinking in terms of your thematic material and your methods. You were saying that your poetry is often a wandering around and you have often tried in your poetry to come to terms with major 20th-century outrages such as Nazi Germany, Hiroshima, now Vietnam. And I was wondering if you feel that those kinds of events present special problems that poets have never faced before.*

KINNELL: Yes, I think it's true. Well, *nobody* has had to face these things before. And most frightening of all, we're the first ones who foresee the end of human life and of our world, and see it in the conceivable future. It makes it a struggle, almost futile, to write. But we know that poetry — that what poetry represents and expresses — is all that can save us. Therefore, while it's a struggle, it's an exhilarating one. To some degree or another we have all been rendered into what you might call "technological beings." We are part of a technological society consecrated to controlling, using and disposing of the natural, this is a part of the consciousness we all have. Poetry simply can't spring out of that consciousness, therefore writing is more difficult. But if poetry has any function, it is to return oneself and perhaps even others to a sense of their natural beings.

Q: *This returning of our selves to our natural beings, is that the destiny that you conceive for yourself in your wandering or for 20th-century Christian man, the speaker of* The Book of Nightmares?
KINNELL: Yes.

Q: *Do you have a notion of how to get there or is it still a wandering?*
KINNELL: If I have, it's in that book. If I haven't, it isn't.

Q: *One thing that may be close to what you're talking about is*

*something that we were discussing the other day partly as a result of
reading your book. We were wondering about the curious phenomenon that, although many poets are connected with universities, it
seems almost impossible to write a poem about university life in our
age. It seemed to us that the university drives poets into deliberately
seeking out other kinds of experiences such as direct contact with
nature, for their poems. Do you feel those pressures as a teacher
and poet?*

KINNELL: I think the university has become a substitute for life —
a more pleasant version of it. In the university people have lots of
time and can talk about the most interesting things any time they
want; they can smoke a joint; sleep with their girl friend; read; lie
about. Four years are stretched out, often, into ten years, twelve
years — of a sort of new kind of human life. People who drop out
of universities wanting to go out into the real world tend frequently
to scurry back after a year or two of being a waiter or a waitress.
It's a peculiarly modern kind of life because you don't really know
what makes it go. It's not like living on a farm. Therefore, because
all needs are easily filled and because it's essentially a mystifying kind
of life, it's the wrong place for a poet to live, particularly when one
is young. There are at least a dozen Master of Fine Arts programs
in this country where people study how to write poetry. Most of
them then go out and start teaching others to write poetry. Something
is missing in between. College is a very good place for someone who's
young. But once it's over, it would be much better to be with people
who deal with the physical world, to work alongside people who
work hard for a living and who earn what they need and no more
than they need, who do something that's related to the earth and
which is useful to others.

Q: *Was there a time in your life when you did just that, and do
you feel that these experiences were important to you as a poet?
I know a lot of your early poems deal with hunting and rural life.*

KINNELL: I started out teaching, and I've ended up teaching, but
in between I spent probably twelve years picking up my living as I
could. I've had jobs as a cook, a tree climber (cutting infected limbs
on elm trees), on an assembly line, as a journalist in Iran. These
were all jobs that gave me a lot, though it was hard to write, to find
the energy to write, while working at something else. I also spent
years without any job. In the last five years I've taught one semester
here, one semester there, taking a year off when I could. At least

half of the time in the last five years I've been teaching. I now teach at Columbia part time. I guess what I would not like to do is to teach in a small college with a campus, get tenure, have all my friends be professors, and so on. I do love teaching if I can do it a little bit — like once a week. This is what I have at Columbia; it's perfect right now. We have no campus; I have nothing to do with the university life; I have all the joys of teaching, while it remains only a very small part of my life.

When one gets older and no longer has unlimited energy, it's hard to know what kind of job other than teaching would give him that necessary laziness he's got to have in order to write. I don't think many of us can work a full day, go home, take care of the children, put them to bed, read them their stories, and then sit down at 9:30 to write a poem, and then at 11:00, go to bed . . . I don't think I can do it.

Q: *What do you teach at Columbia?*

KINNELL: I teach a workshop in poetry writing.

Q.: *Do you ever teach any literature courses or do you mostly do creative writing courses?*

KINNELL: Last spring, I taught a literature course at Queen's College. I think I would like to teach the 19th-century novel, or the Russian novel. But I've mostly taught creative writing. That's what they seem to hire me for.

Q: *Do you feel that it helps you in your poetry to be teaching creative writing or perhaps in a different way to be teaching literature?*

KINNELL: I think not. No, I don't think it helps. And provided I don't do too much teaching, I don't think that teaching detracts from my work. I just like teaching, that's all.

Q: *Are you ever drawn to work in some other genre, or another medium? You have that one novel, for example; do you plan any more?*

KINNELL: I don't know; it could happen. I had not really planned to write that novel, it happened that I wrote it through peculiar circumstances. It could happen again that I would write a novel, but I rather doubt it because life is short and novels are long.

Q: *How about theater. Has it ever occurred to you to attempt a play?*

KINNELL: No, I have a feeling that I couldn't write for the theater. I think it has something to do with my sense of time. My sense of time isn't right for the theater. I'd like to write for a movie, though. Words can be purified in a movie; they can say only the essentials, and one can let the film say everything else, including the passage of time.

Q: *But you haven't really pursued that notion any further?*

KINNELL: No.

Q: *Do you see any relationship between the medium of film and poetry?*

KINNELL: I've seen a lot of movies in which the script is junk, and yet they have a genius filming it and marvelous actors. If they'd had a poet writing the script they could have a supreme movie. It's because our culture is compartmentalized. In France, for example, the writers, the movie makers, and the theater people know each other. But here the poets know the poets, and the film makers know the film makers, etc., but they rarely know one another, and so there is rarely any collaboration.

Q: *You've had an interest in translation over the years, an interest shared by a fair number of American poets. Does translating help you with your own poetry?*

KINNELL: I translated mostly for selfish reasons — because I wanted to know the poetry which I was translating. It's the best way to enter the poetry of a language that is not your own. I don't think it's affected my poetry any more than the very close reading of any poet has.

Q: *Do the poets you chose to translate have some particular interest for you, or do you translate as a form of discipline?*

KINNELL: I've translated three poets. I translated Bonnefoy and Villon because I couldn't understand them just reading them and wanted to very much. I translated Yvan Goll because his widow is a very charming and persuasive person.

Q: *Denise Levertov mentioned that she translated occasionally as a way of keeping herself going during a dry spell. Do you ever do that?*

KINNELL: I've never done that, no.

Q: *Is there any exercise that you do in such circumstances? Or do you just force yourself to write? Denise Levertov mentioned doing that, although she hates doing it.*

KINNELL: No, I don't. What I do if I don't feel like writing a poem is write prose. Since this last book came out, for example, I've been writing a lot of prose.

Q: *Do you mean fiction?*

KINNELL: No, I don't know what you call it, but I'm sort of writing about poetry.

Q: *Do you ever do reviews or is there any kind of critical prose that you want to do, say perhaps writing about Whitman?*

KINNELL: I'm writing what might turn out to be a book about poetry. A number of the things we've mentioned in this conversation have been things I've been writing about. In fact I think I've quoted from my text on occasion. Whitman plays a large part in this book.

The Church of Ash

BY LAURENCE LIEBERMAN

THE HARD EDGE OF W. S. Merwin's scrupulous negativity is the fiercest poetic discipline around. Readers can hardly fail to assimilate into their ears the violence of vacancy—the exacerbating vacuum—produced by shorn parings of our excesses he leaves behind him, littered on the path following his poems. In the ten years since the publication of *The Moving Target*, the first of four volumes developing his radical new aesthetics, Merwin's artistry has steadily deepened in the anger of an uncompromising honesty that pares away falsities, layer by layer, always leaving him in a condition of final exposure, vulnerability, nakedness. As in his style of writing, so in his style of spiritualizing—an utter divesting of defenses, the risk of more and more perfect defenselessness. He would denude himself of all possessions, all conceivable forms or modes of ownership, even stripping away the charter to his name, his face, since to own anything is to be enchained, shackled, to be owned in turn.

The soldiers have burned down all our churches of wood, whether our names were carved on the doors or written in the humble black of the charcoal floors. The only church left *standing* is made of ash; nobody owns it, and beautiful nameless spirits worship in its pews:

> we have a church where the others stood
> it's made of ash
> no roof no doors
>
> nothing on earth
> says it's ours

—"Ash"

Merwin would found the church of the poem, then, from imperishable materials, words of ash. It is to be a poetry of no signatures, no possessorship, a stamp of impersonality on the timbers of every line and stanza. Once complete, the poem is set free from the hand of its maker, its word carpenter to be owned by no one, by no place, by no time; thus,

A review of *Writings to an Unfinished Accompaniment*, by W. S. Merwin, reprinted from *The Yale Review*, by permission of the Editor.

like the free nomad-spirit that breathed luminous, unconditional life into the art, the works will be indestructible, and inexhaustible in their power to nourish free spirits of countless readers who partake of their bounty.

Merwin's aspiration is to become an empty nobody, an impersonal expertly trained thing—a tool, an instrument, a pure vehicle for the "one truth," the vision that suddenly fills the fertile, incubating emptiness: the state in which the spirit has completely freed itself from comforts, needs, habits, freed from a human personality, freed from the body's claims, freed from the demands of other beings, freed from the brand-marks of colleagues, family, country:

> If it's invented it will be used
>
> maybe not for some time
>
> then all at once
> a hammer rises from under a lid
> and shakes off its cold family
>
> its one truth is stirring in its head
> order order saying . . .
>
> —"Tool"

This is the state of uttermost self-purification, disaffiliation, dispossession that Merwin has cultivated with unwavering tenacity in his last four volumes of original poetry, and throughout his prodigious career as this country's foremost living translator of verse from other languages. It is a condition of maximum plasticity and availability, a priming and predisposing of the receptive ear to become a psychic medium for the poetry of foreign tongues, as well as for deep images springing from the subconscious mind, or from the racial preconscious: images germinating in the visionary dream-life which have the authority and unshakable finality about them of last basic necessities; images which are as indispensable to survival in worlds of the spirit stretching to its outer limits, on the verge of breaking into new uncharted territory, as the barest physical necessities—a little water, roots, scant body covering—are crucial to survival in the desert.

Regrettably, he cannot sustain this level of peak accessibility, since the habits of our cumbersome sensory apparatus operate in most of our routine daily living at levels of imprecision and inefficiency far less sensitive, less in touch with the hidden spirit in words, images, or objects than is necessary to support the scrupulous fidelity to quantities, nuances, shades, hues, lusters—quieter brilliancies, faded grays, softer delicate radiances—that Merwin's spirit of aspiring perfectibility demands for his art. Hence, the disturbing perplexity, approaching a cosmic vertigo, of psychic states in which we have fallen hopelessly out of touch with the spirit centers, registered in poems like "Habits," "Something I've Not Done." Suddenly, we may feel alienated, or dissociated, from our own delicate—if unwieldy—senses: our eyes, our ears, our tongues, our hands, our lungs—yes, even the most intimately undeliberated act of our breathing itself, every breath we take, or give back, may seem to work against us, to be at war with our wills, or to operate in a dimension so far removed from our conscious awareness, we may feel as if our sense organs have been invaded by alien identities, beings, presences:

> Even in the middle of the night
> they go on handing me around . . .
>
> even when I'm asleep they take
> one or two of my eyes for their sockets . . .
>
> when I wake and can feel the black lungs
> flying deeper into the century
> carrying me
> even then they borrow
> most of my tongues to tell me
> that they're me
> and they lend me most of my ears to hear them
>   —"Habits"

This state of the psyche seems linked to the immense frustration, born of a relentless perfectionism, in "Something I've Not Done":

> Something I've not done
> is following me
> I haven't done it again and again
> so it has many footsteps
> like a drumstick that's grown old and never been used
>
> In late afternoon I hear it come closer
> at times it climbs out of a sea
> onto my shoulders
> and I shrug it off
> losing one more chance . . .

To be always obsessed with doing, making, crafting—as is this inexhaustibly prolific writer—is to be perennially haunted by the ghosts of the "not done," to be possessed by the demons of the one failure, the one forgetting, the one loss amid a horde of gains: it is an aesthetic of tirelessness, forbidding rest or ease of spirit, much less gaiety, exuberance, or comic ebullience.

Behind all our words and acts, behind each very signing of names, lurk absences, vacancies, emptinesses. Active, not passive, voids. Dynamic silences. Alert negative spaces. This mysterious sector of our mental life, usually hidden from us, is vivified with astonishing poignancy in a dozen-odd impressive short poems of a strikingly new species in Merwin's proliferating canon. They are stark, direct in delivery, coolly remote and stingingly intimate at once, like daggers of hot ice: raw, naked, brutally overexposed—in the sense of a photo with too much glare drowning the outlines of things, but so hypnotic in their quiet chanting we cannot look away, or even a little to the side to shield our eyes, and we can't keep our gloveless, perishable hands off of them. The missing things embraced behind the lines of the poem exert an immense negative pull working invisibly upon the reader's ear. If we examine the few words and lines that are present, with much white space surrounding them on the page, we can hardly locate the source of the great suction that freezes a reader's ear to the poem, invisible like the lines of force of a powerful electromagnet.

The remarkable artistry in this cluster of poems is no idle exercise or mere exhibition of verbal legerdemain—the poems make an unmistakable impact on the conscience of our unique American generation. In the peculiar way they make moral designs upon us, I have never read anything like them. They would shock readers into illumination of the slow, irreversible dyings of the true spirit within us, within animals, within things: the slow retreat of the mysterious inner beauty of each thing and being which *is* its life, its identity, its sole reality; the slow withdrawal from us of the spirit because of our neglect, our innocent blindness to all the inner secret life that we fail to recognize, and which enacts its slow judgment upon us by simply turning away forever, turning its back on us, as in "The Place of Backs":

> When what has helped us has helped us enough
> it moves off and sits down
> not looking our way
>
> after that every time we call it
> it takes away one of the answers it had given us,

or by staying hidden, locked inside our helpless waiting pencils, as in "The Unwritten":

> Inside this pencil
> crouch words that have never been written
> never been spoken
> never been taught

> they're hiding
>
> they're awake in there
> dark in the dark
> hearing us
> but they won't come out
> not for love not for time not for fire,

or, again, as in "Something I've Not Done," "Every morning / it's drunk up part of my breath for the day," and the spirit is eaten up from within us, and eats ourselves up, bit by bit, during all our most unnoticed, ostensibly harmless, daily routines:

> while we sign our names
> more of us
> lets go
>
> and will never answer

In the consistent moral vision that informs these poems, a prophecy builds: Merwin foresees the total desertion, or secession, of the spirit from our inner life space; not that the spirit will cease to exist on the planet we'll soon have depopulated of every animal species but our own—the spirit will simply take up its residence in exclusively nonmortal dwellings, and quite happily flourish without our feeble collaboration:

> While we talk
> thousands of languages are listening
> saying nothing

In another cluster of poems—"The Current," "Surf-Casting," "The Chase," "The Way Ahead"—the metaphysical keystone is the dissection and anatomizing of our age's cosmic greed, our measureless possessiveness and need for conquest. In these poems of the most bitter moral and political indignation since the antiwar poems of *The Lice*, Merwin translates the international politics of grasping into a personal, spiritual condition which can be satisfied by nothing short of the dream of total acquisitiveness: a vast illimitable gluttony that seeks to swallow everything alive, that would empty the sea of all forms of life in one or two great gulps; and the swindle is all a disguised projection of our human identity onto the extrahuman world, at bottom, the most devastating self-betrayal that can be imagined, in a barren attempt to fill the void in the self left by the spirit's mutiny.

We are "surf-casting," having "practised a long time / with the last moments of fish." We employ our own irreplaceable toes for bait ("you have ten chances"). Our quarry is "the great Foot." The utter futility of the quest blinds us to the obvious barren terms: it is the vain blundering attempt to repossess willingly amputated parts of our very being, squandered segments of the body of the self. Having depleted all of the available game in the world, we continue the obsolete charade of the hunt, our own foot for prey, which we do not recognize as a projected hunk of ourselves any more than we have recognized for centuries that all the animal legions we have decimated and all but exterminated were of the one spirit with our flesh, sharing our life, an extension and continuation of our own bodies, like our limbs. The current that surrounds the fish and also partakes of their body fluids is continuous in spirit with the blood currents that flow in our arteries and veins, though "for a long time" we've been "forgetting that we are water." Our blindness to our closest familial kind in the animal kingdom—flesh of our flesh, blood of our blood, of the one family—has progressed to the bizarre extremity of the terms of the last hunt. It must be the last, since we fish for our own "great Foot" using our toes as bait, and we will win, we know it, we'll always win:

> if only the great Foot is running
>
> if only it will strike
> and you can bring it to shore
>
> in two strides it will take you
> to the emperor's palace
> stamp stamp the gates will open
> he will present you with half of his kingdom
> and his only daughter
>
> and the next night you will come back
> to fish for the Hand

There are bewildering ambiguities of tone in "Surf-Casting," as in "The Way Ahead." The process that unfolds in the poem resembles, in many of its particulars, the spare exacting discipline of Merwin's own most advanced aesthetic of the poem: the painstaking rituals practiced in pursuit of the perfecting of skill, mastery of both the mechanics of a craft and the profound intimate awareness of the best conditions, the most suitable climate for its flourishing, are, it would seem, set forth sympathetically, and ironically, at once:

> It has to be the end of the day
> the hour of one star
> the beach has to be a naked slab

> and you have to have practised a long time
> with the last moments of fish
> sending them to look for the middle of the sea
> until your fingers
> can play back whole voyages . . .

The prophecy of "Surf-Casting" foresees the next stage in "The Way Ahead," envisioning a time in the near future when all nonhuman creatures will have been removed by us, but in our demented fantasy lives, a hierarchy of larger and smaller creatures, an entire undiminished encyclopedic animal kingdom, will continue to flourish and populate our dreamscape:

> A winter is to come
> when smaller creatures
> will hibernate inside the bones
> of larger creatures
> and we will be the largest of all
> and the smallest . . .

"The Way Ahead" is an agonizing oracular performance—all prophecies, all riddles, seemingly optimistic on the surface, but ringing hollow at the center. The poem has Orwellian overtones, true to the tenor of our American present historical moment. What is so disturbingly powerful in the poem is the way its visionary apparatus—the exquisite images, the authentic oracular tone persuading the ear by hypnosis, incantation, persuading the imagination with genuine fabling, mythologizing, riddle-making—all these immaculate skills flawlessly participate in the sellout that hangs us, an aesthetic soft sell matching the political machinations of our day. The poem's power is enhanced, I feel, because Merwin dares to let his own instrument, his visionary medium at its most heightened pitch of clarity and revelation, fall under the grimmest judgment:

> A Monday is to come
> when some who had not known
> what hands were for
> will be lifted and shaken
> and broken and stroked and blessed
> and made

The poet spares neither himself nor his most exalted art from the ferocity of his denunciation. The poem's valiant risk is in resisting the temptation to take comfort in the aloofness of an aesthetic removed from the crimes of innocence, of allowing ourselves to be violated, brutalized, mutilated, our spirits butchered, as we absentmindedly hasten the progress toward our own genocide, and Merwin invites the poem's craft to illustrate how our profoundest visionary myths and arts may be twisted to serve the fatal ends:

> Feet are already marching there
> fields of green corn and black corn are already
> throwing up their hands
> all the weeds know and leap up from the ditches
> every egg presses on toward those ends
> for this the clouds sleep with the mountains
> for this in the almanacs of the unborn
> terrible flowers appear
> one after the other
> giving new light
>
> A light is to come

How much rage is contained in the parody of political optimism in this passage, closing the poem. All living things left—the few survivors of each diminishing species—are fooled by the Nixonian cant of the propaganda machine preaching better times in "The Way Ahead," advocating escape from the pain of the present into the future. All flora and fauna, then, are tricked into hurrying into the premature void of extinction, mistaking their doom, their "first day of ruin," for a "new light" that "is to come."

Our misdeciphering the tragic events of our time goes hand in hand with our misreading, or mishearing, of the words:

> When the pain of the world finds words
> they sound like joy
> and often we follow them
> with our feet of earth
> and learn them by heart
> but when the joy of the world finds words
> they are painful
> and often we turn away
> with our hands of water

Merwin instills a profound belief, here, that everything depends on our learning to find our way back into touch with the true spirit behind the life of words. Our tragedy is our hopeless disaffiliation from the saving, healing powers of our own native tongue, and what could be more desolately mistaken than misreading joy for pain, pain for joy?

However, I find Merwin's new voice most attractive when the quality of intellectual rage, the impulse to scathing moral judgment, is transmuted into a drama of the long spirit battling with itself, the full intensity of judgment turned inward which, for all its censuring of failures to measure up to standards set by its highest aspirations, is tempered by a compassionate acceptance. In "Division," an austere myth resonating with overtones from American Indian folklore, a dominant saving quality of whimsy, caprice, archness invests the vision with a fortification of human warmth that is, I feel, the most welcome new emotional undertone in a handful of the best new poems in this book—a quality of tempering mercy and self-forgiveness, a willingness to fail:

> People are divided
> because the finger god
> named One
> was lonely
> so he made for himself a brother like him
> named Other One
>
> then they were both lonely
>
> so each made for himself four others
> all twins
>
> then they were afraid
> that they would lose each other
> and be lonely
>
> so they made for themselves two hands
> to hold them together
>
> but the hands drifted apart . . .

There are surges here of the human light of feeling radiating from humility before weakness exposed, indeed weakness exalted beyond all spite that mistakes its whimpers for meagerness of soul. What abides in these lines is the refreshing quality of quiet ardor, a gentle self-mockery, with all mere human negativity purged out of the judgment, that assures me that this poem could utterly charm the shrewd ears of children, whose infallible capacity to detect some varieties of fraudulence has never been adequately explained or acknowledged. I can only hope that this emergent quality of gaiety and buoyancy, which approaches ecstatic generosity of spirit in the beautiful new poem which ends the book, "Gift," consummate in its serenity and happiness of earned spiritual independence, is the forerunner to the next major rebirth in the work of this poet of many radical self-restylings, this prince of alchemists:

> I have to trust what was given to me
> if I am to trust anything
> it led the stars over the shadowless mountain
> what does it not remember in its night and silence
> what does it not hope knowing itself no child of time . . .

> I call to it Nameless One O Invisible
> Untouchable Free
> I am nameless I am divided
> I am invisible I am untouchable
> and empty
> nomad live with me
> be my eyes
> my tongue and my hands
> my sleep and my rising
> out of chaos
> come and be given

Still another remarkable new development in many poems of this volume is the power with which ordinary inanimate objects—a wharf, a house, a room, a hammer and nail, a door hauled on someone's shoulders, a burning plank of wood—are endowed with supernatural presence, or haunted being:

> O venerable plank burning
> and your pegs with you
> the hordes of flame gaining
> in the marks of the adze
> each mark seven times older than I am
> each furthermore shaped like a tongue
> you that contain
> of several lives now only a dust
> inside the surfaces that were once cuts
> but no memory no tree
> even your sparks dust
> toward the last some of your old pitch
> boils up through you
> many children running
> into a shining forest

The objects are pictured—or silhouetted, rather, so few the details selected—with hallucinatory clarity and maximum suggestiveness, at once. I'm reminded of the drawings of Matisse, in which a single curved line of subtly varied sharpness and intensity suggests intricately not only the shape and position of the model's neck, arch of back, buttock, calf, and a possible gesture, or swerve, of movement; but hints enigmatically the exact mass and density and texture of the missing precincts of flesh—flank, loin, shoulder. By a secret power, by invisible craft, the few lines and dots and fleck-marks hint—but to hint with precision and exactitude is to inescapably command the viewer's eye—the larger, weightier, missing quantities of the figure which blossom in the vacancy, the eye's masterfully controlled hallucinated versions of forms filling in the blank white space, the explosive negative areas, which comprise immeasurably more of the canvas than the *positives*, the areas literally filled with pencilings.

As the draftsman the eye, so does the impresario-poet command the reader's ear. To a degree surpassing every other poet of my acquaintance, writing in English or whatever language, W. S. Merwin has developed with increasing mastery in his last four volumes of verse a Matisse-like notation, a fantastic linguistic shorthand, in which the few irreducible lines and images chosen (or has he mastered, rather, the power of perfect submission, passivity, in allowing the inevitable lines and images to choose *him*, the translator's genius?) guide the reader's ear by unerringly exact bridges across the very hinges— invisible overlaps and interlockings—between the words to the silences behind, or surrounding, the spoken utterances. This wizardry is accomplished by chains of sound and echoes, the echoes of echoes, the tones and overtones—all matings that tie or bind sound to silence, tongue to its dumbness, voice to its muteness; and always, in Merwin's art at its best, that which is given, or revealed nakedly, releases by invisible art those quantities which are withheld, buried, concealed, but *contained* in the silence, and, therefore, inescapably picked up by the reader's ear, and poignantly heard, leading the reader into the heart of a vision of quietly gathering intensity, balanced halfway between sound and silence. Or rather, not vision—the scores of eyes and eye-images in this book are always closing, or going blind—but *audition*, an integrated totality of incantatory chantings, the insistently felt and intensely heard presences of sound building cumulatively in the silences, the apparent voids of voice, as orchestration builds into a central awakening and reverberation within a listener's ear, resonating wholenesses of the heard and ultra-heard. But no, Wallace Stevens anticipated me by exactly fifty years in the search for an alternate word, beyond *vision*, to take account of an utterly new music in the poetic art of our American language: a *harmonium*.

James Wright and the Dissolving Self

BY CHARLES MOLESWORTH

SUSAN SONTAG SAID that the two chief elements of the modern sensibility are "homosexual aesthetic irony and Jewish moral earnestness." Perhaps the first qualifier in each triplet is excessive, but certainly most modern artists have traces of both qualities in some combination. In looking at his career, we can see that James Wright has moved from irony to earnestness. Because in his poetry the artist is still the suffering hero, because the outsider is still the seer, and most of all because the self is problematic even beyond the snares of the world, James Wright is modern. Because of the peculiar way these themes and subjects are articulated in his poetry, and through the course of his career, however, he might be more accurately considered a post-modern poet. But that may mean nothing more than Wright prefers the immersion of sentiment to the suspension of irony, in other words, that he acknowledges his own romanticism.

The problem of the self in the lyric poem, essentially a problem left over from the great English Romantics, animates Wright's poetry from its very beginnings. The problem can be simply stated, though seldom does Wright offer it, or resolve it, in simple terms. The lyric poem, as it approaches song as one of its aesthetic limits, threatens to dissolve the self in which it originates. Melody and pulse capture the discerning eye and the articulating voice and return them both to the status of natural forces. On the other hand, the lyric poem vindicates and justifies the self; its very structure is co-terminous with the discovery of the self which its very voicings make possible. Two *loci classici* epitomize the polar possibilities of this tension: where Keats, listening to the nightingale singing, says "Now more than ever seems it rich to die," and Shelley's command to the west wind, "Be thou, Spirit fierce,/My spirit! Be thou me, impetuous one!" The voice that sings conjures a world, and that world may not have a place in it for the singer; then again, it may delight in pointing out that the world *is* the singer.

Whether the self is to be dissolved by its song or whether the song will dissolve the world into the singer: this unresolved problem remained to haunt the chief poets of the modern era. When Eliot says "the more perfect the artist, the more completely separate in him will be the man who suffers and the mind which creates," we realize that he has come up with a radical solution to the problem. The ironic mode offers one way to deal with this set of concerns. By dividing the self over the possibilities of emotional evaporation and intellectual concentration, by choosing neither to lose the self in feelings nor to locate it in unequivocation, the poet both acknowleges the perennial depth of the problem as well as its existential fascination.

But when the Eliotic hegemony dissolved in the late '50's, the problem returned with a different set of possible resolutions. Williams reminded us that "the descent beckons," and Roethke turned his words over to the wind. A new spirit of release, of abandonment, took over in American poetry. At one level, the new solution was a new subject matter; confessional poetry, often using irony as its dominant mode, sought to explore the "man who suffers." But there was another way to descend into the self, as Williams also noted "A/ world lost, a world unsuspected." This other way traversed and released the buried memories of the preternatural, the mystical lost world which offered, in the wake of its discovery, a new man. But to re-discover this world, or more exactly the gnostic discipline that would open this world, the poet must immerse himself not simply in his own suffering, but in the principles of suffering itself; as he does so he must form for himself, not a tragic view, but a beatific one. As Juan Ramon Jiménez says, in Wright's translation:

> And life begins to grow
> within us, the delightful daylight
> that cannot be switched off,
> that is thinning, now, somewhere else.
>   Ah, how lovely, how lovely,
> truth, even if it is not real, how lovely!

Wright begins his search, again using a poem from Jiménez, for a "divine plainness," that will "pierce the familiar certainty," and "place a new soul into whatever is real."

This search leads Wright away from the irony so valued by Eliot and indulged in so often by his imitators, toward a poetry of sentiment, in which emotions are allowed freer play and the self is celebrated rather than divided. Yet such a celebration of the self takes place only when the self turns over its powers to its own emotions, its own consciousness, when, in other words, the soul is willing to dissolve the ground of its own being. Such dissolution, of course, some people identify simply as ecstasy. Wright's ecstasy, however, is not for ecstasy's sake, nor is it simply for the poem's sake. It is for Wright's own sake, it is the only way he has of realizing himself — realizing both in the sense of "becoming real" and "coming to know." Again quoting Williams: "The descent / made up of despairs / and without accomplishment / realizes a new awakening: / which is a reversal /of despair." This is the way Wright has chosen for himself. And in so choosing, he is willing to go "without accomplishment," indeed, he is even willing to sacrifice an accomplishment very dear to him, the meticulous control and craft of his own verse.

If by style we mean the intersection of a peculiar temperament, syntax, and mode of perception, then Wright has become one of the most stylish of contemporary poets. His poetry has accrued to itself several various terms of description: deep image, Neo-Imagist, Jungian, American surrealist, etc. The first of these is the most natural term, since it appears in *The Sixties* magazine (once *The Fifties,* now, sporadically, *The Seventies*) where, with Robert Bly, Wright worked out much of his poetic. The term "deep image" connotes the non-discursive, the archetypal. We are put in mind of Pound's description of the image as "an intellectual and emotional complex in an instant of time." For Pound the energy was stored in the tense but complementary relation between "complex" (the polysemous, the traditional, the ordered, "poetry as a criticism of life") and "instant" (the concision, the sculptured edge, the "make it new" commandment). Wright accepts all this, but goes further, into the pre-conscious, if not the unconscious of the poet, beneath tradition, beyond orders of meaning into fields of light and fears of darkness.

He has been quoted as saying, with the publication of *The Branch Will Not Break,* that "whatever I write from now on will be different . . . I am finished with what I was doing." Which is to say, he had left the aesthetic modes of the '50's behind him. But such Pauline fervor, such evangelistic absolutism is bred into Wright's midwestern sensibility from the very beginning. Even though he now teaches in New York City, we will see that his view of the metropolis still contains a wide border of Lutheran mistrust of deeds, along with a concomitant trust in redeemed, and redeeming, consciousness.

In his first book, *The Green Wall* (1957), a Yale Younger Poet selection chosen by W. H. Auden, Wright exhibits a consciousness, and a conscience, of an outsider, a harsh sentimentality that locates its most adequate objects in condemned prisoners and oppressed women. At least three of the poems have female personae, and Wright has spoken of his conscious imitation of Robert Frost. When the persona of a poem is male, the women presented are often shown to be insubstantial: "I sought, bewildered, for her face, / No more than splendid air, gone blind," or "The blue dusk bore feathers beyond our eyes, / Dissolved all wings as you, your hair dissolved, / Your frame of bone blown hollow as a house . . ." The subtle articulation of sound effects in that last line, plus the controlled, and controlling simile, represent the dominant style of Wright's early work. Wright's control here is truly admirable, and his volume in the Yale series remains one of the best titles in what is almost bound to be a spotty list. The verse stays so polished, so delightful just as artifice, without ever becoming empty or facile, that one cannot help but wonder if Wright had not used up the dominant mode of the '50's with his very first book. But Wright's vigorously humane intelligence keeps the book from being more than a collection of set pieces.

It is no wonder that the poem that remains the sharpest, "Sappho," is about a Lesbian relationship, spoken by the Lesbian as she laments the return of the other woman to her husband. The Lesbian in part accepts her social role as "sinner," yet almost because of her being ostracized, her perceptions are clearer, and her emotions more authentic. By submitting she dominates. It's a moving poem, almost never anthologized, and besides demonstrating Wright's use of the outsider, it shows an extremely effective free verse line at work in the service of a psychological realism that manages to avoid stylization. Because of that, it forecasts what is to come for Wright. It is not the average '50's poem, unless one considers that it ends in inanition.

With the publication of *Saint Judas* (1959) Wright began to demonstrate some of the less refined sentiment that marks his later work. This sentiment combined with a heightened rhetoric and a cultivated awe, through the use of open simple images that widened rather than defined the poems' emotional drifts. An abundant use of simple rhyme, archly phrased rhetoric, and a not-quite-relaxed colloquialism occasionally mar some of the poems. The book is, to me, less interesting than *The Green Wall* because it lacks a variety of personae, and its central existential "I" seems too theatrical ("I cannot live or die," or "I looked behind me where my wings were gone"), though sometimes it has just the right mixture of boldness and disgust ("Order be damned, I do not want to die, / Even to keep Belaire, Ohio, safe.").

Three poems deserve special mention in this volume, however. The best poems are "The Cold Divinities" and "At the Slackening of the Tide." This is the last stanza of the former:

> But slowly twilight gathered up the skiffs
> Into its long gray arms; and though the sea
> Grew kind as possible to wrack-splayed birds;
> And though the sea like woman vaguely wept;
> She could not hide her clear enduring face,
> Her cold divinities of death and change.

Simple, emotional, not afraid to be vulnerable, this stanza presents the sea as perhaps only a midwesterner can see it. The religious feeling of "cold divinities" seems just right because it avoids piety and yet is both eternal ("enduring face") and human ("like woman vaguely wept"). There is a beauty and a passiveness here, associated with the mythically feminine, which we will see again and again in the later two books as they celebrate "the mysterious lives / Of the unnamed poor." The pervading feeling here forces on the poet, and us, a realization of the limitation of the self, as Wright verges on a total loss of self in the face of nature's unyielding immensities. Yet the effect of the emotion results from Wright's personification of the sea in such controlled and stirring terms. The self seems to both lose and find itself in the imputed hypostasis of the sea.

The third poem of continuing interest from this volume is "The Morality of Poetry," whose very title signals a shift from the highly controlled, autotelic verse emulated by most of the then current theorizers. After saying "Before you let a single word escape, / Starve it in darkness; lash it to the shape / Of tense wing skimming on the sea alone . . . ," Wright describes his failure to formulate a poetics:

> Woman or bird, she [the moon] plumes the ashening sound
> Flaunting to nothingness the rules I made,
> Scattering cinders, widening, over the sand
> Her cold epistle falls. To plumb the fall
> Of silver on ripple, evening ripple on wave,
> Quick celebration where she lives for light,
> I let all measures die.

The poet abandons measure, the principles of ordered utterance, in favor of the measure of things themselves, knowing both the beauty of moon-light and the regularity of nature will constitute his sacramental offering. This, I believe, is one of the central tenets of Wright's poetry, and it is through the unremitting adoption of this belief that Wright found his own later style. This movement from control and measure, from the strictures represented by verse, to the mysteries of self-less absorption in the reverberating patterns of nature marks a dangerous threat, as well as a wondrous promise, that Wright had been avoiding since *The Green Wall* and that continues to haunt him in the last poem of *Shall We Gather at the River* ("Come up to me, love / Out of the river, or I will? Come down to you.") Here is the conclusion of "The Morality of Poetry":

> I send you shoreward echoes of my voice:
> The dithyrambic gestures of the moon,
> Sun-lost, the mind plumed, Dionysian,
> A blue sea-poem, joy, moon-ripple on wave.

The poet discovers a reaffirmative poetic by emulating the release of Dionysus, by gaining a beatific vision of and through nature. Pausing a moment at the mid-way point of Wright's career, it is noteworthy that at least two things appear in both of Wright's first books: love is imaged as stone, and someone drowns. The hard measured emotions contrast sharply with the fluid rechannelings of the self; the cold light of the moon must be taken up by the changing sea.

Wright's next two books mark a decisive break from his previous mode, a break much debated and discussed, viewed as a significant step forward or, by some, as an abandonment of skill and intelligent balance. Both *The Branch Will Not Break* (1963) and *Shall We Gather at the River* (1968) employ a kind of surrealism, at least a kind of surrealist succession of disparate images, whose very isolation constitutes the tissue of the poem's structure, as well as its affective texture. The peculiar emotional *feel* of these later Wright poems is what is distinctive about them. In places their virtual tonelessness seems to insist that they are "gestures of the moon," cold, implacable, and yet somehow fragile. The by now famous "Lying in a Hammock . . ." poem, with its flat concluding statement, "I have wasted my life," leaps out or falls limp in the reader's face, giving or taking little quarter with safe notions about poetic logic. Yet a close examination of "Lying in a Hammock" will reveal that the last line is *not* a surprise; if anything it has been over-prepared for, and that, I think, is really why it gets anthologized so often. With a few adjustments it can be assimilated into a sensibility that still prizes the ironic suspension of self among several possibilities. Only in its final statement does it collapse all these possibilities into an unequivocal admission. The "black trunk," the "distances of the afternoon," the horse manure that "blaze[s] up into golden stones" are all extremely poeticized images. The poem itself, however, doesn't cloy because its disjunctive syntax, its refusal to subordinate or balance the clauses, rejects the control of irony and distance for the sentiment of helpless, unexcused self-victimization.

One thing should be said about these later poems: occasionally some of the lines are badly *written*, however they might be sincerely *felt*. "Tonight, / The cancerous ghosts of old con men / Shed their leaves." "A cop's palm / Is a roach dangling down the scorched fangs / Of a light bulb." What is most striking about the lines out of context is how overwrought, emotionally speaking, the adjectives are, and yet poetically undercharged. "Cancerous," "scorched," and "dangling" are slack, hackneyed, and falsely plangent. The excess feeling also causes the metaphors to blur; in fact, we are back close to something like the "emotional slither" that Pound so castigated in late Victorian poetry. The problem for Wright is to find a mode, and a diction, that will allow him to break open his consciousness with affective suddenness without succumbing to mere pathos.

Here is a poem from *Shall We Gather* that will illustrate most of the features of the late, developed style:

OUTSIDE FARGO, NORTH DAKOTA

Along the sprawled body of the derailed Great Northern freight car,
I strike a match slowly and lift it slowly.
No wind.

Beyond town, three heavy white horses
Wade all the way to their shoulders
In a silo shadow.

Suddenly the freight car lurches.
The door slams back, a man with a flashlight
Calls me good evening.
I nod as I write good evening, lonely
and sick for home.

The specific geographical location, the alienated landscape ("derailed"), the ordinary gesture overfraught with significance (lines 3-4), the sudden leap to another perspective in the second stanza (notice how the temporal dimension here is mythical, featureless, a kind of ablative absolute), the world of shadows and sudden disruptions, and finally the central consciousness of the poem completes (or destroys?) itself in the last, abrupt moment. A majority of those characteristics go to make up almost every poem in the last two books. One way to read this particular poem, and others like it, is to reread it; that is, like a periodic sentence, the controlling action comes only at the end, and we must go back and reevaluate all the relationships in the poem on that basis. Is this poem "really" about the interior life of the poet? If so, isn't its appropriation of all those external realities a selfish, egocentric act, rather than a selfless, ecstatic one? Are the horses there because the numinous, mythical aspects of nature are necessary to give the poem depth (why the number three, for example)? Keats said he hated poetry that "had designs" on him. Surely this is that kind of poem; surely what few "literary" effects it allows itself are all in the service of taking *us in*, rather than getting the poet *out into*, the mood of the poem.

These are certainly "shoreward echoes of [a] voice," such faint emanations that even as the moment occurs in the poem ("Calls me good evening") it becomes no more than a poetic gesture ("I write good evening"). Here the myth of the person is central. Again Keats can help, for he defines negative capability as being in doubts and uncertainties without "any irritable reaching after fact and reason," and something like this is operating in Wright's poetry. But where is the joy of which Wright spoke? Instead he admits "I speak of flat defeat/ In a flat voice." When he begins a poem "My life was never so precious/ To me as now," the next line is flooded with self-consciousness: "I gaze unbelieving at those two lines." Even as early as *Saint Judas* Wright's sense of himself as a writer ("I croon my tears at fifty cents a line") has been fitful, serving by turns as his greatest burden and his only salvation ("I have nothing to ask a blessing for,/ Except these words.").

This central, personal myth — that the poet must lose himself in things, for only there will he find his tongue, the only agency of his true survival — lies pervasively installed in all of Wright's poetry. That is why images of birds ("I want to be lifted up / By some great white bird unknown to the police"), and animals and insects, recur constantly along with that sense of darkness, of a world hidden inside the seen world, which promises an inhuman illumination. The myth of the social outsider, the creature whose antinomian purity is a reservoir of hope, however distant and unrealizable, merges perfectly with this redemptive view of the poet. And the scene of the poet-outsider's redemption is more and more often the body in or by which the expanded consciousness and the rediscovered word is made articulate. As Wright says at the end of "Poems to a Brown Cricket":

> Here, I will stand by you, shadowless,
> At the small golden door of your body till you wake
> In a book that is shining.

He speaks "To the Poets in New York" and the message, of alienation, of loss of self, of rebirth, remains the same:

> You strolled in the open, leisurely and alone,
> Daydreaming of a beautiful human body
> That had undressed quietly and slipped into the river
> And become the river:
> The proud body of an animal that would transform
> The snaggled gears and pulleys
> Into a plant that grows under water.

There is an awesome fear of the fallen human body here that reminds me of Thoreau, and an embracing of the mundane in order to transform it that clearly echoes William Carlos Williams. And there is an Orphic mythifying of nature that recalls Goethe and Emerson. But behind it all I hear most strongly, if not most clearly, the voice of Keats: "O for a life of Sensations rather than of Thoughts . . . the simple imaginative Mind may have its rewards in the repetition of its own silent Working coming continually on the Spirit with a fine Suddenness."

The mind coming on the spirit with a fine suddenness: this is just different enough from Pound's "intellectual and emotional complex in an instant of time" to be very different indeed. Instead of sharp tension and ironic movement through the phrase (cf. Pound's "Franchise for circumcision" or "His true Penelope was Flaubert," the *mot juste*), we have a different sort of movement, one which doesn't value the single line so much as the reverberations at the end of the stanza. But such prosodic speculation is only part of the story (see, for example, Robert Bly's polemic against "technique" in *Naked Poetry*); behind this shift is a change of heart, a transvaluation of value which has reached far beyond Eliot and Pound. It mixes anti-intellectualism, symbolic looseness, Shelleyan inflation, un-ironic theatricality, all at the same time it retains much of the rigor and clarity of the Imagist revolution of the first two decades of the 20th century.

In addition to his four previously published books, Wright includes thirty-three new poems and thirty translations in his *Collected Poems* (1971). The translations are from poets such as Trakl, Neruda, Vallejo, and Jiménez, whose short poems seem especially close to Wright's celebratory, non-ironic spirit. The new poems are uneven in quality, often self-indulgent ("Nobody else will follow/ This poem but you,/ But I don't care"), sometimes bathetic ("I don't even know where/ My own grave is."), and it is easy to see why Wright did not issue them as a separate volume. Many concerns and images reappear from the earlier books, though the scene of the poem is now as likely to be the city as the country. The self-doubt and self-laceration has intensified, and it insists that we, all of us, are implicated.

> We can kill anything.
> We can kill our own bodies.
> Those deer on the hillside have no idea what in hell
> We are except murderers.
> They know that much, and don't think
> They don't.
> Man's heart is the rotten yolk of a blacksnake egg
> Corroding, as it is just born, in a pile of dead
> Horse dung.
> I have no use for the human creature.
> He subtly extracts pain awake in his own kind.
> I am born one, out of an accidental hump of chemistry.
> I have no use.

Even assuming "hump" is a misprint for "lump" and that some other typographical corrections might smooth out the syntax of the third-to-last line, this passage fails for a wide range of reasons, not the least of which is its use of "mangled figures of speech" which Wright laments in the "young poets of New York." "The kind of poem I want to write is/ The poetry of a grown man," he pleads, but this doesn't seem to be it.

That last quote is from "Many of Our Waters: Variations on a Poem by a Black Child," the Phi Beta Kappa poem delivered at William and Mary in 1969. The longest of the new poems, it contains the worst and the best of Wright, that is, his best sentiments and his worst writing, a "scattering poem" by his own admission. These two stanzas illustrate the difficulties:

> I know something about the pure clear word,
> Though I am not yet a grown man.
> And who is he?
>
> The long body of his dream is the beginning of a dark
> Hair under an illiterate
> Girl's ear.

The "illiterate" lets us know Wright is a sentimental liberal; the syntactical elaboration of the metaphor demonstrates how involuted and indefinable his perceptions are; the modifiers "long" and "dark" signal that he wants to remain a simple, passionate poet; the assurance of the first assertion is balanced by the humility of the unadorned second line. But do we have here an example of the "pure, clear word," or an elaborately ironic joke which is really at Wright's expense? Surely, he can't think that his comparison really illuminates anything except his own momentary illiteracy. Yet perhaps he wants that illiteracy to be what rescues the sentiment, rescues it by its dumb, insistent, yet beautiful earnestness. Read in the context of all of Wright's poems, we have to take the poem without irony, even if that makes the poem much less successful. When one becomes as deliberately vulnerable as Wright has become, ordinary strictures about emotional control and artistic clarity are beside the point.

> If you do not care one way or another about
> The preceding lines,
> Please do not go on listening
> On any account of mine.
> Please leave the poem.
> Thank you.

Some poems seem only an exit for themselves, so they can only be left behind. We leave knowing what is meant, but we take no new meanings with us. When an ironic poem fails, it's because it's been too carefully suspended above its own feelings, but when a sentimental poem fails, it's because it merely immerses us in ourselves. The plainness of Wright's feelings threatens to bring a stop to the inventiveness of his words.

The risks involved in following out the dictates of his new style are considerable, and by his occasional, nervous self-consciousness Wright indicates that he is well aware of them. So far I think the rewards have been mixed for his poetry, whatever their effects on him personally. What is most challenging about the questions raised however, is that they must have made Wright, and they will surely make us, reconsider assumptions about the very nature of the self, especially as that nebulous and protean entity exists in poems. Is form itself a way of asserting and aggrandizing the self, or a way of turning the self over to larger forces? No simple talk about keeping the persona separate from the author, or extrapolating from an ironic distance, will suffice in clarifying these problems. For the reader as well as the writer the poem can be a "momentary stay against confusion," but we take up poems and we lay them down in the exigent world. Whether we are enlarged or dissolved by them, or enlarged by being dissolved, depends in crucial ways on *how* and *why* their authors took them up in the first place. Finally, the dumbest, but most important, question we can ask of a poem is "Is it sincere?" The question is dumb because even when we can answer it, we haven't been told much. But it's something we must know.

Wright is, I believe, a sincere man, and when his poems are most successful, it's not simply because he has found a controlling form for his emotions. More inexactly, it's because the question of control has been put aside, for the voice that speaks uncovers and exhausts itself simultaneously. A good lyric poet — and Wright is that — understands that every divinity, especially the musically divine, controls and reveals itself in death and change.

The Poems of Howard Nemerov: Where Loveliness Adorns Intelligible Things

BY JAMES M. KIEHL

DESPITE MY ABSTRACTING a phrase from "Blue Swallows" and for the moment seeming to return it to a banal notion that poems are merely ornamental, I believe that Nemerov's poems are often great imaginative instruments that lead us far out. They take us to the ground of being to watch the dragonfly become, transformed from brutal night below and ascending to the sun ("The Dragonfly"). They further lead us, as in "The Beekeeper Speaks . . . And Is Silent," to listen to the stars beyond the sun. And despite the typical lucidity of Nemerov's poems and despite his usual achievement of splendid images, his poems are not always easily grasped. "Celestial Globe," for example, "Turns all things inside out," including the human head, until the poem virtually baffles thought. "Interiors," presenting a medieval milieu, is only obscurely lit and dimly figured according to human sexual sensation.

Often Nemerov's poems lead us into thought, about ourselves and our circumstances, beyond our usual conceptual and perceptual categories. We are offered passages across boundaries as formidable as death itself if we can come to see that "flowers light the sun": "When you have known how this may be / you have already lived forever . . ." ("Small Moment"). And before the poet of "Blue Swallows" himself falls into stoney-eyed silent rapture before the world he would take us to, he at last disclaims even his own medium as if most certainly to point the way one last time:

> O swallows, swallows, poems are not
> The point. Finding again the world,
> That is the point, where loveliness
> Adorns intelligible things
> Because the mind's eye lit the sun.

The world referred to is clearly not our usual world of conventionally "Remarkable things" ("Sightseers"):

> *Click,* the Vatican,
> *Click,* the Sphinx,
> *Click,* in the Badlands,
> The enormous nostrils
> Of the Fathers. . . .

Us usual sightseers, bearing "Tabernacle or pyx / Priestly with symbols / In silver and black," come to worship only graven images.

Nemerov's poems would lead us instead to the wonderful, unaccounted for, and hitherto scarcely spoken of world of "everything that is." They lead us to everything "In the world" beyond our usual categories of apprehension such as angel (spirit) at one hand and stone (substance) at the other ("Angel and Stone"). They take us to "the incommensurable" world scarcely imaginable beyond our motion picture thinking ("The First Day"), to the unclockable "now" ("Moment"), to the uncharted "somewhere" ("Somewhere") beyond where "history is" ("Blue Swallows") or "history was" ("Sightseers"). His poems would take us back to the miraculous otherworld all our philosophers derive us from. "Firelight in Sunlight" offers a splendid phenomenal paradigm of such returns, as it shows us how sunlight (the world's primary energy) returns to itself. If our mood is yet more flamboyant, our home with the gods, in "The First Point of Aries" or in "The Companions," will make best sense to us. Or perhaps we will most plausibly get home to the undivided self through the dream-poems like "Sleeping Beauty" or through reveries, by smell, to the child's sense in "Burning the Leaves" or to the beloved vision of "Two Girls."

Seldom are we much aware of our own perceptual conventions. The witty viewer, who speaks to us while watching TV in Nemerov's satire "A Way of Life," is at least partly aware that he confuses several planes of illusion: television fiction, commercial advertisement, and ordinary consciousness. But we are usually quite unaware that we thoroughly order our worlds with our concepts and our language and, consequently, that we get locked into narrowly exclusive views. The pitiable plight of the man, much like ourselves, confined to "a view where every last thing / Is rimed with its own shadow / Exactly" ("The View") shows us our own perceptual predicament. Usually we unwittingly run our hellish race to nowhere ("The Race") and are at last "taken by the darkness in surprise" ("Blue Suburban").

Rarely do we noticeably cross boundaries of being so that, like the people in "Going Away," we are touched "with a strange tonality" of what we have been and, implicitly, of who and where we are. Moreover, such boundary-crossings are risky. In "Brainstorm" we see a man that sees through some of the usual human conceptual categories. He sees himself related to his circumstance — his house assailed by the wind and outside his house, the crows — with unusual but marvelously creditable vision. He sees, for example, that "Houses are only trees stretched on the rack." Thus he brilliantly intuits the total integrity of nature, but his consequent guilt at his usual ignorant human abstraction threatens to entirely overwhelm his ordinary sense of things. And so he sees his own opening awareness as a horrifying craniotomy.

Psychologists, semanticists, and other scientists and philosophers of all sorts have long warned us that the real world is not necessarily coincidental with our words referring to it, our ideas ordering it, or our compelling illusions about its forms and appearances. Nemerov's many dream-poems typically test our senses of reality. His difficult epistemological poem "One Way" describes how words wed thing (other) and thought (self) to bring the world into being for us or, perhaps, to bring ourselves into being, but it concomitantly discloses and warns that our words are not coextensive with the world. Like the ancient prophets and patriarchs that Nemerov thought of in composing "The View from Pisgah," scientists warn us of the folly in mistaking our particular maps for the real territories they refer to and represent. "Projection," about us fearfully coming to the end of our Renaissance self-assurance and certainty, beautifully expresses Korzybski's metaphor.

Our amazingly complex human cultures indicate that, apart from our more notorious conceptual disagreements (about economics or politics or religion), we have been incredibly successful at perceptual and verbal socialization. Highly prizing social order, we determinedly indoctrinate ourselves thoroughly into our languages. "To David, about His Education" describes, with amusing irony, the way we condition ourselves:

> In order to become one of the grown ups
> Who sees invisible things neither steadily nor whole,
> But keeps gravely the grand confusion of the world
> Under his hat, which is where it belongs,
> And teaches small children to do this in their turn.

And the oldest wisdom poetry preserves for us intimates that the human experience of mind is essentially an achievement of imaginative fixation and conventionality. Referring to both *Beowulf* and Freud, "Beyond the Pleasure Principle" notices, for example, that "Our human thought arose at first in myth, / And going far enough became a myth once more." In "The View from Pisgah" human mind is mirages and idolatries, with which to figure the void and by which we seem to escape the unbearable wilderness.

And so, we greatly value the way that language orders our experience for us and are like the absent-minded professor's bright replacement, who prefers the papers to the leaves ("Absent-Minded Professor"). We prefer to stay inside with the orderly and manageable illusions; we are fond of the sense they convey that we control our life and experience. Prizing the order, coherence, and closure — the definition, we say — that our languages furnish, we are disposed to ignore that they are also a "limiting tradition" ("Cybernetics"). Nemerov's Phi Beta Kappa poem on how "the dreams of the desert are digested in art" is fiercely angry that we benignly frame, tame, and pervert the savage otherworldly intuitions that might wake us from our solipsisms ("A Relation of Art and Life"). His Arabian Nights poem, "Somewhere," warns at last that the accounts of life we listen to, the stories we tell ourselves, before we go to sleep betray us by turning life into soporific "sweet seductions / Punishable by death." "The Companions," on the sense of dying to the world's magic and marvel — "There used to be gods in everything, and now they've gone" — is perhaps a complement for "To David, about His Education." More than poignant, the speaker's awareness of having turned away from the world and wonder is redeemingly tragic:

> I must have done, I guess, to have grown so abstract
> That all the lonely summer night's become but fact,
> That when the cricket signals I no longer listen,
> Nor read the glowworms' constellations when they glisten.

But ordinarily we have only grown abstract and only come to fact. We have unwittingly come to assume that our particular categories are indigenous to nature. Our ignorance is an insidious trap, and even intending to avoid it may not save us from it. Consider the gentle ironies in "Elegy for a Nature Poet" about how a man, more than usually sensitive to the world, died:

> And now, poor man, he's gone. Without his name
> The field reverts to wilderness again,

> The rocks are silent, woods don't seem the same;
> Demoralized small birds will fly insane.
>
> Rude Nature, whom he loved to idealize
> And would have wed, pretends she never heard
> His voice at all, as, taken by surprise
> At last, he goes to her without a word.

Especially in our own time, however, the best thinkers, in the natural sciences and elsewhere, are more and more aware that they approach absolute limits in their capacities to describe and order the world. One of the characters in Nemerov's little drama, "This, That, & the Other," observes: "The physicists are vexed between the wave / And particle." The poet in "Angel and Stone" concedes "it is hard to imagine what life must be like." "The First Day" begins:

> Below the ten thousand billionth of a centimeter
> Length ceases to exist. Beyond three billion light years
> The nebulae would have to exceed the speed of light
> In order to be, which is impossible: no universe.
> The long and short of it seems to be that thought
> Can make itself unthinkable, and that measurement
> Of reach enough and scrupulosity will find its home
> In the incommensurable.

One response, by the sciences, to such limitations is to come back upon themselves to devote attention to their own modes of expression and perception. They are at last noticing that their own modes are analogic and metaphoric, and consequently they are learning the same sort of diffidence poets acquire as a "negative capability."

It is especially this new scientific awareness, I think, that explains why Nemerov noticeably exploits "scientific" images and concepts. Particularly important to him is the idea that our mode of observation significantly determines what we see or, more broadly, that being is not a thing but a Gestalt. Correspondingly, so many of his finest poems are reflexive — that is, they present the topic of their own expressiveness — exactly because he recognizes that the limit of expression is such a universally important intellectual problem. In "Writing" the poet makes lovely analogies, such as skaters' marks scored in ice and looking like script in a foreign language, and seems to conclude: "It is as though the world / were a great writing." But he sees further, and the poem continues:

> Having said so much,
> let us allow there is more to the world
> than writing; continental faults are not
> bare convoluted fissures in the brain.
> Not only must the skaters soon go home;
> also the hard inscription of their skates

> is scored across the open water, which long
> remembers nothing, neither wind nor wake.

In "Blue Swallows" the poet urges us "to see / The real world where the spelling mind / Imposes with its grammar book / Unreal relations on the blue / Swallows." And in "Holding the Mirror Up to Nature" the poet speaks as if frustrated and distraught:

> Some shapes cannot be seen in a glass,
> those are the ones the heart breaks at.
> They will never become valentines
> or crucifixes, never. Night clouds
> go on insanely as themselves
> though metaphors would be prettier;
> and when I see them massed at the edge
> of the globe, neither weasel nor whale,
> as though this world were, after all,
> non-representational, I know
> a truth that cannot be told, although
> I try to tell you. . . .

This sort of distress, perhaps traditionally suffered by "the serious poets with their / crazy ladies and cloudy histories" and mostly disdained by scientists we suppose, has now become the hardcore study of our sciences. Striving for ever more-precise descriptive accuracy, they have anxiously come at last to uncertainty principles and may yet lose themselves in Nemerov's Black Museum "When all analogies are broken" and "The scene grows strange again" ("The Black Museum"). And so, "The Human Condition" portrays the recently-familiar modern sensibility:

> In this motel where I was told to wait,
> The television screen is stood before
> The picture window. Nothing could be more
> Use to a man than knowing where he's at,
> And I don't know, but pace the day in doubt
> Between my looking in and looking out.

Or, from a radically different point of view, the poet, as if one long suffering, will vindictively and almost hysterically celebrate the breakdowns of the "iron characters," of all the self-righteously certain "keepers of the public confidence" ("The Iron Characters").

In some of Nemerov's poems, such as "The Daily Globe," the poet is simply detached from and amused at the psychic bondage into which we have fallen and at the instruments by which our illusions are sustained. The newspaper comic strip recurs, we notice, as one of Nemerov's expressions of our simple-minded stupor. In "Life Cycle of the Common Man," for example, we "behold the man":

> Walking into deep silence, with the ectoplastic
> Cartoon's balloon of speech proceeding
> Steadily out of the front of his face, the words
> Borne along on the breath which is his spirit
> Telling the numberless tale of his untold Word
> Which makes the world his apple, and forces him to eat.

In "Sunday" we are reduced to supposing that our lives and sensibilities are "the horrible funnies flattened on the floor" that God may read on his day off. The movies-idea, which appears in "The First Day," is perhaps Nemerov's most fully elaborated analogue for consciousness — for the conventionalized awareness — that may be mistaken for vital being. But if all these instances imply contempt for our condition, in other poems, like "Projection," the poetic voice seems inclined to pity our plight as victims of our own illusions: "They were so amply beautiful, . . . who could have blamed / Us? . . ."

No matter what tone he takes, however, the poet's recurrent recognition that we are typically locked into particular modes of perception helps him to counteract his accustomed sense of things and to try to see, for a change, how flowers — perhaps Nemerov's metaphor for our sensory organs — may be said to light the sun ("Small Moment"). If the recognition is at first mostly intellectual it nevertheless prepares him and us to seize upon and treasure experiences of grace when they come. With a genius for selecting the objective correlative (and an eye to the antique tradition that souls travel on odors), the poet reports, for example, that while burning leaves "the smell of smoke takes memory by surprise" and marvelously transports him ("Burning the Leaves"). In a poem that amply prepares us for the visual realization, he fuses his view of his own children playing about the fire with an extravagant and poignant sense of himself as a child. In "The Companions" the poet remembers that he once saw the world wonderful. Thus he prepares us to look for the eyes in the stone, to listen for the voice from the elm branch, to discover the glowworms' constellations when they glisten, to be with the gods again.

Actually, Nemerov seldom exploits the vatic myths about poesy or comes on as a prophet. Occasionally, however, he satirizes such posturing. The poet in "On the Platform" scorns the modern poet's podium-persona and the audience that patronizes it. Taking the rostrum on a traditional prophetic occasion, the college commencement, the poet in "A Relation of Art and Life" savages false prophets. But more usual for Nemerov is the lament, with its gentle irony, for the poet as failed prophet in "Elegy for a Nature Poet." Both "The

View from Pisgah" and "The Poet at Forty" expose the poet's sense
of inadequacy with regard to the tradition. About as close as Nemerov
comes to sincerely taking the prophetic stance is in his offering, from
high up in the head of the house, "The View from an Attic Window."

But if he doesn't often or easily posture, Nemerov nevertheless
insistently asserts the substance of the great tradition and reaffirms
that the poet is a visionary. Here are some of his remarks in "The
Muse's Interest," his address to the National Poetry Festival at the
Library of Congress in 1962 and printed in his book *Poetry and
Fiction: Essays*:

> The poet hopes to articulate a vision concerning human
> life; he hopes to articulate it truly. He may not be much of
> a poet, he may not be much of a human being, the vision
> is not so special either; but it is what he hopes to do.

> This "vision" need not be thought of in religious terms,
> as a dramatic one-shot on the road to Damascus; its articu-
> lation may be slow indeed, and spread over many works;
> the early and late parts of it may elucidate one another, or
> encipher one another still more deeply.

> For the substance of this vision the poet listens, he watches,
> and when he speaks in his character of poet it is his convic-
> tion, possibly his illusion, that something other speaks in him.

As special vision is the soul of poetic experience, the poet's art or
craft is to remodel language so that it can embody and express the
new reality he sees. The most usual way this is done is to make
unusual comparisons of things or events so as to partly redefine them
and alter their appearances to us. Such figuring is abundant in
Nemerov's poems, and it is sometimes more witty than it is earnest
and purposeful. Pleasant instances are the power lawn mower likened
to a dinosaur ("Suburban Prophecy"), the corsetted lady as an
antique whaling vessel or as the whale itself ("I Only Am Escaped
Alone to Tell Thee"), or boarding an airliner and taking off as the
rite of Eucharist ("At the Airport"). Others of his analogues are
richly thoughtful and illuminating. In "Sanctuary," a thought taking
shape in the human mind is like a trout in a pool, coming up toward
the surface where it can be seen. And some of his comparisons are
deeply disturbing: an American poet in bed, cowering under his
electric blanket, is like a Vietnamese Buddhist priest who immolates
himself in gasoline fire ("Christmas Morning").

With respect to our language's usual appearances, operations, and
uses, poetry is our language turned extravagant and used somewhat

out of bounds. Good examples are Nemerov's many dream poems that upset the definitions of human waking and sleeping, perhaps by simply inverting them. "Sleeping Beauty" is a superb instance. Not only is it about dreaming as a traditional borderline experience for the human sensibility but it is additionally modeled on the child's fairy tale, another conventional borderline concept. Frequently then, as in "Sleeping Beauty" but as is especially apparent in "Winter Exercise," the inversion of waking and sleeping is extended to a reversal of life and death and of our values for them. You will notice, of course, that I have chosen to characterize Nemerov's poetry generally with one of his own expressions that demands just such simple inversion. "Because the mind's eye lit the sun" not only are things finally lovely but they are even discernible as *things* in the first place.

Beyond the mental play of simple inversion, then, many more of Nemerov's poems broadly effect various boundary-crossings and enlarge upon our usual senses of the language. "At a Country Hotel" presents a dead man who watches from another state of wakeful being, not unlike a dream perhaps, as his widow supervises their children's play with toy boats on the pond. At last, as the children are asleep, their planes of being may, if they dream of their boats, meet with their father's dreams of sailing home to them. In another poem, darkness falls in the public park and longing statues tremble at the brink and nearly spring to life and love ("The Statues in the Public Gardens"). In "The Goose Fish," too, lovers at the shore are haunted by the grinning dead fish, whose judgment of them they try to infer. And in "The Breaking of Rainbows" it is a polluted stream, not even a conventionally animate phenomenon, that is personified and vitalized.

Because poetry is, in various ways, language turned inside out or upside down it is more noticeably challenging to hearers and readers than is the language of ordinary usage. If it often more easily excites visual, aural, and kinesthetic responses, it also demands more active intellectual engagement. It often poses riddles. How, for example, are human limbs like flower-stalks ("Sunday at the End of Summer")? How can flowers be said to light the sun, and how could battlefield be marriage bed ("Small Moment")? What other way could the grinning corpse ("The Goose Fish") tell lovers how to make a world their own than by their making love? And sometimes, as in "Celestial Globe," the riddles about a globe "Whereon I stand / Balancing this ball / Upon my hand" are so acute and mind-baffling, so much

288 JAMES M. KIEHL

"Turn all things inside out," that we become frustrated with language. We may come to sympathize with Nemerov's 40-year-old poet in "Lion & Honeycomb," who had had enough of skill, of cleverly managing the verbal medium, and at last recognizes that he wants only "words that would / Enter the silence and be there as light" to establish "Only a moment's inviolable presence / . . . Perfected and casual as to a child's eye / Soap bubbles are, and skipping stones."

And so it may be that the ultimate refinement of the poet's craft or art in behalf of his vision is to do the thing in words that is as near as possible to doing without words. For it is words and thinking that are in some senses destructive to fullest human life, as Nemerov suggests in his elegy "These Words Also," on the suicide of a young woman. In opposition to the beautiful, vital flower garden outside, inside, letters and nighttime talk and telephone ringing haunted their victim till she died. Perhaps the poet best expresses his vision by the compelling understatement of simply drawing "A Picture" — "Of people running down the street / Among the cars, a good many people. / . . . (hunting down / A Negro, according to the caption)":

> A pretty girl tilted off-balance
> And with her mouth in O amazed;
> A man in a fat white shirt, his tie
> Streaming behind him, as one flat foot
> Went slap on the asphalt. . . .

By praising Flaubert's wish to write a novel about *nothing* — "It was to have no subject / And be sustained upon style alone" — and even more by his gratitude that Flaubert "never wrote that novel" thus leaving it "not deformed by style, / That fire that eats what it illuminates" ("Style"), Nemerov wittily expresses the poet's ambition to transcend his art that so often betrays his vision.

Possessing a brilliant objective correlative, Nemerov's justly celebrated "Vermeer" begins by the poet composedly remarking both on Vermeer's manner in his paintings and on what the poet hopes will be his own manner in celebrating Vermeer's manner: "Taking what is, and seeing it as it is, / Pretending to no heroic stances or gestures, / Keeping it simple." But the poet is soon drawn into a paean on the "marvelous things that light is able to do" and, finding himself "At one for once with sunlight falling through / A leaded window," verges on "the holy mathematic" that "Plays out the cat's cradle of relation / Endlessly" in the composition. Then, as if sensing that again in his art his medium will betray his vision, he changes tactics, self-consciously retreats from the subject, and surprisingly finds it:

If I could say to you, and make it stick,
A girl in a red hat, a woman in blue
Reading a letter, a lady weighing gold . . .
If I could say this to you so you saw,
And knew, and agreed that this was how it was
In a lost city across the sea of years,
I think we should be for one moment happy
In the great reckoning of those little rooms
Where the weight of life has been lifted and made light,
Or standing invisible on the shore opposed,
Watching the water in the foreground dream
Reflectively, taking a view of Delft
As it was, under a wide and darkening sky.

Nemerov appropriately names his poem *Vermeer* — instead of *Light,* for instance — to indicate that illumination comes to us exactly because it is framed.

No doubt, various artists are of differing visionary genius and of differing skill in expression, which partly accounts for the difficulties that poetry may impose on hearers and readers. In several poems Nemerov satirizes would-be poets of little genius. "A Modern Poet" presents a poet not crossing Brooklyn Ferry at sunset and rhapsodizing on the gloriously transfigured cityscape but instead riding a bandwagon "crossing at rush hour the Walt Whitman Bridge" and meanly calculating routes to fame. "Make Big Money at Home! Write Poems in Spare Time!" portrays the wooden-headed would-be poet trying unsuccessfully to write verses on a tree while holding his wooden pencil poised above his pad of wooden paper on his wooden table in his whole wooden house. In yet other poems Nemerov refers more generously to the plights of those who may possess worthy vision but whose skill falls short of expressing it. In "To H. M.: On Reading His Poems," for example, Nemerov consolingly makes a pretty figure to suggest that even should the poet fail at his intention his verse may yet be inadvertently felicitous and worthy. And in "Trees" he touchingly redeems the much-ridiculed verses by Joyce Kilmer.

Furthermore the language of poetry may be regarded as variously challenging because, possibly apart from considerations of vision and expressive skill, poets may choose how much difficulty to impose upon hearers and readers. Poets make decisions, probably not always conscious ones, about how an accommodation should be made in the conflict between requirements of the vision that strains language conventions on the one hand and language recognition needs of the audience on the other hand. In several poems Nemerov portrays poets' awareness of the need to adjust the mode of expression to the audience. "On the Platform" presents a sarcastic poet contemptuous of both himself and his audience for having compromised his vision by his offering and their taking or mistaking a mode of expression he at last discovers to be infelicitous. "From the Desk of the Laureate: For Immediate Release" is about seeing little and, even worse, possessing only an outworn mode of expression not at all suited to an "audience" that is deaf to any music and only reads the news. The poem portrays a spent poet resigning from the front office of the grand old heroic style no longer in vogue (Great Pan, Helicon, the Birthday Ode, Astraea, etc.). With what little dignity remains he retires from that archaic reference and idiom in the early stanzas to anesthetized, antiquated privacy and wry self-deprecation in the tightly rhymed last stanza. Thus not only do various poets compose for different audiences but any poet may vary his sense of audience from one poem to another, as Nemerov appears to do.

Considering the whole spectrum of poetic subjects and styles, we can notice that at one side some poems are relatively private; they are composed only for the poet himself or for a coterie. Most of Nemerov's reflexive poems — that is, poems about poetry — are surely of this sort. In addition to those I've already cited — "Writing," "Holding the Mirror Up to Nature," "The Blue Swallows," "Vermeer," "Lion & Honeycomb," and "In the Black Museum" — we should also notice: "Maestria," "To Lu Chi," and "Shells." And perhaps commanding an even smaller audience are Nemerov's poems on mind and thought. Some of these, though rich and difficult, are relatively easier than others, however, because they develop a substantial coherent image. "The First Day" with its movies-metaphor for human thought and self-consciousness offers a good example:

> It may be said that within limits the Creation is
> A going concern, imaginable because the film supplies
> An image, a thin but absolute membrane whose surfaces
> Divide the darkness from the light while at the same time
> Uniting light and darkness, and whose linear motion,
> Divided into frames, or moments, is at the same time
> Continuous with itself and may be made to pace itself
> Indistinguishably from the pace of time; being also
> Able to be repeated, speeded up, slowed down, stopped,
> And even run backwards, its model represents to us
> Memory, concentration, causal sequence, analysis,
> Time's irreversibility together with our doubt of this,
> And a host of notions that from time long out of mind
> Belong to the mind.

Others, like "Truth" with its buzzing fly that presides over the sleeper's dream and "The Sanctuary" with its trout, are difficult despite elaborately sustaining an image. Perhaps responding to these as a group, including others such as "Thought" and "Idea" as well, is the surest way to fathom their depths.

At the other side of the poetic spectrum are Nemerov's more public compositions; these, by their subjects and modes, are much more easily available to many of us who share the common language. And in "The Muse's Interest" (the National Poetry Festival address) Nemerov remarks, indeed, that he believes his own poems are readily accessible: "I do not think my own efforts in the art raise such barriers of intellect, learning, subtlety, as would defeat the well-intentioned effort of any ordinarily literate person to read what I produce." Obvious examples are his topical poems on exceedingly commonplace things, events, and values. He discourses on the iconography of the U. S. nickel ("Money"). He remodels power-mowing our suburban lawns as a sort of primitive-beast fable ("Suburban Prophecy"). He reinterprets our photo-journalism history of the atomic bombing in "August, 1945." And in "Santa Claus" he invites our indignation at the commercial travesty of our social and religious sentiments. We also get easy access to other poems — "The Distances They Keep" and "Learning by Doing," for examples — because we are well-prepared with socially credited attitudes on fashionable topics of human experience such as depredations of the natural environment. Yet others among Nemerov's poems are broadly available because they employ vulgar idiom. "The Great Society, Mark X" speaks to us the language of the auto ads. "To the Governor and Legislature of Massachusetts" offers us juvenile education and adolescent sport. In "The Sparrow in the Zoo" we get homely literary kinds like fable and proverb. Witty and amusing as they often are, however, these are poems in which "loveliness adorns intelligible things" only in the most peripheral and feeble sense of Nemerov's essential meaning in "Blue Swallows," with which we started.

Nemerov's success at composing in a public voice is nevertheless commendable, as it serves to counter obscurantist fashions that have polluted modern verse and its appreciation. "On Certain Wits: who amused themselves over the simplicity of Barnett Newman's paintings shown at Bennington College in May of 1958" renders unmistakable his contempt of poseurs. Or consider Nemerov's revulsion to verse of no vision tortuously expressed only to indulge pretensions. "On the Threshold of His Greatness, the Poet Comes Down with a Sore

Throat" mercilessly lampoons Eliot's sort of anti-heroic poem that offers an excursion through an esoteric wasteland to presumed transcendence at last but that really only sinks at last into babbling idiocy and graceless self-exegesis.

Nemerov's most primitive and simple poems are related to the ancient riddling and proverb traditions in poetry. "Don Juan to the Statue" exploits vulgar euphemism and turns on several senses of "erection." Similarly, "The Dream of Flying Comes of Age" wryly notices that the pilot's "joystick" has become a "control column." Gnomishly Nemerov is tempted to transform "boys and girls" to "bars and grills" to resolve love-pangs ("Gnomes"). And he portrays the entire course of a human life, by ringing changes on a single word, "innocense"; a single phrase, "That was it." "A Primer of the Daily Round" surveys the alphabet personified, as if cataloguing an entire society's interaction, and ends by remembering how it began by peeling an apple. "Drama," staged in esoteric nomenclature, mock-heroically plays out molluscan love and death beneath the sea. Largely whimsical, these witty stunt-poems disclose Nemerov's fondness for verbal play. In some sense, of course, all poetry is play with the language for new expressive purposes. But these stunt-poems are made mostly for the sake of play itself rather than for any earnest intention to express vision or wisdom.

More purposeful and earnest play with the language occurs with Nemerov's management of elaborate verse forms such as the sestina that helps to measure the sun's descent in "Sarajevo"; the symmetry that facilitates our access to the center or bottom of things in the whole group of his "Runes"; or the several compositional symmetries in "The Human Condition," symmetries that mimic the predicament of the poem's speaker who languishes in a limbo between the world and his view of it:

> Once I saw world and thought exactly meet,
> But only in a picture by Magritte,
>
> A picture of a picture, by Magritte,
> Wherein a landscape on an easel stands
> Before a window opening on a land-
> scape, and the pair of them a perfect fit,
> Silent and mad.

But we have already remarked (in "Lion & Honeycomb") that ultimately the poet comes to repudiate his whole bag of tricks and to desire only "words that would / Enter the silence and be there as light."

This brings us, then, to "The Junction, on a Warm Afternoon," an exquisite sensory poem where we stand at a rural railroad-crossing and watch a slow freight train rise into view around a bend. We watch it pass us, then, so that we can see and ponder its crew looking back at us and acknowledging us looking at them; then at last we watch the train disappear into the distance. The miracle of this poem is mimetic perfection. Out of an initial sketchy and tangled abstraction, corresponding to "The roadside scribble of wire and stick / Left over from last fall," the imagery rises in slow motion to detailed substantiality as it describes the approaching slow freight and the appearance and manner of its crew. At the exact center of the poem and middle of the train's passage past us through the junction, we are led past the old men's meditative pipe-smoking and courteous but remote nods to us to emphatically cross into their feelings and their sense of warm sunlight. Then past the poem's center, we are returned back out to the rich imagery that restores our more-objective view of the slowly passing train. And we are also turned to thoughtfulness about the growing obsolescence of both the old men and their engines. At last the freight disappears "among small trees, / Leaving empty the long, shining rails / That curve, divide, vanish, and remain." And correlatively, the rich imagery has diminished into the lean images that approach severe abstraction. Thus Nemerov's great poem is not only profoundly skillful, even though "He didn't want to do it with skill," but it utterly depends on his skill.

Another sort of playful poem by Nemerov is founded on learning, that is, on somewhat special information. These poems correspond, in a way, to the ones we've already noticed playing with sounds and meanings of words. These learned poems play with public facts and traditional ideas. They are plentifully referential and elaborately allusive, sometimes only for the sake of the play itself and to offer us enjoyable recognitions if we are knowledgeable. Both "The Second-Best Bed" and "Polonius Passing through a Stage" tease Shakespearean lore and literature to something like interpretive variations on traditional themes, for our pleasure. And "Metamorphoses: according to Steinberg" is mostly a descriptive panegyric to the great cartoonist's extraordinary vision and his incisive style that is itself the principal substance of his vision. Others of Nemerov's learned poems are made more for thematic purposes beyond their play. Ulysses appears in the second and fourteenth "Runes" as a traditional intellectual marker that helps direct the entire sequence's passage by water to the still center of being. "To a Scholar in the Stacks" describes traditional bookish scholarships as the scholar's tragic self-incarceration in the depths of cerebral illusion. Appropriate to the scholar's imagination, the depths are rendered in figures from ancient legends about lost wanderings in the Cretan labyrinth:

> Sometimes in darkness and in deep despair
> You will remember, Theseus, that you were
> The Minotaur, the Labyrinth and the thread
> Yourself; even you were that ingener
> That fled the maze and flew — so long ago —
> Over the sunlit sea to Sicily.

Making involuted reference, not unlike that in Keats's "On First Looking into Chapman's Homer," Nemerov's "Celestial Globe" supposes children at the Museum watching "some amateur / Copying Rembrandt's painting / Of Aristotle contemplating / The skull of Homer, that / Dark fire fountaining forth / the twin poems of the war / And of the journey home" as if Homer's mind were either the Museum in which the children stand or the world on which they stand. Although the poem seems immensely playful as the poet imaginatively juggles and compares celestial (inside), terrestial (outside), and cranial (inside and outside) globes, it nevertheless earnestly expresses Nemerov's centrally important idea that the mind's eye lights the sun. All these learned poems, both playful and purposeful, are to varying degrees exclusive. They are, by their erudition, not altogether public and easily accessible. But what is usually not obscure about them, even to the ill-informed hearer or reader, is why or how these learned poems are challenging. Most of us easily enough appreciate that grasping this sort of poem turns mostly on recognizing what are obviously the proper names that occur in it.

Another sizable group of Nemerov's poems, his satires, are also somewhat more complex and demanding than the poems of simple play. For though the satires do play to some extent, they are also visionary, often in the reactive sense that they show us the failures of vision. By Nemerov's dramatic irony, for example, we can patronize Oliver's failure to see the "reality" under his nose ("Make Big Money at Home! Write Poems in Spare Time!"). But the satire does more than merely ridicule an ignorant blockhead. Without accusing us exactly, it compels us to adjust what was likely also our supposition: that a tree as the subject of a poem ought to be "The axle of the universe, maybe, / Or some other mythologically / Respectable tree-contraption / With dryads, or having to do / With the knowledge of Good and Evil, and the Fall." And by further directing our attention so much to wood, the poem leads us to see what we otherwise wouldn't. Or look beneath the hood and notice that Nemerov's parody of the auto-ad hucksterism in "The Great Society, Mark X" does more than merely indict us for being too willing to "buy" a dangerous social machine, inimical to human welfare. A look at the poem's controlling image further shows us that it is literally our obsession with the *things* we consume, such as autos, or with being hell-bent on getting somewhere, as in "The Race," that jeopardizes us.

The satirist's method, typically, is to draw us to his side in a contest he portrays between his views and values and some others. In "Boom!" he mimics the prophetic stance of his adversary the Eisenhower clergyman and pretends enthusiastic assent to the preacher's smug satisfaction with the affluent society. But the satirist's ranting panegyric and his bizarre catalog of the affluent society's material and spiritual wonders soon imputes madness to the preacher and his values. In "One Forever Alien" the satirist speaks as if a long-suffering immigrant martyred at last to American chauvinism. As if a moldering corpse speaking from the grave, he bitterly describes his outsider's frustration and suffering in terms that ironically realize Whitmanesque vision and prophecy about the assimilation of aliens to the American experience:

> When I become the land, when they will build
> Blast furnaces over me, and lay black asphalt
> For hundreds of miles across my ribs, and wheels
> Begin to bounce interminably on the bone;
> When I enter, at last, America, when I am
> Part of her progress and a true patriot,
> And the school children sing of my sacrifice,
> Remembering the burial day of my birth —
> . . . .
> When I shall come among you fleeced as the lamb
> And in the diaper of the grave newly arrayed. . . .

Thus we are moved to empathy with the pitiable outsider's view and to scorn for the traditional American sentiment that might otherwise have been ours. But however he wins us exactly, however he establishes normative views, the satirist's intention to do so constrains him, after all, to make and keep his values clear to us, to express himself in a relatively public way.

As we examine "One Forever Alien" we should notice that, unlike the other satires, it does not invite ridicule of a speaker who sees things in ways that we find ridiculous or contemptible; it does not present a speaker with views and values inferior to our own. To the contrary, it presents a special point of view in which we can vicariously participate and so gives us a new view of things, and, perhaps, an altered sense of ourselves. Thus we come to Nemerov's dramatic poems. "Drama" is a delightful melodramatic play of love and death, between aloof Elysia and importunate Wentletrap. "Debate with the Rabbi" presents the witty play and definition of ethnic experience and wisdom. Richer in vision is the epistemological debate, between This (percept) and That (concept), on snowflakes and sunlight falling on the open water ("This, That, & the Other"). The two characters harmoniously conclude (their colloquy ends as if it had been a litany) as if both apprehension and comprehension have failed:

> The Other is deeply meddled in this world.
> We see no more than that the fallen light
> Is wrinkled in and with the wrinkling wave.

But if we heed their own Shakespearean proverb — " 'By indirections find directions out' " — we see that their culminating vision is a scintillating and dazzling image that figures for us no failure at all.

Only a few of Nemerov's poems, however, actually present several speakers engaged in dialogue and conflict. Instead, I designate as *dramatic* mostly those among his poems that are expressed not in the vaguely defined "poet's" voice of so many poems but in various voices of other better individuated personae. And I find that typically these dramatic poems function to portray the personae speaking as much as to express their particular views. Or as is so clear in the special drama of the satire, there are in these poems several views — for example, both the persona's view of things and Nemerov's implicit view of the persona — which the hearer or reader must accommodate. Having already noticed "One Forever Alien," let us go on to "Redeployment," in which a survivor of warfare seems uncertain that the war is over: "They say the war is over. But water still / Comes bloody from the taps. . . . " He suffers what we rather easily infer are disordered views of his circumstance, and we suppose he is deranged. We come to a strange dilemma, however, as we notice that we depend on his expression for our views of him and that he is somewhat aware that all is not well with him:

> The end of the war. I took it quietly
> Enough. I tried to wash the dirt out of
> My hair and from under my fingernails,
> I dressed in clean white clothes and went to bed.

His barely expressed suspicion that warfare may not be over but that warring forces may be only displaced from the public world to be redeployed within himself poignantly portrays that he is not altogether mad. If we are at all sensitive, we begin to see, I think, that war, far more than its victim, is horribly insane. And we may be moved to adjust somewhat our own presumed healthy sensibilities and conventional sound judgments that certainly affirm the war is over and patronizingly pity the deranged victim. Or consider "History of a Literary Movement" as another dramatic poem that involves us in the interplay of several points of view. Here an anonymous speaker sadly chronicles for us the disintegration of a literary coterie. But the very manner of his expression discloses that his judgments about others are capricious and that he is an unreliable reporter. About his former comrade Brumbach he petulantly remarks: "He was a fat man / Fat men are seldom the best / Creative writers." Finally he unwittingly discloses that he is undergoing treatment that, by both the manner and substance of his expression, we suspect is psychiatric:

> Only Impli and I
> Hung on, feeling as we did
> That the last word had not
> Finally been said. Sometimes
> I feel, I might say, cheated.
> Life here at Bad Grandstein
> Is dull, is dull, what with
> The eternal rocks and the river;
> And Impli, though one of my
> Dearest friends, can never,
> I have decided, become great.

Thus we are reduced to little certainty at all about the reality of what happened apart from the patient's unreliable views, and we come to an unanticipated possibility in the poem's title. Perhaps the movement referred to is the development of conflict, uncertainty, and ambiguity in the very best expression of human vision; that is, in literature; certainly in this fine poem.

As a last instance of Nemerov's dramatic poem and its lesson for us about how extraordinary vision is successfully expressed, let us look at a paradise-lost poem, "Landscape with Figures," in which an acutely self-conscious speaker tells us about his nearly seducing Mrs. Persepolis, who is in the garden with him. Only his awareness, he tells

us, of her awareness of his lustful impulse (and hers too, perhaps:
"her glittering eye") prevents the moment and precludes their spontaneous falling into love-making. Whereupon the speaker turns from
us, as he and she go into the chilling shade of the house, to reflectively
address her about what nearly befell them:

> my dear
> Mrs. Persepolis, beautiful
> Exile from childhood, girl
> In your rough and wrinkled
> Sack suit, couldn't you cry
> Over that funny moment when
> We almost fell together
> Into the green sleep of the
> Landscape, the hooded hills
> That dream us up & down?

Our first appraisal of the poem's imagery is likely to be that the fall
of man has nearly recurred. But as we more carefully puzzle over the
odd specifications about the characters' appearances and manners —
his thinking that the hills are "Brooding some brutal thought / As it
were about myself & / Mrs. Persepolis"; her venemous and hissing
name; her "Wrinkling skin at the wrist / Patterned in sunburnt dia-
monds"; her "glittering eye" that takes his thought "exactly / as the
toad's tongue takes a fly"; or their sudden cold-blooded chill as they
leave the sunlight — we come to guess that the two of them are
snakes. Then we may recall another of Nemerov's fables, "The Race,"
in which he revalues the traditional outcome of the contest between
tortoise and hare to suggest that the earnest, purposive participant is
insane relative to the favorite in his idyllic recumbency. In "The Race"
it is not our wholesome animal nature that fails us after all, but our
purposeful abstracting minds that make us "The silent families /
Mounted in glass / Facing the front" and "strictly passing /
Away. . . ." Thus we are disposed to see that in "Landscape with
Figures" Nemerov regards self-consciousness (knowing) as distancing
us — inside our gardens and houses — from the containing landscape
and as precluding the dream. Perspicaciously, he sees that our failing
is not sensual experience so much as it is our taking thought so much.
  Despite their extravagant vision, these dramatic poems presenting
alien points of view are often gratifyingly public in manner because
the human persona is a traditional intellectual mode for conceptual
coherency. That is, we expect the various expressions of whatever
phenomena have any presumption to human form to be sufficiently
self-consistent to establish a recognizable type or variant. Further,

Nemerov's poems such as "Learning by Doing," "Sunday at the End of Summer," "The Pond," and "A Day on the Big Branch" are yet more public and comprehensible in presenting their visions because their manner is substantially narrative, which is undoubtedly our richest rhetorical mode. Even beyond the *personal* convention available in the dramatic poems, narrative is a framework that furnishes much circumstantial information toward our understanding. Both dramatic and narrative poems provide settings for percept and concept; we get not only views but sure ways of judging the views.

Many of Nemerov's poems are lyrical in mode, not dramatic or narrative. That is, they not only present a single point of view exclusively but they also appear as if they address virtually no audience. They are poems the poet makes for himself. Conscious address to any other audience would, of course, dramatize the speaker, alter his "voice," and remove us from extremely close proximity to the poet's visionary experience. The very great advantage of the lyrical mode is that it offers us, through only an anonymous and mostly negligible *personal* lens, most direct possible access to human thoughts and feelings other than our own. Such poems are not necessarily lyrical in the primitive sense of being suitable for singing, although some of Nemerov's compositions, like his "Carol," are to be sung. Others such as "Sarabande" and "The Breaking of Rainbows" at least refer to musical sensations, and some of the sonnets are, according to their convention, especially musical. "The Fall Again," for example, is a Noah-poem that sounds according to the rainfall and water running in gutter and creek portrayed in it.

Because lyric invites the poet to "speak" as if he were not overtly expressing himself but only feeling and thinking to himself, we might suppose that the poet's vision would be less conventionally intelligible to us, despite our closer proximity to it. If we get to it with as little medium as is possible, we should nevertheless anticipate difficulty sharing its substance. We might expect that vision to be quite private, as if a human mind merely indulged itself in its own association of images and concepts, as if such poems dispensed with objective correlatives. And were we denied the exquisite and richly developed initial image of the trout poised in its pool, the experiences of thought and mind the poet reflects upon in "The Sanctuary" might indeed be indecipherable: "Pure thought, in principle, some way, is near / Madness . . ." ("Idea"). But, in fact, many of Nemerov's lyrics are among his clearest expressions and powerfully draw us into his vision. Some of these lyrical poems, like his sonnets for example, are accessible because their form or topic is either conventional or recognizably variant. But perhaps mostly his lyrics are typically accessible because they are often, at their beginnings, poems of vision in the most common, literal sense. For example, Nemerov, like many poets in the American tradition, is fond of homely images. Like his own fondly elegized Nature Poet, he especially enjoys drawing them from the Book of Nature. The dragonfly, with which he begins the last stanza in his elegy for Christopher, the drowned skater ("The Pond"), is a good example. Nemerov returns to it, we notice, in "The Dragonfly," one of his Emblems in *The Next Room of the Dream* collection. Another easy instance occurs in "Dandelions" that develops the ephemeral plant as an emblem of human life's transciency. And perhaps I best cite "Runes," III, which richly describes the mature heavy-seeded sunflower while also personifying it as a selfish imperialist merchant who is at last over-extended in self-aggrandizement. Altogether the poet sees the flower's fall as deserved, according to human moral principles, and concomitantly delights us by permitting us a growing realization that such principles of ours are rooted in the economy or integrity of our natural environment.

Nemerov's lyrics are often substantially descriptive. Here, for example, is the first stanza from the voluptuously rhymed and timed "Summer's Elegy":

> Day after day, day after still day,
> The summer has begun to pass away.
> Starlings at twilight fly clustered and call,
> And branches bend, and leaves begin to fall.
> The meadow and the orchard grass are mown,
> And the meadowlark's house is cut down.

But perhaps "The Cherry Tree" yet more cogently develops and sustains a single image. The tree, flourishing between the earth and darkness beneath it and the light and sun above, is seen as the durable nucleus of a whole vital system, of "a minor universe." Moreover, at first in the poem, the colorful tree is ripening its cherries "from white to pink, and to blood red." It is regarded as lighting "its many suns," as if the tree expressed sunlight and as if the tree nourished all life and were itself the source that gave being to the universe. But at last in the poem, the tree, having relinquished its fruit, casts its shadow on the earth to disclose that the "one sun" gives light to the tree yet more certainly than the tree gives light to the sun. Thus "The Cherry Tree" suggests that all being occurs in reciprocity between above and below, between light and dark. For indeed, the "bloody stones" and "rotting flesh" fallen to the ground may rise again as the tree renewed. In another poem — "Runes," XII — the poet directs us to "Consider how the seed lost by a bird / Will harbor in its branches most remote / Descendants of the bird. . . ." "The Cherry Tree," we can see, like "Blue Swallows" comes near to showing us that if things are lovely because intelligible, they are intelligible because lovely.

To a considerable extent, all this is delightful play with an image, but unlike the play for its own sake in the stunt-poems, this more advanced play carries us beyond the image and our usual common vision to see more deeply into our condition and circumstance. Consider how exquisite is "The End of Summer School." Most of its stanzas describe delicate autumnal phenomena: a spider's web is silverly bedewed, leaves loosen and begin to fall, slowly ripened apples redden suddenly, seeds spin down, and baby spiders sail away on golden shining threads. But as these soft beauties are observed, their gradual cumulation inexorably becomes the immense hard fact of the cosmos:

> And of the strength that slowly warps the stars
> To strange harbors, the learned pupil knows
> How adamant the anvil, fierce the hearth
> Where imperceptible summer turns the rose.

Some of these poems by Nemerov look as if their sense or vision demanded expression in the particular image found or made. Such is "The Rope's End," a jeremiad that compares the world to a great rope. The poet contends that we have never been sufficiently respectful about the integrity of all being. He indicts us for being vainly puzzled about the world's order — that is, nature — and for not regarding it as the creation that his paradoxically artificial image insists it is. He despairs that our examination itself unravels the rope we presume to examine, undoes the marvelous order we think to comprehend:

> All this
> In the last analysis
> Is crazy man's work,
> Admitted, who can leave
> Nothing continuous
> Since Adam's fall
> Unraveled all.

In others of Nemerov's poems that sustain elaborate images, the poet plays with an engaging image and finds something in it. "Enthusiasm for Hats" is like this. Beginning with puzzled amusement at strangely showy Sunday headgear, the poet first supposes such bizarre costume mysteriously suitable somehow to occasion for worship, despite the apparent indecorum. But he finally suspects that the extravagant hat may unwittingly express, "As manifestations from the mind itself,' otherwise hidden sins and covert madness.

At last we appreciate that our query about whether the vision demands its image or whether an image comes to disclose truth is correlative to our earlier puzzle about whether things are lovely because intelligible, or intelligible because lovely. Do we see things because they are there in nature, or do things exist — that is, are they discernible as *things* — because we see them? In "Blue Swallows," we recall, the poet, in reaction to our common sense, ambiguously insists on the latter proposition "Because the mind's eye lit the sun." But in another mood — in "Projection" — he forgives our presumption:

> They were so amply beautiful, the maps,
> With their blue rivers winding to the sea,
> So calmly beautiful, who could have blamed
> Us? . . .

And we come to feel that both attitudes are the truth, that as Keats' urn says, "Beauty is truth, truth beauty, — that is all / Ye know on earth and all ye need to know." This is the truth, we see, in Nemerov's great meditative poems: some, like "Sanctuary" and "Blue Swallows," leading us in amazement from wonder at our circumstances to wonder at ourselves; others, such as "The Beekeeper Speaks . . . And Is Silent," principally leading us from the self to other; but all of them, after all reciprocal. Finally we should notice that in "Shells," his superb poem about poems among other things, Nemerov explicitly instructs us in this reciprocity. He observes this of the shell, of the poem:

> Its form is only cryptically
> Instructive, if at all: it winds
> Like generality, from nothing to nothing
>
> By means of nothing but itself.
> It is a stairway going nowhere,
> Our precious emblem of the steep ascent,
>
> Perhaps, beginning at a point
> And opening to infinity,
> Or the other way, if you want it the other way.
>
> Inside it, also, there is nothing
> Except the obedient sound of waters
> Beat by your Mediterranean, classic heart
>
> In bloody tides as long as breath,
> Bringing by turns the ebb and flood
> Upon the ruining house of histories,
>
> Whose whitening stones, in Africa,
> Bake dry and blow away, in Athens,
> In Rome. . . .

James Dickey's Muscular Eschatology

BY NORMAN SILVERSTEIN

JAMES DICKEY MAKES MUCH OF THE FACT that in high school a class in poetry was followed by another in manual training. He tends to equate writing poetry to playing the guitar and shooting a bow. "What I want to do most as a poet," he has written in his journals, "is to charge the world with vitality: with the vitality it already has, if we can rise to it."* His favorite sports before World War II were football and track, and his Air Force experience involved eighty-seven missions rewarded with a silver star and two distinguished flying crosses. As a veteran returned to college, Mr. Dickey was graduated from Vanderbilt *magna cum laude* and *phi beta kappa* in 1948, and earned his master's degree in 1950, at the age of twenty-seven. He has never taken a doctorate. After serving as English instructor at Rice, the University of Florida, and elsewhere, he wrote advertising copy for six years in Atlanta and New York. As, after 1958, his poems brought him prizes and grants, he could afford to leave advertising. Especially important for him was the publication of *Into the Stone* in John Hall Wheelock's *Poets of Today* series, in 1960, when he was 37 years old.

In terms of published work, Dickey is the most prolific representative voice of serious poetry of the American '60's. His volumes of poetry include *Drowning with Others* (1962), *Helmets* (1964), *Two Poems of the Air* and *Buckdancer's Choice* (1965), *Poems 1957–1967*, (the paperback edition of which enjoys the same Macmillan format as given to Yeats and Hardy), and *The Eyebeaters, Blood, Victory, Madness, Buckhead, and Mercy* (1970). Dickey has provided a gloss to his poetry in *Self-Interviews* (1970) [*S-I*], "recorded and edited" taped interviews. His novel *Deliverance* (1970) applied to fiction

---

*James Dickey, *Sorties* (New York, Doubleday and Co., 1971), p. 5. Hereafter abbreviated *S*. This volume consists of journal entries and seven essays, including the excellent speeches Dickey delivered as Consultant for the Library of Congress.

the love of narrative adventure that gave his poetry popularity, and it explored suburban character in the face of mystery, a theme that dominates his poetry. Notes for an unpublished novel, *Death's Baby Machine*, about an Air Force cadet who, in 1942, threatens to disestablish the military and to liberate military society, appears in *Sorties*, pages 124-151. In spite of this abundance of literary work, rewarded with publication and with prizes, he is a self-conscious craftsman, aware of his apocalyptic tendency and defensive about it.

Dickey retained a sanguine temperament throughout the apocalyptic '60's. A poet of God and America, he is against nay-sayers and cynical intellectuals. He despises both the idea that "everything is in some way contemptible" and the "bitchy gentlemanly review" which the British write when they "settle for Robert Lowell or, better still, Sylvia Plath " (*S*, p. 98). Sounding somewhat like Jason in *The Sound of the Fury*, he says of New York intellectuals, "You can't really be 'in' up there unless you are with them on their stand against the Vietnam war and virulently anti-American " (*S*, p. 146).

What Dickey admires is hunting, not with a camera — "I think the animal is debased by that" (*S-I*, p. 110) — but with a bow and arrow. He is for self-improvement of body and mind, and admires the athlete for the possibility that exercise will lead, through application, to the physical grace that animals feel instinctively. He accepts the nobility of service in the Second World War. He loves "the large scenes of nature, forms of alien life, fish, sun, silence and — a loaf of bread." Shamelessly, he celebrates the strivings of suburban man to test his body. In his journals, he writes continually about improving his mind through the study of languages. He loves his wife Maxine and his children Christopher and Kevin and transposes his experiences at home into poetry by pushing to metaphysical limits ordinary, mundane, and unheroic events, like a bad sunburn or a short circuit in the suburban house.

There is behind these attitudes a body of thought, a somewhat systematic theory of modern culture that flourished at Vanderbilt 20 years before Dickey took his degrees. Dickey is a Southern poet, not just by fact of birth, but by temperament. At Vanderbilt, he was taught by Mrs. Monroe Spears and later came to know the critic himself, with whom Dickey studied the eighteenth century. Vanderbilt was the home of the Fugitives, who, in the '20's, became the Southern Agrarians. This cultural movement found in fixed forms of poetry parallels of the fixed ante-bellum Southern life they admired. In 1930, in *I'll Take My Stand,* the group, which included, among others, John Crowe Ransom, Allen Tate, and Robert Penn Warren, asserted that their goal was to foster a "distributist" agrarian economy, in opposition to industrialism. Since applied science at the beginning of the Great Depression had rendered industrial labor hard, fierce in tempo, and insecure, they sought to retain the best of the Southern past in the face of industrial encroachment. Not that they rejected science. The good labor of applied science uses a tool or a process for enjoyment and happiness, as Dickey, years later, uses a guitar or a bow. In the religious sphere, the agrarian, as Dickey would later attempt, sought to disengage industrial man from "the illusion of having power over nature" and to restore "the sense of nature as something mysterious and contingent." Since advertising tries "to persuade the consumers to want what the applied sciences are able to furnish," art, its opposite, depended upon a "right attitude — a free and disinterested observation of nature that occurs only in leisure." In their search for order amid industrial chaos, Fugitives encouraged the creation of autotelic, or self-contained poems, capable of multi-leveled interpretation. In particular, they admired, like T. S. Eliot, seventeenth-century metaphysical poets and tended to disparage the Romantics and the Victorians. Economic theory, science, religion and art — parts of an ordered world — required metaphysical poetry to link otherwise distinct phenomena.

While the terms are altered by 1960, the essence of the agrarian scheme retains a hold over Dickey's mind and art. In place of a "distributist" agrarian economy is the suburban house, removed from center cities, and supported with ecological poetry, as when a threatened wolverine cries to die, but not to die out. Dickey also commends tools and processes, as the possible extensions of man's hands, and accepts the great machinery that enables flights to the moon. On the other hand, he moves the agrarian notion of nature as "mysterious and contingent" into an unseemly paganism:

> But let me say that I have always been against traditional religion because my religion has been so personal to *me.* I always felt that God and I have a very good understanding, and the more the ritualistic services go on, the more God and I stand by and laugh. I don't believe that the God that created the universe has any interest in the dreadful kind of self-abasement men go through in religious ceremonies. . . .
> . . . I would have made a great Bushman or an aborigine who believes that spirits inhabit all things. Or that my brother was once a snake, or that I myself was once a turtle.

> *(Self-Interviews,* pp. 78-79)

A nature mysterious and contingent makes Dickey into a mythologue, for, like a theosophist, he can start anywhere and find God, not god, with a small g, but the Lord who creates, intercedes, and aids. Assuming that his career at McCann-Erickson and that writing on the Eddie Fisher show (called *Coke Time*), was an expedient — a bitchy, gentlemanly statement, but I am trying to understand his motive for writing poetry — then Dickey, unlike the agrarians, can come to terms with consumerism, even abetting motivational research and planned obsolescence, provided that advertising frees him for poetry. Freed at last, Dickey can pursue, not the autotelic poem required by the agrarians, but a "tribal simplicity," without "richness in ambiguity" and without "verse measured by multiplicity of reference."

"For a sense of the absolute basics of life," Dickey says, "the language of Eliot and Empson is not right." To the classical restraint of Ransom and the classical themes of Tate, Dickey prefers a "country surrealism," one based on contemporary experience, particularly of the suburban life seen in heroic dimensions. He admires a tribal poetry, as of an Eskimo marveling at wandering caribou, or a Randall Jarrell woman moving from All to Cheer and from Cheer to Joy in a supermarket. He accepts William Stafford walking down Main Street surrounded left and right, fore and aft, by his family because they all comprise an angelic moving-grouping, comparable to a cloud of unknowing. As Dickey describes the task of the poet, it is to "ask the parts of creation to get together." Restating the metaphysical credo admired by the agrarians, he adds, "The deliberate conjunction of disparate items . . . is not so much a way of understanding the world but a way of recreating it from its own parts." Unlike the ontological poetry advocated by John Crowe Ransom, Dickey's poetry is always in process, never "marmoreal." It is "not as much a matter of serene and disinterested choice but of action, the very *heat* of choice " (*S*, p. 173).

The form of his verse, except for some early slant-rhymed couplets, is open, tending toward rhythmic blocks with conversational anapestics, or, later, the "split line," in which the space bar of Dickey's typewriter determines the duration of a caesura. Both open forms appear to be contemptuous of strong metrics, for enjambed lines and stanzas based on conversational rhythms, often deliberately prosaic, confuse the reader who wants to stop at the end of a verse or a stanza before realizing, abruptly, that he should have carried the sense on. Even though the metrics are vague, expletives, as in conversation, fill out many lines — vague *it's* and *there's* forcing a reader to search for antecedent nouns. One cannot quarrel with Dickey's assertion that diction must be "convincing as speech before as poetry," but decorum is violated when unlikely unions of disparate elements are expressed in common speech.

When Dickey read Tate's account of the blending of Southern and Roman experience in the Pindaric "Ode to the Confederate Dead," he said of its blending of disparate elements, ". . . it hit me like a blinding light. . . . the poetic process is . . . that kind of personal connection of very disparate elements under the fusing heat of the poem's necessity, so that they create the illusion of belonging and illuminate each other by providing an insight of association." In one of Dickey's poems, whiskey and a cancer growth engage in a judo match inside his mouth. Diabetes is "a nervous sweetness of my blood" that buzzards sense, leaving a forest fire to find the poet; as he drinks beer on a hot day, he is hallucinated into thinking that he is calling the buzzards to come to him.

Dickey acknowledges that he tries to walk the "razor's edge between sublimity and absurdity" and that sometimes "*both* sides are ludicrous" (*S-I*, page 65). Tate's verse avoids the trap of becoming a joyless puzzle; not so the overstated idea of Mr. Dickey's "Giving a Son to the Sea." After remembering that one of his sons shot him with a toy bullet that said "I love you," the poet sees the grown son descend for a deep-sea dive and send, underwater, the same message. Dickey is not, of course, giving a son to the sea: nobody, thankfully, is dying, as the title implies. And how unconsciously insulting Dickey is when he presumes to tell his blond son that the "I love you" message "hits me most / when I watch you swim, that being your only talent." Is that my *only* talent, dad? In "Mercy," Dickey's protagonist meets his sweetheart at a hospital that reminds him of a convent and talks himself through highfalutin poetic analysis into thinking of her as smelling of disinfectant and perfume. Once again the title, "Mercy," makes of the poem a discordant concurrence of the trivial and the sublime. Unlike Tate, who achieves a classical rigor, Dickey treats Mercy as précieux poets would, with the difference that his treatment lacks a comic sense, their little dance before a mirror being omitted. To the above-quoted phrase about walking the razor's edge between sublimity and absurdity, Dickey adds that a poet whose poems deal with far-fetched situations needs the participation of the reader. One reacts to the far-fetched in his poems as

Dickey does to an admirer of *Helmets,* who wrote on the dedication page alongside "To Maxine: *light* and *warmth*" the marginalia "intellectual and physical." Dickey says, "I suppose that's what I meant but it seemed strange with all that scholarly apparatus." Through *discordia concors,* he does the same thing — exaggerate!

Neo-metaphysical poetry tends to belabor the theme of spiritual paralysis. Because he is "a born believer and not a disbeliever" (*S-I,* p. 65), Dickey eschews cynicism, but not gloom. In *Drowning with Others,* Dickey tends to dissipate poetic feeling into either plain misery or accedium. Sometimes he begins a poem, for example, "Inside the River," with a pleasing enough scene of someone stepping into water, perhaps for a swim. Before he has done, however, the dunking is an immersion. The river becomes holy, a Jordan, in which a swimmer moves as the "deep dead move, opposed to nothing." Nor is bathing alone "sacramentalized." A lifeguard who has failed to save a child during the afternoon waits in a "stable" of boats, while a "fish" leaping makes the lake tremble. Finding the moonlit center of the lake which is also the center of the moon, the lifeguard dreams of being "savior" of the boy who has drowned. He steps over the water. In a Donne-like passage, the dead boy breaks the stone surface of the water with his forehead and smiles; the lifeguard kneels on water, called "the quick of the moon," and holds in his arms an imaginary child of "water, water, water" — repeated three times. The son-Son analogy proliferates as one reads *Drowning with Others.* A poem about an imaginary horse ends with Dickey as father to his own son and as son to his own mother who happens to be in the room. Joining the two sons is an aura — call it the Son of God. In other poems, Dickey "sacramentalizes" hunting. The fox has a holy scent (p. 15). A mystical fog envelops the animals, prefiguring a birth. Wounds of animals are "like the mouths of holy beings." Summoning an animal with a mating call, Dickey listens to the "beast that shall die of its love." In short, Dickey's accedium springs from his "unfinished desire . . . for the Other" (p. 31).

These poems strive after mystical transcendence, and a questionable luminosity encourages belief in mystery in the reader. Mr. Dickey's warmth and sensitivity toward family life, nature, and God, and his hopefulness of finding the "Other" — these qualities make him a mystic-poet. In "The Heaven of the Animals," Dickey describes a new peaceable kingdom where animal instinct is perfected. Each animal accepts its active or its passive role. The fanged animals enjoy their vigor eternal, their prey accepting their fate to be devoured: both are part of an eternity where renewal is endless. This poem answers a passage in which Thomas Aquinas says that animals have no souls. Its theme of endless renewal is based on a Walt Disney sequence in *The African Lion.* It draws from the Bible and from T. S. Eliot the notion of Heaven as a still center (*S-I*, pp. 106-8).

In another poem, the line "I see the tree think it will turn brown" gives more sentience to plants than I believe them to enjoy. When Dickey walks into the room of his sleeping children, he knows that he is their imago — "a god or beast come true at last."

Dickey's affection for metaphysics, together with his desire to celebrate suburban adventure — the razor's edge between the sublime and the absurd — would be viable only if he had a systematic religion, whether inherited or adopted, as with Hopkins, or contrived, as with Yeats. Or if, like Ransom and Tate, he wrote on secular themes. The phrase *personal religion,* which Dickey uses, is a catachresis. *Religion* by definition includes a body of believers, a set of moral laws, a doctrine and a discipline, an eschatology that is fixed, and, perhaps, a soteriology, or a medium through which personal salvation is possible. T. S. Eliot's religious poetry has the Anglican system behind it and provides answers to religious doubt, not, as with Dickey, assertion — and discovery of religion in unlikely places. A vague religion is worse than none, particularly one that is "strong in my work in some wild kind of way." With the luxury of disbelief or non-belief, a poet can be on a quest, without knowing beforehand the fixed destination.

Induced religion hovers about Dickey's intentions, even in poems seemingly unconcerned with last things. You read, for example, the title "Sun," curious about how Dickey, who always seems to be invoking moons, half-moons, and crescents, will treat the solar force, which, in Yeats's phases, stands for objective reality as opposed to the moon's subjective reality and imagination. You may even have in mind the simpler verses of Fergus' "the silver apples of the moon/ The golden apples of the sun." So you read the title.

SUN

and you find the first rhythmic block:

> O Lord, it was all night
> Consuming me

The words O Lord are not just an imprecation but, as you know
from other poems, possibly an overtone, indicating a prayer. But
what is the antecedent of it? Of course, you say, looking back, "It is
Sun." How is it possible that the sun has been consuming him at
night? The sun doesn't shine at night. What is the answer then?
Can it be that the poet is sunburnt? You read on —

> skin crawling tighter than any
> Skin of my teeth.

Your fears seem already to be justified:

> Bleary with ointments, dazzling
> Through the dark house   man red as iron   glowing
> Blazing up anew with each bad
> Breath from the bellowing curtains
>
> I had held the sun longer
> Than it could stay   and in the dark it turned
> My face on infra red:

The rhythms of these lines are threatening, even if the subject is
trivial to readers who are not sunburnt. And the b-pattern implies
a catastrophe — bleary, blazing, bad breath, bellowing. And the
reader is likely to resist the advertising metaphor of bad breath
applied to a night breeze through bedroom windows of a suburban
house.

As the story unfolds, both poet and wife — Mr. Dickey is very
good at describing the white skin beneath the removed straps of
her bathing suit — try to sleep. Written in italics are the specific
words of his prayer; without italics is his comment:

> O Lord
> Who can turn out the sun, turn out that neighbor's
> One bulb on his badminton court
>
> For we are dying
> Of light   searing each other   not able
> To stop   to get away   she screaming O Lord
> Apollo or Water Water   as the moonlight drove
> Us down on the tangled grid
> Where in the end we lay
>
> Suffering equally   in the sun
> Backlashed from the moon's brutal stone
> And meeting itself where we had stored it up
> All afternoon in pain   in the gentlest touch
> As we lay, O Lord,
> In Hell, in love.

Although the sacramentalizing is here diminished — the poem appears
in the section "Falling" of Poems 1957-1967 — the sense of burning

in hell fire, like Paolo and Francesca, makes the sublime ludicrous. The utterance to Apollo is unlikely to have been uttered. A sunburn has been sacramentalized into a minatory eschatology. Yet the strong lines in the cosmic picture of "the sun backlashed from the moon's brutal stone and meeting itself where we lay" are remarkable. This image has the action, the very *heat* of choice Dickey seeks, for the reader can grasp the persistence of sunlight into night, the word *backlashed* implying a cosmic journey of light. Without the narrative and without the locked-in conception that has given the poem its origin — the suburban couple sunburnt — the lines have a *chosiste* power of describing external reality, according to the laws of physics. In cross-references, the one bulb on the badminton court is a miniature moon, the sun at another remove. Because these good details subserve a vague religious idea that there is the Other, one longs to separate from the story the effective image.

The medium through which Dickey reaches toward the ineffable is not vision but hallucination, as in the pain of a sunburn. If he had called the poem "On Being Sunburnt," the reader could anticipate a comic poem. By choosing "Sun" as the title, Dickey prefers the metonymic word that masks the trivial subject. This device is deliberate, being Dickey's means of walking the razor's edge between sublimity and absurdity. Metonymy — or exaggeration — is the chief feature of what he wants to call "country surrealism." He is doubtless aware that his Clevelandisms are "false wit" but he appears to be locked into pursuing the relationship between the suburban life and the divine. Thus, as the poet is lying in his apartment, perhaps with a guitar at his side, he becomes a folk singer of the '30's riding a boxcar until orphans, or railway police, nail him to the boxcar's siding with twenty-penny nails so that as Christ crucified he careens across the West. Thus also the lifeguard of the poem discussed earlier proves to be working in a boy's camp before he goes on to become a Savior-substitute. "Power and Light," with the epigraph from E. M. Forster ". . . only connect . . ." is — believe it — about a suburban husband worrying about a short circuit and trying to ground a wire somewhere in the basement because the lights are out — "like I tell you it takes/ A man to pour whiskey in the dark." These suburban matters — swimming in a lake, suffering a sunburn, grounding a wire, the ins-and-outs of family life, even the feelings of hunters, guitarists, and bowmen whose lives are lived in comfort — are better expressed in fiction than in poetry. The title *Deliverance* retains the traces of the metonymic occupations of Dickey's poetry. The novel happily became an adventure story rather than another illustration of Dickey's "personal religion."

In a decade that demanded of its poets "confession" and "hysteria," Dickey retained a sanguine temperament. While in such poems as "The Lost Son," "Skunk Hour," and "Daddy," Roethke, Lowell, and Plath conveyed tortured mental suffering which he doubts to be a correct subject of poetry, Dickey seems to have been well-disposed to the world, pushing toward the Other as a poetic convenience. He can admire Roethke for having in his poetry outgrown the babyism that marked his life, his wanting to be considered the best and to receive unending compliments. He never quite says what he likes in Roethke's poems, which use French forms and have the control admired by the Southern agrarians. Lowell and Plath he dismisses as "slickly confessional " (S, p. 191). The projective poets he dismisses as having "no personal rhythm" — it all "comes out of the tiresome and predictable prosiness of William Carlos Williams." Robert Bly and James Wright lack "*necessity* of statement"; their works cannot sustain narrative. He is against the idea, fostered by Eliot and Pound, that the poem is "a kind of high-cult *objet d'art,* 'a superior amusement,' as Eliot once termed it." He quotes Camus as saying "There is no shame in being happy." As he spins the crystal ball in a Library of Congress lecture, he opts for a poetry that will, in the words of Richard Jefferies, "Go straight to the sun, the immense forces of the universe, to the Entity unknown; go higher than a god; deeper than prayer; and open a new day." He seeks to have "a purely tribal poetry, something naive and utterly convincing, immediately accessible, animistic, communal, dancelike, entered into, participated in."

The poems written after these hopeful statements in *Eye-Beaters, Blood, Victory, Madness, Buckhead,* and *Mercy* appear to be griefs manufactured by a happy man, well-disposed to the world, an athlete, a successful pilot, a hunter, a faithful husband satisfied with family and career — excited by the craft of poetry for its own sake. More and more he reaches, with the encroachment of middle age, to the past — to forgotten girls, war reminiscences, memories of his children as they were. Becoming a Hemingwayesque grace-under-pressure quarterback in "In the Pocket," a poem dedicated, apparently, to the National Football League, Dickey is about to throw a screen pass. When Number One is "hooking / Into the violent green alive / with linebackers," unable "to beat his man," Number Two goes off-side. Fortunately Number Three is a possible pocket receiver, and Dickey cries out

> throw it hit him in the middle
> Of his enemies   hit move scramble
> Before death and the ground
> Come up   LEAP STAND KILL DIE STRIKE
> Now

This poem, which at last ignores personal religion, stands as an example of a poem without the Other, either by direct appeal or by implication. Dickey means it, perhaps, to be an example of "tribal poetry" or of "country surrealism." But it is, it seems to me, a stream-of-consciousness paragraph from a novel about a football game. The poet has reported the mind of the quarterback, or of a football fan, without the embellishment that brings in an exaggerated comparison. He does not walk the razor's edge between the sublime and the ludicrous. The poem is not an hallucination passing as a vision, nor a joyless puzzle with vague antecedents. Charged though it be with vitality, crafted with words though it be, as a bookcase is planed in a manual training class, it is effective without a joining of the trivial and the sublime.

When Dickey rejected the closed poem admired by Pound, Eliot, and the Southern agrarians, he retained the chief element that unified their poems in his own open, process-directed, free-form verse. They needed to yoke by violence together disparate elements of their received world because they were in search of stability. *Discordia concors* is the means by which troubled poets resolve tensions imposed upon them and evade the disorder of the world outside in ordered autotelic poems. Because Dickey was in love with life as it was given him, in all its mutability, he had no need for the rhetorical figure that was their mainstay and that continued to be needed by Roethke, Lowell, and Plath. Once delivered from this figure of speech, as in "In the Pocket," Dickey, avoiding the conjunction of dissimilars — which explains the uneasiness a reader feels in his prolific apocalyptic '60's poems — will, I think, be less tempted to exalt the commonplace. And the preferred medium for his verbal talents will be the novel.

The New Surrealism

BY PAUL ZWEIG

To LOOK FOR THE influence of surrealism in American poetry today is like looking for references to aquatic mammals in *Moby Dick* (to paraphrase a remark from one of Vladimir Nabokov's immortal quarrels). Since the "silent generation" of the 1950's faded quietly away, and odd sounds started to emerge from previously pacified areas like San Francisco, Minnesota and downtown New York, surrealism has set up shop in the American language, with a spirit of novelty and exuberance it never attained even in France in the 1920's, beyond a handful of admittedly brilliant writers (Breton, Aragon, Artaud, Desnos, Eluard).

The differences between the original French movement and its influence in America are important. There has been no one here with the intellectual stature of a Breton, to theorize in the vigorous style of the *Surrealist Manifestos*, or the *Vases Communicants*. Franklin Rosemont's diatribes are little more than Breton updated and served lukewarm.* Robert Bly's essays in *The Sixties* are by far the most interesting attempt to define a program, and even a morality, based on a surreal vision of the psyche. But Bly is more concerned with spiritual exploration than with surreal language. His plea for "imagery," and against traditional rhetoric, brings him closer to Rilke, Vallejo and Neruda, than to the provocations of Breton. In fact, surrealism in American poetry doesn't really amount to a movement at all, no more than "free verse" or "modernism" do any more. It has become part of the way our language works. It reflects the plunge away from culture and rationality which the poets of the 1960's undertook, wholeheartedly. The surrealist argument never needed to be made in America. When Allen Ginsberg and Frank O'Hara made impolite noises at the garden party of American

*Franklin Rosemont, *Morning of a Machinegun* (Surrealist Press, Chicago).

poetry in the late 1950's, there was a shudder of recognition. A new sort of poetry was born overnight, natural as a nightmare, inventive, belligerently informal. At the heart of the new poetry was an anti-cultural rage aimed at the polite involutions of a decade of neo-Georgian ephemera. It was inevitable that the techniques of surrealist language should appeal to poets like Ginsberg, O'Hara, Koch, Bly, Lamantia. If anything, the transition was too swift. America leaped into dream imagery, free association and the language of insanity, as into a warm bath.

Breton's icy polemic against the police mentality of the ego, and its repressive shock troops: logic, rationality, coherence, style, tradition and literature itself, was turned in America against a more local enemy. Where the French surrealists took on 2,000 years of European tradition, the new poets of America took on Richard Eberhart, W. H. Auden, and Robert Lowell. The enemy never mustered an answer, and the experimental verve of the new poetry spread uncontested, until now it corresponds oddly to Breton's dream of a time when troops of poets would learn to master the techniques of spontaneous language in training centers—we call them creative writing programs—a time when poetry would no longer be written by thin lonely people, but by everyone. (*"La poésie doit être fait par tous, et non par un"*: Breton, quoting Lautreamont.)

Since surrealism is everywhere, it is probably also nowhere. Aside from Phillip Lamantia—the only historical surrealist in America— Bill Knott and a few others, there are not many poets who would actually admit to being surrealists. Instead of a program and a discipline, a debris of techniques, a conglomerate of attitudes has emerged, which loosely recognizes surrealism as their homeland. In the *First Manifesto*, Breton invents a list of eternal surrealists ("Swift, surrealist in nastiness"; "Hugo, surrealist when he's not stupid"; "Poe, surrealist in adventure," etc.). If I may resort to imitation, a forgotten art since Ezra Pound, the list, or non-list of American surrealists would look like this:

Frank O'Hara, surrealist in loneliness
Robert Bly, surrealist in old automobile tires
James Wright, surrealist in Ohio childhood
Charles Simic, surrealist in Yugoslavian folklore
Kenneth Koch, surrealist in the absurd
Paul Carrol, surrealist in jive talk
Allen Ginsberg, surrealist in polymorphous perversity and everything else
Bill Knott, surrealist in suicide
James Tate, surrealist in Bill Knott

Michael Benedickt, surrealist in his funny bone
Diane Wakoski, surrealist in exotic reptiles
Phillip Lamantia, surrealist in the black sun
etc.

Such a compilation (surreal in its very incoherence) means simply that "surrealism" has become almost anything at all. Carefully composed dream poems, incoherent torrents of language, obscure humor, jiving anti-rhetoric, nonsense, fantasy landscapes, images, obscure abstraction, are the offspring abandoned at many doorsteps by a sect of French heretical poets who would probably not recognize their paternity.

2

André Breton's definitions of surrealism in the 1920's gave rise to a tight body of doctrines, arguing a single belief that unreason is, and always has been, truer than reason; that the world of organized intentions floats meagerly on a well of spontaneity which is the source of what Breton called "the marvelous." No matter how a man tries to say what he means, other meanings creep into his words, darker, contradictory, as if, in the act of making sense, he was inhabited by a voice which spoke through him, and against him. It was this countervoice that surrealism set out to cultivate, and revalue: "Our task . . . is to perceive, more and more clearly, what occurs unknown to man in the depths of his psyche. . . ." The surrealists took Freud to witness that man was a prisoner of his intelligence; that the veritable workings of the spirit took place mysteriously in the unconscious, while a simulacrum of life went through the motions in the world of consciousness and culture. The surrealist goal was not to produce works of literature, but to transform the functioning of the mind, to create a liberated, non-repressive vision of reality (a surreality):

> the idea of surrealism aims simply toward the total recuperation
> of our psychic energy, by a means which is nothing more than
> a vertiginous descent within, the systematic illumination of hid-
> den places and the progressive darkening of the other places, a
> continual penetration into the hidden zone . . . its activity has
> no real chance of ending as long as man can tell the difference
> between an animal, a flame or a stone. . . . [*Manifestes du Sur-
> realisme,* Idées, NRF, p. 92]

The surrealists organized a vast prison-break away from the repressive modes of coherence, grammar and sense. What they worked at in the medium of language, they hoped also to produce in the "real" world. Witness their interest in revolutionary action, or Breton's famous provocative definition, in the Second Manifesto: "The simplest surrealist act consists in going down into the street, with a revolver in each hand, and shooting at random into the crowd for as long as possible." Surrealism, for Breton, was a terrorist action, a hygiene of the spirit whose principle, but not sole, domain was language.

Now that the dust of history has settled, one tends to discount Breton's apocalyptic flourishes. Whether or not he would have liked the idea—Breton excommunicated his best friends one after another for the same heresy—surrealism has gone down as a literary (and artistic) movement on the left wing of modernism, slightly to the right of Dada, having produced few durable works of poetry, several famous polemics, and a theoretical text, Breton's *Manifestos*, which has become an important document in twentieth-century cultural history. The surrealist contribution to literature lies not so much in great individual texts, as in a variety of methods transforming the notion of what language could and should do. The most famous of these methods is automatic writing, whose discovery Breton describes as follows:

> At the time I was still extremely interested in Freud, and his methods of examination which I had occasion to try out on patients during the war. I decided to get from myself what one tries to get from them: a monologue carried on as rapidly as possible, without any judgement pronounced by the patient's critical faculties, therefore without reticence of any sort, and which, as accurately as possible, is a form of *spoken thinking.* . . . With this in mind, Phillipe Soupault and I . . . undertook to blacken some paper, without the slightest care about what would result literally from our efforts.

Shooting a revolver into a crowd may have been the simplest surrealist act, but automatic writing—the written equivalent of psychoanalytic free association—would also do. Not, as Breton emphasized elsewhere, to produce glamorous anti-literary masterpieces, but to create a free flow of darkness into light, madness into sanity, unreason into reason; and simultaneously, a self-discipline of the mind reflecting on its internal revolution, learning to know itself in a new way. Automatic writing, for Breton, was a revolutionary yoga, a modern technique equivalent to Loyola's spiritual excercises. By teaching language to respond to the countervoice in the psyche, Breton sought to redefine at every level, the very notion of "sense." In place of a rational, he sought to create a lyrical vision of reality. Automatic writing (and other techniques of randomness, such as cut-outs and paste-ups) became, for the surrealists, the precise equivalent of a revolutionary act, a Bolshevism at the level of language. "Just as Marx's predictions, concerning almost all the exterior events occurring from his death until now, have been accurate, I don't see what contradicts a single word written by Lautreamont, concerning events involving only the spirit."

The mother-discipline of automatic writing gave rise to a series of emphases, all of which elevated the "magic" of unreason. Instead of the sentence, the purest element of language became the image, which Breton, quoting Pierre Reverdy, defines in a way reminiscent of Dr. Johnson describing the "metaphysical poets" of 17th-century England:

> The image is a pure creation of the mind.
> It does not result from a comparison, but from bringing together two more or less distant realities.
> The image will be stronger, and will have a greater emotive power and poetic reality, as the relationships between the two realities are more distant and exact. . . .

Breton gives examples of surrealist imagery: "A church rose up as brilliant as a bell." "I had barely invoked the marble-admiral when he turned on his heels like a horse bucking before the north star, and showed me with his two cornered hat the region where I would spend my life." "During a break in the game, while the players got together around a bowl of flaming punch, I asked the tree if it still had its red ribbon."

As the surrealist movement developed, other manifestations of unreason became sacralized. The surrealists were fascinated by psychosis, considering it to be a sort of psychic heroism. Above all, they argued for the revelatory character of dreams, as in Breton's essay, *Les Vases Communicants*.

In Breton's own day, the movement had trouble keeping itself pure of "literary" ambition. The various techniques of the surreal yoga were all too easily convertible into a new rhetoric. So that by the late 1930's, Breton had excommunicated almost all of the original founders. Artaud, Limbour, Soupault, Vitrac, Desnos, Aragon could not resist becoming poets, and Breton dispatched them one after another, until he stood all but alone, the ultimate heretic; like the aging Milton, splendid and obsessed. The fate of surrealism was exemplary. As a movement it dwindled to a single magnificent voice, Breton's. At the same time, its techniques, cut loose from Breton's discipline, infiltrated the language of literature in dispersed order. It became impossible to disregard them. Surrealism's revaluation of all values fell short of Breton's messianic dream; it was, ultimately, accomplished against, and not with him. In the process, surrealism left the terrain of revolutionary action, and became literature, albeit anti-traditional and angrily subversive. Breton's prophecy, in the Second Manifesto, was not far from the mark:

> The hordes of literally frenzied words that Dada and surrealism acted to set free . . . . will enter slowly but surely into the small moronic towns of literature as it is still taught. . . . People try not to notice that the logical mechanism of the sentence has shown itself to be increasingly incapable of triggering in man the emotional shock which gives real value to his life. On the other hand, the products of that spontaneous or *more* spontaneous, direct or *more* direct activity, such as those offered increasingly by surrealism, in the form of books, paintings and films, and which at first shocked him into a stupor, he now seeks out and more or less timidly asks that they transform his way of feeling.

The apotheosis of literary surrealism came, strangely enough, not in France but in Spain and Latin America, with poets like Lorca, Alberti, Blas de Otero, and especially Neruda. In their works the explosive imagery and the torrential rhythms of automatic writing became charged with Whitmanesque emotion. The Spanish and Latin American poets ignored the anti-worldly purity of the French surrealists. They created a darker, more human surrealism, as in the great poems of Neruda's *Residencia en Tierra*.

3

By the time the "left wing" modernism of the surrealists reached the United States, it had become a scattering of detached ideas and techniques, moving in separate directions, appealing to extremely different writers for different reasons. Robert Bly's argument for surreal imagery, for example, gave rise, in his work, to a poetry of carefully composed figures, with a dreamlike aura, but no attempt at surreal spontaneity. Here is an example of Bly's surrealism, from *The Light around the Body*:

We think of Charlemagne
As we open oysters.
Looking down, we see
Crowds waving from islands inside the oyster shell.
The neck swings to bite the dog.
When the fishermen take in the floats
They find nets some giant fish
Broke through at night.
At dusk we leave. We start north with twenty dogs.
A blizzard begins,
Making us look down.
And the miles of snow crust going past between the runners!
Westward the ice peaks
Like vast maternity hospitals turned white by oyster shells . . .

Bly's imagery here corresponds perfectly to Reverdy's definition.
It is an imagery of disparate realities; it proceeds by leaps and breaks
in the logic of perception. Yet the language of the poem has an
almost classical cleanliness. It is tuned with enormous care. Its
transitions are artful, almost mannered, in a way that would have
enraged the purists of surrealism. This divorce between the mother-
discipline of automatic writing and the literary use of the image
characterizes a number of poets. James Wright, W. S. Merwin, Mark
Strand, Charles Simic are in this vein, as are most of the *Kayak*
poets. Surrealism here becomes a literary technique, a way of "using"
the image to build meanings and paradoxes. The image replaces
rhyme, pentameter and argument as the organizing spirit of the poem,
as in these lines by Simic:

> We have before us
> A magician's coffin
> Sawn in half
> With a girl in it
>
> A knuckle knocking on wood
> For its lips to be read
> A heap of sucked wish-bones
> Snoring on a plate
>
> A bridge
> Over nothing in particular
> A stone that thinks
> Itself a flower
> — *Dismantling the Silence*

At their best such poems embody a new classicism, based on inward
realities. At their worst they give rise to a certain coquetry which
employs the mysteries of the surreal image without actually being
mysterious. These are the Ben Jonsons and Robert Herricks of American surrealism. The style they have created is contradictory. Breton
may be one of their ancestors, but Wallace Stevens or Yeats might
well be another.

Frank O'Hara and Allen Ginsberg start out far closer to the
original discipline of automatic writing. 1956-57 were good years
for literary revolution. That is when *Meditations in an Emergency*
and *Howl* appeared on opposite coasts, two of the most important
first books of poetry to be published in America since the war. O'Hara
like a violin, Ginsberg like a waterfall, let loose the flood of deep
associations. They created a torrential rhetoric that literally washed
away the poetry of the "silent generation." Certain texts in *Meditations in an Emergency* are clearly imitations of the French:

Avarice, the noose that lets oil, oh my dear oh
"La Ronde" erase what is assured and ours, it
resurrects nothing, finally, in its eagerness
to sit under the widely spaced stairs, to be a fabulous
toilette, doesn't imitate footsteps of disappearance

The neighbor, having teased peace to retire, soon
averages six flowering fountains, ooh! spare the men
and their nervous companions that melt and ripen
into a sordid harbor of squid-slipping tarpaulin strips,
quits the sordid arbor of community butcher' girth

The jumping error pins hate on the blossoms of baffles,
densely foraging covered hero-Nero of Maltese, of Moor,
leap, oh leap! against the fame that's in the noose,
sister of yearning, of eclogues without overcoats deeply,
and the trumpet rages over filigreed prisoners

The packaging of the poem into five-line stanzas is not so much evidence of formal intention, as a joke about literary form. The language slips and leaps and interrupts itself with the limberness of the surreal countervoice. The text has no real subject matter; it is what it means: an incoherence of rhythms and images that is oddly seductive. Although passages like this are not the best part of *Meditations in an Emergency*, they form the bedrock of pure style from which the book emerges. O'Hara himself describes the paradox of his poetry: "I will my will, though I may become famous for a mysterious vacancy in that department. . . ." The will that makes meanings struggles bravely with a flood of surreal associations, and the will loses; but the failure is a victory. The poem knocks down the retaining walls of form and meaning. Ordinary situations and rooms and streets become Rimbaudian voyages:

The white chocolate jar full of petals
swirls odds and ends around in a dizzying eye
of four o'clocks now and to come. The tiger,
marvelously striped and irritable, leaps
on the table and without disturbing a hair
of the flowers' breathless attention, pisses
into the pot, right down its delicate spout.
A whisper of steam goes up from the porcelain
eurythra. "Saint-Saëns!" it seems to be whispering . . .

More than a decade later, *Meditations in an Emergency* remains a moving book, perhaps because O'Hara understood the risks, as well as the charms, caused by his "mysterious vacancy of the will." O'Hara was fascinated by the eternal youth of the psyche; but he was elegiac too, in mourning for the drabness of the "logical" world which would never be changed by literature. Perhaps the closing lines of the book describe what O'Hara hoped to create out of his "mysterious vacancy," and what he was afraid to lose:

> Now I am quietly waiting for
> the catastrophe of my personality
> to seem beautiful again,
> and interesting, and modern.
> The country is grey and
> brown and white in trees,
> snows and skies of laughter
> always diminishing, less funny
> not just darker, not just grey.
>
> It may be the coldest day of
> the year, what does he think of
> that? I mean, what do I? And if I do,
> perhaps I am myself again.

If Walt Whitman had met André Breton, he might have written *Howl*. It took half a dozen years, and more, for people to realize that Ginsberg, in *Howl*, had not merely invented a written equivalent of noise, but had opened language so wide, and made it so hungry, that nothing was safe any longer from poetry. Anything could be cut loose from its attachment to logical reality, and sent roaring into a sea of associations. Ginsberg's voice, in *Howl*, *Kaddish* and *Planet News* is omnivorous; its genius is to include and never to exclude. That is its connection to the surrealist practice of automatic writing which is also a method of radical inclusion, a way of putting a parenthesis around the will, while the contents of the psyche pour forth, unjudged. The poetry of *Howl* clarifies a profound implication of spontaneous language: it is an act of love. Not only noble images, but also the crippled children of the psyche will be loved, and the abortions and the terrors and the lonely ones. The surrealists argued that love was the essential revolutionary act. Love was the opposite of reason, because reason selects and judges, while love embraces. This was an argument that Whitman would have understood, and Ginsberg stands halfway between these two master-sources of his psyche, sometimes closer to one, sometimes to the other:

> incomparable blind streets of shuddering cloud and lightning in
> the mind leaping toward poles of Canada & Paterson,
> illuminating all the motionless world of Time between,
> Peyote solidities of halls, backyard green tree cemetery dawns,
> wine drunkenness over the rooftops, storefront boroughs of
> teahead joyride neon blinking traffic light, sun and moon
> and tree vibrations in the roaring winter dusks of Brooklyn,
> ashcan rantings and kind king lights of mind . . .

— Howl

My uncle thinks his Truthcloud's Jewish—thinks his Name is
   Nose-smell-Newark 5 decades—& that's all except there's
   Gentile Images of mirrory vast Universe—
and Chinese Microcosms too, a race of spade microcosms apart,
   like Jewish truth clouds & Goyisha Nameless Vasts
But I am the Intolerant One Gasbag from the Morgue & Void,
   Garbler of all Conceptions that myope my eye & is Uncle
Same asleep in the Funeral Home —?

Planet News.

In poems like these, Ginsberg created an unselective language similar
to the mode of automatic writing, and turned it into a cultural-
revolutionary weapon. But there is an important difference between
the spirit of his poetry and that of the French surrealists. Surrealism,
in France, was attuned to psychic realities. It tended to view the
outer world as a locus of repressions, a negative place to argue against
or to destroy, not to embrace. But Ginsberg makes a further step.
To embrace the rhythms of the unconscious mind, he felt that he
also had to embrace the rhythms of the outer world. Ginsberg's
poems turn crowded pads and bus stations and supermarkets and
Warsaw cafés and his own aging body and his mother's insanity
and crushed beercans and flowers and Wales hilltops, into moments
of illumination. Unlike the surrealists, Ginsberg makes the language
of unreason into an act of *amor fati*, an ultimate generosity which
accepts to perceive the world even at its worst, unfiltered by habits
or conventions or repressive judgments. Even Ginsberg's rage
against the political falsity of America is a form of embracing; it is
a warm, life-including anger. The surrealists were haunted by suicide, and René Crevel actually killed himself on principle. This was
because of an ambivalence in their attitude: unselective self-acceptance mingled dangerously with hatred of the ordinary world. The
language of their texts verges on preciosity, as if their spontaneity
retained an element of judgment resembling Baudelaire's longing
to be "anywhere out of this world." Ginsberg, like Whitman,
broadens the surrealist act, creating a poetry that evokes all the
ranges of experience, a poetry anchored inside of life.

Although *Howl* almost singlehandedly dislocated the tradition-
alist poetry of the 1950's, its specifically literary influence has been
negligible. Ginsberg made the experimental mode of the 1960's
possible, but very few poets could approach the breadth of his
surreal spontaneity. Self-indulgence on the grand scale is harder
than it looks, as many liberated, anonymous poets discovered.
Among younger poets, only Diane Wakoski has been able to create,

at least occasionally, a mode of Whitmanesque surrealism that sustains itself.

Although the surrealists cultivated unreason and absurdity, it would be a mistake to confuse the aims of surrealism with those of "absurdists" like Beckett and Ionesco. The surrealists believed that where sense broke down, the "marvelous" began. Absurdity and fractured meanings did not portray the emptiness of conventional lives. They were excursions into a domain of lyrical reality. The surreal absurd has a mystical intensity which one recognizes in the poetry of Ginsberg, Bly, Wakoski, Simic, Lamantia, Knott. It is a quality which lacks entirely in Kenneth Koch's poetry. Koch plays on the quirks and mannerisms of surrealist language; he is a virtuoso of the absurd image. There is an air of provocative non-sense in his work which echoes the French poets with a lightness of touch verging on coquetry:

Buttes-Chaumont pleased Aragon; the fire department say, "Flint is our religion."
The bone Andes are still pledging facial Switzerland to Peruvian intestinal prisms
Too coffee-like to replace the face; but then that tissue paper is their business.
    Our replica
Of all this is the sunset, a basilica of friendly brassieres—
The government of Switzerland may not be overcome by gonorrhea!
Finland wants "boats." The sheep want to go to Finland.
"Sand will not make you a very thrilling overcoat," the house said to me;
Our peach tree sat down. "Chalk was dreaming of the lightning and thunder."

Koch makes surrealist poetry into a field of fun; but his wit, en route, moves closer to the absurdist snicker than to the intensity of a Breton. Although such distinctions are difficult to make, it is possible that Koch is not as much a surrealist as he seems. His humor has an edge of satire; his ebullient absurdity slides into an original form of social and cultural criticism, as in "The Artist" and "Fresh Air," both enormously funny epics about the impossibility of art. With Koch, as to a certain extent with Michael Benedickt, the elements of surreal language are often put to a more circumscribed use, as absurdist jokes.

Among younger poets, Bill Knott, in particular, calls himself a "hard-core" surrealist. Here are some lines from "Aurealism: A Study":

        Prickly palace now cyclops child
        Fresh from the headlands of wild
        The future is in your *Eye*
        Show us the wonder why
        In seconds light reaches the
        Ground then takes an eternity

> To travel just six feet further
> Down to the girls who move their vagina-lips when they read
> The aurealm the chimerashpere the carnalcopia the forger
> Who signs the worlds name to our lies
> With the flashback flesh of the woman known as the tiny
>   misprints of the rain
>   Her breasts write an hourglass each second
> I perform mouth-to-mouth arms upon her

The poem proceeds by needle-thrusts of imagery, as do most of Knott's works. There is a kind of anonymity in the tone, as if the images emerged without a voice, from out of the language itself. This is a touchstone of the pure surrealist text, which avoids giving any sense of personality, since what is being written belongs to the flow of pure chance, not to the needs and feelings of a "self." Perhaps that is the secret behind Knott's literary "suicide." All of his recent books are signed: "Bill Knott (1940-1966)." In the mode of the original surrealists, Knott may be telling us that his poems are written by nobody; that they come from no place, and mean nothing.

Although Knott acknowledges the surrealists as his masters, there is an element of calculation and intense care in many of his poems, which contradicts the seemingly "automatic" feeling of his images, as in this poem from *Nights of Naomi*:

> Prefrontal lightningbolt too lazy to chew the sphynx's loudest eyelash
> Not even if it shushes you with a mast of sneers
> Down which grateful bankvault-doors scamper
> Because of a doublejointedness that glows in the dark
> Like a soliloquy of walnuts
> Numbed by beaks of headless measuringtape
> So the lubriciousness can tower in peace
> Like a buzzsaw trapped in a perfumery of shrugs
> Lemon
> Or lime
> Only a maze can remember your hair of buttered blowguns.

The lines swing on well-oiled connectives. Line by line, the poem makes thrusts into "the marvelous," yet there is a mannered quality in the rhythms. The poem has a constructed air, as if Knott had to work hard to keep sense out. Is this surrealism, or is it an absurdist exercise in the manner of Koch? The question is difficult to answer, and that may be a mark of Knott's originality as a poet: he is absurd and classical and surreal all at once. A marvelously impossible animal.

Of all the American poets to whom surrealism has mattered, only one, Phillip Lamantia, has created a body of work which reflects the intensity and the original ambition of the French poets. When Lamantia was sixteen, during the 1940's, he met Breton, and became a latter-day member of the movement. His early poems, collected in *Touch of the Marvelous*, are delicate chants of suicide. They move quietly from one incendiary image to the next as if they were telling a story. But the grammar and the division into stanzas serve only to entice the reader into a landscape of total surprise which Lamantia, in one poem, calls "the automatic world":

> Rainbow guns are dancing
> in front of the movie queens
> Everyone is laughing
> flying dying
> never knowing when to rest
> never knowing when to eat
>
> And the fountains come falling
> out of her thistle-covered breasts
> and the dogs are happy
> and the clowns are knifing
> and the ballerinas are eating stone
>   — *Selected Poems*

In these early poems, the leaps of imagery are contained by a song-like quality which had always been latent in the poetry of the French surrealists, and emerged startlingly in the post-surreal works of Desnos and Aragon. But Lamantia never leaves the ground of surrealist surprise. Often the song-quality of his voice resembles the songs of William Blake:

> O the flock of sheep
> breaking their flesh open
> with bones sucked
> from the brothels!
>
> O the grave of bats
> sailing through shops
> with the violent hands!
>
> When will these come?
> When will these go?
>   — *Selected Poems*

Lamantia's early poems are swept by a mystical energy which makes them more gripping than most of the original surrealist texts. The chant of suicide ("I drink from the goblet of suicide") becomes a journey out of the daylight which is self, into the moonlight which dissolves forms into images; it becomes a narrowly intense love-song, as in the poem "I Am Coming":

> I am following her to the wavering moon
> to a bridge by the long waterfront
> to valleys of beautiful arson
> to flowers dead in a mirror of love

to men eating wild minutes from a clock
to hands playing in celestial pockets
and to that dark room beside a castle
of youthful voices singing to the moon.

When the sun comes up she will live at a sky
covered with sparrow's blood
and wrapped in robes of lost decay.

But I am coming to the moon,
and she will be there in a musical night,
in a night of burning laughter
burning like a road of my brain
pouring its arm into the lunar lake.

Lamantia's images are charged with the energy of pain. Unlike Koch's and even Knott's surrealism, Lamantia's has an air of deadliness. Its thrusts of imagery are knife-thrusts. They are compulsive, like a voice squeezed out of a deep hiding place. The poems spray themselves into language, but their core is molten. In the background are shadows of Poe, Rimbaud and Lautreamont.

For a number of years Lamantia, under the influence perhaps of Ginsberg and Robert Duncan, moved toward an expansive mystical style. The compressed thrusts of surrealist imagery gave way to a spacious poetry closer to Whitman or to Blake's prophetic books. Even in *Touch of the Marvelous*, Lamantia had created a language of revelation. In "Trance Ports" (Section Two of his *Selected Poems*), illumination becomes the central subject matter of his poetry:

On a himalaya
this one in sight of heaven
outpouring
prayer of lungs sex eyes
eyes poured in abysms of light. . . .

I never see enough
with those who fly tortoise shell in the infinite hangup
words slow unravelling song

the gods are vomiting
I am entering earth I am walled in light I am where the song
is shot into my eyes O *hypodermic light!*

Lamantia never strayed far from his attachment to surreal language, and his most recent book, *The Blood of the Air*, indicates a return to his origins. The poems are presented as "automatic" texts, less purely lyrical than Lamantia's early poems, but more somber and hallucinatory. The slender chant of suicide has become a vision of apocalypse. In *The Blood of the Air* it is no longer the poet flying into himself on the blade of a knife, it is the world exploding into a debris of deadly images:

The earthquake slivers
The broken nails of the nazis
Mister Fly and his obsidian mask
My father on his razor
Basalt nightmares
Megalithic godplanes click the xylophones
My wracking spit spits
Words are magic beans
Children of the flat-faced musicians
Cross the street into subtropical ice
Manuring down your hand split a hundred ways
By the onyx of baptism
Stop
I'm climbing
To genocide the look of you
A thousand shacks
Human faces
Synthetic clouds
O for the slaughter America pinned on its bottom
I'd give up the rasp of Europe
Beatific visions sprawled on coat hangers
And weigh the silence with real screws
The fists of dawn
I'm still too intelligent
Become waste of years
Cruel whistling from under the snow inside the floorboards
And asleep drugged poet
You're safe striking the buttocks of the dream machine.

                                        — *Blood of the Air*

There is no use trying to "understand" poems like this, any more
than one "understands" an orgiastic dance. One gets the drift of it,
one experiences the freedom of language released into complete un-
predictability. The poems are exercises in meditation, as Breton
originally meant surrealist texts to be. They point to what Rimbaud
first called the "long reasoned unreasoning of the senses." Lamantia's poems blindfold the reader, and lead him through labyrinths
of somber imagery, until he has lost his way, and cannot tell how
he arrived at the cave where the hermit sits. Then he is released,
and left to make up his mind about what has taken place: a descent
into the underworld? a confidence game of seductive images? a Zen
journey into the white heat of impossibility?

Although I have described the main currents of surrealist influence
in America, it is not possible to do thorough justice to the subject,
because the elements of surrealist language have become so wide-
spread. Neither W. S. Merwin nor David Ignatow nor James Dickey
are surrealists, yet the dream element in their poetry parallels the surrealist vision, and may be indebted to it. Although younger poets
like James Tate, Erica Jong, William Matthews and Russel Edson

are not surrealists in any narrow sense, they have clearly been nourished on the indigenous second-growth surrealism of American poetry in the 1960's.

Much of what is good, and often what is terrible, in the anti-cultural language of the 1960's, derives from the use and misuse of surreal attitudes. In the work of our best poets, a new subject matter has been created, based on the language of pure fantasy. It is a poetry of psychic voyaging and dream-states, akin to the archaic tales of shamanism. In the work of lesser poets on the other hand, the surrealist attitudes have become merely sources of rhetoric. The result is an imitative surrealism, a facile belief not in "the marvelous," but simply in irrationality.

In the end, the American surrealism of the 1960's defies description. Having long since come to an end as a "movement," surrealism has become the language our poets speak.

The Poetry of A. R. Ammons: Some Notes and Reflections

BY HYATT H. WAGGONER

MY TITLE IS NOT MODEST, simply descriptive. Mr. Boyers asked me about a year ago to contribute an essay on a contemporary poet to this issue of *Salmagundi* and I agreed to do so if possible, but circumstances of several sorts now make it impossible to write the full-length, fully worked out, appreciative and interpretive article Ammons' poetry deserves and I should like to do. What follows is simply some of the thoughts, and a few reflections on those thoughts, that have come to me as I have read through seven volumes of the poetry, the product of something more than a decade of writing.* I do not own, am not near a library that contains, and so have not seen Ammons' first volume, *Ommateum* (1955), an omission which must qualify anything I may say about Ammons' development.

I write these notes seated in a mountain meadow, facing north toward a spruce woods fringed with poplar and balsam fir, the short-lived forward units of the woods as it edges across an unused pasture beyond the meadow. I have been watching the woods take over the pasture for more than thirty years now but have seen no movement. All I know is that the woods are a hundred or so feet closer to engulfing the spot where I sit and the house behind me than they used to be, and from that I can deduce that they are coming toward us all the time, moving in stillness.

So much for the permanencies of nature. I find this helping me to understand and respond to a good deal of Ammons' poetry, in which nature is the subject, the exemplum, or the setting of a good many of the best passages and poems.

---

* Since this was written, Ammons'-*Collected Poems, 1951-1971* has appeared. I take its publication to be a major event in our poetry. The poems in it that are new to me do not seem to require any major alterations in what I wrote from a knowledge only of the earlier volumes.

Ammons is a visionary poet in the Neoplatonic tradition introduced and best represented in our (American) poetry by Emerson. I would guess that he has read a good deal of Emerson and pondered much on what he has read. Maybe not. Maybe he has read only a little and gotten all his Emersonianism from that little, working out for himself, as Emerson did, the consequences of a few major ideas about the relations of the Many and the One. Or maybe it has come to him at second and third hand, through Pound and Williams, Whitman and Frost, all of whom make their appearance in his poetry. It is clear at least though that he has read "Brahma" — which could have been sufficient for the right kind of mind — for he alludes to it and paraphrases it in "What This Mode of Motion Said" in *Expressions of Sea Level.* Emerson: "When me they fly, I am the wings"; Ammons: "I am the wings when you me fly"; Emerson: "I am the doubter and the doubt"; Ammons:

> I am the way by
> which you prove me
>   wrong,
> the reason you
> reason against me.

Some other "Emersonianisms" in the poetry. (This could be a full-length article itself. It would have to treat important poems in each of the seven volumes I have read.*) "Raft," the opening poem in *Expressions of Sea Level,* a somewhat self-consciously Romantic poem in which the sought-for unity with nature — or with the undefinable Reason behind nature — is distanced by a tone of playful make-believe, is central Emerson: let go, yield, be blown by the winds of spirit. *Spiritus:* breath, wind. The Muse, the deeper self, the Holy Spirit. The boy on the circular raft is swept out to sea by the tides to where the winds control his motion toward the east, the rising sun. Neoplatonists: sun, source of light, life, and goodness; emanation. Christian Neoplatonists: sun = Son. . . . The Romantic sea-voyage; the "innocent eye" of the child. Several poems in the same volume make explicit what "Raft" implies by the story it tells. For instance, "Guide": "the wind that is my guide said this"; and "Mansion":

---

* For such a study, "Hibernaculum" in the new *Collected Poems* would be particularly important. In it Emerson is mentioned by name and linked with Plotinus in a passage that seems to me to say in effect, This is the philosophic tradition that means the most to me. Some of the Emersonianisms are jocular, as when Ammons finds in Shakespeare the same virtues and same defect that Emerson had found, then adds that he is cheered by this because "I can't reconcile the one with the many either."

So it came time
    for me to cede myself
and I chose
the wind
    to be delivered to.

The word *soul* can be used only in actual or implied quotation marks by contemporary poets. Since Ammons takes what the word refers to very seriously, he seldom uses it: there is nothing "so-called" about spirit in his work. Like Emerson, he is ambiguous about what he refuses to name. Emerson usually preferred to define the "Over-Soul," "World-Soul," "The Spirit," "The Real" in negative terms, as he does in the opening of the essay on the subject, following the long tradition of "negative theology." He was surer about Immanence than about Transcendence: "A light from within or from behind," with the ambiguity kept. Only in "Circles," in the early essays, does he drop the subjective-objective ambiguity and attribute unqualified Transcendence to the One: "the eternal generator of circles," that is, the Creator of the circles of physical and spiritual reality. Ammons' poetry keeps both Emerson's theoretic ambiguity and the intensity of Emerson's search for vision.

Ammons has a *mind,* too good a mind to be content with the kinds of superficial Romanticism that are becoming fashionable in contemporary poetry. I would like to call him a philosophical poet — except that description might turn away some of those who should read him, and except also that the phrase is in part intrinsically misleading in its suggestion that he deals principally in abstractions. He deals with the perfectly concrete felt motions and emotions of the particular self he is and, like Emerson again, looks for and often sees "Correspondences" between these motions and those of animate and inanimate nature, both nature-as-observed (winds, tides, seeds, birds) and nature-as-known-about (the chemistry of digestion, entropy).

The title poem of *Corsons Inlet* is such a philosophical poem, treating the relations and claims of logic and vision, order created and order discovered, being and becoming, art and nature. Rejecting any "finality of vision," it still prefers the risk of vision to any "easy victory" in "narrow orders, limited tightness." The poet's task is to try to "fasten into order enlarging grasps of disorder," the task Emerson set before the poet in "Merlin" and "Bacchus." I find significance in the fact that the poem was first entitled "A Nature Walk." If there is no order discoverable in nature, the order of art is a contrivance without noetic value. Ammons, like his Romantic and Transcendental poetic forebears, is not content to make pretty, or even interesting because intricately fashioned, poems. "Corsons Inlet" seems to me at once one of the finest and one of the most significant poems written by any of our poets in recent years. It is a credo, a manifesto, a cluster of felt perceptions, and a demonstration that, up to a point at least, vision *can* be both achieved and conveyed.

Though I am persuaded that my frequent mentions of Emerson up to this point do not distort but rather illuminate Ammons' work, still they might prove misleading if I failed to mention the ways in which the poet's vision is *un*like Emerson's. (Emerson, I should explain, is very fresh in my mind these days, for I have just spent a year rereading and writing about him. But I am still not importing my own preoccupation into Ammons' poetry: Emerson is there, and I happen to be well prepared to notice his presence — in many more ways, and more poems, than I have mentioned or will mention.) Let me try to generalize the difference first. Ammons comes as close to rediscovering the Romantic Transcendental vision of Emerson as any thoughtful and well-informed man of the late twentieth century is likely to be able to, but as a man of our time he simply cannot be a "disciple," he can only learn from, be stimulated by, walk the paths of, and be honest about his differences with, the poet who more than any other foreshadows him, as I see it.

A few of the differences. Ammons allows to come into consciousness, and so into his poetry, much more freely than Emerson did, the existential *angst* that Emerson must have felt but usually repressed. (See "1 Jan." in *Tape for the Turn of the Year* for Ammons' statement on this. The point he makes there — "I know the/violence, grief, guilt, / despair, absurdity" — is clear in all the volumes without being stated.) Death, disorder, entropy (one of his few technical philosophical terms) are never far from the surface of any of Ammons' poems, and frequently they are central in them. Poetry, he says in *Tape,* has "one subject, impermanence." Never unaware of "a universe of horror," Ammons knows that "we must bear/the dark edges of/our awareness," but the goal of his search remains "a universe of light " (*Tape,* "1 Jan.")

A different man in a different age, Emerson erected his defenses against fear and grief stronger and taller than Ammons', though I should say that in his best poetry — in prose as well as in verse — he was sufficiently open to all his feelings, even these, to allow his wonderful intelligence to work freely. Still, it is true, however one may take the fact, that Ammons does not transcend so easily or so far.

Related to this as a symptom is to a cause is the much greater concreteness of the way Ammons' imagination works, and so of his poetic language. As Emerson was more concrete, specific, even local (think of the first line of "Hamatreya") than the Pre-Romantics whose style his often resembles, so Ammons is more concrete, specific, local, and *personal* than Emerson. On this matter, as on style in general, Ammons' affinity seems to be with Pound and Williams, but of course Pound and Williams were more Emersonian than they knew.

A difference that is more strikingly obvious but I think finally less important is that of verse-forms. Emerson's theory, at least the part of it we are most likely to remember, called for organic or open form, but only a few of his best poems put the theory successfully into practice, and then only partially. Ammons, like most of his best contemporaries, has moved all the way toward practicing the theory announced in "The Poet" and elaborated in "Poetry and Imagination." Still, there is not an immeasurable gap, formally speaking, between "Merlin" and "Poetics" in *Briefings*.

Tape for the Turn of the Year, Ammons' "long thin poem" typed on a roll of adding-machine paper, a poetic journal which keeps turning into a poetic meditation, is the most continuously interesting, the strongest, the finest long poem I have read in I don't know how many years. It is as concrete as the *Cantos,* but the facts in it are not exotic lore out of the library and they are not illustrations of theories. It is at once personal and historical, like *Paterson,* but I don't feel, as I do in that poem at times, any attempt to impose the larger meanings. The meanings rise from the facts of personal history, the life the poet led from December 6 to January 10, the meals, the weather, the news, the interruptions, the discrete perceptions, and are presented for just what they are, felt thoughts. *Tape* proves — for me, anyway — the point Ammons makes in it somewhere, that poetry is "a way of/thinking about/truth" even while, as an art form, its distinctiveness is its way of "playing" with language to create untranslatable meanings.

Stylistically, *Tape* is "good Emerson," not so much in resembling Emerson's poems (though it does resemble them in certain ways, at times) as in following-out Emerson's theory. Transcendental poetic theory puts enormous emphasis on the single word, the single image, the discrete perception that may become an intuition. The short lines of the poem would seem merely stylish if they could not be justified in terms of this aspect of Transcendental Poetics. "Stylish" they may be, but the reason for the style emerges from the lines surprisingly, astonishingly. Prosaic, lyric, meditative, philosophic by turns, *Tape* is a wonderful poem. Read it.

Ammons' latest poems strike me as showing two developments. Stylistically, they are somewhat less "open," more thought-out, "reasonable," logically disciplined. They have pulled back a little from the letting-go and letting-out of the earlier work. There is less abandon, more control. Stylistically firmer perhaps, they seem to me less daring. Their style might be described as more "mature," but maturity brings losses as well as gains. The transparent eyeball narrows slightly to shield itself against the too-dazzling light. Ammons said toward the end of *Tape* that after the long, in a sense "dictated," poem he wanted to write short, artful lyrics, and he's doing it. And of course art is artificial. But I hope he will continue to leave openings, cracks maybe, in his conceptual boxes.

In any poet as fine as Ammons, a stylistic change signals a change in sensibility and vision. "Transaction" in *Uplands* ("I attended the burial of all my rosy feelings") describes the new "resignation" (Is this the right word? I'm not sure.) explicitly, but a good many of the poems in the two latest volumes exhibit it.

In *Tape* he reminded us — warned us? — that "I care about the statement/of fact" and suggested that "coming home" meant "a way of/going along with this/world as it is:/nothing ideal," but he still invited us to the dance. Wisdom involves a kind of resignation, I suppose, as one of its elements, but I think of it as contrasting with rashness and inexperience rather than as first cousin to prudence. I should hate to see Ammons become too prudent. I don't think he will.

The most recent poems may be less ambitious philosophically and less openly Romantic-Transcendental in their imaginative questing, but the quest itself has not been abandoned and the conception of how the journey should be undertaken — how thinking, feeling, imagining, responding can find expression and thus be realized, recognized, identified, and shared in a particular verbal object we call "this poem" — has not essentially changed. In the inseparable union of physics and metaphysics in Ammons' imagination, the emphasis may have shifted a little from the *meta* to the *physics,* but the union has not been dissolved, as of course it must not be if poetry is to continue to have noetic value. (Heidegger's "What Are Poets For?" in his recent *Poetry, Language, Thought* is relevant here. What are poets for in a dark time?) "Poetics" in *Briefings* should send any readers of it who don't remember the essay back to Emerson's "Poetry and Imagination." "Ask the fact for the form." Imagination and circles, imagination and possibility, the expanding spheres of possibility — of apprehension, of recognition, of meaning — finding their forms in poems. Here's the poem:

> I look for the way
> things will turn
> out spiralling from a center,
> the shape
> things will take to come forth in
>
> so that the birch tree white
> touched black at branches
> will stand out
> wind-glittering
> totally its apparent self:
>
> I look for the forms
> things want to come as
> from what black wells of possibility,
> how a thing will
> unfold:
>
> not the shape on paper—though
> that, too—but the
> uninterfering means on paper:
>
> not so much looking for the shape
> as being available
> to any shape that may be
> summoning itself
> through me
> from the self not mine but ours.

Harold Bloom is quoted on the back cover of *Briefings* as saying that the lyrics in the book "maintain an utterly consistent purity of detached yet radiant vision." Right on target. But I'd like to shrink the ambiguities of this a bit if I can without putting us and Ammons into a mentalistic box. "Consistent": consistent with all the other lyrics in the volume, yes, but not entirely consistent, in tone or statement, with the best of the earlier lyrics or even with the prayer ("14 Dec.") and the several credos (*credo*: I believe) in *Tape*. A little more defensive, more guarded, more "intellectually prudent." There's a concern with defining differences: ". . . keep me from my enemies'/wafered concision and zeal" ("Hymn IV," *Briefings*). A fear almost that vision may harden into doctrine.

"Purity": Yes, of style, of tone, of vision too. The wonderful thing is that the purity is at once a purity of style and a purity of vision, in both cases (or perspectives: two sides of the same coin) a unique balance maintained between conflicting perceptions of the One and the Many, the Real and the Actual, etc. — to borrow some Emersonian terms for what is not easily talked about in any terms.

"Detached": "Wafered concision" suggests that the detachment is from High Church zealots who localize "the eternal generator of circles" (Emerson's term in "Circles") in the manageable little round wafer of Communion. But the detachment is equally, I think, from the rationalistic formulations of the ineffable that betray an idolatrous attitude not toward a common substance, bread, but toward the results of a process, directed abstract thought. I say this not from the evidence of this poem, which, by its emphasis, might not seem to prompt it, but from the evidence of the whole corpus of the poetry as I have read it.

"Radiant": No need for clarification (if that's the word for what I'm trying to do) here. "Radiant" in the sense that applies to Blake, Emerson, Whitman, Cummings, Roethke.

"Vision": Right again, of course. But "vision" and "visionary" can be a way of throwing positivistic enemies off the scent. Vision of what? Assuming that God is not a "being" among other beings, and so, being unlimited spatially and temporally ("God is the circle whose center is everywhere and circumference nowhere" — the practitioners of the "negative theology," and Emerson, said), is undefinable, still I'd say a sense of God's reality, whether as immanent or as *deus absconditus*, is everywhere present in the poems and should be recognized, for it does more than anything else (of the many factors at work, some unknown, some unknowable,) to give the poems their special *kind* of "vision." Heidegger, "What Are Poets For?" again.

I'd like to make the word *religious* respectable once again among literary critics, rescue it from Freud ("the future of an illusion") and give it to Jung, who used the word not to clobber the naively pious but to point to something real and permanent in human experience. ("Permanent" until *now*, maybe.) Ammons is a poet of religious vision who is as wary of intellectualist abstractions as he is of pious dogmas. *That's* the peculiar feature of the "purity" of his "vision," it seems to me. Peculiar in our time, not peculiar if we think of the poetic visionaries who are his ancestors, whether he knows it or not — and he probably does, for he seems to know everything.

The "veracity" of Ammons' poetry (his word, and Emerson's before him, in "Poetry and Imagination"), the sense it creates in us that the radiance, when it comes, is real, discovered, not invented or faked, is causally related, I suspect, to the steadiness with which the poet has looked into the Abyss. The gains for the imagination from such looking are incalculable, but it must be hard on the nerves. One wants to survive as well as write "short rich hard lyrics," as Ammons is doing now. I want Ammons to do both — that is, survive and write. Perhaps the slight narrowing of the eyelids over the transparent eyeballs I seem to detect in the later work is necessary for the survival. But the transparency remains essential to his kind of vision. Dilemma. Poets age, like the rest of us.

I don't try very conscientiously to "keep up" with all the new poetry in the magazines and the slender volumes, but I can say that of the "new" poets I've read since Roethke's death, Ammons seems to me at or near the top. His poetry is, among other things, more important, a "sign" granted for the strengthening of the faith, the faith that in a dark time light may still be seen, not invented (no "Supreme Fiction," no fiction at all), by the unguarded eye.

At his best (I don't much like "Summer Session 1968"), Ammons is a highly distinguished poet of religious vision who grants the Transcendence but finds his occupation chiefly in searching out the traces of the Immanence. May he survive, save himself for this, and be visited often by the Muse, indulging as little as may be in the writing of merely fashionable poems.

Alan Dugan: The Poetry of Survival

BY ROBERT BOYERS

THE POET ROBERT GRAVES in a memorable lecture series once criticized Ezra Pound's unabashed ambition of writing great poems. For Graves, it is more than enough simply to try to write good poetry. Such a view may perhaps be too easily explained by the fact that it represents the advice of a minor poet to a great poet. Alan Dugan is a good poet who has in his own peculiar way proven what Graves was getting at. By cultivating what is by any standard a confining style, and by exercising his caustic intelligence on a relatively narrow range of subjects, Dugan has created a significant body of work that speaks with authority to a variety of modern readers. One does not get terribly excited about Alan Dugan's work, but one nevertheless returns to it with increasing regularity, for it successfully inhabits that middle ground of experience which our best poets today seem loathe to admit, as though to do so would somehow in itself constitute a denigration of their talents and a disavowal of intensity.

In Dugan, at least, if one is able to hope at all, he hopes to endure rather than to triumph. If one feels trapped, he will strive not for ultimate freedom and total independence, but for the sensation of freedom, temporary, imperfect, illusory. Dugan's spirit is best expressed in the conditional, which is to say that nothing he feels or thinks is very far removed from regret for what might have been, what the speaker might have thought, or done, or said. He asks nothing more of himself than he does of the hermit crab in "Life Comparison," that he do ". . . what is appropriate within his means, within a case," though even within these terms he is a failure. In short, Dugan's poetry succinctly conveys what most of us perennially feel—that even genuine commitment to a life of inconsequence fails to silence the persistent anxiety that we might be somehow less human than even we agreed to be.

It has been generally accepted that Dugan is something of a moralist, and I suppose it is possible to go along with such a view if we understand a moralist to be someone who experiences convulsive fits of nausea from time to time, whenever, that is, he remembers who he is, what he has consented to become, and to what he has given his approval if only by means of undisturbed acquiescence. But then, it might just be that public demonstrations of nausea, a kind of communal vomiting, is all we have left in the way of genuinely viable expressions of response to the modern world. Dugan's is an intensely private, almost a claustrophobic vision, but the poetry is accessible to any kind of sensibility. In this sense, I suppose, most poetry is fundamentally communal if it enlists imaginative participation on the part of readers in whatever it is the poet describes. Dugan's poems do not threaten us as do the poems of writers like Plath and Lowell. At his best, Dugan communicates small perceptions appropriate to the lives of small people, and we listen not because of any glittering eye, but because we feel we should. The voice that apprehends us is as earnest as any we might hope to encounter, and the combination of brittle surfaces and an underlying warmth is relentlessly imposing. I am not sure that Dugan "is exactly what we need," as one observer claimed, but he shows us why we have little right to expect anything more.

To date, Dugan has published three collections: *Poems, Poems 2*, and most recently, you guessed it, *Poems 3*.* In the latest volume, nine of the poems are entitled, simply, "Poem," which should not be terribly surprising to readers of Dugan's verse. His poems have variety, but they might all be drawn together as a single long poem. The same alert but static sensibility is operant in all of them, and the speaker rarely indulges the sort of emotional extremism which might distinguish his more inspired from his more characteristically quotidian utterances. Generally speaking, a Dugan poem begins by positing a problem, often representing a conflict between what the poet would like to think or imagine, and what he must in fact acknowledge as he looks about and within himself. Which is to say that Dugan's poems deal more or less with an extremely limited range of subjects, any combination of particulars in his work being easily reducible to an elementary abstraction in which polarities are anxiously opposed until, under the wry focus of Dugan's imagination, they somehow coalesce. Alternatives become merely matters of perspective, and the wise man gradually learns that as between one choice and another, we had best avoid choices altogether. If there is to be found in Dugan's verse a notion of what is good, one may

*Others have appeared since the original publication of this essay in 1968, including a *Poems 4*.

be sure that it could be a lot better, and if Dugan occasionally permits himself the luxury of criticizing others, one may be certain that these others are only slightly worse than the poet can imagine himself. In Dugan, reticence is not just strategy, but a way of life. If you say too much about someone else, you will find his features growing disconcertingly familiar.

A poem like "Adultery" from Dugan's most recent book is particularly instructive. It is one of those poems in which Dugan's compulsive honesty is manifest to a degree that makes a reader almost as uncomfortable as Dugan must perennially make himself. I quote it in full:

> What do a few crimes
> matter in a good life?
> Adultery is not so bad.
> You think yourself too old
> for loving, gone in the guts
> and charms, but a woman says
> "I love you," a drunken lie,
> and down you go on the grass
> outside the party. You rejoin
> the wife, delighted and renewed!
> She's grateful but goes out
> with a bruiser. Blood
> passions arise and die
> in lawyers' smiles, a few
> children suffer for life,
> and that's all. But: One
> memo from that McNamara and his band
> can kill a city of lives
> and the life of cities, too,
> while L. B. "Killer" Johnson And His Napalm Boys
> sit singing by their fire:
> The Goldberg Variations.
> So, what do a few crimes
> matter in a neutral life?
> They pray the insignificance
> of most private behavior.

The poem is at once impressive in purely formal terms, for its construction is considerably more elaborate and careful than in most of Dugan's poems. There is the opening rhetorical question, repeated with slight but highly significant adjustment toward the end of the poem. There is the self-conscious wordplay working under conditions of great concentration: "can kill a city of lives / and the life of cities, too." And finally there is the curiously logical if distinctly circular patterning of observations which permits the reader to savor the subtle modification of the poet's point of view which the poem has effected. I confess to what is perhaps a disproportionate admiration for poetry in which the dynamic process by which the poem unfolds is capable of forcing a shift in the poet's original intention. This is an essential element of our response to the work of a great poet like Sylvia Plath, and is not without its rewards in Dugan's "Adultery," so different in both texture and authority from anything Plath wrote.

The conflict in "Adultery" is, as suggested, between what Dugan would like to assert, and what he must in fact discover as an honest man. On the one hand is Dugan's intention of contrasting the relative innocence of the average man with the calculating murderousness of "L. B. 'Killer' Johnson And His Napalm Boys," who institutionalize violence and blitherly proclaim its wonders to the world in "The Goldberg Variations." On the other hand is the poet's discovery, in the interests of accuracy, that the "few crimes" of the private life can produce their own peculiarly terrible results, and that the diminutive scale of one's activities is not always assurance against an anxiety which ideally ought to afflict only the patent monsters of our civilization. At the poem's beginning, Dugan is relatively certain of what he has comfortably believed for some time. The opening lines are genuinely rhetorical. The average life is a good life, not glorious, but modestly decent. The adulterous foibles of the middle-aged are nothing more serious than . . . foibles, testimony of the weakness of flesh and the unreality of righteous presumptions. Only what emerges in the scope of a few lines is not merely the ugliness of the pattern, but its utterly predictable contours. The question that must form at the lips is, How is it possible that even the most modest of men should allow such a circumstance to develop as far as it frequently does? Dugan's morality does not counsel him to condemn an action out of hand, but he retains enough sense of our common dignity to demand, quietly, that we be somewhat accountable for what we do. What Dugan calls into question in this poem, as in so many others, is not so much what we do, as how we do things without considering them. Adultery does not present the problem of controlling passion, but of doing something about drift, heedlessness.

The irony of ". . . a few / children suffer for life, / and that's all" is unmistakably a bitter irony. How dreadfully skillful we have become in our rationalizations of what we do. After all, we argue, it is foolish to expect perfection of mere mortals. But then, it is the characteristic sickness of our age that we wear our flawed humanity as a coat of armor, humbly displayed, as protection against any charge that we might be less than we ought. In the course of Dugan's poem, the "good life," gratefully unexamined before, becomes the "neutral life," which is quite different. The notion of neutrality suggests a refusal or inability to commit oneself in any particular direction. Where it is deliberate and considered and contingent, neutrality may be useful. Where neutrality hardens into a comprehensive ethic or a life-style, the individual ceases to think of himself as fundamentally responsible for the things he does. In Dugan's poem, while the speaker would like to plead neutrality and evade guilt, his sincerity and intelligence block his way. The precision with which he chooses his words obviates any possibility of his refusing to make basic choices altogether. Perhaps the most crucial word in the conclusion to "Adultery" is "pray," reflecting Dugan's abject uncertainty in the face of the dilemma he has just projected. Is our "private behavior" for the most part "insignificant," or is it true instead that the semiconscious drift and subtle malignity of the average man constitute a more telling indictment of our humanity than our more overt betrayals of one another?

Dugan's concerns in "Adultery" are to be found with variation throughout his work. In "Not to Choose," the poet acknowledges that he "should be someplace else," that he should refuse to be the slave of habit and deny ". . . the sweat / of inhumane endeavor and its trash: / goods, deeds, credits, debts." But when he finally pays heed to those mysterious voices that urge him to "Choose, choose," he finds it is too late, that he is not ". . . in shape for choices / choices. No! Instead, I leave / the dirty business by the back / window, climb down the fire escape, / and sneak out of town alive / with petty cash and bad nerves. . . ." Dugan feels that he is somehow not of this world, that while situated within it and feeling himself hedged by the most obvious and blunt realities, he is not prepared to deal with it. He can neither accept the world nor reject it, nor conceive a way to alter its course. What he fears most is that neutrality which predicts the death of the spirit, but more and more it appears to him that this is indeed his most authentic reality. In "The Working World's Bloody Flux," the speaker struggles against any inclination to commit himself to a personal and potentially satisfying vision of things. Dugan is a skeptic where the imagination is concerned, and he refuses to hope that his visions or anyone else's can impose even a degree of permanence or order on a frightfully deceptive and chaotic reality. According to Dugan, when one feels most tempted to abandon inhibition, to submit to the imperatives of passion, or simple fancy, one must flee, and failing successful escape, ". . . build a fort of reason in her country." In Dugan we find ourselves desperately clinging to the quotidian, to what we defiantly know, for only in this way can we be spared that ultimate disillusionment we want to try to endure, and yet fear so much. Dugan's is a poetry of a man who almost tries, and who is acutely sensitive to the magnitude of his loss.

Dugan is very much an original poet, which is to say that he never sounds like any other poet so much as he sounds like himself. Still, there is a kind of ennui in this verse that makes me think of Baudelaire, of his compulsive fascination with the details of his own suffering, and of the relentless sincerity that led the great French poet to probe every aspect of what once seemed a morbid sensibility, though now strangely tamed and moral. Eliot's still perfect essay on Baudelaire includes the following observation: "Indeed, in much romantic poetry the sadness is due to the exploitation of the fact that no human relations are adequate to human desires, but also to the disbelief in any further object for human desires than that which, being human, fails to satisfy them." How well this serves as a description of Dugan's poetry, as well as of Baudelaire's. And how clearly it enables us to see the nature of the tensions evoked in such poetry, though Baudelaire's is obviously the more heroic struggle, and consequently produces a wider range of tensions. With Baudelaire it is possible to speak, as Eliot does, of good and evil, of salvation and damnation. Such terms sound faintly preposterous where Dugan is concerned. His structures are too fragile, his temperament too subdued to sustain convictions of that sort. "Baudelaire was man enough for damnation," Eliot wrote, and we cannot but agree. It is difficult to imagine Dugan granting any authority that kind of ultimate dominion. Dugan's, we must remember, is a world in which judgments are relative, in which all relations are at best tentative. It is a world in which one may occasionally refer to impending catastrophe, but in which the dominant reality is "the daily accident" Dugan evoked in his first memorable volume.

And what is "the daily accident" but the inevitable skirmish that reveals our inadequacy, just at the moment when we have finally propitiated nagging doubts, or at least managed temporarily to forget them? Always there is the faceless authority, incomprehensible and unreasonable, and yet impossible to dismiss. Always the vaguely drawn circumstances assume a rigidity that is inexplicable, and yet effectively works to suppress revolt. In so many of Dugan's Kafkaesque structures, the speaker seems willing to go to his own imminent destruction, or at least to some severe punishment, in expiation of crimes he may not have committed. How often in Dugan, as in Kafka, one feels tempted to shake the speaker, to force him to acknowledge the absurdity of the largely abstract proposition to which he has assented, and according to the terms of which he no longer feels free to exercise independent, rational judgment. One thinks, for example, of one of Dugan's early poems, entitled "Tribute to Kafka for Someone Taken":

> The party is going strong.
> The doorbell rings. It's
> for someone named me.
> I'm coming. I take
> a last drink, a last
> puff on a cigarette,
> a last kiss at a girl,
> and step into the hall,
>   bang,
> Shutting out the laughter.   "Is
> your name you?" "Yes."
> "Well come along then."
> "See here. See here. See here."

Dugan's perception in a poem like this is neither of a sociological nor of a political nature. It tells us not so much about the modern world as about the effects of the modern world on a sensibility which has but barely retained the will and energy to defend its right to exist. "Tribute" and poems like it mark the almost total surrender of those pretensions to innocence which according to both Dugan and Kafka are wholly incommensurate with the human being's insistence on his rights as an individual. "See here. See here. See here" suggests the poet's persisting demand for a measure of justice, but not for justice of an ordinary kind. As W. H. Auden wrote of Kafka's hero in *The Trial*: "K. knows he is guilty, he does not know of what, and his whole efforts are directed not to proving his innocence but learning the cause of his guilt."

Like Kafka's characters, then, Dugan begins with the assumption of guilt, largely founded upon his refusal to function comfortably as an accomplice in the ongoing processes of his society. Even when he gives in and follows along, as is the usual case, he dreams of a more stirring and human denouement. Always Dugan posits an irreconcilable opposition between the needs of the individual and the obligations of that individual to his society. And so long as the human brain will continue to examine the realities that threaten and finally overwhelm it, so long will the opposition be renewed. In "Two Hatreds of Action," the Coward sees his degeneration in the following terms:

> Fifes drilled·through my ears
> and found my trouble: brains
> coiled in the greys of self,
> and reamed them with the shrieks
> of civic cadence.

The troubling element is the brain, but without it there is no life worthy of man: "My brains are drummed out / of the corpse and wheedled away." What seems to underlie so much of Dugan's verse is the conviction that the world is a miserable place, but that to be aware of it is in no way protection against its insidious charms. The best one can do is now and again to negotiate a temporary truce, often a bitter agreement in which one vows not to think in return for promises he knows cannot be kept. In one poem, the speaker determines to suspend disbelief, to commit himself to the world so that he may learn from it, to play on "as if all horrors are mistakes." Only, of course, Dugan must know that they are not mistakes, that brutality is more a way of life than a remediable nuisance. In one of his most ambitious and prophetic pieces, "On Zero," Dugan laments the debilitation of those imaginative resources which at one time could enable us better to control and pacify our perceptions, and which could give form and coherence to visions of violence, "and hold them helpless in the will / and tractable to Liberal errands."

For us, Dugan claims, as we have no longer any belief in the vital capacity of the imagination fundamentally to improve the human condition, so we can no longer believe in those generous social instincts to which we have all along attributed our ability to survive. At our best, we endure by cultivating an amused detachment, an absurdist orientation, in which the worst we can possibly experience seems more than a little ridiculous alongside the more crucial perception of nullity as the predominating fact of man's existence. This is the "broad view," or so it has been called. Failing to adopt this kind of "cool," there are other alternatives. These, too, are "Qualifications of Survivors":

> Hide in cesspools, sleep well
> on broken glass, and eat
> shit. Kiss the whips,
> hold the wife for rape,
> and have good luck:
> stumble behind a lamb
> before the bomb burst
> and crawl out of the wreck
> to be the epitaph:
> "The good ones die first,
> but I am not so bad:
> Americans are worse."

This is the poem of a man who has spent years of his life cringing behind office desks, the poem of a man who frequently thinks of himself ". . . as an aging phoney, stale, woozy, and corrupt / from unattempted dreams and bad health habits." And his predictable low-keyed humor, so often remarked upon by others, does little to mitigate the stinging venom of self-contempt that courses through so much of Dugan's work. His is a bitter eloquence. If the cadence is austere, it is rarely impoverished, and the muscular flow of his terse diction is rarely purchased at the expense of complexity. Dugan invites us to witness with him, without any redemptive qualification, the sordid spectacle of our common humiliation. It is a strangely unimpassioned witnessing, but then, as Dugan thoughtfully reminds us, "Americans are worse."

Days and Distances: The Cartographic Imagination of Elizabeth Bishop

BY JAN B. GORDON

> My house, my fairy
>   palace, is
> of perishable
>   clapboards with
> three rooms in all,
>   my grey wasps' nest
> of chewed-up paper
>   glued with spit.
>   — "Jeronimo's House" *

ELIZABETH BISHOP'S ABODES are always "fairy palaces" of incredible interiority where child-like inhabitants construct rooms within rooms — all of which reflect a delicate fragility at the locus of intersection. If not real children, the figures who populate her poems are epistemological primitives whose approach to ordinary existence is never ordinary. *The Diary of 'Helena Morley,'* the first book translated from the Portuguese after Elizabeth Bishop moved to Brazil, is ostensibly the diary of a real child, "Helena," whose life in a Brazilian mining town must have resembled Miss Bishop's early existence, replete with bronchitis, in rural Nova Scotia. When the volume was published in Portuguese in 1942, the then grown "Helena" contributed an introduction:

> And now a word to my granddaughters: you who were born in comfortable circumstances and who feel sorry when you read the stories of my childhood, you do not need to pity poor little girls just because they are poor. We were so happy! Happiness does not consist in worldly goods but in a peaceful home, in family affection, in a simple life without ambition — things that fortune cannot bring and often takes away.

Her world is happy as a direct function of its containment; self-

A¹ All citations from Elizabeth Bishop, *The Complete Poems* (New York, Farrar, Straus and Giroux, 1970).

enclosed, the child experiences evanescence as a corollary to freedom. It is only when the delicate fragility breaks down that the child's world falls apart. In a short story, "In a Village," Miss Bishop has described in vivid detail the child's experience of loss, but once again the perspective is that of adult reminiscence. The story itself is suspended between two sharp sounds: the scream of the now deceased mother and the metallic clang of the village blacksmith's anvil. Death appears merely as an absence surrounded by a world punctuated with the commerce of grief: a fire in a sympathetic neighbor's house; the arrival of parcels of cakes; and cartons of musty personal effects. Her memory thematically resembles those paintings of Brueghel; although the child regards time as having stopped, the countryside moves through all the phases appropriate to the Nova Scotia summer. There is an harmonious balance between the silence of personal grief and the noise of a world that pays little heed to the artificial egocentricity induced by the departure of a loved one. Cows continue to lose their way on the path home; house repairs must be completed before winter sets in; and the blacksmith's hammer continues to serve as a village timepiece. The story exhibits the same tension in its mode of composition, for the progress of chronological time is always interrupted by the circuitous nature of the adult narrator's dramatization of the crisis of childhood loss. Lines of narration proceed only to be broken off with large patches of white space — the spaces of nature struggling with the spaces of absence.

Such a conflict is almost always at the heart of Elizabeth Bishop's craft and is nowhere better illustrated than in a story, written while she was still at Vassar, which appeared in *Partisan Review* in March, 1938. Like so much of Elizabeth Bishop's art, "In Prison" begins with a question about the nature of perception only to eventually move into ontological issues. The result is often deceptive, since the poems, like so many of the short stories, begin as if they were puzzles or riddles while simultaneously demanding that the "pieces" be taken seriously. Yet, precisely because they always begin with a question or series of questions, a number of the poems appear as epistemological exercises. This particular story is a monologue wherein a narrator who seeks some principle of order in a universe which he imagines to be chaotic, comes to the conviction that his imprisonment is part of nature's design. Willing to substitute the paranoia of determinism for what most men define as freedom, Miss Bishop's prisoner recognizes that only incarceration transforms acts of conscience into arenas of potentiality. He focuses upon the details of interiority so that his willed criminality becomes part of the aesthete's intentionality: the hues of sunlight refracted upon the walls of his cell; the harlequinage of nuance in personal dress; the fascination with the traces that food leaves upon a tin plate. For his leisure reading, the narrator devotes himself to a naturalistic tome, an objective catalogue of pseudo-events to which is added layer upon layer of literary criticism. At a certain point in the process, the reader is unable to distinguish the prisoner's criticism of the book from the book itself. There is no authorial intent against which one might commit the *crime* of the intentional fallacy; the book provides the *basis* for a literary criticism, but because of the infinite regress of multiple layering, the critic-criminal never knows where he is, but only what he has lost. Taste has become a substitute for freedom. In this world her solitary speaker extends Hegelian philosophy to its logical limits — freedom is the knowledge of Necessity. His dilemma is that of the man who can live in the universe only to the extent that he remains ignorant of its presence, and the baroque constructions of his imagination resemble that city described from a window in one of Elizabeth Bishop's poems:

> carefully revealed,
> made delicate by over-workmanship,
> detail upon detail,
> cornice upon facade,
>
> reaching so languidly up into
> a weak white sky, it seems to waver there.
> — "Love Lies Sleeping"

On another level, the most acute loss faced by the protagonist of "In Prison" is the absence of the historical. In the environment where every intersection is a corner, there is virtually no lineage. His critical exercise is virtually indistinguishable from the book which serves as its object, and questions of priority and succession pale beneath the metaphysics of the layer. Since time has virtually disappeared, there is no meaning, save in the shade or the nuance — the projection of the inadequacy of taste to make circumscription a synonym for appropriation. The predominant metaphor for this activity is map-making — a sort of charting of poetic voyages which is in part, at least, autobiographical. In her craft, as in her life, geography always triumphs over history. Following her graduation from Vassar in 1934 and a brief sojourn in New York, Elizabeth Bishop went to Paris in 1935, only to return to the United States in 1936 to winter on Florida's West Coast. Obviously enchanted by a fishing trip to Key West, she later elected to live there in 1938 after excursions to Ireland, London, and Italy. Until she went to Mexico in 1943, Elizabeth Bishop lived off and on in the Florida Keys. In 1951 she elected to use the money awarded to her from a number of literary prizes to sail to the Straits of Magellan. En route, she stopped off to visit friends in Rio de Janeiro only to be afflicted by one of her childhood allergies. Forced to remain in Rio for treatment, she settled in nearby Petropolis where she now lives with her friend, Lota de Macedo Soares. She continues, however, to visit the United States, usually for brief visits, serving most recently as writer-in-residence at Harvard.

The course of her life's wanderings has a peculiar pattern. Nova Scotia, the Straits of Magellan, interior journeys into the Amazon estuary — all of these places demarcate geographical boundaries between land and sea. Whether consciously or not, Elizabeth Bishop seems fascinated by geographical *extremities* — fingers of water or land that are the sensory receptors of a larger mass. Straits, peninsulas, icebergs, radio antennas ("The Unbeliever"), wharfs and quais, capes ("Cape Breton"), and promontories are the structures of her world. These are spaces which all share the quality of near isolation; they are almost, but not quite, geologically severed as if, like Miss Bishop herself, they were being constantly pulled back to their origin. And the first poem of her 1945 volume, *North and South*, engages us in the dilemma of that layered struggle between land and sea:

> Land lies in water; it is shadowed green.
> Shadows, or are they shallows, at its edges
> showing the line of long sea-weeded ledges
> where weeds hang to the simple blue from green.
> Or does the land lean down to lift the sea from under,
> drawing it unperturbed around itself?
> Along the fine tan sandy shelf
> is the land tugging at the sea from under?
>
> —"The Map"

The poem itself is a mere study of a map and of the art of cartography. Musing over the color gradations that separate charted from uncharted areas, Elizabeth Bishop's introductory poem is itself a kind of map to the volume. Although the poem commences with one kind of question — does the land lie on the water or does the water lie on the land? — its conclusion involves the necessary transcendence of the epistemological:

> Are they assigned, or can the countries pick their colors?
> — What suits the characters or the native waters best.

> Topography displays no favorites; North's as near as West,
> More delicate than the historians' are the map-makers' colors.
>   —"The Map"

The historical precedence of land or water has nothing whatsoever to do with the aesthetics of the "picture" beneath the glass. Maps pose the question of freedom originally encountered in the early story, "In Prison": the existence of voluntary acts would imply the possibility of choices, and to the contrary, these countries cannot elect their colors. Topography is helpless to accommodate the third dimension and hence reduces all to the flat objectivity of *necessary direction,* itself a paradox. The map which purports to guide us to a location is, from an aesthetic perspective, a neutral space where we lose rather than gain our way. Like Elizabeth Bishop herself, we are wanderers rather than travelers and the "map" is an intermediary surface between those two states of being. She has taken an object known primarily for its utility in getting us from one place to another and restored it to an existence purged of history. In the process, the aesthetic preferences of "character" or "native waters" is sacrificed to the delicacy of the map-maker. Neither land nor water lends shape, but rather the artificial profiles of the cartographer. So obsessed with geographical boundaries, and the precise calibration of latitude and longitude, the printer nonetheless allows "the names of seashore towns [to] run out to sea." Words, whether on maps or in poems, always exceed the intersections to which they point.

But the poetic vision which imagines the most innocuous of events as "marking out maps like Rand McNally's" ("Roosters") surely embodies intriguing premises. It is a world where the poet charts — which is to say, that scale and perspective become primary considerations. Although the genre would seem to be that of the landscape, map-making is really a pseudo-landscape, enacting, to borrow from the vocabulary of Claude Lévi-Strauss, *bricolage.* She is fascinated with this activity, as the poem "Large Bad Picture" testifies:

> Remembering the Strait of Belle Isle or
> some northerly harbor of Labrador,
> before he became a schoolteacher
> a great-uncle painted a big picture.
>
> Receding for miles on either side
> into a flushed, still sky
> are overhanging pale blue cliffs
> hundreds of feet high,
>
> their bases fretted by little arches,
> the entrances to caves

> running in along the level of a bay
> masked by perfect waves.

The subject of the poem is an amateur's attempt to construct a coastal scene on canvas. As the painter becomes involved with the process of "remembering" so in the second stanza the coast line is "receding for miles on either side." There is the characteristic interiorization, followed by the quest for a sterile perfection: the "perfect waves" and later, the black birds "hanging in n's in banks." His feeble landscape lacks grandeur precisely because the painter of the "Large Bad Picture" has substituted *reconstruction* for imaginative construction: the spars of the vessels are like "burnt match-sticks" and the glassy sea resembles the middle of some "quiet floor." In order to capture that tone of the painting, Miss Bishop herself consciously resorts to the same gimmick as her great-uncle:

> In the pink light
> the small red sun goes rolling, rolling,
> round and round and round at the same height
> in perpetual sunset, comprehensive, consoling,
>
> while the ships consider it.
> Apparently they have reached their destination.
> It would be hard to say what brought them there,
> commerce or contemplation.

Her stanzas are artificially linked with "while" and "as" in order to establish simultaneity where none exists in the same way that the schoolteacher-painter has several objects — birds, ships, sun, and an aquatic animal—within an association which appears as a suspension. The conflict in the painting is one between "commerce or contemplation," since some objects move, while others remain static or "perpetual" in their motionlessness. Everything in the poem, like the painting, is strung together with some technique, or word, like "apparently." The terrible painting is simultaneously part cheap commercial oil painting and part the authentic product of an old man's contemplation; like its very lines, this landscape is hung between "receding" and "remembering" in stanzas one and two. And those trapped birds in "n's" above some cliff are "hanging" in Elizabeth Bishop's poem in such a way that we almost hear the "n" trapped between hard "g's." Again, like the world of her travels, everything in Miss Bishop's poetic universe is nearly severed and must be strung together with ferries or bridges or their verbal equivalents.

Like her great-uncle, Miss Bishop is always constructing when she appears to be describing, and the result is a poetry which has the quality of an engineering exercise. There is a tendency to reduce the most complicated poetic issues to "questions" that are exclusively technical in nature. Her poem "Large Bad Picture," then, is a highly self-conscious enterprise — the use of an artificially bad poem to elicit the mood of an artificially awkward oil painting. Although we marvel at the proficiency of the poem, there is something curiously absent in such mastery. The emphasis upon the coalesced perspective tends to be a substitute for any attention to the *personal*. Even though we might wish to meet the grizzled amateur painter, he will always be inaccessible, located somewhere behind his masterpiece. Behind all the present and past participles of "Large Bad Picture" lurks only a world that is somehow already *given*, never in the process of being created. One suspects that this too is part of the map-maker's vision; after all, a poetic universe that is reducible to a map might well imply that the person en route is always among the lost. Compared with so much contemporary poetry that is confessional in its detail of the loss of or dispersal of selfhood, self-negation is a point of departure in Elizabeth Bishop's craft. But it is a self-negation that the reader never records and has no way of measuring, since the loss has occurred *a priori*. For this reason, the poetry often lacks a distinctive teleology. We see no possibility of a therapeutic progression in a world so relativized that "North's as near as West" precisely because hers is at best a two-dimensional craft. There is a certain surface tension always present in Elizabeth Bishop's art that is at least partially the result of the loss of *privilege* in every sense in which we might typically use that word: the narrator's sense of an advantage to perspective; an access to secrets unknown to other protagonists in her poems; or even the subtlety of an untrustworthy vision which might confer aesthetic advantage by granting the reader the right to acknowledge a false subjectivity. She has had far more favorable response from British critics than from those in this country perhaps because the limits of her poetry prevent the kind of self-indulgence that G. S. Fraser referred to as "luxury" in his essay, "Some Younger American Poets" (*Commentary*, May, 1957). Fraser contrasted Miss Bishop's precise diction with that of her American contemporaries and came to the conclusion that she had willingly surrendered a certain polish in order that she might more clearly say exactly what her poems want to say. He equates that equation, unfortunately, with what he terms "an immense sense of responsibility toward a critically cooperative audience." Of course there is a definable responsibility

in such an enterprise only when the word "responsibility" is made
synonymous with a failure to take risks. The etymology of the word
itself involves — as one of its primary meanings — the idea of an
"answer" or a "reply," literally a "speaking again (re-spondere)."
And that quality is seldom characteristic of her poetry because there
is never a voice sufficiently distinctive so as to serve as a vehicle for
an assumed dialogue. Responsibility seldom derives from rhetorical
questions. In short, it is the responsibility of the map-maker: a world
well-drawn and accurate, given the nature of current exploration,
but exhibiting more and more the quality of a guidebook:

> The mosquitoes
> go hunting to the tune of their ferocious obbligatos.
> After dark, the fireflies map the heavens in the marsh
> until the moon rises.
> Cold white, not bright, the moonlight is coarse-meshed,
> and the careless, corrupt state is all black specks
> too far apart, and ugly whites; the poorest
> post-card of itself.
>
> — "Florida"

That very ability to turn a traditional landscape into a guidebook,
complete with a commentary on the state's gnarled race relations,
is a peculiarly unique slant to the contemporary *paysage moralise*.
Travel guides become post-cards at the end of the journey when the
initiate tells the would-be traveler where to go and what to see.

But the landscape itself is altered in the process so that it always
appears to the reader as if it had been reproduced rather than experienced. And the moral vision of such a universe is similarly skewed.
For, as in so many twentieth-century sex manuals, occasions that we
would expect to be of great intimacy are charted for us, perhaps too
narrowly. If personal intercourse with the natural world is part of
the mythos of the guidebook, the reader's potentiality is democratized
at an enormous price. Not only does it always look easier than it is,
but emotional considerations are seldom horizontal. For if the poet
creates the illusion that technique alone assures mastery, then we
study the craft with an idea of learning it only to discover that we
have become cognizant of a world that is all surface. From the map,
as from the do-it-yourself guide to auto repair, we become aware only
of other surfaces. All of this is to say that Elizabeth Bishop's poetry
is always an *expedition* for which preparation is needed and, though
such is surely part of the Christian metaphor for life itself, her vision
is peculiarly technologized since there is no authentic ground for

existence in her scheme. We have the trappings of direction and guidance without the emergence, real or promised, of presence. There is no better or worse, no up or down, but only boundaries that create neutralized spaces:

> At low tide like this how sheer the water is.
> White, crumbling ribs of marl protrude and glare
> and the boats are dry, the pilings dry as matches.
> Absorbing, rather than being absorbed, . . .
>   — "The Bight"

Her images are never organically related nor are they presented in any of Imagism's characteristically durational clusters. Rather her poems appear as if they were strung together, with each metaphoric "set" following the preceding one in some established order of proper priorities. The pattern involves some invisible poetic finger moving across a map and accumulating rather than creating the world: "there is this, and then this, and then this. . . ." The manner is strangely reminiscent of one of Miss Bishop's childhood favorites, Gerard Manley Hopkins, whose verse provides the epigraph to a charming little poem, "Cold Spring." As in Hopkins's progressions, a number of her poems commence *ex nihilo* followed by some highly truncated phrase: "A cold spring:/the violet was flawed on the lawn." Then the universe suddenly proliferates:

> Tufts of long grass show
> where each cow-flop lies,
> The bull-frogs are sounding,
> slack strings plucked by heavy thumbs.
> Beneath the light, against your white front door,
> the smallest moths, like Chinese fans,
> flatten themselves, silver and silver-gilt
> over pale yellow, orange, or gray.
> Now from the thick grass, the fireflies
> begin to rise:
>   — "A Cold Spring"

This type of poem usually concludes with some coda that approximates the tone of Hopkins' "Praise him" in its abbreviated reduplication in emotive language of the phenomenal catalogue:

> And your shadowy pastures will be able to offer
> these particular glowing tributes
> every evening now throughout the summer.
>   — "A Cold Spring"

The progression is from nothingness, through an almost incredible enumeration of the discrete, though evanescent particulars of a landscape, and then to a deliberation upon the human significance of the catalogue. We move from the distinctly non-human to the decidedly human by means of an almost imperceptible intrusion of the possessive pronoun "your" which serves to give the reader a kind of power at the very instant that he is being overwhelmed by the fertility of the scene. The use of "and" to link the human coda to the world of nature that precedes it in "Cold Spring" is one of those partial deceptions that deflect Miss Bishop's craft from a certain sincerity. As spring catches slumbering nature by surprise, so the "shadowy pastures" of the concluding lines catch the reader by surprise. Somehow, the location has been shifted, for these pastures are part of an interior landscape, part of the realm of "offer[ings]" and "tribute." At the very instant of rebirth in the book of nature, the reader is also part of the kingdom of sacrifice in the book of grace. But, like the old man's painting in "Large Bad Picture," the reader is never sure how he got there. The poem proceeds within a false *telos* punctuated by "Now, in the evening" to "Now, from the thick grass" to the "And . . . /now throughout the summer." Yet, the final "now" is not part of the world of presence, but part of the absence of sacrifice and redemption that involves the possibility of return in the future; we have entered a realm of "will be" disguised as "now." Map-making too is an enterprise sufficiently vicarious as to involve a similar confusion between future and present tenses. The cartographer's product is one that continually must be updated, which is yet another way of using the word "now" as a refrain.

This constant struggle with the current in Elizabeth Bishop's art is metaphorically represented as a dialectic involving natural landscape and the claims of history. But again, history in her poems appears not as chronological time nor as the presence of the past, but rather as some symbol for every failed connection. For example, the poem "Argument" from the volume *A Cold Spring* seems a lament for some lost love (one of the very few poems in Miss Bishop's canon that involves anything like intimacy), yet the rift is related in terms of a battle between distance and desire on the one hand, and days and voices on the other:

> Days that cannot bring you near
> or will not,
> Distance trying to appear
> something more than obstinate,
> argue argue argue with me
> endlessly
> neither proving you less wanted nor less dear.
> —"Argument"

History never is part of the kingdom of contiguity, but rather serves an opposite function in the dialogue with space:

> Days: And think
> of all those cluttered instruments,
> one to a fact,
> cancelling each other's experience,
> how they were
> like some hideous calendar
> "Compliments of Never & Forever, Inc."
> —"Argument"

Rather than the accumulation of experience in increments of intensity, the voice of days is merely a record of canceled hopes and fears. It is the absence rather than the presence of connection. The lines themselves are faintly derivative of the kind of emotion that Sylvia Plath wrote about with such poignancy; the female body appears as a calendar torn between the two extremes of human affections: "I *never* want to see you again" and "I shall love you *forever*." The words appear merely as another "compliment," a part of the commercial world affixed to the gift of days as an afterthought. It is something distributed free at holiday time from businesses and corporations we have never encountered in experience. For Elizabeth Bishop, history then is merely another map, a spatialization of relationships that always appears as distance. In the poem "Argument" there is no distinction whatsoever between the language of history and the language of space:

> Distance: Remember all that land
> beneath the plane;
> that coastline
> of dim beaches deep in sand
> stretching indistinguishably
> all the way,
> all the way to where my reasons end?
> —"Argument"

Actually, the two components of this pseudo-dialogue come to participate in the life of the other. Days are related to the cancellation of experience, and distance is inextricably bound to the processes of memory "stretching indistinguishably" to a point where "reasons end." Again, the poet is almost fixated by boundaries, by the extremity where each participant loses domain. It is the realm of peninsular experience, either brackish water or tidal flats, and is surely a second cousin to the terrain of the Brazilian jungle from which our map-maker continually has drawn translations throughout her poetic career. Perhaps these too are but the poetic equivalent of a mercator projection. As the solitary speaker of "In Prison" had discovered, the tiniest reduction of space nevertheless provides the occasion for the metaphoric enlargement of boundaries through psychic projection and reprojection. The recognition of imprisonment participates in and leads to the only kind of freedom to which humans have access.

On David Wagoner

BY SANFORD PINSKER

SINCE, ROUGHLY, the end of the Second World War America has been blessed with any number of accomplished poets. Yet, none seems more consistently satisfying than David Wagoner. At the present moment both the shrill sounds of the public poet and the equally shrill sound of the confessionally private one have escalated their wares to the point of diminishing returns. Which is to say, the social tragedies which surround us — whether they be a lingering war in Vietnam, the ongoing racial agony or man's regular inhumanities to man — have a way of depleting the poetic arsenal without ever quite achieving the desired effect. Perhaps our headlines are too monstrous for *any* poem, even one recited with passion to an audience willing to respond with appropriate indignation. On more personal fronts, the race to confess some "horrible" truth leads to exhaustion, if not the conventionally boring. With no-holds barred — and a society which has made a shambles of restraint — perhaps the only shocking revelation left to tell is that one is (1) heterosexual (2) happily married, on the whole and (3) not particularly fucked up. Such a poet may yet appear — he may even refuse to appear in lime-colored flares and moppish hair — but it is hard to buck a tradition which expects its poets to "come on strong."

Wagoner, it seems to me, comes closest to that dual allegiance to craft and continual surprise which makes a developing body of poetry possible. At a time when fashionable postures and a short life span are nearly synonymous terms, Wagoner continues to produce first-rate poems. Since his impressive debut with *A Place to Stand* in 1958, he has published some four books of poetry. As Robert Boyers has suggested,* *Staying Alive* (1966) was the turning point, the volume in which Wagoner "really came into his own as a poet." And while

* See "The Poetry of David Wagoner," *Kenyon Review*, Spring 1970.

I have no desire to belabor the psychological, there does seem to be a connection between Theodore Roethke's untimely death in 1963 and Wagoner's discovery of a poetic voice that is distinctively his own. Wagoner — like Roethke before him — has been the victim of tedious discussions about "influence" or, worse, a kind of un-acknowledged disciplehood. And not, I suppose, without some cause. After all, the combination of Theodore Roethke's very considerable presence and the shared landscape of a majestic Northwest conspire to make such comparisons inevitable. But poetic assets hardly ever come without poetic liabilities. Which is to say, the natural rivalry between surrogate fathers and surrogate sons is as much a fact of life as it is a powerful literary theme. Life may be lonely center-stage, but there is nothing like the warm bask of the single spotlight to make a poet like Wagoner feel his oats.

And, yet, Wagoner — for all the Northwestern geography in poems like "A Guide to Dungeness Spit" — has retained that ear conditioned by the Midwest from which he came. His most characteristic pitch is a flat, almost wry combination of the matter-of-fact and the mildly self-deprecating. It is a unique note in contemporary letters, for all the kinship to Hoosiers who have come before. Generally speaking, it manifests itself in a quiet astonishment, at once a reverence for the intrinsic magic that is life and a continual surprise as one encounters it again and again. The terms of the astonishment grow inevitably out of dramatic situations which prefer the landscape of actuality to the larger surfaces of unbridled dream. That is, Wagoner may occasionally pitch his material in the bizarre — as he does in, say, "The Keepers" — but whatever lines have been cast upon sensational waters hook back to that curious interaction between man and nature which is his strongest suit. To be sure, Wagoner's playfulness suspends — at least temporarily — much of the serious-ness I have been suggesting. In "The Keepers" the very ambiguity of his title compounds the question of who, exactly, is keeping whom. On a day when "The drizzle and the wind had driven the keepers Indoors," the speaker and a woman observe the zoo uneasily: "Our games rained out like theirs." What follows is a moment out of some half-forgotten chapter of human history, one which combines the Earth Mother with La Belle Dame Sans Merci, the face of Eve with the aspect of Lilith. As a killer whale swims his "flat circle," the woman calls out something the speaker cannot quite hear in the tear-ing wind that is the zoo. The whale, however, evidently can; his

tongue responds — sticking out from a huge head and perfectly pointed
teeth — when suddenly:

> She kissed it, as God is my witness. The whale
> Sank back and swam as it had before.
> She came toward me at the top of the stair,
> As I braced against the wind blowing between us,
>
> And offered me those same lips to be kissed.
> And something I hadn't dared
> Believe in, something deep as my salt
> Rose to the surface of my mouth to touch them.

In the forty-eight poems of Wagoner's most recent collection —
Riverbed (University of Indiana Press: Bloomington, Indiana, 1972)
— the deepest yearnings are often couched in emotions which verge
on surprise. Both whale and man respond to primal needs with
particularly primal gestures. Ultimately, even a sophisticated stance
and the off-rhymes of a line like "She kissed it, as God is my witness"
are subsumed by that which is more basic. Wagoner's tendency is
to come at such moments from an oblique angle we recognize as wit,
but the gentle sense of verbal play always teeters toward a transposed
key, that "something I hadn't dared/ Believe in." At a time when
"religious" poets are still measured by the more sensational yardstick
of a conversion embraced or rejected, Wagoner's poetry speaks of a
reverence for that subtle relationship between man and animal. It is
this spirit which draws his characters to spawning grounds of the
relentless salmon in "Riverbed": "We come back to find them, to
wait at their nesting hollows/ With the same unreasoning hope."
The terrible cost of fertility is mirrored in the lovers who "lie down
all day" beside the dying salmon, partaking of a ritual which lies
beneath both language itself and the surrounding landscape of flat
rocks, swift-flowing streams.

A similar note is struck in "The Fisherman's Wife." Once again
there is a doubling effect: the "wife" cradles a trout (freed, by her
objections, from the fisherman's hook) in much the way that her
instinctive response helps to nurture him. And, yet, it is the fisherman
who catches his wife "by the hair, bringing her back alive" as she
sinks into the lake on her mission of mercy. What begins in a ritualized death ends in an equally ritualized life:

> We sat on edge till the moon came out, but nothing
> Rose, belly up, to mock it at our feet.

Like the lovers in "In the Badlands," the tableau freezes motion at a
point somewhere between accomplished dread and miraculous salva-

tion. Overhead the vultures sail "With our love as the pivot"; a sea of fossils lies beneath them. But at this moment of precious equipoise — a time which calls to mind "Staying Alive" — suspended animation makes for the poetic possibility. In such poems death is warded off and the context is savored in its stead. And, too, there is a quiet astonishment about both the original predicament and one's response to its potential meaning. Love, of course, is the life-sustaining counter, but Wagoner's flat, almost clinical, tone and the gentle contours of ironic wit hold the gush of sentimentality at the necessary arm's length.

Very often Wagoner's brand of secret-sharing at the zoo reminds one of Rilke. In *Staying Alive* an extraordinary poem entitled "The Fruit of the Tree" focused on a curious pear and the equally curious camel who gobbled it up through the bars. In "Waiting with the Snowy Owls," Wagoner balances the moment of communion between nine owls (presumably waiting for the sun to melt "What holds them, to run from them or stir/ The thawed halves of hearts at their feet.") and a similar condition mirrored in his inability to "read or write."

As Wagoner himself has suggested — in a poem entitled "The Words" — his recurrent images seem to be those of

> Wind, bird and tree,
> Water, grass, and light:
> In half of what I write
> Roughly or smoothly
> Year by impatient year,
> The same six words appear.

To be sure, there is nothing quite like beating your potential critics to the punch. And, yet, a *Wagoner Concordance* might prove otherwise, especially where the matter of his congenial themes are concerned. Since *New and Selected Poems* (1969) "magic" has been a constant motif, one which fuses craft and astonishment into a uniquely Wagoneresque key. By this I mean he comes at magic from that sense of first-hand experience usually missing when contemporary poets play at being ancient shamans or ersatz magicians. In poems like "Magic Night at the Reformatory" or "The Escape Artist," one has the sense that both the dramatic situation and the quiet astonishment it produces have been grounded in the actual, in felt reality, as it were. This is not to suggest, of course, that Wagoner neglects the metaphorical possibilities — magicians and poets, after all, have much in common, not the least of which is a trafficking in illusion — but

Wagoner has never quite recovered from that sleight of hand which can hide a clutter of stuff in an innocent hat. With a poem like "The Inexhaustible Hat," Monsieur Hartz (a magician who performed in the 1880's) is singled out for special applause. To be sure, Wagoner provides the selection here — from the standard "swaddle of scarves" to the "grinning skull" which concludes the performance — but his capacity to be surprised about it all really really dulls. As he puts it: ". . . Oh Monsieur Hartz,/ You were right, you were absolutely right! Encore!" The effect is more than one fellow-artist praising another; rather, it is an affirmation of the aesthetic principle involved, a joyous testament to the abundance only Art (which is to say, illusion) can make.

Instead of chanting approximations of the shamans(which have so fascinated other contemporary poets), Wagoner prefers to come at "magic" with the amateur's deep respect for the professional. He is proud to be a member of the Society of American Magicians (the only "organization" of which he has dues-paying, card-holding status) and the skills he developed as a picker-of-locks when he "researched" his novel *The Escape Artist*. All this combines to create something less than the exorcizing efforts of, say, Denise Levertov and something more amenable to the modern ear. After all, chants — for all the romantic energy expended on behalf of their reconstruction — have gone the way of cave-painting and narrative sagas about embattled hunters. Or to put it another way: Wagoner manages to keep amazement and understatement in an equipoise that is the stuff of dramatic tension. Once again, the very flatness of his voice — simultaneously detached and yet savoring its own ironies — contributes to the effect:

> As he stands alone on stage, the Professor
> Shows us he has nothing
> Up his sleeve or under his coattails,
> Then lowers his brows as seriously as a man
> Thinking of being something else, and there,
> Would you believe it, from between his lips
> The white tip of an egg comes mooning out.

In "The Extraordinary Production of Eggs from the Mouth," a professor-magician "eggs us on/ To laugh and gag for him" until the audience, too, becomes a collective chicken in his skillful hands. But like the circle snake — notorious for swallowing its own tail until he disappears inside himself — the eggs return to the source from which they so mysteriously came — and "we see his mouth is absolutely empty."

To be sure, that something apparently pops out of nothing is the essence of the magician's art — and Wagoner retains his fascination for such images. Occasionally — as in "Laughter in the Dark," a poem based on a Nabokov title and dedicated to that consummate trickster — dark shadows have an uncanny way of sliding across a lesson in what Wagoner calls "physics, good taste, and raw anatomy." But laughing in darkness is very different from that instruction in laughter through a shut mouth which opens the poem. In the latter case it "gets us nowhere"; in the former, however, we conjure up psychic residue, the "bent selves, who are no laughing matter." A penchant for the quasi-didactic — a rubric one finds in poems like Dr. Williams' "Tract" or Henry Reed's *Lessons of the War* — links ostensibly scattered strands of the Wagoner canon into something like a cohesive vision. "Staying Alive," for example, is built upon a substructure of survival technique; it provides, among other things, a manual for how to live off the land. In poems like "Do Not Proceed Beyond This Point without a Guide" ("The hemlock had more sense. It stayed where it was,/ . . . Being a guide instead of needing one.") or "The Other Side of the Mountain" ("To walk downhill you must lean partially backwards,/ Heels digging in . . .") much of that spirit is continued. But what has become, for Wagoner, a very congenial mode indeed is not limited to a single analogy between woodsy advice and poetic truth. The dramatic situation of objective instructor and wry detachment allows for that sense of quiet astonishment which infuses his best work. It is the stuff of magic, whether one encounters it on stage, in the forest or, as so often happens, in the relentless absurdities of contemporary life. Readiness, indeed, is all. The found situations become the germs for "occasional" poems, responses to the jingoism of daily life. When, for example, a police recruit (asked by NBC News why he likes police work) claims that "it's not too much of a dull moment, and I'm not in one place at one time," the combination of shoddy speech and unwitting comedy provides Wagoner with an epigraph for a poetic monologue entitled "A Police Manual." What follows is a chilling lesson in standard operating procedures, one which might have been delivered by some sergeant plucked out of a Henry Reed poem and issued an American accent:

> The efficient use of a nightstick as an extension
> Of your arm and armor
> Lies at the heart of patrolling; each human body
> Has tender and vulnerable places whose location,
> By trial and error,
> You may find to your advantage.

To be sure, in poems like "The Naming of Parts" or "Judging Distances," Reed plays off the no-nonsense drill instructor against a more sensitive, even poetically inclined, recruit. Which is to say, tone is a function of the delicately balanced juxtapositions. Wagoner, on the other hand, tends to prop his straightforward response against the epigraph, either by extending its proposition to absurdity (as he does with ingeniously worded math problems in "The Calculation") or by raising self-parody to yet another power (as he does in his delightful intertwining of the stilted rhetoric from *The Insidious Fu-Manchu* and Wagoner called "Six for Sax"). And, yet, for all the punning in, say, "A Victorian Idyll" — based on a bit of innocuous etiquette by Emily Post — Wagoner makes much the same sort of comment on ingrained foolishness as Ionesco's Absurdist manhandling of language achieves in a play like *The Bald Soprano*. That is, he revitalizes language by calling our attention to possibilities, no matter how fantastic, which had not occurred to us before. In an early poem like "Murder Mystery," there is a stock Hawkshaw, stalking his way through the incredible baggage of drawing-room whodunits. It is a world of bumbling questions and instant alibis, the perfect place to pass out "suspicion like lemonade." But in Wagoner's best work metaphor is never isolated to a single line, however much his touch about suspicion and lemonade seems appropriately witty. Rather, the entire fabric of such forms — with their stylized movement from enigmatic crime to incredible solution — becomes the foundation on which his own vision is built. Thus, when Emily Post advises us about how to enter a room ("A gentleman always falls behind his wife . . .") or what to say if the butler asks "What name, please?" ("Whichever one is asked answers, 'Mr. and Mrs. Lake'"), Wagoner responds with a combination of tongue-in-cheek literalness and low-keyed astonishment:

> She came through the room like an answer in long division,
> At the top of her form, trailing a dividend.
> And when her husband fell down, as he always does,
> Flat on his face behind her and met the rug
> Like an old friend, we simply sharpened our charcoal.
> When the quizzical-looking butler said, "What name, please?"
> Someone said wearily, "Mr. and Mrs. Lake."
> It's always like this.

The effect is something like asking Laurel and Hardy to a sophisticated soiree; in short order the custard pies start flying and unbridled farce replaces "manners" on all fronts.

In fact, many of Wagoner's wittiest poems have that civilized touch which magazines like *The New Yorker* (which originally published five of the poems from *Riverbed*) bring to our ongoing comedy of manners. In "Lying Awake in a Bed Once Slept in by Grover Cleveland," for example, historical speculation takes a comic turn, one which looks at the conditions of Cleveland's presidency through a wryly realistic lens:

> One night, this bed was the Ship of State. It sank
> In the middle as deep as its hard slats
> Under the burdens of office
> Which, pound for pound, were seldom greater,
> Sir, than under you.

Wagoner is never one to resist the pun. Like Leopold Bloom, he feasts on life with relish, a half-winking eye out for the comic possibilities we have overlooked. Pop heroes like John Dillinger (whose elegy is written in a delightful combination of historical accuracy and escalating slant rhymes) or Midwestern giants like William Jennings Bryan come with the territory of Wagoner's Indiana childhood. But even an irascible parrot will do in a pinch, as he proves with "Talking Back." There the tag-lines of chaotic learning (the gamut runs from *Every good boy does fine* to *What then? sang Plato's ghost, What then?*) blend into the domestic fabric. And as the parrot "jangles back at motors in general, *Who knows/ What evil lurks in the hearts of men?*" the trauma of noisy breakfast rooms is transposed into a key that is distinctly Wagoner's own.

Riverbed speaks with a lyric voice, one as confident about its abilities as it is mature about its vision. In individual poems like "The Death and Resurrection of the Birds" ("Falling asleep, the birds are falling/ Down through the last light's thatchwork. . ."), "The Ascent of the Carpenter Ants" (in which the drama of ant and starling overpowers even an exterminator's pragmatic advice) or the delicate "psalm" that is "Once More for the Rain," Wagoner continues the opposition between things in motion and those at rest; he speculates about the nature of rusting machines and equally rusting lives ("Trying to Think by a Steel Mill") or Newton's Laws, poetically conceived ("The First Law of Motion"). Wagoner may claim that he is merely "doing life/ For willful failure to report/ On what goes on

and on in the heart," but "Doing Time" is hardly the poem from
Riverbed we would use to write him down. Rather, Wagoner is a
poet wise enough to see moments of rest as the valued occasions they
can be. The "river bed" is where we lie down to see the salmon's
mysterious cycle and remember the riverbed which underlies us all.
It is, in short, a place where quiet astonishments can flourish and
poetry can be made. "Doing Time" may be full of dazzle, of puns
on pregnant words like "sentence" and assorted prison motifs, but it
is the richer, impressively newer voice one hears in *Riverbed* that
makes the difference. And *that* voice urges us to wait, to rediscover
something deeper than public rhetoric or private grief. We feel it most
clearly in a remarkable poem called "Lost":

> Stand still. The trees ahead and bushes beside you
> Are not lost. Wherever you are is called Here,
> And you must treat it as a powerful stranger,
> Ask permission to know it and be known.
> The forest breathes. Listen. It answers,
> I have made this place around you.
> If you leave it, you may come back again, saying Here.
> No two trees are the same to Raven.
> No two branches are the same to Wren.
> If what a tree or bush does is lost to you,
> You are surely lost. Stand still. The forest knows
> Where you are. You must let it find you.

Wagoner has been willing to do just that — and the poetry of *Riverbed* gives witness to an ongoing love affair with the world which is
never quite contained by either a matter-of-factness about his tone
or the fireworks of his verbal wit. Wagoner's may be the "still, small
voice" which, ironically enough, has more attentive ears among fellow
poets than academic colleagues, but if his most recent poetry is any
indication (and I suspect it is) his brand of quiet astonishment will
come to seem increasingly impressive to all readers of our poetry.

Notes on Contributors

John Bayley teaches at New College, Oxford University, and has written such extraordinary works as *The Characters of Love* and *Tolstoy and the Novel.*

Harold Bloom teaches at Yale University and is author of such works as *The Visionary Company, The Ringers in the Tower,* and the controversial *The Anxiety of Influence.*

Robert Boyers has written on contemporary American poetry for such journals as *Partisan, Kenyon,* and *Sewanee* reviews.

Jan B. Gordon has taught for some years at the State University of New York, Buffalo, and has written essays for many journals, including *Salmagundi.*

James M. Kiehl teaches in the English Department at Skidmore College.

Galway Kinnell has written an exquisite long poem entitled *The Book of Nightmares.* Also among his volumes are *Body Rags, Flower Herding on Mt. Monadnock,* and translations from Villon.

Stanley Kunitz's *Selected Poems* won the Pulitzer Prize in 1958; his most recent volume is *The Testing Tree.* Currently he is Poet of the Library of Congress and editor of the Yale Series of Younger Poets.

Joan Hutton Landis did a remarkable interview with Ben Belitt for the magazine *Midway* some years ago. She is doing graduate work at Bryn Mawr.

Laurence Lieberman is a widely published poet and critic, and regular poetry reviewer for *The Yale Review.*

Jerome Mazzaro teaches at the State University of New York, Buffalo. He has written books on Robert Lowell, the Renaissance lyric, and most recently on William Carlos Williams.

Charles Molesworth has published poetry and prose in such publications as *The Nation, Salmagundi*, and *American Review*. He teaches at Queens College in New York.

Howard Nemerov won the first Roethke Memorial Award for *The Blue Swallows* (1968) and has published many volumes of verse, fiction, and criticism, including the recent *gnomes & occasions*.

Joyce Carol Oates won the National Book Award in fiction for the novel *them* a few years back and has published many volumes of fiction, poetry, and criticism, including *The Wheel of Love, Wonderland*, and *Do with Me What You Will*.

Gabriel Pearson is a British critic whose work has appeared with some regularity in the poetry journal *The Review*.

Sanford Pinsker is a younger poet and critic probably best known for the volume *The Schlemiehl as Metaphor*. He teaches at Franklin and Marshall College.

Martin L. Pops is author of a book on Melville and of a forthcoming work on Vermeer. He teaches at the State University of New York, Buffalo.

M. L. Rosenthal is the well-known poet and critic, author of such works as *The New Poets* and *View from the Peacock's Tail*. He teaches at New York University.

Norman Silverstein was regular film critic of *Salmagundi* and professor of English at Queens College in New York before his untimely death in the Summer of 1974.

W. D. Snodgrass is author of such works as *Heart's Needle* and *After Experience*. He has taught for some years at Syracuse University.

Hyatt H. Waggoner is author of such important works as *American Poets: Puritans to the Present*. He has taught for many years at Brown University.

Paul Zweig is Chairman of Comparative Literature at Queens College in New York and author of several books of poetry and criticism, including the widely admired *The Heresy of Self-Love*.